INTRODUCTION TO
SPORTS LAW & BUSINESS

NINTH EDITION

PHIL BREAUX

B.A. LOUISIANA STATE UNIVERSITY 1969

J.D. LOUISIANA STATE UNIVERSITY LAW SCHOOL 1972

INSTRUCTOR, LOUISIANA STATE UNIVERSITY E. J. OURSO COLLEGE OF BUSINESS

PAUL BREAUX,

J.D. HARVARD LAW SCHOOL 2008; B.A. U. OF TEXAS 2005; B.B.A. U. OF TEXAS 2005.

AARON BROOKS

J.D. HARVARD LAW SCHOOL 2008; B.S. UNIVERSITY OF CENTRAL ARKANSAS 2005.

Printed in the United States of America.

ISBN: 1-60250-137-8 (978-1-60250-137-9)

Table of Contents

Preface

Introduction

It is often said that sports have become less like a game and more like a business. Critics charge that commercialization is destroying the essence of athletic competition. The growing influence of business in sports is undeniable. It should be noted, however, that business has always been involved in athletic events--and not just at the professional level. Has the role of business increased in the last few decades? Absolutely. Has that been harmful to sports? Probably in some respects. There is little debate, however, that without the economic incentives and financial support of the business community, the enormous growth, popularity and availability of sports would not have occurred. The association of business with athletic events is a reflection of the pervasive role sports has in our society.

Television, radio, and the Internet are integral parts of our culture. The relationship between these mediums and sports is telling. Sporting events are the most reliable and coveted content for broadcasters. The television rights to the National Football League's games, the Olympics and the college basketball playoffs are worth billions of dollars. Each year some of the most watched programs on television are *Monday Night Football*, the Super Bowl and the NCAA college basketball championship. Sports talk shows on radio stations are more popular than ever, as are Internet Websites devoted to sports.

Owners of professional franchises have always been viewed as businessmen. Historically, athletes were merely players in the game. Times have changed. Minimum salaries in the major leagues are in excess of $200,000 and a few player contracts are in excess of $100 million--not including endorsements. Professional athletes have become much more sophisticated in understanding the economics of the game and this knowledge has produced enormous benefits for the players. Sports are not *like* a business, but in fact are multi-billion dollar entertainment industry that continues to flourish.

Like any other industry, the world of sports has business disputes. As the industry has grown, so has the number and significance of the conflicts. In 1994, for the first time in more than 90 years, there was no World Series in professional baseball. A strike by the players ended the season and the much-anticipated championship contest. Efforts to bring a quick end to the strike were made by countless parties, including some of the most powerful members of Congress and the President of the United States, to no avail. The strike, which at the time was the longest in sports history, lasted for 232 days. The National Basketball Association (NBA) imposed a lockout in 1998 that almost caused the cancellation of the entire season. Not to be outdone, the National Hockey League (NHL) lost the entire 2004-05 season to a lockout. The labor disputes cost the leagues and the players hundreds of millions of dollars. The staggering losses are based on business, not sports, issues.

Relocation of professional franchises, the use of public funds to build professional facilities, and the application of federal laws prohibiting discrimination against people with mental and physical impairments who participate in sports are but a few of the business, social, political, and legal issues with enormous consequences affecting professional sports today.

College and high school sports are not insulated. Practically every college in the country with an athletic program had to make major changes to comply with Title IX, a federal law regarding athletic opportunities for female students. Sanctions from the NCAA, which regulates many college athletic programs, can cost a university hundreds of thousands of dollars and severely damage the image of the institution. The NCAA also pays a price for its authority. The organization faces legal challenges to it rules from schools, athletes, coaches, and private companies. The NCAA lost a class action filed by coaches that challenged a restricted earnings rule imposed by the organization. The judgment against the NCAA was settled in excess of $50 million. On the high school level, rules concerning student-athlete transfers, residency, hold-backs, home-bound students, and drug testing are often challenged in court.

Given the enormous economic stakes and substantial rights involved, legal conflicts in the sports world are inevitable. The disputes in sports are not settled on the playing field. The problems are resolved, as in any other industry, through negotiation by the parties or by the application of laws and the judicial system. This book is an attempt to provide the reader with an understanding of some of the business and legal issues that arise in sports.

The Text

The title of this book, <u>Introduction to Sports Law and Business,</u> requires some explanation. The material presented will focus on a number of laws used in sports, including antitrust, labor, agency, contracts, torts, workers compensation and intellectual property. The legal principles discussed, however, are not limited to sports. That is, with few exceptions, the laws discussed are not exclusively for sports. As a result of the phenomenal growth in sports, however, a considerable body of law has developed that addresses disputes in the sports context. This text will discuss this expanding area of the law. Although the title, "Sports Law", may be technically incorrect, the term does provide a fair description of the subject presented.

A comment about the chapter titles: Some of the chapters are titled by the legal subject addressed, such as, courts, contracts, agency, antitrust, labor law, intellectual property, torts, and workers compensation. Other chapters focus on a particular sport, such as the major professional leagues or colleges and are titled accordingly. Although the method used to name chapters is not consistent, it was deemed the most appropriate approach to identify the subjects.

The book is divided into four parts. Although the chapters may be read in any order, the authors have two recommendations. The authors urge that Part I be read first. The chapters in Part I not only offer material on the particular subjects, but will assist the reader's comprehension of the other chapters in the text. The formal resolution of disputes in the sports industry is discussed throughout the book. It is essential for the student to first understand the procedure and remedies explained in Chapter 1. The material on Contracts and Agency in Chapters 2 and 3 is relevant to the chapters in Part II and Part III. More importantly, however, it is imperative that the student grasp the brief, but basic, aspects of Antitrust and Labor Law in Chapters 4 and 5 before reading the chapters on the professional leagues.

In addition, the authors suggest that the chapter on Major League Baseball (MLB) be read before reviewing the chapters on the other professional leagues. A review of the history of the reserve clause and free agency in MLB will make it easier to understand the same issues in the other professional leagues.

Caveat

The topics presented in this text are complex. This material does not purport to present a thorough analysis of the various subjects addressed. A complete understanding of the legal issues presented would require a knowledge of law that the readers of this book are not expected to possess. In addition, the issues discussed are extremely dynamic. Changes are occurring almost on a daily basis. Information in this material that was accurate at the time of publication may no longer be correct. As the title suggests, however, this book is designed to *introduce* the student to some of the major legal and business issues in sports. It is hoped that the information will serve as a foundation for those interested in the subject.

Part I

Dispute Resolution—
Courts, Arbitration, Administrative
Hearings, and Legislation

Although this book is written for students who do not have any previous legal background, it discusses a number of legal issues and proceedings. The reader must first become familiar with how legal disputes are often resolved.

COURT SYSTEMS

Court decisions will be presented throughout this text. It is therefore important for the reader to be able to understand basic aspects of the judicial system.

There are two separate court systems that operate in the United States. The federal government has courts throughout the country, and each state also has its own separate court system. Whether a case goes into state or federal court depends on the nature of the dispute; for purposes of this material, it is not necessary to understand the reasons for this determination.

State and federal courts are structured in a similar fashion. Cases are first tried in courts that are generally called either trial or district courts. The trial may or may not have a jury. Each trial or district court is located within a geographic area referred to as a circuit. Each circuit has an appellate court. After a case is heard at the trial level, a party who is not satisfied with the decision may appeal to the appellate court in that circuit. Appellate courts do not try the case again, but merely review the record of the trial court and arguments of counsel to determine if a reversible error occurred at the trial level. An appellate court can respond to the trial court's decision in a number of ways. The appellate court can *affirm* the trial court's decision, which means the decision of the trial court will be upheld, or *reverse* the decision and rule in favor of the other party. The appellate court can also modify the decision of the trial court or send the case back (remand) to the trial court with further instructions. Decisions at the appellate court level are made by a panel of judges, usually three (3) in number. A decision must be supported by a majority of the judges. If a judge on the panel does not agree with the majority, that judge may write a *dissenting* opinion that reflects his disagreement with the majority decision. The dissenting opinion does not have the force of law; it is merely an expression of disagreement with the majority opinion.

The highest court in the federal court system is the United States Supreme Court. The U.S. Supreme Court functions in the same manner as an appellate court. There are nine justices on the U.S. Supreme Court. If a party is not satisfied with a decision reached by a federal appellate court, an application for an appeal can be made to the U.S. Supreme Court. The U.S. Supreme Court accepts only a limited number of cases for review. The Supreme Court can affirm, reverse, remand, or modify, a decision just as an appellate court may do. Most state court systems have the equivalent of a supreme court, which serves as another court of appeal in the state system.

Court opinions are generally lengthy, and a considerable amount of information has been deleted from the cases presented in this text. The purpose of the editing was to eliminate information not particularly relevant to the issue being discussed so the decision would be easier to read and comprehend. A more thorough understanding of the case may be obtained by reading the entire opinion.

In a civil (non-criminal) case, the party who files the lawsuit is generally referred to as the *plaintiff, petitioner,* or *claimant.* The opposing party is called the *defendant.* For example, *White v. NFL* is the caption of a suit filed by Reggie White, the plaintiff, against the NFL, the defendant. The "v." in the caption is simply an abbreviation for "versus." The party who lost in the trial court and brought an appeal is referred to as the *appellant,* and the other party is called the *appellee* or *respondent.* In civil cases, the plaintiff's name will be listed first in the caption of the case at the trial level. Captions can be confusing, however, because some courts list the appellant's name (who may be the defendant) first when the case is appealed. In a criminal case, the party accused is called the *defendant.* The party bringing the action is not, however, called the plaintiff, but is referred to as the *state* or *government. U.S. v. Walters,* for example, is a criminal case in which the United States prosecuted a sports agent, Norby Walters, the defendant, on criminal charges. With a few exceptions, this material will discuss civil, not criminal, cases.

COURT REMEDIES

There are various remedies that can be awarded by a court to a successful party in a civil lawsuit. The most common relief provided by a court in a civil case is *monetary damages.* The monetary award compensates the injured party for the loss suffered as a result of the wrongful conduct of the other party. The plaintiff has the burden of proving the amount of damages due. Some contracts stipulate the amount of damages in the event of a breach. These stipulated damages are called *liquidated damages.*

Another important remedy that can be provided by a court is an *injunction.* An injunction is generally a court order prohibiting a party from engaging in specified conduct. In most cases, the party seeking injunctive relief requests a temporary, preliminary, and/or a permanent injunction. The request for a temporary or preliminary injunction is determined at a hearing set a relatively short time after the request is filed. If granted, a temporary injunction is only valid for a short period of time. A preliminary injunction remains in force until a trial is held to determine if a permanent injunction should be granted. Injunctions are usually applied where monetary damages are difficult to determine or where immediate and irreparable injury will result if the conduct is allowed to continue. Injunctions are used extensively in sports disputes and will be referred to in a number of cases presented in this text.

Specific performance and *rescission* are two additional remedies that a court may grant in contract actions. Specific performance is an order for the breaching party to perform the obligation provided in the contract. This remedy is usually only available when the subject matter of the contract is unique, for example the sale of land. Rescission is an order that rescinds, or sets aside, the contract and relieves the non-breaching party from performance. A rescission also requires the breaching party to return any benefit received from the non-breaching party.

ARBITRATION AND
ADMINISTRATIVE HEARINGS

Arbitration is a method of resolving problems outside of the court system. Parties to a contract may agree in advance that if a dispute arises it will be submitted to private arbitration for a decision. Arbitration is a process that allows an arbitrator, a private citizen with expertise in the subject matter, to hear a matter and render a decision much like that of a judge in a court proceeding. Decisions by an arbitrator are generally subject to court review. The review is, however, limited to the legitimacy of the arbitration process. Many of the disputed issues in professional sports are resolved by arbitration pursuant to league rules.

Many public bodies, such as public schools, colleges and governmental agencies, require disputes to be submitted to an *administrative hearing*. Universities and the National Collegiate Athletic Association (NCAA) often use administrative hearings in connection with alleged improper conduct. An administrative hearing is conducted similar to an arbitration or court proceeding. Decisions made in administrative hearings may generally be challenged in court.

LEGISLATION

This material will cite specific laws that are often referred to as legislation or statutes. The federal law citations used in the material are from the United States Code, which is abbreviated as U.S.C., and is preceded by the chapter number and followed by the section number, for example, 15 U.S.C. 1.

Contracts

Although most people are familiar with the concept of a contract, few recognize the essential role contracts play in our daily lives. Our economic system could not function without the use of contracts. Contracts can be extremely complex and involve millions of dollars. Many contracts, however, are entered into on a routine basis with little thought by the parties. Some of the more common types of commercial activities that utilize contracts are sales, leases, loans, services, credit cards, employment, and insurance. Contracts are used extensively in almost every aspect of sports, and contractual issues will be discussed throughout this text. This chapter provides a brief description of the basic elements of contracts and some examples of contract disputes in sports.

INTRODUCTION TO CONTRACTS

DEFINITION OF A CONTRACT

A contract is a *legal* relationship between two or more parties. A definition that is often used for contracts is that it is an agreement that is enforceable by law. In most cases, however, a court will not compel a breaching party to perform the terms of a contract. A better description is that a contract is an agreement in which the law provides a *remedy*--in the event of a breach and injury. The remedy usually awarded is monetary damages to the injured party. Regardless of the remedy, however, the essential aspect of a contract that separates it from other agreements is that the law provides some type of legal recourse to the injured party against the party who breached the contract.

CONTRACT FORMATION

Contracts can be formed by the mere conduct of the parties. Purchasing gas or groceries are examples of contracts that are often accomplished without uttering a word. These types of agreements are called implied contracts. Most contracts, however, are formed by written or verbal communications and are called express contracts. Although some types of contracts are required by law to be in writing, oral contracts are generally valid—if proven. Oral contracts can, however, be very difficult to prove. Contracts that involve important rights or significant sums of money should always be in writing or in some documented form, such as an electronic communication.

EFFECTIVE COMMUNICATION

The most important aspect of a contract is effective communication. Most contract disputes are the result of an ambiguous agreement, that is, a contract that uses vague language or which fails to address issues that arise later. Oral contracts, by their nature, are extremely vulnerable to different interpretations and memories. Conflicts over oral contracts often lead to swearing matches between the parties as to who said what. Both parties will have difficulty proving the terms of such an agreement.

Written contracts are not immune from ambiguities. Written contracts, like oral contracts, are formed with words. Most words have more than one meaning. Even simple contracts may require the use of thousands of words and hundreds of sentences. Many people take communication skills for granted, but it is difficult to write a contract on a complex matter with absolute clarity. There are contract disputes involving millions of dollars where the resolution was based on the placement, or lack of, a comma.

A contract should expressly state the rights and duties of each party on any matter that might arise related to the contract. Every effort should be made to foresee any possible set of circumstances that might occur and to address the situation in the agreement. Parties often draft contracts with little or no regard for the unexpected. If an unforeseen event occurs, the contract is of little assistance.

ELEMENTS OF A CONTRACT

The four essential elements of a contract are mutual assent, consideration, legality, and legal capacity.

Mutual assent: In order to have a contract, one party must make an *offer* that is *accepted* by the other party. A person who makes an offer is called an *offeror*. The person to whom the offer is made is called an *offeree*. An offer is a definite proposal made by the offeror to the offeree. The acceptance by the offeree must acknowledge an agreement to the terms of the offer. Generally, an acceptance must indicate an agreement to the exact terms of the offer. There are situations, however, in which an acceptance may be valid even though it is not a *mirror image* of the offer. An offer and acceptance provides the mutual assent necessary for a contract to exist.

Consideration: Consideration is defined as the price that is paid to make the offer and acceptance binding. Consideration in a contract simply means that each party is giving, or more often, *promising* to give something of value to the other party. The result is that each party gives and receives something from the contract.

Consideration from each party does not have to be equal in value, but must be bargained for by the parties.

Consideration often appears in a contract in the form of promises. For example, if a professional team promises to pay an athlete a certain sum of money to play, and the athlete accepts the offer, both parties have provided the necessary consideration. A contract has been formed even though the team has not paid the money and the athlete has not played for the team. The *promises* to perform, not the performance, create the consideration for the contract. A breach of contract occurs if either party fails to perform according to the agreement.

Legality: The essence of a contract is that it has the force of law. For a contract to be valid, the object of the agreement must be legal. Courts will not recognize or provide remedies for the breach of a *purported* contract or a provision in a contract that is illegal. Many of the cases presented in this material are challenges to the legality of contracts. In particular, some of the more significant cases in professional sports involve claims that an alleged contract violates antitrust law and is, therefore, illegal.

Legal Capacity: Parties to a contract should have legal capacity. Generally, parties who have not reached the age of majority (18 years of age in most states) or who have a mental impairment that would prevent them from understanding the nature of the contract lack contractual capacity. A contract with a party who lacks legal capacity may be void, that is, no contract exists. In many situations, however, the law provides that the contract is voidable. A voidable contract is enforceable--at the option of the party who lacks capacity.

REAL ASSENT

Even if all of the necessary elements of a contract exist, the agreement may not be enforceable if one party can prove that real assent was lacking in the formation of the contract. For example, if the contract was brought about through duress (a wrongful force or threat) or fraud (a misrepresentation of a material fact), the contract may be rescinded by the party who was the victim of the duress or fraud.

CONTRACT REMEDIES

The essence of a contract is that the law provides a remedy in the event of a breach of the agreement by one party and an injury or loss by the other party. Remedies that may be awarded by a court in the event of a contract breach include damages, injunctions, specific performance, or recision.

PAROL EVIDENCE RULE

The parol evidence rule essentially provides that if there is a written document that is intended to represent the entire contract between the parties, a party is not allowed to introduce evidence in a trial that would change the terms of the contract. The rule is an attempt to discourage parties from signing a written contract, but, at the same time, agreeing on terms different from those stated in the contract. At first glance, it might appear that the rule is obvious and need never be invoked. Parties often, however, sign written agreements and, at the same time, agree to other terms which are not incorporated into the written contract.

There are exceptions to the parol evidence rule. Evidence of a subsequent or later agreement modifying the contract can be introduced at trial. Also, the rule does not prevent evidence that attempts to explain an ambiguous provision in a contract.

FORCE MAJEURE

Force Majeure, which means superior force, clauses are sometimes placed in contracts. Essentially, the clause exempts a party from nonperformance due to certain conditions beyond the control of the party. Floods, storms, earthquakes, and other "acts of God" are typical examples of events that might be listed as excusing a party from performing on a contract. Many of the leases on the arenas for NBA teams contain clauses that included labor strikes or lockouts as force majeure events. These provisions became very significant during the 1998 NBA lockout and allowed most teams to avoid their rental obligations on the arenas during the lockout.

MOST-FAVORED-NATIONS CLAUSE

A *most-favored-nations* clause is a provision in a contract that prohibits one party to a contract from granting more favorable terms to another party in a similar contract. In the context of a lease contract, it is a provision that no other lessee utilizing the same facility or a facility owned by the same lessor will have more favorable terms in its lease than the terms that were given to the original lessee. *Most-favored-nations* clauses may apply when two tenants occupy different facilities owned by the same lessor, when two lessees occupy the same facility, or when one lessee anticipates the occupation of the facility by another lessee at some point in the future. The New Orleans Saints' lease at the Superdome contains a provision that benefits the Saints in the event the Stadium District leases the facility to another tenant, for example, a Major League Baseball team. The clause states

> If at any time during the term of this Agreement, Manager should enter into a lease agreement with any other entity, other than the NFL, for use of the Superdome for...professional sporting events, and should such lease contain financial terms which, in aggregate, are more favorable than the financial terms and conditions in this Agreement, then, at the option of the Club, Manager and club shall enter into an amendment in this Agreement which shall incorporate the terms and conditions deemed to be more favorable by the Club with due regard to the relative revenues produced and games played in the Superdome by their respective organizations.

A significant dispute over a *favored-nations clause* erupted between the Baltimore Orioles and the Maryland Stadium Authority (MSA) regarding the use of the Orioles' park at Camden Yards. The Orioles' lease with MSA contained a favored-nations clause that required MSA to grant rent abatement and lease modifications to achieve parity between the Orioles and any NFL franchise that might move to Baltimore. After the Orioles lease was executed, the MSA granted extremely generous lease terms to attract the NFL's Baltimore Ravens to a new football stadium. The Orioles submitted a demand for arbitration on the provision to the American Arbitration Association. The demand claimed that the MSA had failed to honor the parity provision. The Orioles argued that eleven elements of their lease were deficient in comparison to the Ravens' lease. In July 2001, the arbitrators ruled in favor of the Orioles on three of the claims. As a result of the ruling, the Orioles were given the right to sell the naming rights to its stadium and to conduct non-baseball events at the stadium. In addition, the MSA was required to contribute $10 million to the Orioles' Ballpark Improvement Fund. The arbitrators rejected the other claims including those that involved the number of private suites, the disparity in the audio/visual equipment, parking differences, and tax issues. Both parties claimed victory.

SPORTS CONTRACTS

COACHES' CONTRACTS

A team or school's contract with a coach is an employment contract. Most employment contracts are classified as *at-will* under the law, that is, an employer can terminate the employee at any time and without *cause*. The employer is only obligated to pay the employee the wages earned up to the time of the termination. The employee has no right to continued employment or compensation. There are a number of exceptions to the at-will rule. Federal and state laws prohibit employers, in some circumstances, from terminating an employee for various reasons, such as age, race, sex, and physical impairments. Civil service employees generally can only be terminated for *cause*. Employment contracts with unions and tenured teachers are generally exempt from the at-will rule.

Head-coaches in the professional leagues and the major sports schools almost always have contracts for a specified term, generally 3 to 5 years, and are not at-will contracts. Generally, an employee hired for a stated period can only be terminated for *cause* during the contract term. Termination by the employer before the expiration of the term entitles the employee to damages for the breach.

It is common for a coach's contract to provide that the contract may be terminated prior to the expiration of the term for *cause*. The meaning of *cause* may include a breach of the contract, criminal conduct, and, for college coaches, violation of NCAA or conference rules. *Cause* for termination should be explained as clearly as possible in contracts. For example, will an arrest for a misdemeanor offense such as driving while intoxicated constitute sufficient *cause* to terminate the contract? Or, will a conviction or a misdemeanor be sufficient?

Several years ago, the University of Minnesota's basketball program was a tremendous success on the court. The player's classroom performance was less impressive. A scandal erupted at the school when an administrator alleged she had been paid for years to provide improper academic support to basketball players. The coach denied the allegations, but was eventually terminated. He was paid more than $1 million dollars in the buyout. The public backlash over the scandal and additional evidence of academic fraud, however, forced the university to file suit against the coach to recover the buyout funds. The school's contract with the coach provided that no buyout was required if he was fired for "just cause." The term "just cause" included a major violation of a Governing Association rule (NCAA). An arbitrator ruled that the coach had to refund more than $800,000 of the buyout to the school. The payment, however, could be made over an eleven-year period.

Moral turpitude clauses are generally included in a coach's contract to address conduct that may not be illegal or directly related to the job, but is not in keeping with the image the school wants to project. The clauses are useful, but problematic. What if a coach is photographed at a private party with one hand clutching a beer and the other firmly around one of the school's cheerleaders? Can a coach be terminated if he uses a school credit card to pay for expenses incurred at a club that features scantly dressed female dancers? Would it matter if the coach is married?

Determining if *cause* exists may require factual findings and subjective decisions, especially on a "morals" clause. Some contracts designate an impartial party to ascertain if the moral conduct in question constitutes *cause*. If the contract is terminated for *cause*, the coach is generally not entitled to any additional compensation.

Coaches are often terminated before the expiration of the term in the contract without *cause*. The employer will, however, usually have to pay damages for the breach of the contract. In most situations, the compensation approximates the present value of the remainder of the contract. When a coach's contract is terminated without *cause*, one problem is trying to determine whether the damage calculation should be limited to base salary or include other perks, such as shoe contracts, media appearances, and camps.

A general rule of law is that an injured party must make a reasonable effort to mitigate his damages, that is, to make some effort to reduce the amount of damages. This duty is often expressed with specific language in a contract. A common mitigation provision in a coach's contract requires the coach to make a good faith effort to find new employment. The contract may also provide that any new salary for a certain period will serve as an offset or credit on the damages due from the previous employer for the breach.

Terminating coaches without *cause* before their contract expires and paying damages to cover the balance of the contract term has long been a common practice. For many years, however, the reverse was not true. That is, if a coach terminated his contract early—usually for a better-paying job—the coach did so without paying any damages to his employer. The premature and unexpected departure by the coach, however, usually caused a hardship on his ex-employer.

Many colleges now include provisions in their contracts that require a coach to pay damages in the event he chooses to terminate the contract before the expiration of the term. In 1994, Louisiana State University (LSU) terminated its head football coach and reached a tentative agreement to hire Pat Sullivan as a replacement. Coach Sullivan was still, however, under contract at Texas Christian University (TCU). Sullivan's contract with TCU required Sullivan to pay a substantial sum to TCU if he, Sullivan, terminated the contract before its expiration. The payment TCU insisted on receiving was apparently too high, and Sullivan eventually declined the LSU job.

After Sullivan declined the job, LSU hired Gerry Dinardo. Coach Dinardo was, however, also under contract, with Vanderbilt, at the time he accepted the LSU position. Vanderbilt filed suit against Coach Dinardo as a result of his early departure. Vanderbilt was successful in its breach of contract case against Coach Dinardo. The court of appeal's decision follows.

Vanderbilt University v. DiNardo (1999)

Gerry DiNardo resigned as Vanderbilt's head football coach to become the head football coach for Louisiana State University. As a result, Vanderbilt University brought this breach of contract action. The district court entered summary judgment for Vanderbilt, awarding $281,886.43, pursuant to a damage provision in DiNardo's employment contract with Vanderbilt. DiNardo appeals, arguing that the district court erred in concluding: 1) that the contract provision was an enforceable liquidated damage provision and not an unlawful penalty under Tennessee law; 2) that Vanderbilt did not waive its right to liquidated damages; 3) that the Addendum to the contract was enforceable; and 4) that the Addendum applied to the damage provision of the original contract.

We affirm the district court's ruling that the employment contract contained an enforceable liquidated damage provision and the award of liquidated damages under the original contract. We conclude, however, that there are genuine issues of material fact as to whether the Addendum was enforceable. We, therefore, reverse the judgment awarding liquidated damages under the Addendum and remand the case to the district court.

On December 3, 1990, Vanderbilt and DiNardo executed an employment contract hiring DiNardo to be Vanderbilt's head football coach. Section one of the contract provided:

The University hereby agrees to hire Mr. DiNardo for a period of five (5) years from the date hereof with Mr. DiNardo's assurance that he will serve the entire term of this Contract, a long-term commitment by Mr. DiNardo being important to the University's desire for a stable intercollegiate football program...

The contract also contained reciprocal liquidated damage provisions. Vanderbilt agreed to pay DiNardo his remaining salary should Vanderbilt replace him as football coach, and DiNardo agreed to reimburse Vanderbilt should he leave before his contract expired. Section eight of the contract stated:

Mr. DiNardo recognizes that his promise to work for the University for the entire term of this 5-year Contract is of the essence of this Contract to the University.... Accordingly, Mr. DiNardo agrees that in the event he resigns or otherwise terminates his employment as Head Football Coach (as opposed to his resignation or termination from another position at the University to which he may have been reassigned) prior to the expiration of this Contract and is employed or performing services for a person or institution other than the University, he will pay to the University as liquidated damages an amount equal to his Base Salary, less amounts that would otherwise be deducted or withheld from his Base Salary for income and social security tax purposes, multiplied by the number of years (or portion(s) thereof) remaining on the Contract.

On August 14, 1994, Paul Hoolahan, Vanderbilt's Athletic Director, went to Bell Buckle, Tennessee, where the football team was practicing, to talk to DiNardo about a contract extension. (DiNardo's original contract would expire on January 5, 1996). Hoolahan offered DiNardo a two-year contract extension. DiNardo told Hoolahan that he wanted to extend his contract but that he also wanted to discuss the extension with Larry DiNardo, his brother and attorney.

Hoolahan telephoned John Callison, Deputy General Counsel for Vanderbilt, and asked him to prepare a contract extension. Callison drafted an addendum to the original employment contract, which provided for a two-year extension of the original contract, specifying a termination date of January 5, 1998. Vanderbilt's Chancellor, Joe B. Wyatt, and Hoolahan signed the Addendum.

On August 17, Hoolahan returned to Bell Buckle with the Addendum. He took it to DiNardo at the practice field where they met in Hoolahan's car. DiNardo stated that Hoolahan did not present him with the complete two-page addendum, but only the second page, which was the signature page. DiNardo asked, "what am I signing?" Hoolahan explained to DiNardo, "It means that your contract as it presently exists will be extended for two years with everything else remaining exactly the same as it existed in the present contract." Before DiNardo signed the Addendum, he told Hoolahan, "Larry needs to see a copy before this thing is finalized." Hoolahan agreed, and DiNardo signed the document.

DiNardo explained that he agreed to sign the document because he thought the extension was the "best thing" for the football program and that he "knew ultimately, Larry would look at it, and, before it would become finalized, he would approve it." Hoolahan took the signed document without giving DiNardo a copy.

On August 16, Larry DiNardo had a telephone conversation with Callison. They briefly talked about the contract extension, discussing a salary increase. Larry DiNardo testified that, as of that date, he did not know that Gerry DiNardo had signed the Addendum or even that one yet existed.

On August 25, 1994, Callison faxed to Larry DiNardo "a copy of the draft Addendum to Gerry's contract." Callison wrote on the fax transmittal sheet: "let me know if you have any questions." The copy sent was unsigned. Callison and Larry DiNardo had several telephone conversations in late August and September, primarily discussing the television and radio contract. Callison testified that he did not recall discussing the Addendum, explaining: "The hot issue . . . was the radio and television contract." On September 27, Callison sent a fax to Larry DiNardo concerning the television and radio contract, and also added: "I would like your comments on the contract extension." Larry DiNardo testified that he neither participated in the drafting nor suggested any changes to the Addendum.

DiNardo first claims that section eight of the contract is an unenforceable penalty under Tennessee law. DiNardo argues that the provision is not a liquidated damage provision but a "thinly disguised, overly broad non-compete provision," unenforceable under Tennessee law.

The term "liquidated damages" refers to an amount determined by the parties to be just compensation for damages should a breach occur. Courts will not enforce such a provision, however, if the stipulated amount constitutes a penalty. A penalty is designed to coerce performance by punishing default. In Tennessee, a provision will be considered one for liquidated damages, rather than a penalty, if it is reasonable in relation to the anticipated damages for breach, measured prospectively at the time the contract was entered into and not grossly disproportionate to the actual damages.

The district court held that the use of a formula based on DiNardo's salary to calculate liquidated damages was reasonable "given the nature of the unquantifiable damages in the case."

DiNardo contends that there is no evidence that the parties contemplated that the potential damage from DiNardo's resignation would go beyond the cost of hiring a replacement coach. He argues that his salary has no relationship to Vanderbilt's damages and that the liquidated damage amount is unreasonable and shows that the parties did not intend the provision to be for liquidated damages.

DiNardo's theory of the parties' intent, however, does not square with the record. The contract language establishes that Vanderbilt wanted the five-year contract, because "a long-term commitment" by DiNardo was "important to the University's desire for a stable intercollegiate football program" and that this commitment was of "essence" to the contract.... Thus, undisputed evidence, and reasonable inferences therefrom establish that both parties understood and agreed that DiNardo's resignation would result in Vanderbilt suffering damage beyond the cost of hiring a replacement coach.

This evidence also refutes DiNardo's argument that the district court erred in presuming that DiNardo's resignation would necessarily cause damage to the University. That the University may actually benefit from a coaching change (as DiNardo suggests) matters little as we measure the reasonableness of the liquidated damage provision at the time the parties entered the contract, not when the breach occurred, and we hardly think the parties entered the contract anticipating that DiNardo's resignation would benefit Vanderbilt.

The stipulated damage amount is reasonable in relation to the amount of damages that could be expected to result from the breach. As we stated, the parties understood that Vanderbilt would suffer damage should DiNardo prematurely terminate his contract and that these actual damages would be difficult to measure.

We also reject DiNardo's argument that a question of fact remains as to whether the parties intended section eight to be a "reasonable estimate" of damages. The liquidated damages are in line with Vanderbilt's estimate of its actual damages. Vanderbilt presented evidence that it incurred expenses associated with recruiting a new head coach of $27,000.00, moving expenses for the new coaching staff of $86,840, and a compensation difference between the coaching staffs of $184,311. The stipulated damages clause is reasonable under the circumstances, and we affirm the district court's conclusion that the liquidated damages clause is enforceable under Tennessee law.

DiNardo claims that the Addendum did not become a binding contract, and, therefore, he is only liable for the one year remaining on the original contract, not the three years held by the district court.

DiNardo also claims that the Addendum never became a binding contract, because Larry DiNardo never expressly approved its terms. DiNardo contends that, at the very least, a question of fact exists as to whether the two-year Addendum is an enforceable contract. Under Tennessee law, parties may accept terms of a contract and make the contract conditional upon some other event or occurrence. DiNardo argues that the Addendum is not enforceable, because it was contingent on Larry DiNardo's approval.

…Vanderbilt . . . contends that, if Larry DiNardo found any of the language in the simple two-page Addendum objectionable, he should have objected immediately. Finally, Vanderbilt argues that if we decide that Larry DiNardo's approval was a condition precedent to enforceability, the condition was satisfied by Larry DiNardo's failure to object.

Viewing the evidence, in the light most favorable to DiNardo, as we must, we are convinced that there is a disputed question of material fact as to whether the Addendum is enforceable. There is a factual dispute as to whether Larry DiNardo's approval of the contract was a condition precedent to the Addendum's enforceability. Gerry DiNardo testified that he told Hoolahan that the contract extension was not "final" until Larry DiNardo looked at it. . . From [various] facts, a jury could conclude that Larry DiNardo's approval was required before the Addendum became a binding contract.

. . .

Accordingly, we affirm the district court's judgment that the contract contained an enforceable liquidated damage provision, and we affirm the portion of the judgment reflecting damages calculated under the original five-year contract. We reverse the district court's judgment concluding that the Addendum was enforceable as a matter of law. We remand for a resolution of the factual issues as to whether Larry DiNardo's approval was a condition precedent to the enforceability of the Addendum and, if so, whether the condition was satisfied by Larry DiNardo's failure to object.

We affirm in part, reverse in part, and remand the case to the district court for further proceedings consistent with this opinion.

****

On remand, the court ruled that Coach Dinardo owed Vanderbilt for the years in the contract extension.

Some coaches have the bargaining power to avoid any type of payment in the event the coach terminates the contract before the expiration of the term. Tubby Smith, when hired by the University of Georgia as the basketball coach, obtained a provision in his contract that allowed him to leave Georgia before the expiration of the contract term without penalty or restriction. This negotiation turned out to be very beneficial. During his contract with Georgia, Coach Smith received an offer to coach one of the most successful college basketball programs in the country—Kentucky—which he accepted.

An employer's termination of a coach before the expiration of the contract without *cause* generally entitles the coach to damages for the remainder of the contract term. The early termination may, however, cause irreparable harm to a coach and impair future employment opportunities. Can a coach object to the termination and sue for specific performance on the contract for the remainder of the term? Should a coach be entitled to an injunction to prevent the firing and be allowed to coach for the remainder of the contract term over the objection of the employer?

Can a school that has a coach under contract prevent him from taking another coaching job?

Northeastern University v. Donald A. Brown, Jr., et al. (2004)

This civil action arises from an alleged case of "contract jumping" by Donald A. Brown, Jr. ("Brown"), at the alleged instigation of and "tampering" by the University of Massachusetts at Amherst ("U.Mass.") and its athletic department.

In 1960, Judge J. Skelly Wright in *Detroit Football Co. v. Robinson,* (1960) described these types of "contract jumping cases" with players and coaches as follows:

> This case is but another round in the sordid fight for football players [or coaches] ... It is a fight characterized by deception, double dealing, campus jumping, secret alumni subsidization, semi-professionalism and professionalism. It is a fight which has produced as part of its harvest this current rash of contract jumping suits. It is a fight which so conditions the minds and hearts of these athletes [and coaches] that one day they can agree to play [or coach] football for a stated amount for one group, only to repudiate that agreement the following day or whenever a better offer comes along.

Brown has been the head football coach at Northeastern University ("Northeastern") since 2000. On or about July 8, 2003, Northeastern entered into a written Employment Agreement ("Contract") with Brown pursuant to which Northeastern agreed to employ Brown as its head football coach through the end of the 2007-2008 football season. At the time that he signed the Contract in 2003, Brown and his assistant coaches received substantial salary increases from Northeastern.

Article VIII of the Contract, captioned "outside employment," provided as follows:

> Coach [Brown] agrees to devote full time and effort to the University and agrees not to seek, discuss, negotiate for, or accept other employment during the term of this Agreement without first obtaining the written consent of the President of the University. Such consent shall not be unreasonably withheld.

Article IX of the Contract, captioned "Liquidated Damages," provides that, "[e]xcept as otherwise noted herein," if Brown leaves Northeastern prior to the end of the contract period, then Brown "shall pay to the University as liquidated damages

$25,000" and that in the event of an acceptance of such amount by Northeastern, it would be deemed to be "adequate and reasonable compensation to the University.""

In January 2004, six months after signing his contract with Northeastern, at the conclusion of the 2003-2004 football season, Brown told Northeastern's Athletic Director David O'Brien (O'Brien) that Brown wished to speak to another college (not U. Mass.) from whom Brown claimed to have received an inquiry. O'Brien asked Brown "what it would take" to keep Brown from interviewing with that other college. Brown and O'Brien proceeded to discuss a one-year extension to Brown's contract, a raise in his and his staff's salaries, and other football program enhancements, and Brown agreed to those terms. Thereupon, Northeastern agreed to grant him a one-year extension to his contract and to enter into a new contract with him through June 2009 with concomitant salary increases.

However, before a contract could be drafted and signed, the Acting Athletic Director of U. Mass., Thorr Bjorn ("Bjorn"), called O'Brien to seek permission to speak to Brown about coaching football at U. Mass. O'Brien notified Bjorn that Northeastern would not grant permission and that Northeastern had a contractual right to prevent such discussions. The next day, O'Brien called Bjorn again and confirmed that O'Brien and Northeastern would not give permission to U. Mass. to speak with Brown.

On Friday evening, February 6, 2004, Brown called O'Brien and told O'Brien that U. Mass. Athletic Director John McCutcheon had offered him the U. Mass. football coaching job, that he, Brown, had accepted it, and that he then turned it down. Over the weekend of February 7-8, 2004, and although he had told several student football players that the rumors that he was leaving were not true, Brown cleared out his office. On Monday, February 9, 2004, Brown handed his letter of resignation to O'Brien, and O'Brien said that Northeastern would do what it needed to do to protect its legal rights.

Thereupon, U. Mass. issued a press release around 5:30 p.m. on Monday, February 9, 2004, to notify the newspapers and media outlets that it hired and signed Brown to be the new football coach at U. Mass. U. Mass. is a member of the same football conference as Northeastern, and the teams play each other every year. Northeastern's entire football program and its playbook will be available to U. Mass. Their recruitment practices and methods will be known to U. Mass. These two universities compete with each other in the same league, compete for fans to attend their games, compete for media coverage, compete for many of the same football recruits, and compete with each other for television to cover their games on a regional basis. There should be no doubt that college sports and the revenue that they draw are a major business for a university. At times, at some universities, football and basketball programs appear to be more important than the universities' duty to educate and their duty to instill in college students basic concepts of ethical conduct and adherence to legal and moral obligations.

There appears to the Court that there is no question that Brown willfully and intentionally breached his contract with Northeastern. He signed his contract and straight-out violated it. He gave his word to Northeastern and the student-athletes that he was not leaving Northeastern when in fact, within a day, he was cleaning out his room to move to U. Mass. Unfortunately for Northeastern, its student-athletes, and its football program, Brown's word was no good and his promises were lies. There also appears to be no question that U. Mass. actively induced the breach when it had been told of the restrictions on Brown's talking to other potential football employers and of his existing long- term contract with Northeastern.

Both defendants raise the issue that Article IX of the Contract contains a liquidated damage clause in the event that Brown leaves before the Contract is completed. In this case, there is absolutely nothing to indicate that the liquidated damage clause in Article IX was intended as an alternate to performance. While Article IX does state that in the event of an acceptance of such amount by Northeastern, it would be deemed to be "adequate and reasonable compensation to the University," Article IX deals with the money losses to Northeastern in the event Brown would leave as football coach. It appears to the Court that Article IX does not in any way prohibit injunctive relief, and merely deals with financial payments for money losses incurred by Brown for leaving the University and breaching the contract. Or, as stated in Restatement (Second) of Contracts, § 361: "Specific performance or an injunction may be granted to enforce a duty even though there is a provision for liquidated damages for breach of that duty."

This Court finds that the irreparable harm suffered by Northeastern and its probable chance of success on the merits far outweigh the irreparable harm, if any, to Brown or U. Mass. and their negligible chance, if any, to prevail in this case. A preliminary injunction will not at this time issue directed to U. Mass., and said request is denied without prejudice. A preliminary injunction will issue to the defendant, Donald A. Brown, Jr.

****

Several days after issuing the preliminary injunction, the trial court reversed the decision and set aside the injunction. The court ruled that the liquidated damage payment was the only relief Northeastern was entitled to under the contract.

Ohio State fired its coach O'Brien for alleged NCAA violations. O'Brien filed suit.

O'Brien v. Ohio State University

[The court examined the letter sent to O'Brien from Ohio State explaining the university's decision to fire him, which in the section discussing his $6,000 gift to Radojevic's family stated:]

In particular, it is a recruiting inducement in violation of NCAA Bylaw 13.2.1. Despite the fact that the University was no longer actively recruiting Mr. Radojevic after he signed his National Letter of Intent, he is considered a 'prospect' according to NCAA rules until he officially registers and enrolls in a minimum full-time program of studies and attends classes for autumn quarter. Furthermore, for each of the past five years, you violated NCAA Bylaw 30.3.5 which, by your signature on the annual NCAA Certification of Compliance form, requires you to confirm that you have self-reported your knowledge of any NCAA Violations. We have self-reported this matter and other allegations related to the program to the NCAA.

> Section 4.1(d) of your employment agreement requires you to 'know, recognize and comply' with all applicable rules and regulations of the NCAA and to 'immediately report to the Director of Athletics and to the Department of Athletics Compliance Office' if you have 'reasonable cause to believe that nay person has violated such laws, policies, rules or regulations.' You have materially breached this important term of your contract.

> Upon review of the language used by the parties in Section 4.1(d), the court finds that plaintiff could breach his duties thereunder if either he fails to comply with NCAA rules or he has reasonable cause to believe that an NCAA violation has occurred and that he fails to immediately report it to the director. . .

> [After discussing conflicting testimonies from current and former collegiate athletic officials regarding the duty to report the gift, the court continued . . .] Ultimately, the determination whether plaintiff committed a major infraction of NCAA rules and what sanctions, if any, may be imposed upon defendant will be made by the NCAA Committee on Infractions and not this court. As of the date of publication of this decision, the NCAA has yet to decide the issue. In this case, in order to determine that plaintiff breached Section 4.1(d) of the employment agreement, the court need only find that plaintiff had reasonable cause to believe that he committed an infraction when he made the loan to the Radojevic family. The circumstances surrounding plaintiff's decision to make the loan combined with plaintiff's subsequent words and conduct convince the court that plaintiff had reasonable cause to believe that he had committed an infraction.

> Plaintiff testified that he found out about the professional contract in September 1998 and that he was certain at that time that Radojevic was not eligible to play college basketball. Yet Radojevic signed an NLI and he was brought in for an official visit. [A testifying expert] was unable to think of any reason why Radojevic would be offered an NLI and invited to make an official visit to the school if plaintiff were convinced that Radojevic was ineligible to play.

> Plaintiff's words and conduct are not those of a person who was sure that Radojevic would never play college basketball. Indeed, plaintiff acknowledged on cross-examination that if Radojevic had been reinstated, he would not have been eligible to play because of the loan plaintiff made to his family. Plaintiff testified that he would have had to reveal the loan if reinstatement had been granted.

> In consideration of all of the evidence presented, the court finds that in December 1998 plaintiff had reasonable grounds to believe that he had violated NCAA Recruiting Bylaw 13.02.1 by making a loan to the family of Alex Radojevic. Plaintiff's conduct in making the loan and then failing to report it to the director was a breach of Section 4.1(d) of the contract.

> Under common law, "a 'material breach' is a failure to do something that is so fundamental to a contract that the failure to perform that obligation defeats the essential purpose of the contract or makes it impossible for the other party to perform

under the contract." Defendant contends that plaintiff's conduct in violating NCAA rules and thereafter failing to immediately report the violation constitutes a "material breach" of the employment agreement and provides defendant with sufficient cause to terminate plaintiff's employment pursuant to paragraph 5.1(a).

[I]t is clear that defendant reasonably expected plaintiff to refrain from violating NCAA rules, to monitor assistant coaches and players to assure their compliance with those rules, to exercise a reasonable degree of vigilance to uncover any violations, and to immediately report any suspected violations.

Defendant argues that plaintiff's breach of Section 4.1(d) deprived it of the benefit it reasonably expected from the employment agreement in three ways: subjecting defendant to NCAA sanctions; adversely affecting defendant's reputation in the community; and breaching the trust between plaintiff and defendant's athletic director.

In assessing the potential harm to defendant in the form of NCAA sanctions, the court is mindful that the NCAA notice of allegations lists a total of seven violations in the men's basketball program; six of those allegations involve a player other than Alex Radojevic. Thus, the extent of the harm to defendant in the form of NCAA sanctions that can be fairly attributed to the Radojevic matter is difficult to predict.

Moreover, a defense based upon the four-year limitation period is clearly available to defendant with respect to the Radojevic matter. The court finds that even though defendant has elected not to avail itself of this defense in proceedings before the NCAA, the availability of this defense is a mitigating factor in determining the extent that defendant is or will be deprived of the expected benefit of Section 4.1(d).

Finally, the NCAA has not sought any sanctions arising from plaintiff's execution of allegedly false NCAA compliance certificates and the evidence shows that the NCAA rarely penalizes member institutions for such violations.

With respect to self-imposed sanctions, [Ohio State's compliance officer] testified that member institutions, such as defendant, frequently self-impose penalties in advance of the NCAA findings in an effort to demonstrate good faith. The hope is that the NCAA will ultimately conclude that the self-imposed sanctions are sufficient and that no further penalty will be imposed.

In September 2004, defendant self-imposed sanctions in response to the NCAA allegations. Those sanctions included the forfeiture of two scholarships in the 2005 recruiting class and a post-season ban for the 2004-2005 season. There was no testimony in this case whether those sanctions were imposed solely as a result of the Radojevic matter. However, even if the court were to assume that all of the sanctions relate to the alleged recruiting violation involving Radojevic, the evidence shows that these sanctions are not as debilitating to defendant's basketball program as defendant suggests. [An associate athletic director] testified that at the time the post-season ban was imposed, she did not believe that the team was good enough to merit a post-season tournament invitation. With regard to the two scholarships forfeited by defendant for the 2005 recruiting class, the evidence demonstrates that the loss may not result in significant harm to the basketball program given defendant's expectation that the recruiting class for the 2005-2006 year will be one of the best in its history.

Upon consideration of the relevant circumstances for determining materiality, the court finds that plaintiff's failure of performance was not material. Although plaintiff breached Section 4.1(d) by making and then failing to timely disclose a loan, the extent to which defendant was deprived of the benefit it reasonably expected from the employment agreement was not as significant as defendant contends. For example, the evidence shows that the NCAA sanctions and the injury to defendant's reputation that can be fairly attributed to the loan are relatively minor. Additionally, while plaintiff may not be able to cure either the reputational injury or the NCAA sanctions, the evidence shows that the breach of trust could have been repaired. In comparison, plaintiff's forfeiture of salary and benefits is substantial. Furthermore, while plaintiff's conduct prior to disclosing the loan was not completely consistent with good faith and fair dealing, plaintiff did make a good faith effort to resolve the dispute. Defendant chose a course that was adversarial.

Because plaintiff's failure of performance was not material, defendant did not have cause for termination. Because defendant did not have cause for termination, defendant was contractually obligated to pay plaintiff in accordance with the provisions relating to termination other than for cause. Defendant breached the contract by refusing to pay plaintiff.

With respect to Section 4.1(d) of the instant agreement, it is clear to the court that NCAA compliance is important to defendant; it is one of the specified duties of the coach. However, Section 5.1(b) of the contract contemplates a chain of events whereby plaintiff could retain his employment in the face of an ongoing major infractions investigation by the NCAA and that he could remain so employed absent the imposition of certain serious sanctions. From this language the court concludes that the parties did not consider plaintiff's performance under Section 4.1(d) of the contract to be so critical that a failure of any kind would justify immediate termination for cause. If defendant reasonably expected perfect compliance, Section 5.1(b) would not have been made part of the agreement.

In summary, Geiger's June 8, 2004, letter speaks to a single, isolated recruiting infraction by plaintiff and plaintiff's failure to timely disclose that violation. The evidence shows that the violation consists of a loan made to the family of a prospect for humanitarian reasons. The evidence also demonstrates that such prospect was ineligible to participate in intercollegiate athletics at the time that the loan was made. Although plaintiff breached his contract by making the loan under these circumstances, the court is persuaded, given the contract language, that this single, isolated failure of performance was not so egregious as to frustrate the essential purpose of that contract and thus render future performance by defendant impossible. Because the breach by plaintiff was not a material breach, defendant did not have cause to terminate plaintiff's employment. Defendant's decision to do so without any compensation to plaintiff was a breach of the parties' agreement.

****

The court ordered Ohio State to pay O'Brien liquidated damages as determined by his contract, and in 2008, the Ohio Supreme Court declined to hear the university's appeal, which effectively ended the lawsuit. At a glance, one would think it absurd that a school must pay damages when it fires a coach for breaking NCAA rules, especially considering that in 2006 the NCAA imposed penalties upon Ohio State and O'Brien for recruiting violations. The result of the case emphasizes the importance of contractual language. Recently, on an appeal to the NCAA, O'Brien's sanctions were reduced to allow him to resume coaching in 2008.

EMPLOYMENT CONTRACTS FOR PROFESSIONAL ATHLETES

The employment contracts of the players in the four major professional leagues of football, basketball, hockey, and baseball are discussed in later chapters. A comment about the application of the at-will rule on the players' contracts in the NFL is, however, appropriate at this juncture.

Many players in the National Football League (NFL) have multi-year contracts. Although these contracts are for a term, the players are, to a large extent, at-will employees pursuant to their contract. The standard contract that NFL players must sign contains the following provision:

> If at any time, in the sole judgement of Club, Player's skill or performance has been unsatisfactory as compared with other players...then Club may terminate this contract. In addition, during the period any salary cap is in effect, this contract may be terminated if, in Club's opinion, Player is anticipated to make less of a contribution to Club's ability to compete than another player...

Technically, the player may not be an at-will employee. The employer must have a reason or *cause* to release the player. The *cause*, however, can be simply that, in the opinion of the coach, the player's skills are lacking. That is, even though a player may sign a four-year contract, he can be released immediately. The player would not be entitled to any further salary unless his contract was guaranteed. Guaranteed contracts are common in the National Basketball Association (NBA) and in Major League Baseball (MLB), but are rare in the NFL. As will be explained in a later chapter, a player in the NFL, and in the other leagues, does have some protection if he is released due to a sport-related injury.

In February 2005, an arbitrator ordered Ricky Williams to return more than $8 million in signing bonuses to the NFL's Miami Dolphins as a result of Williams's sudden retirement in 2004. His contract contained the following provision:

> If player is in default, then upon demand by Club Player shall return and refund to the Club any and all incentive payments previously paid by Club and relinquish and forfeit any and all earned, but unpaid incentives.

Williams and the NFLPA, the player's union, challenged the arbitrator's ruling in court. The Judge noted it had limited authority to overturn an arbitrator's decision. The court construed the provision as a valid liquidated damage clause and upheld the ruling.

An interesting twist on the at-will rule involved a dispute between the boxer, Mike Tyson, and his former trainer, Kevin Rooney. After Rooney was fired, he filed suit against Tyson alleging Tyson orally agreed to use Rooney as his trainer "for as long as Tyson fought" and to pay Rooney ten (10%) percent of Tyson's earnings. A jury awarded Rooney $4.4 million, but the trial judge set aside the jury's award. The case was appealed.

Rooney v. Mike Tyson (1997)

Kevin Rooney appeals from a decision of the United States District Court vacating a prior jury award of $4,415,651 in damages for breach of his oral employment contract with defendant Michael Gerard Tyson and granting Tyson judgment as a matter of law.

I. Background

Rooney claims that, pursuant to an oral contract in 1982 between himself and Cus D'Amato, Tyson's legal guardian and manager, he was to train Tyson until Tyson turned professional, whereupon he would be Tyson's trainer "for as long as [Tyson] fought," and would be paid ten percent of Tyson's boxing earnings. Based upon this agreement with D'Amato, Rooney trained Tyson for twenty-eight months, without compensation, until Tyson turned professional in March 1985.

In September 1984, D'Amato arranged for Tyson to enter into a written contract with Reel Sports, Inc., a firm owned by Jim Jacobs and William Cayton. Tyson granted Reel Sports the authority to designate his boxing manager and agreed with their decision to make Jacobs the manager. This contract was effective from June 30, 1984 (Tyson's eighteenth birthday) until June 30, 1991. Rooney alleges that, prior to Tyson's first professional fight, D'Amato told Jacobs and Cayton on several occasions that Rooney would be Tyson's trainer for the duration of his professional fighting career and that he would be paid ten percent of Tyson's boxing earnings. But, he concedes that there was never any written agreement to this effect. D'Amato died in 1985, while Tyson was enjoying ever-increasing success as a professional boxer. At the same time, rumors abounded that Rooney would be replaced by a more established trainer. Rooney claims that he therefore confronted Jacobs and that Jacobs allegedly reaffirmed the "contract." According to Rooney, although Jacobs offered to put the agreement in writing, he (Rooney) declined the offer and said that a handshake was sufficient. The rumors of Rooney's replacement persisted, however. And so, in 1987, in response to a press inquiry, Tyson authorized Jacobs to say that "Kevin Rooney will be Mike Tyson's trainer as long as Mike Tyson is a professional fighter.... " A videotape of this press statement was sent to Rooney. Thereafter, Rooney continued to train Tyson and was paid fully for each of Tyson's professional fights.

In 1988, Tyson was involved in both a highly publicized divorce and a lawsuit against Cayton. That same year, Rooney appeared on television where he commented on the divorce and seemingly also sided with Cayton. This apparently angered Tyson, and on December 9, 1988, Rooney read an article in the New York Post stating that Tyson would no longer train with him. Rooney then brought the present action against Tyson claiming a breach of the 1982 employment contract.

By its verdict, the jury made clear that it believed Rooney's allegations.

This case presents a series of questions relating to the scope of the New York employment-at-will rule. The New York Court of Appeals has consistently applied a strict rule that "absent an agreement establishing a fixed duration, an employment relationship is presumed to be a hiring at-will, terminable at any time by either party."

Some federal courts have held that, in New York, terms of duration ending upon retirement or on the reaching of retirement age are too indefinite to sustain employment other than as "at-will." For example, the courts have found: "Oral assurances of lifetime employment or a suggestion that an employee would be fired only for cause without more are insufficient to support a claim for breach of employment contract under New York law"; an employer's verbal assurances that an employee would be retained through normal retirement age do not specify a sufficiently definite term of employment; an employer's promise of "long term employment" is "even less definite than a permanent appointment or employment until retirement, neither of which states a clear and definite limitation on the employer's right to discharge". When the term of duration is specified, with reference to one party's engagement in a profession, however, some federal courts have held such contracts were definite. See *DON King Prods., Inc. v. Douglas*, upholding a three-year promotional contract that would be "automatically extended to cover the entire period [the boxer is] world champion and a period of two years following the date on which [the boxer] thereafter cease[s], for any reason, to be so recognized as world champion".

While these federal cases have relied on the decisions of various New York courts, there is, nevertheless, no clear holding by New York's highest court on the scope of the at-will employment rule. These and other issues concerning the reach of the New York at-will rule are highly germane to the case before us. Accordingly, in certifying a question of the validity of the particular contractual relationship before us, we are not asking the New York Court of Appeals to interpret a contract or to decide a case for the federal courts, but, rather, to elucidate a series of open and recurring questions of New York law.

II. Certification

We certify the following question to the New York Court of Appeals: Does an oral contract between a fight trainer and a professional boxer to train the boxer "for as long as the boxer fights professionally" establish a definite duration, or does it constitute employment for indefinite duration within the scope of the at-will rule?

****

Under New York state law, an employment contract that does not have a fixed term is presumed to be at-will. The Tyson case was in federal court. The issue before the federal court was whether under New York law an employment agreement for the duration of a career was sufficient as a fixed term and, therefore, not subject to the at-will rule. The federal court certified the question to the New York State court for an answer. New York's highest court of appeal ruled that the contract did have a duration that was sufficiently ascertainable. Therefore, the at-will concept did not apply, which meant Rooney was entitled to the award.

SCHOLARSHIPS

Athletic scholarships are routinely granted to student-athletes by colleges and universities. What is the legal relationship between the student and the institution as a result of a scholarship? What are the rights and responsibilities of the respective parties? Most schools prefer to treat the scholarship as an educational grant without any substantial quid-pro-quo (something for something). One reason schools prefer this view is that they do not want the relationship to appear as an employment contract.

The Internal Revenue's position regarding athletic scholarships raises interesting issues. According to the IRS, section 117(b)(2) of the Internal Revenue Code, a school's scholarship payment of tuition, fees, and books is not recognized as income. Payment of room and board, however, is taxable income to the student. The fact that the IRS treats part of a scholarship as income supports the "pay-for-play" argument that student-athletes on scholarship are, in fact, employees of the school.

Recognizing student-athletes as employees of a school would have an enormous impact. Employee status could trigger antitrust, labor, and workers' compensation consequences. Colleges shudder at the thought. The employee designation would also, of course, conflict with the NCAA's position as to the *amateur* status of student-athletes. Most courts that have addressed the issue have held that a scholarship is a contract, but not one of employment. How to classify the contract and what remedies are available in the event of a breach are more problematic.

An athletic scholarship generally involves a National Letter of Intent (the offer) submitted by a school to a student. The student signs the Letter of Intent (acceptance), and the school extends a scholarship promise in the form of a financial aid agreement. In addition, the student and the athletic director may execute several other documents, including a Drug Consent form, Disability Insurance, Gambling Statements, Summer Employment, NCAA Statements, and Agent Affidavits. All of these agreements are bundled and comprise the contract agreement between the student and the school.

The Kevin Ross case was a sad commentary on college athletics. The suit revealed the misplaced priorities that many colleges have undertaken in pursuit of establishing winning teams and the price paid by some athletes. Ross, an ex-student, filed suit against Creighton on a number of theories. The trial court dismissed Ross's suit. The trial court's focus, however, was on Ross's *tort* or *educational malpractice* claim. Tort law and the court's opinion on that issue are addressed in a later chapter. The case was appealed, and the appellate court reversed the trial court's dismissal of the *contract* action and ruled that Ross was entitled to a trial on that issue.

Ross v. Creighton Univ. (1992)

In the spring of 1978, Mr. Ross was a promising senior basketball player at Wyandotte High School in Kansas City, Kansas. Sometime during his senior year in high school, he accepted an athletic scholarship to attend Creighton and to play on its varsity basketball team.

Creighton is an academically superior university. Mr. Ross comes from an academically disadvantaged background. At the time of his enrollment at Creighton, Mr. Ross was at an academic level far below that of the average Creighton student. For example, he scored in the bottom fifth percentile of college-bound seniors taking the American College Test, while the average freshman admitted to Creighton with him scored in the upper twenty-seven percent. According to the complaint, Creighton realized Mr. Ross' academic limitations when it admitted him, and, to induce him to attend and play basketball, Creighton assured Mr. Ross that he would receive sufficient tutoring so that he "would receive a meaningful education while at CREIGHTON."

Mr. Ross attended Creighton from 1978 until 1982. During that time he maintained a D average and acquired 96 of the 128 credits needed to graduate. However, many of these credits were in courses such as Marksmanship and Theory of Basketball, and did not count towards a university degree. Mr. Ross alleges that he took these courses on the advice of Creighton's Athletic Department, and that the department also employed a secretary to read his assignments and prepare and type his papers. Mr. Ross also asserts that Creighton failed to provide him with sufficient and competent tutoring that it had promised.

When he left Creighton, Mr. Ross had the overall language skills of a fourth grader and the reading skills of a seventh grader. Consequently, Mr. Ross enrolled, at Creighton's expense, for a year of remedial education at the Westside Preparatory School in Chicago. At Westside, Mr. Ross attended classes with grade school children. He later entered Roosevelt University in Chicago, but was forced to withdraw because of a lack of funds. In July 1987, Mr. Ross suffered what he terms a "major depressive episode," during which he barricaded himself in a Chicago motel room and threw furniture out the window.

The Contract Claims

In counts two and three of his complaint, Mr. Ross alleges that Creighton breached an oral or a written contract that it had with him. When read as a totality, these allegations fairly allege that Creighton agreed, in exchange for Mr. Ross' promise to play on its basketball team, to allow him an opportunity to participate, in a meaningful way, in the academic program of the University despite his deficient academic background. The complaint further alleges, when read as a totality, that Creighton breached this contract and denied Mr. Ross any real opportunity to participate in and benefit from the University's academic program when it failed to perform five commitments made to Ross: (1) "to provide adequate and competent tutoring services," (2) "to require [Mr. Ross] to attend tutoring sessions," (3) to afford Mr. Ross "a reasonable opportunity to take full advantage of tutoring services," (4) to allow Mr. Ross to red-shirt, and (5) to provide funds to allow Mr. Ross to complete his college education.

It is held generally in the United States that the "basic legal relation between a student and a private university or college is contractual in nature. The catalogues, bulletins, circulars, and regulations of the institution made available to the matriculant become a part of the contract." Indeed, there seems to be "no dissent" from this proposition. As the district court correctly noted, Illinois recognizes that the relationship between a student and an educational institution is, in some of its aspects, contractual. It is quite clear, however, that Illinois would not recognize all aspects of a university-student relationship as subject to remedy through a contract action. "A contract between a private institution and a student confers duties upon both parties which cannot be arbitrarily disregarded and may be judicially enforced." However, "a decision of the school authorities relating to the academic qualification of the students will not be reviewed. Courts are not qualified to pass an opinion as to the attainments of a student ... and ... courts will not review a decision of the school authorities relating to academic qualifications of the students."

There is no question, we believe, that Illinois would adhere to the great weight of authority and bar any attempt to repackage an educational malpractice claim as a contract claim. As several courts have noted, the policy concerns that preclude a cause of action for educational malpractice apply with equal force to bar a breach of contract claim attacking the general quality of an education. "Where the essence of the complaint is that the school breached its agreement by failing to provide an effective education, the court is again asked to evaluate the course of instruction ... [and] is similarly called upon to review the soundness of the method of teaching that has been adopted by an educational institution."

To state a claim for breach of contract, the plaintiff must do more than simply allege that the education was not good enough. Instead, he must point to an identifiable contractual promise that the defendant failed to honor. Thus, ... if the defendant took tuition money and then provided no education, or alternately, promised a set number of hours of instruction and then failed to deliver, a breach of contract action may be available. See *Zumbrun*, 1972 (breach of contract action allowed against university when professor declined to give lectures and final exam, and all students received a grade of "B"). Similarly, a breach of contract action might exist if a student enrolled in a course explicitly promising instruction that would qualify him as a journeyman, but in which the fundamentals necessary to attain that skill were not even presented. In these cases, the essence of the plaintiff's complaint would not be that the institution failed to perform adequately a promised educational service but rather that it failed to perform that service at all. Ruling on this issue would not require an inquiry into the nuances of educational processes and theories, but rather an objective assessment of whether the institution made a good faith effort to perform on its promise.

We read Mr. Ross' complaint to allege more than a failure of the University to provide him with an education of a certain quality. Rather, he alleges that the University knew that he was not qualified academically to participate in its curriculum. Nevertheless, it made a specific promise that he would be able to participate in a meaningful way in that program, because it would provide certain specific services to him. Finally, he alleges that the University breached its promise by reneging on its commitment to provide those services and, consequently, effectively cutting him off from any participation in and benefit from the University's academic program. To adjudicate such a claim, the court would not be required to determine whether Creighton had breached its contract with Mr. Ross by providing deficient academic services. Rather, its inquiry would be limited to whether the University had provided any real access to its academic curriculum at all.

Accordingly, we must disagree respectfully with our colleague in the district court as to whether the contract counts of the complaint can be dismissed at the pleadings stage. In our view, the allegations of the complaint are sufficient to warrant further proceedings. We emphasize, however, the narrow ground of our disagreement. We agree—indeed we emphasize—that courts should not "take on the job of supervising the relationship between colleges and student-athletes or creating in effect a new relationship between them." We also recognize a formal university-student contract is rarely employed and, consequently, "the general nature and terms of the agreement are usually implied, with specific terms to be found in the university bulletin and other publications; custom and usages can also become specific terms by implication." Nevertheless, we believe that the district court can adjudicate Mr. Ross' specific and narrow claim that he was barred from any participation in and benefit from the University's academic program without second-guessing the professional judgment of the University faculty on academic matters.

Affirmed in part, remanded in part.

****

Does a school that awards an athletic scholarship to a student guarantee a quality education? What are some situations that might provide a student-athlete with a valid cause of action for breach of contract against a school?

In 1990, Congress passed the Student-Athlete Right To Know Act. The law requires the Department of Education to publish comparative athlete graduation rates from different schools. The NCAA followed with a similar rule, which allows student-athletes the right to obtain graduation information on schools.

Would a student who was given an athletic scholarship by a college be entitled to damages if, after enrolling in the college, he was informed the sport—for example, wrestling—had been eliminated and his scholarship revoked? It is almost certain that the college would be liable for the promised benefits, such as tuition, but for how long? In addition, the student would still miss the opportunity to participate in the sport. Is the student entitled to damages for that loss and, if so, how would the court determine the amount of compensation?

Athletic scholarships are rarely terminated due to poor athletic performance. The contracts are, however, granted on one-year renewable terms. Can a coach remove an athlete from the team or revoke the scholarship if the student skips practice or fails to put forth a reasonable effort? Can the school take away a scholarship if a football player skips spring football practice to study or to run track at the school? These types of issues should not only be discussed during recruiting, but also addressed, in writing, in the scholarship contract.

The issue of a student-athlete missing practice in order to devote more time to his studies was raised in *Taylor v. Wake Forrest* (1972). In *Taylor*, the player was on a football scholarship. Taylor quit going to practice, allegedly to study and improve his grades. The school withdrew the scholarship because of his refusal to participate with the team. Taylor filed a lawsuit to have the scholarship reinstated. The court found that Taylor knew the scholarship required both academic and physical obligations. The court held Taylor's failure to participate in practice was a breach of his "contractual obligations," and the school was allowed to terminate the scholarship. After the *Taylor* decision, the NCAA adopted a rule providing that whenever a student's athletic ability (or participation) is taken into consideration in any degree in awarding financial aid, such aid shall not be awarded in excess of one academic year.

The Brian Fortay case in Florida involved a recurring problem in the college recruiting process. In 1989, Fortay was a star high-school quarterback. The University of Miami's coach, Jimmy Johnson, recruited Fortay and allegedly promised him that he, Johnson, would never leave Miami. This promise was made because of reports that an NFL team was trying to hire Johnson. Johnson also allegedly promised Fortay that he would groom him as Miami's starting quarterback. Three weeks after Fortay committed to Miami, Johnson announced he was leaving Miami to coach the NFL Dallas Cowboys. The new coach, Dennis

Erickson, persuaded Fortay not to switch schools and allegedly made promises, as Johnson had, that Fortay would be his first Heisman trophy winner. Erickson, however, chose Geno Torretta as his quarterback, who, to add to the injury, *did* win the Heisman trophy. Fortay left Miami for another school, but, by the time he was eligible to play, he no longer excelled. Fortay filed suit against Miami, Johnson, Erickson, and others. The coaches denied making the promises, but unbeknownst to them, Fortay and his Father had secretly taped many of the conversations. The tapes were ruled inadmissible pursuant to Florida law, and most of Fortay's claims were dismissed prior to trial. The court ruled, however, that Fortay could present his claim of breach of oral promises in the recruiting effort to a jury. An undisclosed settlement was reached before the case was tried.

Many high school athletes select a college based on the head coach. What rights, if any, does an athlete, such as Fortay, have if the coach resigns after the student passes up other opportunities and commits to the school?

ACADEMIC COUNSELORS

High school and college athletes rely extensively on academic counselors. In *Sain v. Cedar Rapids Community School District* (2001), a guidance counselor who gave a student incorrect course information was sued by the student. The student was a high school senior who had a full scholarship to play NCAA Division I college basketball. In order to be eligible to play, he was required to complete a certain number of NCAA approved courses during high school. The student was enrolled in an approved English class, but asked his guidance counselor if he could switch to another class. The counselor mistakenly told him that the second class was NCAA approved, but later discovered it was not. As a result, the student's scholarship was revoked. The counselor argued he did not owe a duty to the student, but the court disagreed and held that he could be sued for breach of a duty.

Hendricks v. Clemson (2003) was an action brought by R. J. Hendricks against Clemson for advice provided to him by a Clemson advisor. Hendricks played baseball at St. Leo College a Division II school in Florida, and was majoring in Hotel Management. Although Hendricks was on a scholarship, St. Leo permitted him to speak with and transfer to Clemson. Clemson did not offer a degree in Hotel Management. Following the recommendations of a Clemson advisor, Hendricks elected to major in Speech and Communications and enrolled in 15 hours. Shortly thereafter, the advisor realized she had made a mistake and that Hendricks's course load did not meet NCAA requirements. She instructed Hendricks to drop one course and pick up two others so he would be carrying 18 hours. Later, the advisor realized that Hendricks needed to carry 20 hours to comply with NCAA rules that require students to have completed at least 50% of the course requirements for a major to be eligible in their fourth year. The advisor admitted her mistake and requested a waiver from the NCAA. The waiver was denied, and Hendricks was not allowed to play at Clemson. He returned to St. Leo and played baseball, but was not on a scholarship. Hendricks filed suit alleging negligence, breach of contract, and breach of a fiduciary duty. The South Carolina Supreme Court reversed the lower court and ruled in favor of Clemson on each cause of action, including the action in contract.

For support, Hendricks and the Court of Appeals cite cases from several jurisdictions that have acknowledged the possibility that "the relationship between a student and a university is at least in part contractual." (citations omitted). ... Clemson admits that some aspects of the student/university relationship are indeed contractual, but argues Hendricks has not pointed to an identifiable contractual promise that Clemson failed to honor in this case. We agree. Hendricks fails to point to any written promise from Clemson to ensure his athletic eligibility, and submits no real evidence to support his claim that such a promise was implied. He did not discuss NCAA academic eligibility until he was already enrolled at Clemson. His conversations with Kennedy-Dixon in June, according to both his deposition and Kennedy-Dixon's deposition, were limited to what major would most easily transfer back to St. Leo.

A similar result was reached in *Scott v. Savers Insurance* (2003). Ryan Scott was a high school senior with exceptional hockey skills. He received scholarship offers from several Division I schools. He and his parents were advised by the high school's guidance counselor that a course, Broadcast Communication, would meet the NCAA's test as a core English course. Scott later accepted a scholarship offer that was conditioned on his compliance with the NCAA's rules. The NCAA rejected the course, and Scott lost the scholarship. Scott filed a tort and breach of contract suit against the school. The court dismissed both actions. With respect to the contract action the court stated

We conclude that no contract exists to support a breach of contract claim in the present case because any alleged promise by the District to provide counseling services was a promise to perform a preexisting legal obligation.

The tort, or negligence, action was dismissed based upon the state's immunity.

TICKETS TO SPORTING EVENTS

Little thought, other than price and seat location, is generally given to the contract that occurs as a result of the purchase of a ticket for a sporting event. Several ticket incidents, however, have resulted in litigation over the rights and responsibilities of ticket holders.

The 1997 Mike Tyson—Evander Holyfield heavyweight boxing match was highly promoted and sold on a pay-per-view basis to almost 2 million subscribers. The fight was abruptly stopped after Tyson took his *second* bite of Holyfield's ear. Two class action lawsuits were filed by pay-per-view customers against Tyson and his promoters alleging several causes of action, including breach of contract. The plaintiffs' alleged that Tyson intentionally caused the fight to be stopped prematurely and, thereby, deprived the plaintiffs of what they were entitled to on the contract, that is, the viewing of a properly conducted boxing match. The litigation was ultimately dismissed, but the cases raised interesting questions about the rights of spectators to sporting events.

The Denver Broncos paid about $400,000 in a settlement of a class action suit filed on behalf of about 22,000 season-ticket holders. The lawsuit was filed after the Broncos announced in 1995 that the owners of the tickets could not sell the tickets on the open market.

Two class action lawsuits were filed in May of 1998 by season-ticket holders of the Florida Marlins. The plaintiffs were angered by the Marlins trade of players who won the World Series the year before. The latest round of trades left the Marlins with just two of the position players who were in the Series lineup. As a result of the trades, the Marlins salary of $53 million in 1997 dropped to less than $24 million for the 1998 season. The plaintiffs acknowledged that trades are part of the game. They contended, however, that advertising and promotional materials sent by the Marlins assured the fans a quality team would be on the field. The Marlins sent a marketing letter out asking fans to "get excited" about a powerful lineup featuring Gary Sheffield and Bobby Bonilla. A few months later, the two players were traded. The plaintiffs claim that they were misled into buying season tickets. WQAM, the flagship radio station of the Marlins, also filed suit against the team as a result of the player purge. The station claimed it lost substantial advertising dollars and suffered a ratings plunge.

Does a season-ticket holder have a contractual right to purchase season tickets in future years? The answer, of course, depends on the terms of the contract. *In Re Liebman* (1997) was a bankruptcy case where the court had to determine if the trustee of the bankruptcy estate had a contractual right to sell the debtor's *right* to what the court described as "something greatly prized in the Chicagoland area—season tickets to the Chicago Bulls basketball games." The Bulls claimed that the debtor did not have a property interest in the tickets and that only a license, revocable by the Bulls, existed. The court agreed with the Bulls and stated

> The few bankruptcy opinions that have addressed this issue are divided. See *In re Harden*, 1996 (Phoenix Suns season ticket holder had no property interest that could be sold by the trustee. Although, they generally gave the season ticket holder an opportunity to renew, there was no guarantee, nor any legal right, that the Suns would extend the offer to renew); *In re Tucker Freight Lines, Inc.*, 1984 (Notre Dame's past practice of selling the debtor season tickets for over forty years did not create any contract). *In re Walsh*, 1994 (season tickets to the Charlotte Hornets were property of the estate where the debtor was one of the original subscribers and had paid a $10,000 deposit for the right to purchase up to 100 tickets each year); *In re I.D. Craig Service Corp.*, 1992, (right to renew season tickets for the Pittsburgh Steelers was property of the estate that could be sold by the trustee over the objection of the Steelers, where the longstanding policy was to permit automatic renewal and transferability of season tickets).
>
> The key factor that distinguishes the cases relied upon by the Bulls from the cases relied upon by the trustee is how the sports franchise treats the renewal rights of season tickets holders. The Bulls' policy is clearly stated in all pertinent material: The season ticket invoice states that "[s]eason tickets are offered on a one-year basis"; the playoff ticket invoice says that "[e]ach season and playoff ticket is a revocable license"; various letters sent to season ticket holders state that "[t]he Bulls reserve the right to review all accounts before offering season tickets for the [next] season." The Bulls also prohibit the transfer of season tickets except in very limited circumstances. The written policy provides: "NEW CONTRACTS ARE NOT TAKEN FOR PERSONAL ACCOUNTS. WE DO NOT CHANGE NAMES, ADD NAMES, NOR DO WE

TAKE CARE OF NAMES AND ADDRESSES. SEASON TICKETS ARE NOT TRANSFERABLE AND THEY ARE A REVOKABLE (sic) LICENSE. SEASON TICKETS ARE OFFERED ON A ONE-YEAR BASIS ONLY." (Emphasis in original).

Chaussee v. Dallas Cowboys Football (1997) involved a breach of contract suit by several season-ticket holders against the Cowboys. The plaintiffs held seats on "Row A," which was originally the front row of the upper deck. The Cowboys, however, built Row 1 in front of Row A. Row A ticket holders were not amused and filed suit. The court found that the Cowboys had given the plaintiffs exactly what they had agreed to—seats on Row A and that the Cowboys had not contracted to keep Row A the front row. The suit was dismissed.

One couple filed suit against the NCAA, because they were forced to buy a third ticket from a scalper after security refused to let them enter without a ticket for their seven-month old infant. The couple claimed the infant had to be breast-fed every two hours and, therefore, could not be left at home. The suit claimed that the NCAA policy unjustly discriminated against women who breast feed because an infant could not, and did not, use a seat. The outcome of the suit is unknown.

A season ticket holder filed an antitrust action against the University of Miami after the school notified him he had to make a $1,200 donation to keep his 50-yard-line seats at the Orange Bowl. The suit alleges that the policy is similar to an illegal tying agreement, because he is being forced to buy an unwanted product in order to purchase the desired product. The ticket holder dropped the suit, citing a desire to purchase season tickets in the future, but this type of practice is common among college athletic departments.

Fans who misbehave at games can be ejected and even have their ticket privileges for future games revoked. Most courts have held that tickets to events are a revocable license granted at the option of the facility manager. Many personal seat licenses (PSLs) in professional sports require fans to sign agreements governing their conduct. Tickets to the U.S. Open Golf Championship usually include a warning that the ticket can be revoked for failure to obey course marshals' orders including demands for silence during play.

In *Yarde Metal v. New England Patriots* (2003) the Patriots revoked the rights of a 20-year season-ticket holder to continue to purchase the tickets. The revocation came after one of Yarde's employees was disorderly at a game. A disclaimer on the back of the ticket stated the ticket was a revocable license and that the right of revocation was reserved to the team. The court found that the license characterization was based on the "minimal property" theory and upheld the team's revocation. The court did suggest, however, that it may no longer be correct to apply a license theory to season-ticket holders and that contract law may be appropriate to the agreements.

Ticket holders who are confined to wheelchairs have filed suits against sports facilities alleging that they were denied sight-lines over standing spectators. The claims are that the impaired parties are denied the opportunity to see the most exciting plays of the games because of the location of their seats and the inability to see when fans in front of them stand. These suits are based on federal laws, discussed in a later chapter, which prohibit discrimination against impaired persons, but they also raise contractual issues.

Agency Law and Sports Agents

Sport agents have become an integral part of professional sports. Almost every professional athlete and coach, and many college coaches, are represented by agents. A few agents have achieved star status themselves as a result of the athletes they represent. These "super agents" not only represent their clients, but exert considerable influence in the negotiations between unions and management in the professional leagues. This chapter will discuss some of the issues and regulations involving sports agents. It is necessary, however, to first review some basic aspects of agency law.

AGENCY

Agency is a legal relationship between two parties: a principal and an agent. An agency agreement authorizes the agent to speak and act on behalf of the principal. The acts of the agent on behalf of the principal, if within the scope of the agent's authority, become legally binding on the principal with respect to third parties who relied on the agent's authority to represent the principal. Agency is essential to contractual relationships in the business community. Corporations and LLCs are recognized by the law as a "person," but, in reality, they are mere documents and could not function without the ability to act through agents.

An agency relationship is consensual and does not have to meet the consideration requirements of a contract. However, most agency relationships are contracts that provide the agent with compensation for acting on behalf of the principal. A principal can create an agency relationship by written or verbal authorization and, in some cases, by conduct.

An agency relationship is similar to an employer-employee or principal-independent contractor relationship. An employer has the right to control the physical conduct of employees, but a principal does not control how an independent contractor performs a job. Agents may or may not be employees or independent contractors. For example, an attorney hired by a client is usually viewed as an independent contractor, not an employee, and may also be an agent.

An agent will usually inform a third party that he is acting as an agent and identify his principal. This is referred to as a *disclosed agency*. If an agent advises a third party that he is an agent, but does not identify his principal, the agent is described as a *partially disclosed* agent. If the agent does not reveal his principal or his agency status, an *undisclosed agency* exists. In a partially disclosed and undisclosed agency, the agent may be liable to the third party on the contract. As a general rule, however, if the agency status is known to the third party, the principal, not the agent, will be bound on the contract formed with the third party.

EXISTENCE AND SCOPE OF AGENCY

Many of the disputes in agency matters deal with whether an agency relationship exists. An agency agreement does not have to be in written form, but like any important contract, it should be. A written document minimizes the potential for disagreements among the agent, principal, and third parties. The document should, of course, accurately and completely reflect the understanding between the parties.

In 1997, PGA Tour player Lee Janzen filed suit in Florida against his agent, seeking to terminate their representation agreement. In 1995, Janzen signed a written agreement with his agent's firm, Leader Enterprises. The contract provided for Leader to serve as Janzen's exclusive agent in exchange for a fee of 20% of the value of endorsements. Janzen's suit alleged that Leader claimed it was a "preeminent marketing and representation company in the area of professional sports on a worldwide basis." The company, however, only provided three endorsement contracts to Janzen. Janzen argued that three contracts were far below what he should have received based on his performance.

The written contract included a term of three years. Janzen's suit, however, claimed that he was *orally* assured that he could cancel the contract at any time. In Florida, as in most states, the parol evidence rule applies to such disputes. The rule prohibits the introduction of evidence that changes the terms of a written contract (see Chapter 2 , Contracts). There are, however, exceptions to the rule. For example, evidence of *subsequent* modifications to the contract are generally admissible. In order to be successful, Janzen had to establish that his case met one of these exceptions.

Claims like Janzen's are common and illustrate that important contracts should always be memorialized in writing. The document should accurately describe the terms of the agreement, and any later modifications to the contract should also be in writing.

The use of agents to form *contractual* relations is common in business. Agency questions, however, also arise in disputes involving *torts*. The law of torts will be discussed in a later chapter, but includes most non-contractual wrongs. If an agent commits a tort and negligently injures a third party in the course and scope of the agent relationship, the principal may also be liable to the third party for the wrongful injury committed by the agent.

In *Hanson v. Kynast* (1994), Hanson, an Ohio St. student, was paralyzed while playing a lacrosse game against Ashland. The injury came as a result of being thrown down by an Ashland player, Kynast. Hanson filed suit against Kynast and Ashland. The suit alleged that Kynast was an agent of Ashland and acting within the scope of his authority when he injured Hanson. The court dismissed Ashland from the case, emphasizing that Kynast was not on scholarship, no fees were charged to watch the game, and the Ashland players purchased their own equipment. Does this reasoning suggest that a scholarship athlete is an agent of a school when playing the sport? Consider the following case:

Kavanagh v. Trustees of Boston University, et al. (2001)

On December 22, 1998, the university hosted a men's intercollegiate basketball game against Manhattan College. The plaintiff, Kenneth Kavanagh, was a member of the Manhattan College team. Following a contested rebound during the second half, the referee blew his whistle to signal a foul, and some elbowing and shoving ensued among a few of the competing players. When Kavanagh intervened to break up a developing scuffle between one of his teammates and a university player, he was punched in the nose by another university player, Levar Flok. Folk was immediately ejected from the game. Kavanagh was treated for what turned out to be a broken nose and returned to play later in the same game.

At the time of this incident, Folk was in his senior year. He had been recruited for the university's basketball team by its coach, Dennis Wolff, and came to the university on a full athletic scholarship. As part of the recruitment process, Wolff had met with Folk's high school coaches, who described Folk as a "good kid" and expressed no reservations about his character or comportment on the basketball court. Until the incident involving Kavanagh, Folk had not been involved in any physical altercation during a game and had never been ejected from a game. He had no prior history of physical confrontations or fights with either his own teammates or opposing players.

Kavanagh contends that Folk's status as a scholarship athlete playing for the university made him an agent of the university and that the university is therefore vicariously liable for any torts committed by Folk while playing for the university's basketball team. We reject the proposition that the doctrine of respondeat superior renders schools liable for the acts of their students, and decline to treat scholarship students any differently from paying students for these purposes.

A student's status as student does not, by itself, make the student an "employee" or "servant" of the school the student attends. Neither party understands the student's relationship with the school to be one of employment. Students attend school to serve their own interests, not the interests of the school. "The student is a buyer of education rather than an agent. . . . [A] student retains the benefit of that education for himself rather than for the university. "While schools may benefit in various ways from the presence of a particular student, or may benefit in the future from a former student's later success, the student does not attend school to do the school's bidding. Kavanagh has cited no authority for the proposition that the relationship between school and student is that of principal and agent, master and servant, or employer and employee.

The fact that a college or university has facilitated a student's ability to attend that institution by providing a scholarship or other financial assistance does not transform the relationship between the academic institution and the student into any form of employment relationship. While scholarships may introduce some element of "payment" into the relationship, scholarships are not wages. See *Rensing v. Indiana State Univ. Bd. of Trustees*, (noting that NCAA rules prohibit payment to student-athletes and that proceeds of athletic scholarships are not taxable as income). Rather, scholarships pay specific forms of expenses that the student would incur in attending school -- tuition, books, room and board -- and thereby provide the student with an education. Nor does a scholarship student "work for" the school in exchange for that scholarship. The benefits that may accrue to a school from the attendance of particularly talented athletes is conceptually no different from the benefits that schools obtain from the attendance of other forms of talented and successful students -- both as undergraduates and later as alumni, such students enhance the school's reputation, draw favorable attention to the school, and may increase the school's ability to raise funds. A school recruits and provides financial aid to students that it thinks will be good for the school in some respect, and the fact that a particular recruited scholarship student may provide the expected benefit to the school does not affect the nature of the school's legal relationship with the student. Again, scholarship or financial aid notwithstanding, neither side understands the relationship to be that of employer-employee or principal-agent.

It is undeniable that a successful athletic program, particularly in popular sports like basketball, can garner substantial revenues for colleges and universities, both directly from the sporting activities themselves (e.g., gate receipts, sale of broadcasting rights) and indirectly from the attention those activities attract (e.g., increased alumni giving). In recent years, the enormity of the revenues at stake in collegiate sports has prompted some to recommend that colleges and universities be allowed to compensate student-athletes for their "services" and thereby transform them into employees. It is recognized, however, that the current relationship of a player to a school remains that of scholarship student, not employee.

Kavanagh argues that scholarship athletes should nevertheless be treated as "agents" of their schools because it is said that they "represent" their schools. When one speaks of an athlete, or any other student, as a "representative" of his or her school, the term is not being used in its legal sense. Rather, it connotes only that a student's performance will reflect on the school and will be seen as indicative of the school's quality. Students do not "represent" their schools in the sense of being able to bind their schools to agreements, or to act on behalf of their schools. That Folk and his teammates "represented" the university whenever they competed, in the sense of demonstrating the school's capability to field competent and sportsmanlike teams, did not make the university vicariously liable for any torts committed by players in the course of competition.

****

SPORTS AGENTS

In 1959, L.S.U.'s Billy Cannon was "everybody's All American" and the winner of college football's most coveted award, the Heisman trophy. On November 30,

Cannon again received recognition for his outstanding ability when he was selected by the Los Angeles Rams as the number one pick in the NFL draft. Immediately after the draft, the Rams' General Manager, Pete Rozelle, arranged a meeting in a hotel room with Cannon. During the meeting, Cannon signed an NFL contract to play for the Rams. The urgency of Cannon's contract signing was due to Rozelle's concern about competition from the American Football League (AFL). At the time, the AFL was a competing league that was aggressively trying to lure top players away from the NFL. Rozelle's fear was well-founded—two weeks later, Cannon signed with the Houston Oilers of the AFL. On December 30, Cannon sent a letter notifying the Rams that he would be playing for the Oilers. The Rams responded by filing suit against Cannon for breach of contract, *Los Angeles Rams v. Cannon* (1960).

In Cannon's dealings with the Rams (and presumably with the Oilers), he had no agent or attorney. The judge, who ruled in Cannon's favor, was apparently influenced by Cannon's lack of representation.

> While some, particularly those schooled in - to use the vernacular - the "game of dough" may view my interpretation of the transaction as a "Pollyanna" approach and entirely unrealistic it should be borne in mind that Cannon, while having been a highly publicized college ball player, was, in fact, and still is, it would appear, a provincial lad of 21 or 22, untutored and unwise, I am convinced, in the way of the business world. While he had entertained ambitions for years to get into professional football the proposition submitted to him by the Rams came by telephone apparently without prior notice while he was away from home and in New York for the purpose of receiving one of many rapidly accumulating honors that were being bestowed upon him. He was *without counsel or advice* and the whole transaction, including the signing of the alleged contracts, was completed in less than 48 hours. When Cannon arrived at the Warwick Hotel on Monday morning he did not know whether the Rams had acquired the right to draft him. He was immediately brought before the press and, as Rozelle testified, he Rozelle, heard Cannon make the statement to the effect that he would sign a contract with the Rams following the L.S.U. and Mississippi game in the Sugar Bowl on New Year's Day. ...
>
> In view of the foregoing it is my conclusion that the accepting of possession of the check for $10,000 by Cannon was not an acceptance of payment under the alleged contract.

Cannon's situation was not unique. The accepted practice at that time was for players to represent themselves regarding their professional contracts. Attorneys or agents who specialized in representing athletes were virtually non-existent. Legendary Green Bay Packers Coach Vince Lombardi immediately released a key veteran player when he retained an agent. But times have changed since the days of Billy Cannon. Today, a player projected to go in the top rounds of a professional draft will be solicited in some form or another by more than 100 sports agents. Even college players who are not likely to be drafted are often contacted by several agents. Representing professional athletes has become a high-profile line of work. There is no mystery to the attraction: Average salaries and bonuses for players are in the millions of dollars and increasing each year. For a select group of athletes, even larger sums are earned from commercial endorsements.

The athletes entering the professional ranks have exceptional skill in their respective sports, but often have little or no experience in business affairs. There is a tremendous need for assistance with respect to negotiating what is best for the player on a number of issues. In addition, because of the vast sums of money involved, professional advice on management and investment of the income is critical.

Some advisors to players in the professional leagues have suggested that the players do not need agents and can be effectively represented by an attorney versed in contract law and the applicable collective bargaining agreement (CBA). The idea is that the athlete can save money by paying an attorney an hourly rate or flat fee rather than a percentage of the athlete's contract.

Another approach is to pay an agent a percentage of the amount obtained by the agent above the first offer made to the player. Professional athletes, especially those drafted in the early rounds and free agents are going to generate substantial first-offers regardless of who represents them. In the National Basketball Association, there is very little negotiation over the salary for a rookie entering the League. Pursuant to the CBA, the player's salary is based on a scale according to the player's draft position.

There are, however, a number of important issues other than salary and bonus that must be addressed during negotiation of a professional athlete's contract. Contract provisions pertaining to the term, guarantees, incentive clauses, voidable years, and options may be part of the negotiation process. In addition, agents generally do more than negotiate team contracts, often providing tax assistance and long-term financial planning for the player. The nature of the professional athlete's job provides for large sums of money over short periods of time (the average NFL career lasts about four years), and the agent must often ensure that the player develops financial responsibility. Agents may also assist in making teams aware of a player's talent and availability and provide advice with respect to endorsement contracts and dealing with the media. In many cases, an agent is the first person an athlete will call if a personal problem arises.

The expansion of free agency has arguably increased the importance of agents in contract negotiations for veteran players. On the other hand, the existence of rookie salary controls has diminished the role of the agent with respect to first-year players, especially in the NBA.

However, the agent occasionally tries to provide too much advice. In 2007, Alex Rodriguez had just completed one of the most impressive offensive seasons in the history of Major League Baseball, with more than 50 home runs and 150 runs batted in. Rodriguez was eligible to opt-out of his contract with the New York Yankees, and the Yankees made it known publicly that if he chose to do so, they would not pursue him on the free agent market. The team made this decision in part because they would lose a multi-million dollar subsidy from the Texas Rangers (Rodriguez's previous team) to help pay his hefty salary. Rodriguez's agent, Scott Boras, had previously achieved the largest contract in professional sports history for Rodriguez, and Boras made it clear that after several impressive seasons, he thought Rodriguez would command an even larger contract in 2007. Boras had Rodriguez's decision to explore the free agent market announced live during Game 4 of the World Series, a move heavily criticized by several commentators.

After a few weeks of exploring offers from other teams, Rodriguez decided to contact the Yankees and attempt to re-negotiate a new deal with the team. The team had initially decided not to pursue a contract any further, but told Rodriguez that it was willing to talk directly to Rodriguez, as long as there was no involvement by Boras. The two parties reached an agreement without Boras, and Rodriguez ultimately had to settle for as much as $20 million less than the Yankees would have been willing to pay before he opted out. Boras was heavily criticized for misreading the market and for adopting overly firm negotiating tactics with the Yankees; as a result, his relationship with Rodriguez was significantly damaged to the point that Rodriguez announced on national television that the two were no longer on speaking terms. The rift illustrates how things can occasionally go massively wrong for an agent who tries to play too active a role in the professional life of a client.

FIDUCIARY DUTY AND CONFLICT OF INTEREST

Agents have a fiduciary relationship with the principal, that is, a position of trust and confidence. The agent owes the principal the utmost in loyalty, diligence, and disclosure. An agent is liable to the principal for any loss suffered by the principal caused by the agent's breach of the fiduciary duty. In *Detroit Lions v. Argovitz* (1984), the Lions filed suit on their behalf and on behalf of the top collegiate player they had signed, running back sensation Billy Sims. The suit sought to release Sims from another contract he had signed with a team from a competing league, the Houston Gamblers. The defendant, Argovitz, had served as Sims's agent in the contract negotiations with the Gamblers. As it turned out, Argovitz was also a part owner of the Gamblers and had an obvious conflict of interest. The court set aside Sims's contract with the Gamblers and stated:

> The relationship between a principal and agent is fiduciary in nature, and as such imposes a duty of loyalty, good faith, and fair and honest dealing on the agent. A fiduciary relationship arises not only from a formal principal-agent relationship, but also from informal relationships of trust and confidence.
>
> In light of the express agency agreement, and the relationship between Sims and Argovitz, Argovitz clearly owed Sims the fiduciary duties of an agent at all times relevant to this lawsuit.
>
> An agent's duty of loyalty requires that he not have a personal stake that conflicts with the principal's interest in a transaction in which he represents his principal.
>
> A fiduciary violates the prohibition against self dealing not only by dealing with himself but also by dealing on his principal's behalf with a third party in which he has an interest such as a partnership in which he is a member.
>
> Where an agent has an interest adverse to that of his principal in a transaction in which he purports to act on behalf of his principal the transaction is voidable by the principal unless the agent disclosed all material facts within the agent's knowledge that might affect the principal's judgment.
>
> We conclude that recision is the appropriate remedy. We are dismayed by Argovitz's egregious conduct. The careless fashion in which Argovitz went about ascertaining the highest price for Sims' service convinces us of the wisdom of the maxim: no man can faithfully serve two masters whose interests are in conflict.

There are a number of potential conflicts of interests that might arise with respect to an agent's representation of an athlete. The salary cap in the professional leagues has added a new set of situations in which a conflict may arise. Because of team caps, in order to meet one player's salary demands, other players may have to accept less. An agent who represents more than one player on a team may find that increasing the salary of one client results in a reduction in salary or release of another client. Serving both clients could put the agent in a difficult position.

AGENT CERTIFICATION

The players in each of the four major professional leagues (football, basketball, baseball and hockey) are members of and represented by unions. The players in the NFL are represented by the National Football League Players Association (NFLPA), the players in the NBA by the National Basketball Players Association (NBPA), the players in the MLB by the Major League Baseball Players Association (MLBPA), and the players in the NHL by the National Hockey League Players Association (NHLPA). Each union has the exclusive right in the respective collective bargaining agreement with management to certify agents. Without certification, an agent is not allowed to represent a player in the league.

Each union determines what is necessary for agent certification. In order to become certified by the NFLPA an applicant must 1) have a college degree; 2) attend a two-day seminar; 3) pass an exam; and 4) submit an application with a fee. In 2001, the NFLPA passed a rule that an agent must represent at least one player in a three-year period to maintain certification status. The NBPA has similar requirements, but an applicant without a college degree may be certified if established negotiating skills exist. The MLBPA will not certify an agent unless he represents at least one player on a 40-man roster.

AGENT COMPETITION

The sports agency business has experienced a movement toward the mega-firm in the last decade, as a few large entertainment companies began to acquire the largest sports agencies. As a result, companies like SFX, Octagon, IMG, and Assante dominate the sports agency business. These huge firms have enormous budgets, the best training facilities, and access to the business contacts necessary for endorsement deals. Although some of the mergers have been unsuccessful, the super-firm trend will probably continue in the future, making it difficult for small sports agency firms to attract clients.

Anyone interested in becoming a sports agent should be aware of the intense competition. A few years ago, the NFLPA had approximately 1000 certified agents, but over half of the agents had no clients. The new rule requiring an agent to represent at least one player in a three-year period greatly reduced this number. The number of agents who do not have clients is similarly high in the NBPA, but the MLBPA has less than a hundred certified agents (largely because of its rule that an agent must have at least one client on a club's 40-man roster).

Competition among agents is so fierce that the NFLPA's disciplinary committee has a grievance process to handle complaints between agents. Agents who have clients taken from them by other agents may file claims against the offending agent for contract interference and seek sanctions from the NFLPA. Each year, there are a number of agents who claim another agent stole a client.

In April 2002, the number one pick in the NFL draft was David Carr, a highly talented quarterback out of Fresno State. On January 1, before the draft, Carr selected Frank Bauer as his agent. On January 16, however, Carr terminated Bauer's contract after receiving an anonymous letter trashing Bauer and linking his associate to a murder. Carr then signed with Octagon, one of the larger sports firms in the country. Although Bauer did not accuse Octagon of being the source of the mysterious mailing, he did file a third-party contract interference suit against Octagon. The following year, Andrew Joel filed suit against Octagon for tampering and third-party contract interference. Joel had superstar Michael Vick as a client, but Vick switched to Octagon.

Eric Fleisher represents some of the top players in the NBA. He won a judgment of more than $4.5 million against his former partner, Andy Miller, claiming that Miller had engaged in unfair competition when he started his own firm and solicited Fleischer's clients, including Kevin Garnet, one of the most outstanding players in the NBA.

The competition and stakes in the athlete representation business was demonstrated in the high-profile, mud-slinging litigation between Leigh Steinberg and David Dunn. Steinberg was one of the first agents to make a significant mark on the representation of NFL athletes, representing the first overall pick in the NFL draft an unprecedented *eight* times. He partnered with Jeff Moorad, a successful MLB agent, for a number of years, and in 1991, David Dunn joined the firm that was to become Steinberg, Moorad and Dunn (SMD). In 1999, the firm was acquired by Assante, and SMD became the athlete representation division of Assante. At the time of the acquisition, Dunn signed a 5-year employment contract that provided he was to assign all contracts rights to SMD. The contract also included non-compete and non-solicitation agreements.

In February 2001, Dunn resigned and formed another firm, Athletes First, with several other ex-SMD employees. Shortly thereafter, a large number of SMD's athlete clients terminated their relationship with SMD and signed with Athletes First. SMD filed suit alleging breach of contract, breach of fiduciary duty, and intentional contract interference.

The trial was widely publicized and included charges and counter charges of alcoholism, sexual misconduct, dishonesty and other personal attacks. The jury returned a verdict of over $40 million against Athletes First and almost $3 million against Dunn personally. The NFLPA also began the process to decertify Dunn's agency status.

Speakers of Sport, Inc. v. Proserv, Inc. (1999)

The Plaintiff, Speakers of Sport, appeals from the grant of summary judgment to the defendant, ProServ, in a diversity suit in which one sports agency has charged another with tortious interference with a business relationship and related violations of Illinois law. The essential facts, construed as favorably to the plaintiff as the record will permit, are as follows.

Ivan Rodriguez, a highly successful catcher with the Texas Rangers baseball team, in 1991 signed the first of several one-year contracts making Speakers his agent. ProServ wanted to expand its representation of baseball players and to this end invited Rodriguez to its office in Washington and there promised that it would get him between $2 and $4 million in endorsements if he signed with ProServ—which he did, terminating his contract (which was terminable at will) with Speakers. This was in 1995. ProServ failed to obtain significant endorsements for Rodriguez and after just one year he switched to another agent who the following year landed him a five-year $42 million contract with the Rangers. Speakers brought this suit a few months later, charging that the promise of endorsements that ProServ had made to Rodriguez was fraudulent and had induced him to terminate his contract with Speakers. Speakers could not sue Rodriguez for breach of contract, because he had not broken their contract, which was, as we said, terminable at will. Nor, therefore, could it accuse ProServ of inducing a breach of contract. But Speakers did have a contract with Rodriguez, and inducing the termination of a contract, even when the termination is not a breach because the contract is terminable at will, can still be actionable under the tort law of Illinois, either as an interference with prospective economic advantage or as an interference with the contract at will itself.

There is in general nothing wrong with one sports agent trying to take a client from another if this can be done without precipitating a breach of contract. That is the process known as competition, which though painful, fierce, frequently ruthless, sometimes Darwinian in its pitilesssness, is the cornerstone of our highly successful economic system. Competition is not a tort, but on the contrary provides a defense (the "competitor's privilege") to the tort of improper interference. It does not privilege inducing the breach of a contract conduct usefully regarded as a separate tort from interfering with a business relationship without precipitating an actual breach of contract, but it does privilege inducing the lawful termination of a contract that is terminable at will.

There would be few more effective inhibitors of the competitive process than making it a tort for an agent to promise the client of another agent to do better by him. It is true as Speakers argues, that the competitor may not make a promise that he knows he cannot fulfill, may not, that is, compete by fraud. Because the competitor's privilege does not include a right to get business from a competitor by means of fraud, it is hard to quarrel with this position in the abstract, but the practicalities are different. If the argument were accepted and the new agent made a promise that was not fulfilled, the old agent would have a shot at convincing a jury that the new agent had known from the start that he couldn't deliver on the promise. Once a case gets to the jury, all bets are off. The practical consequence of Speakers' approach therefore, would be that a sports agent who lured away the client of another agent with a promise to do better by him would be running a grave legal risk.

The threat to the competitive process is blocked by the principle of Illinois law that promissory fraud is not actionable unless it is part of a scheme to defraud, that is, unless it is one element of a pattern of fraudulent acts. By requiring the plaintiff show a pattern, by thus not letting him rest on proving a single promise, the law reduces the likelihood of a spurious suit; for a series of unfulfilled promises is better (though of course not conclusive) evidence of fraud than a single unfulfilled promise.

Consider in this connection the characterization by Speakers' own chairman of ProServ's promise to Rodriguez as "pure fantasy and gross exaggeration"—in other words, as puffing. Puffing in the usual sense signifies meaningless superlatives that no reasonable person would take seriously, and so it is not actionable as fraud. Rodriguez thus could not have sued ProServ in respect of the promise of $2-$4 million in endorsements. If Rodriguez thus was not wronged, we do not understand on what theory Speakers can complain that ProServ competed with it unfairly.

The promise of endorsements was puffing in the sense of a sales pitch that is intended, and that a reasonable person would understand, to be aspirational, rather than enforceable. It is not as if ProServ proposed to employ Rodriguez and pay him $2 million a year. That would be the kind of promise that could found an enforceable obligation.

It is possible to make a binding promise of something over which one has no control, such a promise is called a warranty. But it is not plausible that this is what ProServ was doing. So understood, the "promise" was not a promise at all. But even if it was a promise (or a warranty), it cannot be the basis for a finding of fraud because it was not a part of a scheme to defraud evidenced by more than the allegedly fraudulent promise itself.

We add that even if Speakers could establish liability under either the torts or the deceptive practices act, its suit would fail because it cannot possibly establish, as it seeks to do, a damages entitlement (the only relief it seeks) to the agent's $42 million contract. The contract was negotiated years after he left Speakers, and by another agent. Since Rodriguez had only a year-to-year contract with Speakers – terminable at will, moreover – and since obviously he was dissatisfied with Speakers at least to the extent of switching to ProServ and then when he became disillusioned with ProServ of not returning to Speakers fold, the likelihood that Speakers would have retained him had ProServ not lured him away is too slight to ground an award of such damages. Such an award would be the best example yet of puffing in the pie-in-the-sky sense.

AFFIRMED.

****

AGENT REGULATION

Each union for the four major leagues has the exclusive authority to certify agents who represent players in the respective leagues. The union certification process seeks to exclude individuals with questionable criminal or ethical backgrounds and requires a level of education or experience on the part of the agents. The unions can sanction or cancel an agent's certification for violation of the union's regulations. In 1998, the NBA declared a lockout. An agent who represented several NBA players publicly criticized the union's negotiations with management. After the lockout was settled, the NBPA revoked the agent's certification. The NFLPA also canceled Tank Black's certification after it was proven he had bilked a number of his clients out of millions of dollars and violated several criminal laws in the process.

There is a growing demand for additional regulation of sports agents. One of the most troubling sports issues for colleges has been the relationship of sports agents and student-athletes. The conduct by the agent often amounts to violations of regulations set by the National Collegiate Athletic Association (NCAA). Alleged and actual violations of NCAA rules are reported on a regular basis.

The NCAA has enormous power over member institutions. NCAA violations can result in sanctions against the school, but can also directly impact coaches and student-athletes with the loss of eligibility and scholarships. As a result of NCAA violations, schools may incur severe financial penalties, including the forfeiture of television appearance rights, the NCAA basketball tournament, and football bowl games.

Although the NCAA controls the member schools, it has no authority over sports agents. In the past, agents have flaunted the NCAA rules with impunity. Times are changing. The damages and adverse publicity have forced universities, the NCAA, prosecutors, and legislators to take a number of steps to punish agents for conduct that is harmful to the universities or its athletes.

In 2004, the NFLPA adopted a rule that requires agents to list "runners" that are employed and the amount of compensation paid to them. The rule also provides that agents are responsible for the acts of the runners. The rule was prompted by the disclosure that an agent had agreed to pay 40% of his 3% agent commission to an influential writer for the writer's assistance in getting a number-one NFL draft pick to sign with the agent. It was also brought to light that one "runner" had recruited at least two first-round draft picks for one agent and that the same runner was working for two other agents.

A more recent rule implemented by the NFLPA prohibits agents from contacting third-year players ("true" juniors) until January, after their third, or junior, season. The rule, designed to remove excessive pressure on younger student-athletes to prematurely end their eligibility and enter professional football, forces those players who do declare early for the NFL draft to drastically accelerate the process of selecting advisors. For example, Arkansas running back Darren McFadden found in 2008 he had only a few weeks to evaluate and settle upon an agent before the pre-draft NFL combine that has become so crucial for a player's professional prospects. Hence, while the rule may give many student-athletes additional peace of mind and privacy, it sacrifices for a few exceptional players the opportunity to conduct an elaborate process to find an NFLPA-certified contract advisor.

CIVIL AND CRIMINAL PROSECUTION OF AGENTS

It is hard to imagine a more colorful insight into the sordid aspects of the sports agent business than the Norby Walters affair. Hollywood could not have written a better script.

In 1985, Norby Walters and his partner, Lloyd Bloom, decided to get into the athlete agent business in a big way. Over the next three years, Walters signed about 58 athletes to contracts during their college eligibility. The scheme involved post-dating the contracts and keeping them secret until the player was no longer eligible for college sports. Walters recruited the athletes the old-fashioned way—he gave them money and other enticements. Walters invested almost a million dollars in the venture. Unfortunately for Walters, his athlete clients were also less than honorable. Almost all of Walters's recruits decided not to honor the agreements and chose to be represented by other agents. Compounding the fiasco, most of the athletes did not return the money that Walters had advanced.

Walters made some attempts to recover his losses in the courts. Walters also sought "collection" help from his associates, who allegedly had ties to organized crime. True to their reputation, threats of broken legs were made by the enforcers to the athletes. One female employee of a rival agency was severely beaten. Word spread that organized crime was trying to gain an influence on collegiate and professional sports. The F.B.I. investigated, and Walters was charged with a 75-count indictment of mail fraud and Racketeer Influenced Corrupt Organization (RICO) violations. The mail fraud charges were based on Walters causing the universities to give scholarships to athletes who verified their eligibility through the mail, but who were, in fact, ineligible. Walters ultimately entered a conditional guilty plea that was set aside on appeal.

United States v. Norby Walters (1993)

Norby Walters, who represents entertainers, tried to move into the sports business. He signed 58 college football players to contracts while they were still playing. Walters offered cars and money to those who would agree to use him as their representative in dealing with professional teams. Sports agents receive a percentage of the players' income, so Walters would profit only to the extent he could negotiate contracts for his clients. The athletes' pro prospects depended on successful completion of their collegiate careers. To the NCAA, however, a student who signs a contract with an agent is a professional, ineligible to play on collegiate teams. To avoid jeopardizing his clients' careers, Walters dated the contracts after the end of their eligibility and locked them in a safe. He promised to lie to the universities in response to any inquiries. Walters inquired of sports lawyers at Shea & Gould whether this plan of operation would be lawful. The firm rendered an opinion that it would violate the NCAA's rules but not any statute.

Having recruited players willing to fool their universities and the NCAA, Walters discovered that they were equally willing to play false with him. Only 2 of the 58 players fulfilled their end of the bargain; the other 56 kept the cars and money, then signed with other agents. They relied on the fact that the contracts were locked away and dated in the future and that Walters' business depended on continued secrecy, so he could not very well sue to enforce their promises. When the 56 would neither accept him as their representative nor return the payments, Walters resorted to threats. One player, Maurice Douglass, was told that his legs would be broken before the pro draft unless he repaid Walters' firm. A 75 page indictment charged Walters and his partner Lloyd Bloom with conspiracy, RICO violations (the predicate felony was extortion), and mail fraud. The fraud: causing the universities to pay scholarship funds to athletes who had become ineligible as a result of the agency contracts. The mail: each university required its athletes to verify their eligibility to play, then sent copies by mail to conferences such as the Big Ten.

Mr. Walters admitted to the conduct. He fought the case on what is commonly referred to as a "technicality." His argument was that in order to have violated the applicable mail fraud law it would have to be shown that he received some value from the school by fraud. Mr. Walters beat this rap. The law was later amended to include Walters's conduct.

In its decision, the appellate court stated:

Walters is by all accounts a nasty and untrustworthy fellow, but the prosecutor did not prove that his efforts to circumvent the NCAA's rules amounted to mail fraud.

****

The damage went beyond Walters and his associates. The trial testimony revealed that many of the talented players were making no progress toward their degree and were, with their school's blessing, simply majoring in "staying eligible." One of Walters's clients was a talented basketball player at the University of Alabama. After signing with Walters, the player helped Alabama advance in the NCAA tournament. As a result of the scandal, Alabama was forced to forfeit the two games it won and the $250,000 it received from the NCAA tournament. Walters later reimbursed the school in order to avoid criminal prosecution in state court. Most of the athletes involved with Walters entered pleas that required them to reimburse their schools for the costs of their scholarships. Walters's partner, Bloom, was not so lucky. He was "whacked" in his home in 1993.

Another incident involving a sports agent and college athletes was the widely reported "Footlocker" scandal in Florida. In 1993, a number of Florida State football players went on a rather extravagant shopping spree, spending about $6,000 at a Footlocker store. The shopping was financed by an unregistered sports agent, Raul Bey, and was a violation of NCAA rules. FSU suspended four players for 2 games before the 1994 season due to the incident. The NCAA put FSU on probation for failing to properly monitor agents on campus. The one-year sanction was the lightest penalty that could be assessed for a major violation. Another major violation in a 5-year period could, however, result in a "death sentence" by the NCAA.

FSU appealed the NCAA ruling, but lost. The agent was sentenced to one year in jail for violation of Florida's agent registration law. Bey was also ordered to reimburse FSU for the $10,000 it spent investigating the matter and was fined $2,000. The agent in the Florida State case was easier to prosecute than Walters because the Florida charges involved violations of a specific state sports agent law rather than the general federal mail fraud statutes used in the *Walters* case. This was not the last time that FSU ran into trouble for rule violations; in 2007, for its bowl game against Kentucky, the school suspended 36 football players, including several key starters, for their roles in an academic cheating scandal involving an online course offered by the school.

In 1995, Marcus Camby was a student at the University of Massachusetts, and, although only a junior, was considered the top pro prospect in college basketball. After the season was over, Camby declared he would enter the NBA draft.

Immediately after his announcement, reports began circulating that Camby had accepted gifts and money from agents while playing college ball. After a six-month investigation, criminal charges were filed against an aspiring sports agent. Camby admitted accepting at least $1,000 and other "favors" from the agent while still eligible. When Camby chose another agent to represent him, the original agent allegedly demanded that Camby pay him 4% of his basketball salary and 25% of his endorsement earnings. The agent who was dumped by Camby threatened to go public with the payments and to "bring U. Mass. down" if Camby refused to cooperate. The agent was charged with first degree larceny by extortion and the promotion of prostitution. U. Mass lost more than $150,000 it had earned from the NCAA basketball tournament as a result of Camby's conduct.

In 1997, Penn State's football team was led by Curtis Enis, a Heisman Trophy candidate. Unfortunately, Enis attended the Heisman ceremony wearing a suit purchased for him by a sports agent. As a result, Enis was not allowed to play in Penn's final game of the season—a bowl appearance. Criminal charges were filed against the agent, who pled guilty, and was fined and sentenced to perform community service. The NFLPA suspended the agent's license for two years and fined him $15,000.

William "Tank" Black appeared to be on top of the sports world after the 1999 NFL draft. Black had more top-round draft choices than any other agent, an impressive feat by any standard. Within a few weeks after the draft, however, reports began circulating that Black had made illegal payments to get new clients during their college eligibility and had even tried to bribe coaches. Some of Black's new clients fired him, and the NFLPA, the SEC, and several states went after him. Black was convicted of multiple criminal counts and is now in prison. Black's clients lost millions of dollars as a result of his bogus investment schemes.

STATE AND FEDERAL LEGISLATION

A large number of states have laws regulating sports agents. Most state laws require all "agent contracts" to contain warnings that execution of the agreement will result in the student-athlete's loss of college eligibility and a time frame, such as three days, for the student to rescind or withdraw from the contract. Most of the laws also require notification to the coach or athletic director of the signing within 72 hours or before participation in a sporting event on behalf of the school.

The agent laws, however, also contain a number of variations. The Alabama law defines "athlete" as, "any person who is employed or seeks to be employed under a professional sports services contract…or as a professional athlete." The law uses a different definition for "student-athlete" which includes any individual who plays intercollegiate sports in Alabama. According to the law, apparently anyone who desires to play professional sports fits the definition of an "athlete." Arkansas has a similar definition for "athlete" but exempts Arkansas lawyers from the definition of "athlete agent." Colorado's definition of "student-athlete" includes any student who participates in intercollegiate sporting events; the law does not limit the definition to students in Colorado. The Kansas law covers college athletes, but by definition does not include high school athletes. The Oklahoma law encompasses "NCAA athletes" and thus excludes college athletes from NAIA institutions. The Texas law includes only football and basketball players in its definition of "athlete."

Most laws require some form of registration and a criminal and/or civil action against an agent who violates the law. Several states also provide for a criminal or civil action against the athlete involved in the violation. Laws that require an agent to meet certain conditions, such as registration, in order to speak to a student-athlete may face First-Amendment constitutional challenges. The penalties that may be imposed or damages that may be awarded for violations range from $1,000 to $100,000. Some state laws allow action only by the schools, while others permit any injured party to recover damages.

A common theme in most state sports agent laws is an attempt to force agents to comply with the applicable NCAA regulations. Noncompliance with the various laws has, however, been widespread and is well known. This should come as no surprise. Until recently, the sanctions for violations in most state statutes have been minor and rarely enforced. Only a handful of states have punished agents for violations. There has been a growing demand for a crackdown on sports agents who break the rules. This demand is fueled by the adverse publicity and enormous costs suffered by schools sanctioned by the NCAA for violations involving agent misconduct.

A number of states are changing their laws to provide stronger sanctions. Some of the state laws provide that the relationship between a school and scholarship athlete is one of contract and that a school has a cause of action for contract interference for violation of the law. Many of the sports agent laws allow an injured party to recover general damages from an agent who violates the law and causes damages. Due to the amount of money that can be earned, and forfeited, by a school from television appearances, bowl games, and NCAA tournaments, the agent's financial exposure is considerable.

Violations of NCAA rules, and therefore the agent's exposure to substantial damages, may be easier to commit than expected. The NCAA's rules are broad and can include communications with a relative or friend of the athlete. How close a relative or friend is needed to trigger the rule? Could offering a ride to someone who is walking to the stadium amount to a violation? Would buying the relative or friend of an athlete a soft drink or popcorn at the game constitute a benefit?

In 1996, the University of Southern California filed what was reported to be the first civil suit by a school against an agent for the recruitment of its athletes. The action was based on the violation of California's sports agent law and on a contract interference theory. The school maintained that the agent had caused the athletes to violate NCAA regulations that resulted in violations of the scholarship contracts with the school. The case was settled on terms requiring the agent to pay the school approximately $50,000 and to agree not to contact the school's athletes. The NFLPA also suspended the agent's license for one year.

Congress got into the picture with The Sports Agent Responsibility Trust Act of 2004. The law requires the following in bold print on agent-athlete contracts:

> Warning to student athlete if you agree orally or in writing to be represented by an agent now or in the future you may lose your eligibility to compete as a student athlete in your sport.

The federal law provides financial penalties for violations that can be enforced by the Federal Trade Commission or the state attorneys general.

UNIFORM ATHLETE AGENT LAW

The increased attention on sports agents and the tougher laws have also increased the criticisms of the various state statutes. The multiple registrations and bonding fees place a substantial burden on agents who operate simultaneously in a number of states. Trying to remain in compliance with the various laws of each state is difficult for agents who represent athletes throughout the country.

The National Conference of Commissioners on Uniform State Laws (NCCUSL) is an organization composed of judges, law professors and attorneys that has proposed more than 200 laws since its inception in 1892. At the urging of parties interested in seeing uniformity in the laws regulating athlete-agents, the NCCUSL worked on model legislation for almost four years. A final draft of the Uniform Athlete Agent's Act (UAAA) was approved on August 2, 2000. By 2002, Alabama, Arizona, Arkansas, Delaware, Idaho, Indiana, Mississippi, Nevada, Tennessee, Utah, West Virginia, the District of Columbia, and the U.S. Virgin Islands had adopted the UAAA. Several other states are currently considering adoption. It is likely that in the next few years a majority of the states will have enacted the UAAA.

The UAAA requires an agent to register with a state to practice as a sports agent in that jurisdiction. An athlete-agent may not initiate contact with a student-athlete unless the agent is registered. The law, however, provides for reciprocity. That is, an agent who has registered in one state may easily register in another state without being required to go through all of the original steps involved in registration.

An "athlete-agent" is broadly defined, but excludes a spouse, parent, or grandparent of the student-athlete. "Student-athlete" includes any athlete who "engages in, is eligible to engage in, or may be eligible in the future to engage in any intercollegiate sport."

The UAAA requires that the contracts between the athlete and the agent must contain information such as the fees to be paid the agent, the services to be provided, and an acknowledgment of understanding by the athlete. The UAAA prohibits certain acts such as giving an athlete anything of value while the athlete still has collegiate eligibility. The Act requires the agent to give the college notice of the contract within 72 hours or before the athlete's next game, whichever comes first. The contract may be canceled by a student-athlete within 14 days of execution, and the student-athlete is not required to pay or return any consideration to the agent in the event of cancellation.

The UAAA does not address the punishment for failure to comply with the Act or the cost of registration. These issues are left up to each state.

Antitrust Law — The Reserve Clause and Free Agency

No issue in professional sports has caused as much controversy between owners and players in the four major professional leagues as the struggle over the reserve clause and its counterpart, free agency. The dispute began over a century ago, and the issue has dominated professional sports for the past 40 years. An understanding of antitrust law is necessary to understand the legal challenges involved in the conflict over the reserve clause and free agency.

ANTITRUST LAW

The term "monopoly" generally refers to a business that, due to its size, has little to no competition. The lack of competition allows the monopoly to control prices or output and denies consumers the benefits of a free market. Monopolies have existed in this country since colonial days. Before the colonies declared independence, the English Crown granted exclusive rights to certain trading companies, which resulted in "royal monopolies." The monopolies were not well received by the colonialists. Resentment of monopolies was later reflected in anti-monopoly language found in some early state constitutions. The concern over monopolies during colonial days, however, paled in comparison to what was to develop later.

After the Civil War, the growth of American industrialization led to the formation of unprecedented concentrations of wealth and power. "Captains of industry," "robber barons," and other similar terms were used to describe men who established businesses of enormous size and control. Through various methods, a few people were able to eliminate most competitors and dominate the respective market. "Trusts" were devices set up so that owners of stock in several companies transferred their securities to a set of trustees, which entitled them to a share of the pooled earnings of the jointly managed firms. The trustees retained a monopoly in the industry and controlled the market. Prices for goods were not determined by the free market, but by monopolistic control. As a result of the increasing concentration and abuse of wealth in a number of industries, federal antitrust legislation, the Sherman Act, was passed in 1890. The Act states in part

Section 1: Every contract, combination in the form of trust or otherwise, or conspiracy, in restraint of trade or commerce among the several States, or with foreign nations, is declared to be illegal. Every person who shall make any contract or engage in any combination or conspiracy hereby declared to be illegal shall be deemed guilty of a felony.

Section 2: Every person who shall monopolize, or attempt to monopolize, or combine with any other person or persons, to monopolize any part of the trade or commerce among the several states, or with foreign nations, shall be deemed guilty of a felony.

Section 1 of the Sherman Act prohibits two or more persons from acting together to restrain trade. An example of a Section 1 violation would result if major automobile manufacturers or fast-food chains met and decided to raise the prices on their products by an agreed amount. Another example of a violation would be if the same companies agreed to divide up the country into exclusive markets so they would not face competition from one another.

Section 2 prohibits any person from obtaining a monopoly in the relevant market that causes injury to competition in that market and includes unilateral action. The fact that a company operates a monopoly alone is not unlawful. It is how the company achieves or maintains that status that determines if the conduct violates the law.

Violation of federal antitrust law is a felony. Criminal actions in antitrust impose a sentence of up to three years and fines of up to $350,000 on an individual violator and up to $10,000,000 per violation on corporate offenders.

The criminal sanctions of the Sherman Act have not been used in sport disputes. The Act, however, also provides for a civil action by an injured person. The civil action allows an injured party to file suit and, if successful, to recover treble damages. Civil antitrust actions have been used extensively in professional sports disputes. Players in the major team sports have filed a number of actions against the respective leagues and club owners alleging violations of the Sherman Act.

The goal of antitrust law is to prevent a single firm or a related group from obtaining excessive market power. The relevant market can be a geographic market or a product market. Generally, monopoly power is illustrated by a business operating in a product market—selling goods or services to consumers. Antitrust actions brought by players against professional teams do not fit into this category.

In the context of an antitrust action by professional players against a league, the power is held by the buyers of the services, the team owners. The players are the "sellers" of the service. The players have little, if any, choice as to where they market their talent. This situation is referred to as "monopsony" power. The reserve clause and the draft rules create a monopsony market power that limits a player's opportunity to sell his services on the open market.

Market power by a monopoly seller can easily lead to exploitation of consumers. But, excess power by a firm buying goods and services for production can, in theory, bring about lower costs to consumers. That is, although the players may suffer lower salaries as a result of the monopsony, fans may benefit, in theory, from lower ticket prices.

A literal application of the Sherman Act would find many, if not most, useful and legitimate contracts as illegal. To avoid this harsh and unwanted result, the courts have formulated rules that limit the types of restraints that violate antitrust law.

The courts have created two different types of illegal antitrust conduct with respect to restraint of trade issues: 1) *per se* violations, where the violation is so unreasonable on its face that courts hold it to be illegal *per se*, and 2) conduct that violates antitrust law pursuant to the *rule-of-reason* analysis.

Examples of *per se* violations include price fixing, market allocations, group boycotts and tying arrangements. Under the rule-of-reason approach, agreements only violate antitrust law if they *unreasonably* restrain trade. The complaining party must present evidence of the effect that the agreement has on trade. The rule-of-reason analysis requires a court to weigh the anticompetitive and procompetitive effects of the agreements to determine if the restraint is illegal. If the procompetitive effects of the agreement outweigh its anticompetitive effects, the court must determine if the restraint imposed is justified by a legitimate purpose and is no more restrictive than necessary.

UNIQUE FEATURES OF PROFESSIONAL LEAGUES

The complexity of antitrust law is compounded when applied to the business of professional sports. Professional leagues are different from other businesses in a number of ways with respect to antitrust law. For example, how should the teams of a major professional league be treated for antitrust purposes? One view is that teams in a league are one entity engaged in a joint venture by the various teams. This concept is referred to as the "single entity" theory. That is, the agreements reached among the teams cannot be subject to a Section 1 antitrust action because only one entity is involved.

If a professional league is a single entity, does that mean it is vulnerable to a Section 2 monopoly claim? Most courts have rejected the argument that a sports league is a monopoly. The courts have found that the leagues face competition not only from other sports, but from movies, concerts, and other entertainment that seeks disposable income.

The majority of court decisions on the issue have treated the teams in each league as separate entities competing with each other. Under this approach, teams in a league are vulnerable to a Section 1 violation as a result of their joint agreements.

Using a Section 1 approach to professional sports leagues, however, raises other issues. Unlike other businesses, professional teams in a league *must* communicate, cooperate, and contract with each other on a multitude of topics, such as the rules of the game, schedules, and playoffs. Without cooperation and agreements among the teams, there could be no league. In addition, the teams in a league must, if need be, assist in keeping their "competitors" in business. Although the teams compete on the field and in the market for fans, players, and coaches, a professional league, unlike any other business, cannot survive without competitors. These unique features have created additional problems in regard to how the antitrust laws should be applied to professional sports leagues.

RESERVE CLAUSE AND FREE AGENCY

The term *reserve clause* in the context of professional sports leagues refers to contractual provisions that prohibit or restrict a player from contracting with another club without the consent of the player's current team. The restriction on the player is enforced pursuant to agreements among the owners of the teams in the league and by language in the player's contract. The various contractual provisions are collectively referred to as the reserve clause. That is, the original team *reserves* the rights to the player.

Owners of professional franchises have long defended the reserve clause as being necessary to maintain a competitive balance among the teams in the league. The owners' argument is that without the restriction on the players, the best athletes would move to the team that was willing to pay the highest salaries. The wealthiest team would acquire the best talent and dominate the league. The latter would lead to a lack of interest by fans that would in turn lead to the failure of the weaker teams, not only on the field, but on the business ledger as well. Without a sufficient number of teams to compete, the entire league would eventually fail.

There is merit to the argument that the reserve clause has contributed to maintaining competitiveness in the various professional leagues. There is also evidence to the contrary. Regardless, it is undeniable that restricting a player's movement pursuant to the reserve clause impairs the athletes' ability to earn higher salaries. A player who can only play for one team has very little leverage to negotiate better pay. If the team does not make a satisfactory offer, the player's only choice is to choose another profession, which is rarely an acceptable option for a professional athlete. The effect of the reserve clause on a player's salary is substantially reduced when competing leagues are available for players. The impact of the reserve clause may also be minimized when, on rare occasions, a player is talented enough to play in another professional sport, although the new sport might have a reserve clause of its own. Overall, the reserve clause works as a direct benefit to team owners in the form of lower salaries for players.

Professional athletes have always desired the opportunity to sell their skills on the open market. The player's position is that this approach allows an athlete to earn the top salary that the market is willing to pay for his services. The right of players to bid their services to any team, free of the reserve clause, is generally referred to as *free agency*. The reserve clause, cherished by owners, directly conflicts with the right of free agency sought by players.

For over a hundred years, professional players and team owners have fought over free agency and the reserve clause. The owners won most of the early battles, but the struggle intensified during the past 40 years. The dispute has been the focus of a number of court battles, arbitration proceedings, strikes, lockouts, and collective bargaining between players and owners.

The reserve clause restrictions on a player are based on contractual agreements between a player and his team and among the teams in a respective league. Contract terms are generally brought about through negotiations between the parties. The rights and responsibilities set forth in the contract are largely determined by the bargaining power and negotiating strength of the respective parties. The strongest party in the negotiations generally obtains the more favorable terms in a contract. In the past, owners had much greater bargaining power than players.

The owners used this position of strength to maintain the reserve clause in player contracts. In the past two decades the bargaining power of the players has increased and the owners' strength has diminished. This shift has led to erosion of the reserve clause and greater free agency rights for players.

The law allows parties the freedom to contract for any lawful terms. The essence of a contract is that it is an agreement between the parties that can be enforced through the law. That is, if one party to a contract fails to perform according to the contract, the law provides the injured party a remedy, generally in the form of monetary damages or injunctive relief. It is important to note, however, that there are limits to contractual freedom. The courts will not enforce a contract that provides for conduct prohibited by law. Other chapters will discuss a number of lawsuits filed by professional athletes alleging that the reserve clause in their contracts violated antitrust law and were, therefore, unenforceable.

Labor Law

Prior to the late eighteenth century, most people worked on farms, at their homes, or for individual craftsmen. Very few employers had a large number of employees under their control. The Industrial Revolution, however, radically altered the employer-employee relationship. The term "Industrial Revolution" refers to the social changes that occurred as a result of the industrialization of our society. The Industrial Revolution began in England in the late 1700s and spread to the U.S. in the early 1800s. The transformation created a new and ever-growing class of employees—factory workers. The concentration of power in the major industries resulted in a large number of workers who were at the complete mercy of their employers. Employees, including children, were powerless to confront employer abuses with respect to wages and working conditions.

At the turn of the century, outrageous working conditions forced workers to organize in an attempt to counteract powerful employers. Many of the employers viewed the movement by workers as a threat to their existence and were determined to stop workers from organizing. A long and violent struggle ensued between labor and management over the right of employees to organize. Eventually, federal laws were passed to recognize and protect the right of workers to form unions.

From the 1940s through the 1960s, unions in the U.S. grew in number and strength. At its peak, union membership was approximately 50% of the non-agricultural workforce in the United States. Since the 1970s, however, the union movement has been on a steep decline. In 1996, it was estimated that union workers constituted about 19% of the (non-agricultural) workforce.

The players in the four major professional leagues in the U.S.—the National Football League, the National Basketball Association, Major League Baseball and the National Hockey League—each have union representation. Unlike the trend in other industries, the players' unions have never been stronger. Players in the WNBA and the AFL (the Arena Football League) have also recently formed unions. Later chapters will discuss the enormous role of unions in professional sports.

LABOR LAW PROCEDURE

NATIONAL LABOR RELATIONS ACT (NLRA)

There are a number of federal laws that make up this country's labor policy, but at the core is the National Labor Relations Act (NLRA), also known as the Wagner Act. The NLRA authorizes a majority of employees in a *unit* to elect a representative (union) to negotiate with an employer on behalf of the employees. Generally, the first step in an election is that a union campaigns for the right to represent employees in collective bargaining. The process continues to an election that is monitored by the National Labor Relations Board (NLRB). If the union wins the election, it gains the authority to represent the employees in collective bargaining.

COLLECTIVE BARGAINING AGREEMENT (CBA)

Collective bargaining is the process by which union representatives negotiate employment conditions for the entire bargaining unit. The NLRA requires both parties to bargain in good faith on *mandatory* subjects, such as wages, hours, and working conditions. The parties may also negotiate on other issues that are referred to as *permissive* subjects. Bargaining in good faith means a sincere effort to reach an agreement is being made. For example, employers are prohibited from unilaterally imposing rules on mandatory subjects without first engaging in negotiations. Good faith negotiations may require employers to disclose information about profits and losses. Employers, especially owners of professional teams, were initially very reluctant to share this information. Good faith bargaining does not, however, require that an agreement be reached.

Due to the nature of the industry, professional sports union contracts are negotiated through multi-employer collective bargaining. That is, one CBA applies to all of the separate employers (teams) in a league. A CBA is binding on the employer(s) and employees for a certain term, usually from three to seven years. As the expiration of the CBA term approaches, the parties are required to negotiate in good faith to reach a new CBA. The mandatory terms of the old CBA continue in effect if the term expires during negotiations.

If the parties cannot agree on a new CBA, the negotiating status is referred to as an *impasse*. *Impasse* exists when the parties have exhausted the possibility of reaching an agreement and further negotiations would be fruitless. *Impasse* is determined by considering a number of factors, such as the history of the negotiations, the good faith of the parties, the nature of the issue which is in disagreement, and other relevant matters. Significantly, after an *impasse* is reached, an employer may unilaterally impose terms that were encompassed in the employer's pre-impasse proposals. After *impasse,* the parties may seek mediation or arbitration to resolve the differences. Or, the parties can resort to the ultimate weapons in labor law: the employees can strike, or management can impose a lockout.

A strike is a declaration by employees that they will not work. An employer can replace striking workers and is not obligated to rehire the workers once the strike is ended. The employer cannot discriminate, however, against individual workers for exercising their right to strike. A lockout is a declaration by the employer that the workers cannot return to work. In professional sports, a lockout suspends team-player activities such as signing free agents or draft picks, trades, practice at the team's facilities, and, certainly, the games. A lockout is allowed as long as the employer intends to support its economic position at the bargaining table. A lockout is impermissible if the motive is to interfere with the CBA process. In the 1998 NBA labor dispute, an arbitrator ruled that management did not have to wait for an impasse to impose a lockout. Threats of a strike and lockout are common in the collective bargaining process, but are rarely used. Instead, the parties generally maintain the status quo of the old CBA until one, or both, of the parties make concessions in the bargaining process.

AGENCY SHOPS AND RIGHT TO WORK

The CBA between the NFL and the NFLPA contains a standard *agency shop* provision that requires all players to pay union dues or provide an equivalent service fee. This provision is permitted by the National Labor Relations Act (NLRA). The NLRA also allows states to enact right-to-work laws that prohibit unions from forcing employees to pay dues as a prerequisite of employment. Virginia and Louisiana are right-to-work states.

In 1993, a large number of players on the Washington Redskins team refused to pay their union dues. Their position was undoubtedly a stand to demonstrate their objection to the recently enacted salary cap in the new CBA. The NFLPA, the players' union, notified the league and teams that the players should be suspended from playing the last game. The players' position was that Virginia was the site of their training facilities and was the controlling location for purposes of the law. The NFLPA's position was that the District of Columbia was the players' job site. The matter went to arbitration, and the arbitrator ruled that Washington, D.C., the location of home games, was the appropriate location, and, therefore, the dues should be paid. The dispute went to court, but in the meantime, the season was continued and no player was suspended. The lower courts ruled in *NFLPA v. Pro Football* that Virginia law applied. On appeal, the appellate court found the issue had become moot and dismissed the case. The court reasoned that the relief sought was the suspension of the players for the last game of the season. By the time the appellate court got the case, the last game had already been played.

NON-STATUTORY EXEMPTION

Collective bargaining by its nature results in an agreement to restrain trade and, on its face, could be viewed as a possible violation of antitrust law. (Antitrust law is discussed in Chapter 4.) To accommodate labor policy, however, the legislature and the courts have created exceptions to the antitrust law. One exception, created by the courts, is referred to as the "non-statutory" labor exemption. The exemption allows the terms of a CBA to be exempt from antitrust law. The reasoning is that the restraints imposed by the CBA—for example, how much workers will be paid— were agreed to by the union that had bargaining power similar to the employer and, therefore, should be upheld in furtherance of labor law promoting collective bargaining. The scope of the non-statutory exemption has been at the center of many labor disputes in professional sports.

PLAYERS' UNIONS

Each of the four major professional leagues has a union that represents the players in the league. The unions are the National Football League Players Association (NFLPA), the National Basketball Players Association (NBPA), the Major League Baseball Players Association (MLBPA), and the National Hockey League Players Association (NHLPA). Although most people are aware of the role sports agents play in representing professional athletes, few are aware of the enormous service provided to the players by the unions.

The unions bargain with the leagues for the players on a number of issues, including minimum salaries, grievance procedures, conduct on and off the field, club discipline, arbitration, salary caps, and free agency. The agreement between each union and the league is called the Collective Bargaining Agreement (CBA). Under labor law, the union has the exclusive right to negotiate on behalf of all employees in the unit. The unions in the four professional sports leagues have, however, waived their right to negotiate salaries, except for the minimum, for individual players.

The language in a CBA can be complex. Some writers have compared the CBAs, in terms of clarity, to the Internal Revenue Code. It is imperative, however, that anyone interested in the rights of players in the professional leagues become familiar with the applicable CBA.

CERTIFICATION OF AGENTS

Each CBA provides the union with the exclusive right to certify agents to represent athletes in the respective league. No agent may contract with a league on behalf of a player unless the agent is first certified by the league's union. For example, the NFL Collective Bargaining Agreement states in part

> The NFLMC (National Football League Management Council) and the Clubs agree that the Clubs are prohibited from engaging in individual contract negotiations with any agent who is not listed by the NFLPA as being duly certified by the NFLPA in accordance with its role as exclusive bargaining agent for NFL players.

The certification process involves submitting an application to the respective union. The application primarily seeks information on education, criminal or ethical misconduct, and past or existing representation of athletes or leagues. Applications to the NFLPA, NBPA, and NHLPA from lawyers or those with suitable education or experience are generally granted. The NFLPA imposes a non-refundable fee to process the application and an annual registration charge for certified agents. The NBPA and the NHLPA also have annual fees. The MLBPA does not charge a fee; however, an agent will not be certified until a player on a 40-man roster of a major league club designates the agent as his representative.

A union's right to certify agents was challenged by an agent in court, *Collins v. NBA*, as an antitrust violation. The agent had previously represented Kareem Abdul-Jabbar, one of the NBA's most outstanding players. The union had removed the agent's certification. The court upheld the union's authority. The courts have also held in antitrust challenges that a CBA is binding on all players within the particular unit, including rookies who were not in the union when the CBA was negotiated.

STANDARD AGENT REPRESENTATION CONTRACT

One significant measure taken by the unions with respect to the players pertains to the agent-player contract. Each union has a Standard Representation Contract (SRK). This is a contract form that an agent must use in connection with his representation of the player. The SRK dictates most of the terms between the agent and player with respect to the team contract. For example, the NFLPA's standard agent contract provides that an agent's fee cannot exceed 3%. The SRK specifies which revenues are used for the calculation of the agent's commission and the timing of the payment. The NFLPA contract form also provides that an agent is not entitled to receive his commission until the player is paid. There are a number of other provisions in the SRK that protect the player from agent abuse. Appendix A is a copy of the NFLPA's Standard Representation Agreement.

STANDARD PLAYER CONTRACT

Each union also has a Standard Player Contract (SPK) that must be used by the team when contracting with a player. The SPK provides uniformity in the contracts for all players and incorporates many of the provisions set forth in the CBA. The standard player contract spares the team and the player or his agent from having to negotiate a number of terms that are applicable to all players pursuant to the CBA. Appendix B is a copy of the standard NFL's Standard Player Contract.

SIGNIFICANCE OF CBAS

The importance of the CBAs and the enormous impact they have on the relationship the professional players have with their respective teams and leagues cannot be stressed enough. Later chapters will discuss some of the more significant aspects of the CBAs in each of the four major leagues.

Part II

Major League Baseball (MLB)

For almost a century, baseball was referred to as America's "National Pastime." Until the 1980s, Major League Baseball (MLB) was the undisputed top professional sports league in the country. In the last few decades, however, MLB has had to share the spotlight with the NFL, NBA, NHL, professional golf, tennis, and NASCAR. Despite this competition, MLB still dominates with respect to fan attendance; in 2005, MLB had 76 million fans attend games, far outnumbering the NBA's 23 million and the NFL's 22 million.

Competition from other sports is not the only problem MLB has faced. For a number of reasons, the labor relationship between management and players in professional baseball has been far more contentious than in any other sports league.

With two recent exceptions, no new CBA in baseball has been reached without a work stoppage. In 1972, the players called a strike that led to the cancellation of 86 games. In 1976, the owners declared a lockout that shut down spring training for 24 days. In 1981, the players struck and caused a mid-season work stoppage. The player's struck again in 1985, albeit for only a couple of days.

In 1994, MLB endured a long and costly strike that seriously diminished its standing with the public. Fans were slow to return to the game after the strike was settled, but a combination of factors in 1998—most notably Mark McGuire and Sammy Sosa's record home run show—seemed to reinvigorate the game. As will be discussed later in the chapter, however, all was not well in baseball land. In early August 2002, the players and clubs agreed upon a new CBA at the last minute to avert another strike. Remarkably, 2006 witnessed a friendly negotiation between the parties that without significant conflict resulted in an agreement to continue play uninterrupted through 2011.

RESERVE CLAUSE HISTORY

The first professional baseball leagues were formed in the early 1870s. The infamous "reserve clause" was not far behind. In the 1880s the owners of the teams in the two existing leagues, the National League and the American Association, met secretly and agreed that each team would not recruit or sign a certain number of the top players on other teams. The owners primarily wanted to prevent a bidding war for the best players that would increase the salaries of the players and, thereby, reduce the profits of the team owners.

Initially, the reserve clause was limited to several players. In a few years, the secretive nature of the restrictive agreement was ignored and the concept was expanded to all players in the major and minor leagues. Various provisions in the players' contracts were included that, in effect, prevented players from signing with other teams without the consent of their original teams. The result of this contractual restraint meant that once a player signed with a team, that player could not play with another team unless and until the original team allowed the transfer. The "hold" or "reservation" in the contract by the original team became known as the "reserve clause." By virtue of the clause, the owners had a virtual transferable property right in the players.

In the early 1900s, professional baseball had two leagues: the National League and the American League. In 1913, the Federal League was founded to join the two existing leagues. The National and American Leagues refused to embrace the new league. In response, the Federal League began enticing the top players from the two leagues with higher salaries. The Federal League also filed suit against the leagues. The suit was eventually settled. The raided players were returned to their original teams, and the Federal League received a cash settlement and disbanded. One of the teams in the Federal League, the Baltimore Club, did not agree to the settlement and filed an antitrust suit. The suit, and the resulting decision, became part of baseball's lore.

Federal Base Ball Club of Baltimore, Inc. v. National League of Professional Base Ball Clubs (1922)

This is a suit for threefold damages brought by the plaintiff in error under the Anti-Trust Acts. The defendants are the National League of Professional Base Ball Clubs and the American League of Professional Base Ball Clubs, unincorporated associations, composed respectively of groups of eight incorporated base ball clubs, joined as defendants; the presidents of the two Leagues and a third person, constituting what is known as the National Commission, having considerable powers in carrying out an agreement between the two Leagues; and three other persons having powers in the Federal League of Professional Base Ball Clubs, the relation of which to this case will be explained. It is alleged that these defendants conspired to monopolize the baseball business, the means adopted being set forth with a detail which, in the view that we take, it is unnecessary to repeat.

The plaintiff is a base ball club incorporated in Maryland, and with seven other corporations was a member of the Federal League of Professional Base Ball Players, a corporation under the laws of Indiana, that attempted to compete with the combined defendants. It alleges that the defendants destroyed the Federal League by buying up some of the constituent clubs and in one way or another inducing all those clubs except the plaintiff to leave their League, and that the three persons connected with the Federal League and named as defendants, one of them being the

President of the League, took part in the conspiracy. Great damage to the plaintiff is alleged. The plaintiff obtained a verdict for $80,000 in the Supreme Court and a judgment for treble the amount was entered, but the Court of Appeals, after an elaborate discussion, held that the defendants were not within the Sherman Act.

The decision of the Court of Appeals went to the root of the case and if correct makes it unnecessary to consider other serious difficulties in the way of the plaintiff's recovery. A summary statement of the nature of the business involved will be enough to present the point. The clubs composing the Leagues are in different cities and for the most part in different States. The end of the elaborate organizations and sub-organizations that are described in the pleadings and evidence is that these clubs shall play against one another in public exhibitions for money, one or the other club crossing a state line in order to make the meeting possible. When as the result of these contests one club has won the pennant of its League and another club has won the pennant of the other League, there is a final competition for the world's championship between these two. Of course the scheme requires constantly repeated travelling on the part of the clubs, which is provided for, controlled and disciplined by the organizations, and this it is said means commerce among the States. But we are of opinion that the Court of Appeals was right.

The business is giving exhibitions of base ball, which are purely state affairs. It is true that in order to attain for these exhibitions the great popularity that they have achieved, competitions must be arranged between clubs from different cities and States. But the fact that in order to give the exhibitions the Leagues must induce free persons to cross state lines and must arrange and pay for their doing so is not enough to change the character of the business. According to the distinction insisted upon in *Hooper v. California*, the transport is a mere incident, not the essential thing. That to which it is incident, the exhibition, although made for money would not be called trade of commerce in the commonly accepted use of those words. As it is put by defendant, personal effort, not related to production, is not a subject of commerce. That which in its consummation is not commerce does not become commerce among the States because the transportation that we have mentioned takes place. To repeat the illustrations given by the Court below, a firm of lawyers sending out a member to argue a case, or the Chautauqua lecture bureau sending out lecturers, does not engage in such commerce because the lawyer or lecturer goes to another State.

If we are right the plaintiff's business is to be described in the same way and the restrictions by contract that prevented the plaintiff from getting players to break their bargains and the other conduct charged against the defendants were not an interference with commerce among the States.

****

Simply put, in *Federal Baseball* the U.S. Supreme Court granted professional baseball an exemption from antitrust law. The decision has generated enormous confusion and debate over the years, especially on two issues. First, the case is often described as holding that professional baseball is not a business. This is an inaccurate description – what the Supreme Court found was that the business of baseball does not affect interstate commerce enough to trigger the antitrust laws. The second, and even more significant issue, is whether the antitrust exemption is limited to baseball's reserve clause.

Another challenge to the reserve clause in baseball, *Toolson v. New York Yankees*, reached the U.S. Supreme Court in 1953. George Toolson was a capable player who was stuck in a New York Yankees' farm system loaded with talent. Toolson wanted a release from the Yankees to increase his chances of making it to the majors with another team. He filed a suit challenging the Yankees' reserve clause hold on him. In *Toolson*, the Court described the *Federal Baseball* decision as "dubious," but upheld the exemption. The Court in *Toolson* did not rely on the interstate commerce reasoning used in the *Federal* case, but cited congressional inaction and baseball's reliance on the exemption as support for upholding the prior decision. The *Toolson* opinion, although short, stated that baseball's "business" was not subject to antitrust laws. That language is used to support the argument that the exemption created in the *Federal Baseball* case is not limited to baseball's reserve clause.

The criticism of the *Federal Baseball* and *Toolson* decisions became more pronounced for two reasons: (1) Major League Baseball expanded to the point where no one could claim in good faith that it did not affect interstate commerce, and (2) the courts held that the other professional sports leagues *were* subject to antitrust laws. In 1972, another highly publicized case challenging baseball's antitrust exemption, *Flood v. Kuhn*, made its way to the U.S. Supreme Court. Many observers believed that the Supreme Court would reverse the *Federal* and *Toolson* decisions in the *Flood* case and end baseball's *unique* antitrust exemption. The Supreme Court, however, upheld the exemption yet again and prevented players from attacking professional baseball, or its reserve clause, on antitrust grounds.

Curt Flood was an outstanding player for the St. Louis Cardinals for twelve (12) years. He had the nerve—or misfortune—of demanding a substantial raise that incensed the team's owner. Flood was then traded without being consulted. Upon learning of the trade, Flood wrote a letter to the owner that contained the following declaration:

> *After twelve years in the Major Leagues, I do not feel that I am a piece of property to be bought and sold irrespective of my wishes.*

Flood filed suit challenging the reserve clause as an antitrust violation. His case went to the U.S. Supreme Court. Excerpts from the majority and dissenting opinion of the case, set forth below, provide insight to the players' frustration and the Court's curious reasoning.

Flood v. Kuhn (U.S. St. Ct. 1972)

The petitioner, Curtis Charles Flood, born in 1938, began his major league career in 1956 when he signed a contract with the Cincinnati Reds for a salary of $4,000 for the season. He had no attorney or agent to advise him on that occasion. He was traded to the St. Louis Cardinals before the 1958 season. Flood rose to fame as a center fielder with the Cardinals during the years 1958-1969. In those 12 seasons he compiled a batting average of .293. His best offensive season was 1967 when he achieved .335. He was .301 or better in 6 of the 12 St. Louis years. He participated in the 1964, 1967, and

1968 World Series. He played errorless ball in the field in 1966, and once enjoyed 223 consecutive errorless games. Flood has received seven Golden Glove Awards. He was co-captain of his team from 1965-1969. He ranks among the 10 major league outfielders possessing the highest lifetime fielding averages.

But at the age of 31, in October 1969, Flood was traded to the Philadelphia Phillies of the National League in a multi-player transaction. He was not consulted about the trade. He was informed by telephone and received formal notice only after the deal had been consummated. In December he complained to the commissioner of Baseball and asked that he be made a free agent and be placed at liberty to strike his own bargain with any other major league teams. His request was denied.

Flood then instituted this antitrust suit in January 1970 in federal court for the Southern District of New York. The defendants were the Commissioner of Baseball, the presidents of the two major leagues, and the 24 major league clubs. In general, the complaint charged violations of the federal antitrust laws and civil rights statutes, violation of state statutes and the common law, and the imposition of a form of peonage and involuntary servitude contrary to the Thirteenth Amendment and 42 U.S.C. Sec. 1994, 18 U.S.C. Sec. 1581, and 29 U.S.C. Sec. 102 and 103. Petitioner sought declaratory and injunctive relief and treble damages.

Flood declined to play for Philadelphia in 1970, despite a $100,000 salary offer, and he sat out the year. After the season was concluded, Philadelphia sold its rights to Flood to the Washington Senators. Washington and the petitioner were able to come to terms for 1971 at a salary of $110,000. Flood started the season but, apparently because he was dissatisfied with his performance, he left the Washington club on April 27, early in the campaign. He has not played baseball since then.

The Legal Background

Federal Baseball Club v. National League, (1922), was a suit for treble damages instituted by a member of the Federal League (Baltimore) against the National and American Leagues and others. The plaintiff obtained a verdict in the trial court, but the Court of Appeals reversed. The main brief filed by the plaintiff with this Court discloses that it was strenuously argued, among other things, that the business in which the defendants were engaged was interstate commerce; that the interstate relationship among the several clubs, located as they were in different States, was predominant; that organized baseball represented an investment of colossal wealth; that it was an engagement in moneymaking; that gate receipts were divided by agreement between the home club and the visiting club; and that the business of baseball was to be distinguished from the mere playing of the game as a sport for physical exercise and diversion....

(Quoting from the *Federal* decision):

The business is giving exhibitions of baseball, which are purely state affairs... But the fact that in order to give the exhibitions the Leagues must induce free persons to cross state lines and must arrange and pay for their doing so is not enough to change the character of the business. ... [T]he transport is a mere incident, not the essential thing. That to which it is incident, the exhibition, although made for money would not be called trade or commerce in the commonly accepted use of those words.

If there is any inconsistency or illogic in all this, it is an inconsistency and illogic of long standing that is to be remedied by the Congress and not by this Court. ... Under these circumstances, there is merit in consistency even though some might claim that beneath that consistency is a layer of inconsistency.

Justice Marshall dissenting:

To non-athletes it might appear that petitioner was virtually enslaved by the owners of major league baseball clubs who bartered among themselves for his services. But, athletes know that it was not servitude that bound petitioner to the club owners; it was the reserve system. The essence of that system is that a player is bound to the club with which he first signs a contract for the rest of his playing days. He cannot escape from the club except by retiring, and he cannot prevent the club from assigning his contract to any other club....

The importance of the antitrust laws to every citizen must not be minimized. They are as important to baseball players as they are to football players, lawyers, doctors, or members of any other class of workers. Baseball players cannot be denied the benefits of competition merely because club owners view other economic interests as being more important, unless Congress says so.

Has Congress acquiesced in our decisions in *Federal Baseball Club* and *Toolson*? I think not. Had the Court been consistent and treated all sports in the same way baseball was treated, Congress might have become concerned enough to take action. But, the Court was inconsistent, and baseball was isolated and distinguished from all other sports. In *Toolson* the Court refused to act because Congress had been silent. But the Court may have read too much into this legislative inaction.

Americans love baseball as they love all sports. Perhaps we become so enamored of athletics that we assume that they are foremost in the minds of legislators as well as fans. We must not forget, however, that there are only some 600 major league baseball players. Whatever muscle they might have been able to muster by combining forces with other athletes has been greatly impaired by the manner in which this Court has isolated them. It is this Court that has made them impotent, and this Court should correct its error.

We do not lightly overrule our prior constructions of federal statutes, but when our errors deny substantial federal rights, like the right to compete freely and effectively to the best of one's ability as guaranteed by the antitrust laws, we must admit our error and correct it. We have done so before and we should do so again here.

****

In addition to losing his case, Curt Flood was isolated and ostracized by management and players alike. His suit paved the way, however, for future challenges that would eventually break the absolute and permanent right owners held over players. Many years later, and after Flood's death, federal legislation would be enacted in honor of the man who fought a lonely and losing battle for what he believed was right.

The *Flood* opinion made several references to baseball's "reserve system" being exempt from the antitrust laws. That language was later used to support the argument that all other aspects of professional baseball, for example the draft and the minor leagues, were not exempt from antitrust. The counter-argument was that *Flood's* case was limited to the reserve clause and that the court had no reason to address other aspects of baseball. Thirty years after *Flood*, in *Major League Baseball v. Crist* (2003), a federal court ruled that baseball's exemption is a federal right and strongly suggested the exemption applied to the entire operation of professional baseball.

LABOR LAW AND THE RESERVE CLAUSE

Although Major League Baseball has historically been exempt from antitrust scrutiny, the League has been subject to labor law. The Major League Baseball Players Association (MLBPA) was formed in the early 1950s. In the beginning, the association was dominated by owners, but in the late 1960s, the power of the players began to grow. The transformation was due primarily to the leadership of one man, Marvin Miller, who was hired to run the union. Miller knew little of baseball, but he was a superb labor negotiator. The Players' Association eventually organized into a union and entered into Collective Bargaining Agreements (CBAs) with management.

Most disputes regarding a CBA term are settled through arbitration. In the beginning, the CBA designated the Commissioner of Baseball as the arbitrator. At Miller's insistence, the Commissioner was eventually relieved of this duty (power) and neutral arbitrators were given the responsibility. The pendulum was starting to swing.

In 1974, James "Catfish" Hunter, a pitcher for the Oakland Athletics, etched his place in baseball history, but not on the diamond. The owner of the Athletics, Charles O. Finley, refused to honor a contract with Hunter after learning that the agreement would not provide the anticipated tax deductions. Hunter was unable to obtain any relief from Bowie Kuhn, MLB's commissioner at the time. A grievance was filed on Hunter's behalf by the union. The matter was heard by an arbitrator, Peter Seitz. Seitz voided the contract and Hunter became a free agent. Hunter then signed a contract with the New York Yankees for what was then an astonishing $3.25 million. Hunter's lucrative deal confirmed the players' belief about the value of free agency.

In the same year, two players, Andy Messersmith and Dave McNally, refused to sign new contracts at the end of the season. Each player continued to play for their teams during the next year pursuant to the automatic one-year extension in their contract. At the end of the '75 season, however, Messersmith and McNally submitted their status as free agents to arbitration. Again, the matter was in the hands of Mr. Seitz. Some commentators have criticized the league for not exercising its right to fire Mr. Seitz, who had already ruled against them in the Catfish Hunter arbitration. The arbitrator's decision in the Messersmith matter had a profound impact on baseball. Portions of the opinion are below and provide an excellent history and analysis of the reserve clause as it existed at that time.

Messersmith Arbitration (1976)

The Reserve System of the leagues is nowhere defined in a sentence or a paragraph. Reference is commonly and frequently made in the press and by the news media to a "Reserve Clause"; but there is no such single clause encompassing the subject matter. It seems fair to say, on the basis of what has been presented, that the "Reserve System" refers to a complex set of rules of the leagues (and provisions in the collective Basic Agreement and the Uniform Players Contract) related to the objective of retaining exclusive control over the service of their players in the interest of preserving discipline, preventing the enticement of players, maintaining financial stability and promoting a balance or a relative parity of competitive skills as among clubs. Such "exclusive control," it is said, is exercised by a Club placing the name of a player on its "reserve list" which is distributed to the other clubs in both leagues. A player on such a list, assert the leagues, cannot "play for or negotiate with any other club until his contract has been assigned or he has been released" and may not be the subject of "tampering."

This system of reservation of exclusive control is historic in baseball and is traceable to the early days of the organized sport in the 19th century. Over the years, the scheme and structure of provisions designed to establish and maintain that control has been changed in expression. The leagues assert that the system was designed, initially, to combat the institutional chaos that resulted when players under contract with one club defected to another. In an effort to deal with the problem, it is represented, various versions of reserve clauses had been adopted...

In 1947 the renewal clause in the Uniform Players Contract (which had been in effect since 1930) was amended for that reason to provide as follows:

> ...... *the Club shall have the right by written notice to the Player...to renew this contract for the period of one year on the same terms,* except that the amount payable to the Player shall be such as the Club shall fix in such notice; provided, however, that said amount, if fixed by a Major League Club shall be an amount payable at a rate of not less than 75% of the rate stipulated for the preceding year.

This provision was carried forward in all forms of the Uniform Player Contract subsequently used, including those signed by these grievants......

Messersmith signed a one-year contract with the Los Angeles Dodgers in 1974. This contract was duly renewed by the Club for what is commonly called the "renewal year" of 1975.

The Players Association (Union) claims that Messersmith, having served out and completed his renewal year on September 29, 1975, was no longer under contract with the Los Angeles Club and, accordingly, was a free agent to negotiate for the rendition of his services with any of the other clubs in the leagues; but that the clubs "have conspired to deny Mr. Messersmith that right and have maintained the position that the Los Angeles Club is still exclusively entitled to his services."

No one challenges the right of a Club to renew a Player's contract with or without his consent, under Section 10(a), "for the period of one [renewal] year." I read the record, however, as containing a contention by the leagues that when a Club renews a Player's contract for the renewal year, the contract in force during that year contains the "right of renewal" clause as one of its terms, entitling the Club to renew the contract in successive years, to perpetuity, perhaps, so long as the Player is alive and the Club has duly discharged all conditions required of it. This is challenged by the Players Association whose position it is that the contractual relationship between the Club and the Player terminates at the end of the first renewal year. Thus, it claims that there was no longer any contractual bond between Messersmith and the Los Angeles Club on September 29, 1975.

The league's argument is based on the language that the Club "may renew this contract for the period of one year *on the same terms*"; and that among those "terms" is the right to further contract renewal.

In the law of contract construction, as I know it, there is nothing to prevent parties from agreeing to successive renewals of the terms of their bargain (even to what had been described as "perpetuity"), provided the contract expresses that intention with explicit clarity and the right of subsequent renewals does not have to be implied. ...

I am not unmindful of the testimony of the Commissioner of Baseball and the Presidents of the National and American League given at the hearings as to the importance of maintaining the integrity of the Reserve System. It was represented to me that any decision of the Arbitration Panel sustaining the Messersmith and McNally grievances would have dire results, wreak great harm to the Reserve System and do serious damage to the sport of baseball.

Thus, for example, it was stated that a decision favoring these grievants would encourage many other players to elect to become free agents at the end of the renewal years; that this would encourage clubs with the largest monetary resources to engage free agents, thus unsettling the competitive balance between clubs, so essential to the sport; that it would increase enormously the already high costs of training and seasoning young players to achieve the level of skills required in professional baseball and such investments would be sacrificed if they became free agents at the end of a renewal year; that driven by the compulsion to win, owners of franchises would over-extend themselves financially and improvident bidding for players in an economic climate in which, today, some clubs are strained, financially; that investors will be discouraged from putting money in franchises in which several of the star players on the club team will become free agents at the end of a renewal year and no continuing control over the players' services can be exercised; and that even the integrity of the sport may be placed in hazard under certain circumstances.

I do not purport to appraise these apprehensions. They are all based on speculations as to what may ensue. Some of the fears may be imaginary or exaggerated; but some may be reasonable, realistic and sound. After all, they were voiced by distinguished baseball officials with long experience in the sport and a background for judgment in such matters much superior to my own. However, as stated above, at length, it is not the Panel (and especially the writer) to determine what, if anything, is good or bad about the reserve system. The Panel's sole duty is to interpret and apply the agreements and undertakings of the parties. If any of the expressed apprehensions and fears are soundly based, I am confident that the dislocations and damage to the reserve system can be avoided or minimized through good faith collective bargaining between the parties. There are numerous expedients available and arrangements that can be made that will soften the blow - if this decision, indeed, should be regarded as a blow. This decision is not the end of the line by any means. The parties, jointly, are free to agree to disregard it and compose their differences as to the reserve system in any way they see fit.

****

The arbitrator, Peter Seitz, ruled that the two players were free agents after the 1975 season. Seitz was fired immediately after his decision. The ruling was unprecedented and sent management into a frenzy. Players in Major League Baseball had become free agents without the concurrence of management. Contrary to popular belief, however, the arbitrator did not rule that the reserve clause was *per se* unenforceable. The arbitrator simply found that in order for the reserve clause to be upheld, it must be expressly stated in the contract, which did not exist in the Messersmith arbitration. The decision was taken to court and the ruling was upheld.

BASIC AGREEMENT

When the CBA expired, after the Messersmith decision, the players' union and management began serious collective bargaining negotiations over free agency, with the two sides having opposite goals. Although a temporary lockout was imposed by management, a new CBA was reached in 1976. Significant aspects in the CBA, referred to as the "Basic Agreement," with respect to free agency, included the following provisions:

1. During the first two years, a player had to accept the team's offer.
2. For the next 4 years, a player was bound to his team, but could submit his salary determination to arbitration.
3. After 6 years, the player could become a free agent.

GUARANTEED CONTRACTS

One major effect of the Basic Agreement was that it brought about a considerable change in the length and nature of many contracts. Prior to the Basic Agreement, almost every contract was for a one-year term and was not guaranteed. By 1980, at least 35% of the contracts were guaranteed for at least a three-year period. Today, most of the top players in Major League Baseball have contracts that are guaranteed for a term well beyond one year.

SALARY ARBITRATION

The provision in the Basic Agreement allowing free agency status after six years was a monumental achievement for the players. The right of salary arbitration was, perhaps, even more important. Salary arbitration has allowed many players to minimize the adverse impact of the antitrust exemption and reserve clause. In 1987, the right to arbitration was changed to three years. In 1991, another modification was reached that allowed players with at least two years of Major League service the potential for arbitration. To qualify for arbitration, the player must have accumulated at least eighty-six days of service in the preceding season and rank in the top 17% in total service of the players in that category. Players with six or more years of major league service who did not qualify for free agency could also select salary arbitration. This situation covers players who elected free agency within the previous five years and are, therefore, ineligible for free agency.

The salary arbitration proceeding used by Major League Baseball merits discussion. The method and results have proven to be extremely beneficial to the players and have become the "agony of defeat" for owners.

The baseball arbitration procedure is based on the "final offer selection" as opposed to conventional arbitration. The argument is that conventional arbitration would encourage each side to submit sums that would be unrealistically slanted in their favor with the belief that the arbitrator would usually split the difference. Under the "final offer" approach, the parties execute a standard contract, but the salary amount is left blank. Each side submits one final salary offer and statistics to support its offer. The factors considered by the arbitrator include the quality of the player's contribution to the team during the past season, the consistency of the player's contribution, the length of the contribution, past compensation, comparative salaries, the record of the club in standings and attendance, and other relevant data. Within 24 hours, the arbitrator selects one of the submissions and writes it into the contract. The arbitrator can only use one of the figures submitted, that is, the one by the player or the one by the club. The arbitrator cannot play Solomon and split the baby.

Opponents of baseball's arbitration claim that it is a win-win process for the players and cite statistics that support their position. From 1984 to 1994, due in large part to arbitration, average salaries for players increased over 300%. In 1970, the average salary in MLB was $29,000. By 1994, the average had risen to $1.2 million.

Citing the "average" salary in baseball (and other sports) can, however, be misleading. In 1995, the average salary in baseball was above $1 million. In that year, however, about 12% of the players got more than 50% of the total payroll. A more telling figure on salaries is the median salary (half the players earn more, half less), which was much lower than the commonly cited average salary. Since 1983, the average salary has gone up around tenfold, but the median salary increase has been much less.

Opponents of arbitration argue that arbitrators take into account the salaries of free agents and other factors in determining awards that unfairly skew the result in favor of the players. Supporters of the arbitration process argue that the dramatic increase in salaries is due to the "monopoly" that owners have and exploit by not paying fair wages in the first two or three years of play, when arbitration is not available to the player. In addition, some argue the dramatic increases are justified as a result of the minimum wage paid to players while in the minor leagues.

BASEBALL COLLUSION

A discussion of the reserve clause and free agency struggle between players and management in baseball would not be complete without addressing an activity on the part of management that severely strained the relationship between the players and the owners in the 1980's.

The Players Union had successfully negotiated the right to "free agency" for players who had six years in the League. Without the players' knowledge, however, the owners made a confidential agreement that other teams would not bid or seek to sign any of the players who became "free agents." Free agents began receiving offers from their original team at an even lower salary than the previous year. The players finally realized that "foul play" was at hand. The players could not challenge the conspiracy on the basis of antitrust because of the court-created exemption. The players could, however, file a grievance pursuant to labor law. The CBA provided the following with respect to setting salaries:

> Players shall not act in concert with other Players and Clubs shall not act in concert with other Clubs.

The players were able to prove collusion occurred among the owners in direct violation of the CBA. A settlement was eventually reached in 1990 on the players' claim. The agreement required the league or teams to pay about $280 million in damages. The Players Union had the enormous problem of determining how the money would be divided between the affected players.

1994 STRIKE

In order for a sports league to exist, there must be some balance to the competitive ability of the teams. The talent available to a team is greatly influenced by its financial strength. Baseball franchises are located in large urban areas, but some locations are clearly better markets and provide more revenue to their respective teams. In the 1990s, revenue from nationally televised games was shared equally by the teams. The bulk of gate receipts, however, was kept by the home team: 90% in the National League and 80% in the American League. This distribution favored teams in large markets and those with modern stadiums that featured various amenities. The largest part of the revenue disparity was due to regional television income, which was not shared. Teams like the New York Yankees could earn in the range of $50 million from regional television, while other teams were unable to earn more than $10 million. The difference in club earnings had a direct effect on salaries paid to the players. For example, in 1994, the Atlanta Braves paid an estimated $52 million in salaries while the San Diego Padres paid about $15 million to its players. Interestingly, in the 1996 season, the Padres were a playoff contender. The three teams with the highest payrolls in 1996—the Yankees ($61 million), the Orioles ($55 million) and the Braves ($53 million) were, however, among the final four teams in the playoffs.

Entering the 1990s, several baseball franchises in the smaller markets were reportedly under severe financial strain. One of the few issues where management and players were in agreement was that something needed to be done to help the financially weaker clubs. The dispute was over who should pay, and what method should be used to strengthen the weaker teams. Management's position was that the poorer teams were suffering as a direct result of players' escalating salaries. The owners argued that changes were necessary to save baseball, including salary caps (like the NFL), further restrictions on free agency, and the abolition or limitation of arbitration. The players countered with studies that showed the problem had little to do with player salaries and was due to how the League negotiated and distributed broadcast revenue. Unlike other leagues, most revenue in the MLB was not shared equally among the clubs.

In 1993, the League discussed a plan of having the larger clubs share local television revenue with smaller-market teams, to provide some relief to the weaker clubs. The plan, however, was conditioned on the players accepting a salary cap and restrictions on arbitration and free agency. There was also discussion of a "salary tax," which would impose a tax or penalty on teams that exceeded salary cap limits. The players were adamantly opposed to management's proposals. The players argued that the proposals would reduce salaries and free agency rights and be a detriment to competition.

When the CBA expired in 1993, the players and management could not come to terms on how the problems resulting from the discrepancies in club earnings should be addressed. In August of 1994, the players called a strike. The players had a $200 million strike fund in place. The timing of the strike favored the players, who by that time had earned about two-thirds of their salaries for the season. The most profitable time for the owners – the playoffs and the World Series – was just approaching as the strike began. Efforts were unsuccessfully made by those in and out of baseball (including the President of the United States and some of the most powerful members of Congress) to bring the parties together. In 1994, for the first time in 90 years, there was no World Series. (In 1904 the National League champion refused to play in the World Series because it felt the American League was an inferior league.)

ENDING THE STRIKE

In December 1994, the owners declared an impasse and unilaterally imposed their terms in the players' contracts. The players refused to sign the contracts and filed charges of unfair labor practices with the National Labor Relations Board (NLRB). The owners' defense was that the changes made were on permissive, not mandatory, subjects of collecive bargaining, and changes to permissive subjects are permitted. The NLRB brought the matter to court and obtained an injunction preventing the owners from implementing the changes in *Silverman v. Major League Baseball Player Relations Committee* (1995). The Basic Agreement was amended in 1990 to provide for treble damages for labor violations, so the court's ruling in *Silverman* exposed the League to substantial losses. The injunction, issued on March 31, 1995, brought an end to the strike. The players resumed play in the 1995-1996 season under the terms of the old CBA. The strike lasted 232 days and, at the time, was the longest in the history of professional sports and the first to cancel a season. It is estimated the strike cost the players and owners approximately $1 billion.

The Judge's ruling in *Silverman* kept the old CBA in place until one of three things occurred:

1. a new CBA was reached between the parties
2. the court determined that a genuine impasse existed
3. a final ruling was issued on the Unfair Labor Practice charges filed by the NLRB against owners (which the owners postponed several times)

Negotiations between the players' union and management were ongoing in an attempt to address the problems by reaching a new CBA. In August 1996, the parties appeared to be approaching an agreement, but another "deal killer" arose. In the past, players had received "service time" credit for days missed during a strike. This credit was important because it was used to determine when a player became a free agent. The union insisted that the players should receive the full 75 days credit lost during the 232-day strike. Late in the negotiation process, the owners announced they would give the credit—except to the 20 or so players who would immediately become free agents as a result of the time. The union and players were outraged.

In November 1996, the negotiators for the players' union and management reached a tentative agreement. It was assumed that each negotiator had authority on behalf of his respective party to commit to the terms. The CBA needed to be approved by three-fourths of the owners. The owners, led by Jerry Reinsdorf of the Chicago White Sox, voted 18-12 against the proposal. It appeared that a new deal was dead and that Major League Baseball was in for more turmoil. Within days of the rejection, though, the White Sox signed Albert Belle to a record $52.5 million contract. A number of owners who had supported Reinsdorf in his opposition to the proposal were furious. Reinsdorf had complained vehemently about escalating player salaries; that same man was now paying a salary in excess of anything ever offered in baseball. Belle's record salary would pressure other owners to raise salaries. Immediately after the Belle contract was announced, the owners met again and voted 26-4 in favor of the proposed CBA. Reinsdorf's contract with Belle appeared to do what Congress, the White House, and the courts could not: it forced the parties to reach an agreement on a labor deal. The battle that had been waged between the owners and players since December 7, 1992, had finally come to an end.

1996 COLLECTIVE BARGAINING AGREEMENT

The 1996 CBA contained some new and significant provisions that included the following:
1. interleague play
2. an agreement to submit a joint proposal to Congress to end baseball's anti-trust exemption as it applies to movement of players in the Major League (All other aspects of the exemption would continue.)

3. three-man panels (as opposed to one-man) on half of all arbitration proceedings.
4. a payroll tax on players salaries of 2.5%, which expired in 1999.
5. an increase of the minimum salary to $150,000, with escalators to raise it to $200,000 in 1999.
6. a luxury tax on the five teams with the highest salaries.

The new CBA also resulted in about 13 players gaining free agency status. Spanish-speaking players (almost 20% of the league) were entitled to English courses at the expense of the clubs, and players would get single rooms on road trips.

The luxury tax was thought to be the most important part of the CBA. The tax was an attempt to create a drag on salaries and provide a direct benefit to small-market clubs. It was hoped the tax would provide relief to small-market teams. As it turned out, however, the impact was minimal.

CURT FLOOD ACT

In 1998, Congress enacted legislation amending the Clayton Act, 15 U.S.C. 12, by adding section 27. The new law was called the Curt Flood Act in honor of Curt Flood's courageous, albeit unsuccessful, attempt to challenge the reserve clause. The law removed baseball's antitrust exemption on issues relating to "employment of Major League Baseball players to play baseball at the major league level." That is, the law prohibited the application of the antitrust exemption established in the court decisions in *Federal Baseball, Toolson,* and *Flood* as to major league players. The law did not apply to any other aspect of the antitrust exemption. Excluded from the law and still subject to the antitrust exemption are 1) minor leagues; 2) the draft; 3) the Professional Baseball Agreement that sets forth the relationship of the Major League Clubs and their Minor League affiliates; 4) franchise relocation; 5) baseball's intellectual property rights; 6) The Sports Broadcasting Act (15 U.S.C. 1291); and 7) the relationship between professional baseball and umpires.

The passage of the Curt Flood Act was hailed as a major triumph. People in and out of baseball, including members of Congress, declared that the law would help prevent labor disputes such as the devastating strike of 1994 that cancelled the end of the season and the World Series. They were wrong for two reasons:

First, the Curt Flood Act was largely symbolic; the Act had little, if any, effect on the labor negotiations between the parties. In 1996, the U.S. Supreme Court rendered a decision in *Brown v. Pro Football.* In *Brown* the Court held that as long as the parties to a collective bargaining process engaged in conduct authorized by labor laws, they could not sue each other for antitrust violations. That is, in order for a professional baseball player, or any other athlete in the leagues with collective bargaining agreements, to bring an antitrust action against the league, the union would first have to be decertified. The players would have to give up all of the benefits obtained, and the rights provided, by labor law. Although the players in the NFL successfully employed this tactic once, it was highly unlikely that baseball players or the players in any of the other leagues, including the NFL, would undertake such a step again.

Second, the 1994 strike had nothing to do with the antitrust exemption. The major issue in 1994 was how to handle the growing revenue disparity among teams; the Curt Flood Act did nothing to affect this disparity.

BASEBALL'S REVENUE DISPARITY

The 1994 strike cost the players and teams hundreds of millions of dollars. The costs did not stop, however, when the strike ended. The stigma of the strike continued for the following seasons, as MLB dealt with angry fans, poor television ratings, and lagging attendance. The 1998 season, however, was one to remember. Attendance was up, an unknown veteran pitched a no-hitter, the Yankees set a record for wins, and fans saw unprecedented interleague play. The highlight of the year, however, was the home run race between Sammy Sosa and Mark McGuire. Even people who did not follow baseball were caught up in the frenzy. Baseball was back.

To the casual observer, everything had returned to pre-strike normality. But no matter how exciting the game was, the *business* of MLB had the same problems. The revenue disparity that brought on the 1994 strike not only remained, but was growing more pronounced. In 1999, eight players in the league each earned more than the entire roster of the Montreal Expos team. The Los Angeles Dodgers gave Kevin Brown a contract worth more than $100 million, about the same amount that was needed to buy the Kansas City club at the time. Brown's salary for 2000 was almost $16 million, slightly less than the entire payroll of the Minnesota Twins. On the opening day of the 2002 season the New York Yankees' payroll was near $125 million, while Montreal's was approximately $35 million. Alex Rodriquez alone was earning $25 million a year with the Texas Rangers.

The disparity problem went even further than the teams at the very top and bottom of the salary scale. There was a growing perception among fans and some owners that post-season play was limited to a few teams that were on the top of the salary scale. This idea may have led some owners to conclude that there was no point in adding $10 million to the payroll, even if it was available, if it would not be enough to make the team a playoff contender. The team might not be a champion, but at least it would be profitable. This attitude had been one of the major obstacles in negotiations with the players, for players were reluctant to make salary sacrifices to help "poorer" teams when there was no guarantee that this sacrifice would be used for players' salaries.

The huge disparity in salaries was a direct result of the difference in team revenue. Gate receipts were part of the problem. In 2000, the home team kept 80% of the proceeds in the American League; and the National League take was 90% of the gate. Some teams had new fan-friendly stadiums that generated far more revenue than their competitors, who continued to play in older stadiums routinely designed for football. The bigger problem, however, was television revenue. MLB teams shared equally in the income derived from national television contracts. The teams, however, did not share income from regional television deals. Some teams, like the New York Yankees and Boston Red Sox, were in very large markets and had a history of winning. In 2001, the Yankees earned approximately $57 million from local broadcasting rights. Financial experts estimated in 2007 that the YES network, the Yankees regional sports network (RSN), might alone command a value upward of $1 billion. In contrast, Montreal only brought in about $500,000 that same year.

It had been demonstrated that large salaries in baseball did not guarantee a winning season. But a low payroll almost ensured that a team would not be a contender. In certain periods, the teams ranked with the top four payrolls made the postseason playoff over 90% of the time, while teams ranked in the bottom 10 in payroll made the postseason less than 10% of the time. In 1998, the difference in the average salary for the five teams with the highest and the lowest salaries was $45 million. There had always been a relationship between a high payroll and winning; the correlation appeared to be increasing. Many fans and players of lower salary teams believed there was no hope for a run at the playoffs. Everyone agreed that attitude was not good for baseball. The league adopted some revenue sharing measures, but critics complained it was not sufficient. There was mounting support to require rich teams like the New York Yankees to share a greater portion of their regional television money with the poorer teams.

It is easy to understand why teams like the Yankees would not readily embrace shifting larger sums of money to other teams. However, the opposition to the revenue distribution was not limited to the high-revenue teams. A number of critics argued that the revenue sharing amounted to corporate welfare that punished teams that were successful and rewarded those that were not.

There were some who argued, however, that the impact of revenue disparity among teams was much ado about nothing. The Yankees payroll in 2006 was $206 million. The shortsop for the Yankees, Derek Jeter, earned $20.6 million, which was equal to the entire payroll of the Marlins—and Jeter was not the highest paid Yankee player. But when the Yankees were eliminated from the playoffs in 2006, MLB was ensured that for 7 years in a row there would be a different World Series champion, a mark of parity that had eluded the NFL and NBA.

CONTRACTION AND MLB CLUB OWNERSHIP

As the new century began, there was a growing consensus that baseball had to undergo some major changes. The seriousness of the situation was made clear when immediately after the 2001 World Series, Bud Selig, MLB's Commissioner, announced that the league was considering contraction of at least two teams. That suggestion would have drawn laughter just a few years earlier. No one, however, was smiling now. Although specific teams were not identified, the Montreal Expos, the Minnesota Twins, and the Florida Marlins were considered likely targets. Montreal's average home attendance in 2001 was around 8,000, less than a number of minor league clubs. Lawsuits in both Minnesota and Florida were filed to stop the action. The opponents to contraction won court battles that would seriously delay, if not stop, the elimination of the teams in those states. Congressional hearings were held to "encourage" the league to abandon the contraction idea. The legal and political action taken ensured that contraction would not occur in 2002, but the threat remained.

In addition to the threat of contraction, MLB saw an unprecedented game of musical chairs among owners. John Henry, the owner of the Florida Marlins, bought the Boston Red Sox. Henry sold the Marlins to Jeffrey Loria, who owned the Montreal Expos. Loria bought the Marlins for $158 million and sold the Expos for $120 million to the Baseball Expos LP—a partnership of major league baseball owners. This was the first time in MLB's long history that the League actually owned a team. At the time of the sale, the contraction of the Montreal Expos seemed inevitable.

MLB realized, however, that the club could be saved and probably sold for a profit if it was placed in another suitable market. In 2005, MLB relocated the team to Washington, D.C., and renamed the team the Nationals. The Nationals temporarily played in the outmoded Robert F. Kennedy Memorial Stadium, but the relocation deal came with a commitment from the local government for a new stadium scheduled to be open in 2008. MLB's asking price was $450 million.

The pennant race in the summer of 2002 was largely overshadowed by the intensive labor negotiations. Numerous issues were on the bargaining table, such as contraction and drug testing. The two potential deal-breakers, however, were revenue sharing and a payroll tax. There was considerable fear that trying to force the richer teams to share revenue with the poorer teams and the attempt to impose a salary tax on the top payroll teams could bring about another work stoppage. It was well recognized that a strike or lockout would have devastated MLB. Revenue sharing and payroll taxes were especially complicated because the opposition came not only from the players, but also from the wealthiest teams that would pay more in revenue sharing and that were the targets of the salary tax. As negotiations intensified the player's union set August 30 as a strike deadline. On the morning of August 30, an agreement on a new CBA was reached.

2002 COLLECTIVE BARGAINING AGREEMENT

Significant aspects of the 2002 CBA included the following:

REVENUE SHARING:

Revenue sharing from national and local revenue was established. About one-third of the sharing came from an uneven split of national revenue. In addition, 34% of each team's local revenue was determined, minus some deductions, and the teams paid or received the difference between their figure and the league average. In 2005 alone, over $300 million was transferred from high-income to low-income teams.

PAYROLL TAX THRESHOLD:

A tax on payrolls that exceeded certain thresholds was implemented. In 2003 the threshold amount was $117 million, in 2004 the sum was $128 million, and in 2005 and '06, it was $136.5 million.

PAYROLL TAX RATES:

In 2003, the tax rate was 17.5%; in 2004 the rate was 22.5% for first-time offenders and 30% for second-time offenders. In 2005 the rate was the same as in 2004, but third-time offenders paid 40%. In 2006, there would be no tax for first-time offenders, but second-time offenders faced a 36% rate and third and fourth-time offenders had a 40% rate. In 2005, the Yankees and Red Sox paid payroll taxes of $34 million and $4 million, respectively.

MINIMUM SALARY:

The minimum salary increased to $300,000 in 2003 and 2004, with cost-of-living adjustments in 2005 and 2006.

CONTRACTION:

Management agreed that there would be no contraction through the year 2006. The owners could attempt to eliminate two teams in 2007, but they had to notify the union by July 1, 2006. The players agreed not to challenge a contraction in 2007 with the National Labor Relations Board.

DRUG TESTING:

Random survey testing for all players was agreed to in 2003. If 5% or more of the players tested positive, mandatory random testing was to be put in place for 2004 and 2005. If 2.5% or fewer tested positive, mandatory random testing would be replaced by survey testing. A first positive test would lead to treatment, and further positive tests would bring suspensions ranging from thirty days to two years.

WORLDWIDE DRAFT:

The league and the union agreed to form a joint committee to establish rules for a worldwide draft to be put in place in 2003. Management proposed thirty-eight rounds, and the union suggested twenty rounds.

UNSIGNED DRAFT PICKS COMPENSATION:

Teams that failed to sign their draft picks in the first round of the amateur draft would receive an additional pick in the same slot the following year. Teams that failed to sign second-round picks would receive a pick at the end of the second round.

EXPIRATION DATE:

The agreement had an expiration date of December 19, 2006, with a provision that play would continue in 2007 under the 2006 terms if a new agreement was not reached.

2006 COLLECTIVE BARGAINING AGREEMENT

In October 2006, MLB and the MLBPA agreed upon a five-year CBA that would allow play to continue uninterrupted through the 2011 season. After the 2011 season baseball will have experienced 16 years without a strike or a lockout – the longest period of labor peace in the history of its collective bargaining relationship. There was surprisingly little conflict or fanfare during the negotiations, and both Commissioner Selig and MLBPA Director Donald Fehr expressed an appreciation for the trust and cooperation that now existed between the two sides. Moreover, both parties viewed continued labor peace to be a vital part of continuing baseball's recent surge in popularity – the league had set new attendance records each of the past three seasons, and had taken in more than $6 billion in revenue during the 2007 season.

Significant aspects of the 2006 CBA included the following:

REVENUE SHARING

The net transfer of the revenue sharing plan remained the same as the current plan, and would adjust according to revenue and changes in disparity. Marginal tax rates for recipients of the plan were significantly lower through the use of a new central fund redistribution mechanism, from 40% for high revenue and 48% under the old CBA to 31% under this agreement. This was the first time that all clubs face the same marginal tax rate. There was also a new provision requiring revenue sharing recipients to spend receipts to improve on-field performance retained with modifications. The Commissioner's Discretionary Fund would continue at $10 million a year, with a cap of $3 million per Club per year.

COMPETITIVE BALANCE TAX

The structure from the 2002 CBA remained intact, but the threshold amounts for the tax were reset to $148 million in 2007, $155 million in 2008, $162 million in 2009, $170 million in 2010, and $178 million in 2011.

AMATEUR DRAFT

Clubs that failed to sign first *or* second round picks would receive the same pick in the subsequent draft as compensation. Clubs that failed to sign a third round pick would receive a sandwich pick between rounds three and four in the subsequent draft as compensation.

DRAFT CHOICE COMPENSATION

Free agents had historically been divided into three categories (Type A, B, and C), depending on skill level. Type C free agents were eliminated in 2006. In the same year, compensation for Type B players became indirect (a sandwich pick) as opposed to direct compensation from the signing Club. In 2007, Type A players were limited to the top 20% of each position, down from 30%, and Type B players became 21% - 40% at each position, down from 31% - 50%. The salary arbitration offer and acceptance dates were moved to December 1 and December 7, and Minor League players could now be protected from the Rule 5 draft for an extra year (to four or five years).

BENEFIT PLAN

The Players Benefit Plan received a $154.5 million average annual contribution, and there were improved benefits for some retired players.

MINIMUM SALARY

In the Major Leagues, minimum salaries would be: $380,000 in 2007, $390,000 in 2008, $400,000 in 2009, and a cost-of-living adjustment for 2011. In the Minor Leagues, the minimum salaries would be: $60,000 in 2007, $62,500 in 2008, and $65,000 in 2009.

FREE AGENCY

Players traded in the middle of a multi-year contract no longer had the right to demand a trade, although players who currently held that right from the last CBA were grandfathered in and could still demand a trade. The December 7, December

19, January 8, and May 1 deadlines were eliminated, and the date to tender contracts was moved from December 20 to December 12.

OTHER HIGHLIGHTS

The All-Star game winner continued to have home-field advantage in the World Series. There would be no contraction during the term of the agreement. Drug-testing rules would stay unchanged, and both sides agreed to further discuss HGH testing in the future.

MLB'S SALARY DISPARITY

Following the 1994-95 strike, MLB revenue increased at a higher rate than player salaries. The huge disparity in salaries among teams, however, remained. At the beginning of the 2006 season, the New York Yankees' team salary was almost $200 million, the highest in the league. The Yankees had three players, Alex Rodriguez, Derek Jeter, and Jason Giambi, earning over $20 million. The second and third teams in terms of salary amounts were the Boston Red Sox ($120 million) and the Los Angeles Angels ($103 million). On the other end of the spectrum, the Florida Marlins started the season with a total payroll under $15 million. Seventeen of the Marlins' players were making $327,000, the league's minimum. The New York Yankees produced around $300 million in local revenue in 2005, while teams at the bottom generated less than $50 million.

It appeared revenue sharing in MLB was necessary to maintain a competitive balance. But the owners held widely different views on how it should work. There was an understanding that the wealthier teams should share some revenue with the lower-end teams, but the challenge was to ensure that the high-revenue teams and low-revenue teams continued to have an incentive to generate more local revenue. In addition, the league had to ensure that the teams on the receiving end of revenue sharing spent it in manner that would enhance their team's performance.

DRUG TESTING

Despite the complaints over MLB's massive salary disparity, the league was in the midst of an unprecedented level of growth and success. From 2000-2006, there were seven different World Series champions. The average player salary increased from $1 million in 1992 to $2.8 million in 2006, and fan attendance had never been higher. There was labor peace for more than a decade, and a five-year CBA was reached without any threat of a work stoppage. However, over the past few years, a cloud of suspicion regarding drug use has begun to threaten the public opinion that is essential to the success of the league. As the "National Pastime," baseball enjoys a special place at the heart of American culture, but this position is far from guaranteed. After the 1994 baseball strike, for example, it took years for the public to warm to the game again. If baseball does not adequately address the "steroid era," it could face a similarly damaging crisis of public confidence in the game.

Pursuant to the CBA, the league currently only employs a urine-testing program to check for steroid use. All players are randomly selected for testing once a season, and the Commissioner has the authority to issue additional tests at unannounced times. For non-steroid drug abuse, the league currently does not randomly test; instead, investigation is based on "reasonable cause." In other words, when a member of the Health Policy Advisory Committee receives evidence that a player has used banned substances within the past year, the Committee calls an immediate conference. If a majority votes in favor, the player is tested within 48 hours.

No player has been accused of steroid use more than Barry Bonds, the new all-time home run leader. It is perhaps fitting that while the last great home run race (involving Sammy Sosa and Mark McGwire) reinvigorated and restored the popularity of the game, the Bonds home run chase greatly damaged it. Bonds ended the 2006 season needing only 22 home runs to pass Henry "Hank" Aaron for first place on the all-time list, and on August 7, 2007, Bonds hit his 756th homer and took over the top of the list. While the "run to the record" was finally over, the real drama was just beginning.

Amidst rumors and accusations of steroid use by Bonds, Commissioner Bud Selig decided not to attend the record-breaking game, instead sending the Executive Vice President of Baseball Operations. Analysts have also debated whether Bonds should end up in the Hall of Fame or an asterisk placed by the record as a result of the steroid controversy.

Bonds was first connected to steroids in 2003, when his trainer (and BALCO) was indicted by a federal grand jury for supplying anabolic steroids to athletes. As a player who gained a significant amount of strength later in his career, speculation naturally began that Bonds might be a user. In 2006, a heavily publicized book (*Game of Shadows*) was released, alleging that Bonds used a variety of steroids. The saga culminated on November 15, 2007, when Bonds was indicted by a federal grand jury for perjury and obstruction of justice in connection with his testimony in the 2003 criminal investigation of BALCO. The outcome of the trial is unknown at this time.

Bonds is far from the only player suspected of steroid use. Following the publication of *Game of Shadows*, which accused several current and retired players of steroid use, several members of Congress expressed concern about the effectiveness of MLB drug policies. This concern led Commissioner Selig to appoint George Mitchell, former Senate Majority Leader, to investigate the use of performance-enhancing drugs in baseball.

After conducting hundreds of interviews with players and looking through over 100,000 pages of documents, the investigation culminated in the Mitchell Report, a much-anticipated 409 page report released December 13, 2007. Shockingly, 88 current or former players were named in the report, including stars such as Roger Clemens and Miguel Tejada. Several analysts and former players derided the report as nothing more than glorified rumors and innuendo, but Selig classified it as a "call to action." The report recommended three changes to MLB's drug policy: (1) MLB should investigate drug use beyond the urine test; (2) MLB should increase its effort to educate players on the health dangers of steroids; and (3) when the League and the MLBPA begin negotiations again, they should be guided by modern standards. It is yet to be determined which changes, if any, MLB will make in response to the report, but it is safe to assume that significant action will be taken.

MINOR LEAGUES

The relationship between the minor leagues, often referred to as "farm clubs," and Major League Baseball is interesting and unique. Minor league teams that are affiliated with the Majors are members of the National Association of Professional Baseball Leagues (NAPBL). The agreement between the NAPBL and MLB is set forth in the Professional Baseball Agreement (PBA). The arrangement between the two groups is complex, but essentially provides that the MLB will pay most of the salaries, meal money, and umpire expense for the minor leagues. The minor league clubs pay some of their travel expenses and a fee to MLB.

Minor leagues are classified at different levels and the more-talented players are expected to advance from lower classifications to higher ones and eventually to the Major Leagues. Minor league teams that are affiliated with Major League teams (some minor league teams are independent) obtain their players on assignment from Major League clubs. The affiliated minor league teams do not control the contract of their players.

THE DRAFT

Years ago, there was no limit to the number of rounds in MLB's draft. In 1998, however, a limit of 50 was imposed. Unlike the draft in the NFL or NBA, a high school graduate or college student with remaining eligibility could be drafted by a Major League team without his consent or declaration. The draftee was not required to sign a contract with the club, but he could not negotiate with other teams. A drafting club had exclusive bargaining rights to the player until the next draft. Once signed, the player was bound to the team for at least three-and-a-half years. The team could keep the player an additional three years by placing him on the forty-man major league roster and optioning him to a minor league affiliate. A maximum of fifteen optioned players was allowed per team, along with the twenty-five active players on the roster. After the initial three-and-a-half years, any player not put on the forty man roster could be drafted by another major league team at the Rule 5 draft held at the winter meetings. To retain a Rule 5 player, the acquiring team had to keep the player on the active twenty-five man major league roster for the entire next season. If not, the player had to be offered back to his original team for the acquiring fee.

The minor league structure was such that a player entering the minors could stay there for six-and-a-half years without the right to offer his services to other teams. The pay in the minors was nominal. The season runs from two to five months, with salaries as low as $700 per month. There were little or no benefits, and the travel accommodations were minimal. A player could be released at any time. Approximately ten percent (10%) of the players in the minors made it to the Majors, and only one in fifty in the Majors stayed for six years or longer.

If a drafted high school player did not enter the league, but instead enrolled in a four-year college, he was not eligible for the draft again until his junior year or his twenty-first birthday. A player entering a junior college could be drafted again in his first or second year of college.

Traditionally, signing bonuses for drafted players were low compared to the other leagues. In the last few years, however, million-dollar bonuses have become the norm for those taken in the first round of the draft. The average signing bonus for a first rounder went from around $246,000 in 1990 to approximately $913,000 in 1995. Multimillion dollar bonuses for first and second round draft choices are not out of the ordinary.

Some drafted players with leverage have been able to demand that their contracts guarantee that they will be assigned to a higher level club or invited to Major League spring training at a designated time. Funds for college expenses are also included in contracts for many players who have not entered college or completed their college education.

Mistakes by some teams on draft procedure provides insight into the enormous value of the reserve clause to owners—and free agency to players. In the 1996 draft, Kris Benson was the number one pick. Benson was rewarded with a record signing bonus of approximately $2 million. Travis Lee was chosen second; John Patterson fifth; Matt White seventh; and Bobby Seay, twelfth. The teams drafting Lee, Patterson, White, and Seay inadvertently failed to tender a written contract within the proscribed time, as required by league rules. The rule violation resulted in each player immediately being classified as a free agent. Normally these players would have entered the minor leagues and then played in the Majors for six years before achieving free agency status. As a result of their unexpected free agency, the players were able to offer their services to the highest bidder. Lee, who had been offered a bonus of approximately $1.5 million by the team that drafted him, signed a contract with a bonus reportedly close to $10 million. Patterson, White, and Seay obtained bonuses for millions of dollars in excess of their previous offers. These rare situations illustrate the enormous value of free agency to players.

The 1997 draft also provided an interesting development. In 1997, J. D. Drew was considered to be one of the best players entering the draft in years. Prior to the draft, Drew's agent made it clear that his client would not sign a contract unless it was worth approximately $10 million. This demand was far in excess of any amount ever paid to a drafted player, but was comparable to what Travis Lee and the others who had managed to achieve instant free agency status had received. Drew was chosen second by the Philadelphia Phillies. Philadelphia, however, refused to make an acceptable offer to Drew. Under MLB rules, if Philadelphia did not sign Drew to a contract by May of the following year, Drew would again be subject to the draft in 1998, but could not be drafted by Philadelphia without his consent. Drew and his agent had other plans. Drew signed and played as a professional with the Northern League, a league independent of the Majors. Drew then argued that since he had played professional ball, he was no longer subject to the draft and was a free agent. Up until the time of Drew's action, the draft was called the "amateur draft" by MLB. MLB quickly, and without union approval, changed the name of the draft to the "first year draft" and modified the rules to cover Drew. Drew and the players' union challenged the action by MLB in arbitration. The arbitrator ruled that he had no jurisdiction or authority to rule on the matter because Drew was not a member of the union. The arbitrator did state, however, that if he had authority, he would rule that MLB's actions were improper. The issue raised by Drew was referred to other administrative bodies within MLB. In the meantime, Drew was selected in the 1998 draft by St. Louis and agreed to a contract worth about $7 million over a four-year period.

National Football League (NFL)

The first major professional football league was formed in the 1920s in Ohio and was called the American Professional Football Association. In the following year, the league changed its name to the National Football League. In the 1950s, the league became a viable professional sports league, and in the 1960s, the modern NFL emerged. Today, the NFL is the crown-jewel of professional sports.

RESERVE CLAUSE HISTORY

Like their baseball counterparts, the owners of professional football teams implemented various restrictions to prevent players from changing teams. The first case challenging the reserve clause in professional football was *Radovich v. National Football League*, decided by the U.S. Supreme Court in 1957. Radovich wanted to move from Detroit to California to play because of an illness in his family. He was denied the move and later was boycotted by the other teams in the NFL. He sued the league on antitrust violations. The NFL assumed, understandably, that it would receive the same exemption the Supreme Court had given professional baseball. The NFL was wrong. Although the Court did not award Radovich damages, it did hold that the Sherman Act applied to professional football.

ROZELLE RULE

A few years later, R. C. Owens played out his contract and changed teams without any compensation paid to the former team. The NFL responded by adopting the "Rozelle Rule." The rule was named after the NFL Commissioner, Pete Rozelle. The Rozelle Rule provided that compensation would have to be paid by the acquiring team to the team losing the player. The compensation would be in the form of draft choices, trades, or payments as established at the sole discretion of the Commissioner. There was no doubt that any team that signed a veteran player from another team would pay a heavy price. There was no free agency under the Rozelle Rule. The players were subjected to the Rozelle Rule from 1963 through 1976.

MACKEY V. NFL

In the mid 1970s, a major legal action was filed against the NFL by John Mackey, a top NFL player. The suit alleged that the Rozelle Rule was a violation of the antitrust law. In 1976, the trial court ruled that the Rozelle Rule was a *per se* violation of antitrust law. The appellate court found that the Rozelle Rule was unilaterally imposed by the clubs in 1963, and therefore not entitled to the nonstatutory labor exemption. The appellate court held that the Rozelle Rule was not a *per se* violation, but a violation of antitrust under the Rule of Reason test. The court explained the Rule of Reason as follows:

The focus of an inquiry under the Rule of Reason is whether the restraint imposed is justified by legitimate business purposes and is no more restrictive than necessary. In defining the restraint on competition for players' services, the district court found that the Rozelle Rule significantly deters clubs from negotiating with and signing free agents, that it acts as a substantial deterrent to players playing out their options and becoming free agents, that it significantly decreases players' bargaining power in contract negotiations; that players are thus denied the right to sell their services in a free and open market, that as a result, the salaries paid by each club are lower than if competitive bidding were allowed to prevail, and that absent the Rozelle Rule, there would be increased movement in interstate commerce of players from one club to another.

In conclusion the court noted:

> We note that our disposition of the antitrust issue does not mean that every restraint on competition for players' services would necessarily violate the antitrust laws. Also, since the Rozelle Rule, as implemented, concerns a mandatory subject of collective bargaining, any agreement as to interteam compensation for free agents moving to other teams reached through good faith collective bargaining might very well be immune from antitrust liability under the nonstatutory labor exemption.

> It may be that some reasonable restrictions relating to player transfers are necessary for the successful operation of the NFL. The protection of mutual interests of both the players and the clubs may indeed require this. We encourage the parties to resolve this question through collective bargaining. The parties are far better situated to agreeably resolve what rules governing player transfers are best suited for their mutual interests than are the courts. However, no mutual resolution of this issue appears within the present record. Therefore, the Rozelle Rule, as it is presently implemented, must be set aside as an unreasonable restraint of trade.

The Mackey case was eventually settled with a total payment of more than $13 million to several players. The union had won a major court battle. Union support waned, however. Only about half of the players in the league paid union dues after the court victory.

RIGHT OF FIRST REFUSAL

After the Mackey decision, a new 5-year CBA was entered into in 1977 by the players' union and management. The new CBA eliminated the Commissioner's complete discretion with respect to draft compensation. Under the new agreement, the Rozelle Rule was replaced with a provision known as the "First Right of Refusal" or "Option Clause." Under this provision, the draft compensation would now be determined by a predetermined objective formula. The provision allowed teams to match any offer that was made by another team to its players. If the original team did not match the offer from the new team, the original team was entitled to compensation set by a formula for draft choices. The new CBA provided that a team could maintain exclusive rights on a free agent if the player did not receive an offer from another team by paying the player 110% of his previous salary. Although the 1977 CBA purported to give some freedom to players, in truth, the players gained nothing. Between 1977 and 1987, although several hundred players were "free agents ," only a few players changed teams at the end of their contracts.

STRIKES — 1980s

In 1982, the players' frustration with their inability to obtain desired changes in the new CBA on free agency reached a breaking point. The players staged a strike that lasted approximately 57 days resulting in the cancellation of several games. The strike was ended and the players were able to obtain concessions on benefits, but the owners did not budge on the issue of free agency. The owners reportedly had arranged a $150 million line of credit to carry them through the strike. The failure of the strike was a setback for the players and a major victory for management. In 1987, after unsuccessful negotiations, the NFL players struck again. Replacement players were recruited by owners to continue the season. The strike lasted approximately 27 days before the players returned. The players lost an estimated $80 million in salaries for the games they did not play. Owners, however, reportedly saved more than $500,000 each week as a result of the lower salaries paid to the replacement players. Once again, the strike was a major loss for players and a victory for management. A new CBA would not be reached by the parties until 1993.

To be effective, a union must be able to maintain a strike for a considerable amount of time or convince management that the employees (players) are willing to go the distance on the strike to obtain concessions. This posture is more difficult in professional sports than other industries. Most players last only a few years in the professional leagues. This is particularly relevant in the NFL where the average turnover for players each season is about 25%. In addition, the compensation for playing is much higher than most players will be able to earn when they leave the game. A strike, even for a short period, is very costly to a professional athlete, especially to a football player.

The success of a strike can also be influenced by the financial strength of the union. The players' union, the National Football League Players Association (NFLPA), relied primarily on revenue from the NFLPA Group Licensing program, which generated substantial income from licensing agreements, such as "player trading cards." Prior to the strikes, NFL Properties, management's licensing operation, had lured about 700 veterans to its program and away from the union's licensing division. This change caused a substantial loss of income to the union.

THE DURATION OF THE NON-STATUTORY EXEMPTION

In 1987, despite the unsuccessful strike, the players were determined to obtain some relief from the restrictions on free agency. Bargaining and strikes had proved unsuccessful for the players. The only other avenue available to the players was to challenge the reserve clause restrictions in court on antitrust grounds. One legal problem this challenge would face was that the players, through their union, had previously agreed to the free agency restrictions in the Collective Bargaining Agreement. Generally, the courts have ruled that terms in a CBA are exempt from antitrust law. The exemption is referred to as a *non-statutory exemption*. The name is based on the fact that the exemption was created by the courts rather than through legislation (which would be a "statutory" exemption).

A major question to be resolved before the players could bring an antitrust action was the duration of the non-statutory exemption. Did the exemption expire at the same time as the CBA? If not, did the exemption continue in effect after termination of the CBA, as long as the parties were negotiating in good faith and *impasse* had not been reached? Or did the exemption continue beyond the point of *impasse*? The reason this issue was so important was because as long as the exemption was applicable, the NFL would be immune from antitrust. Without the exemption, however, the NFL was extremely vulnerable to an antitrust action. The consequences of a successful antitrust suit were severe, not the least of which was the award of treble damages. This issue of when the non-statutory exemption expires would prove to be an extremely significant question in later litigation involving the NFL and the NBA.

POWELL LITIGATION

A series of cases, *Powell* 1-3, dealt with the players' challenge to the free agency restrictions. A major issue in the litigation was the duration of the non-statutory exemption. At the time the litigation began, Marvin Powell was the President of the National Football League Players Association (NFLPA), and Mr. Powell was named as the plaintiff in the suits. In *Powell* 1, the trial court ruled that the non-statutory exemption was not applicable after an *impasse* had been reached. The court of appeal reversed the decision and held that the exemption applied as long as there was a labor relationship between the parties. The appellate court stated the following:

> The parties are now faced with several choices. They may bargain further, which we would strongly urge that they do. They may resort to economic force. And finally, if appropriate issues arise, they may present claims to the NLRB. We are satisfied that as long as there is a possibility that proceedings may be commenced before the Board, or until final resolution of Board proceedings and appeals therefrom, the labor relationship continues and the labor exemption applies.

A dissenting opinion contained the following prophetic warning:

> The majority purports to reject the owners' argument that the labor exemption in this case continues indefinitely. The practical effect of the majority's opinion, however, is just that – because the labor exemption will continue until the bargaining relationship is terminated either by a NLRB decertification proceeding or by abandonment of bargaining rights by the union.
>
> The only basis for NLRB action thus would appear to be a petition for decertification. Certainly, the owners will not file such a petition knowing full well that, if they do, they will subject themselves to antitrust scrutiny. Certainly, the Union will not file such a petition when the price will be the loss of collective bargaining rights. The only likely source for a petition to decertify is a group of high-salaried, highly skilled players who believe that they could do better without a union. It follows that the end result of the majority opinion is that once a union agrees to a package of player restraints, it will be bound to that package forever unless the union forfeits its bargaining rights.

The Court of Appeal's opinion in the *Powell* cases on the extent of the nonstatutory exemption would not only be upheld, but was expanded by the U.S. Supreme Court in a later case. The decertification step referred to in the dissenting opinion, however, was a tactic the players would later employ with great success.

PLAN B

In 1988, the NFL owners unilaterally (without player involvement or bargaining) instituted Plan B. Plan B allowed each team to protect 37 players on its "reserve" list. Protected players, even if their contract expired, were not permitted to move to other NFL teams unless their current team chose not to match the new offer. Plan B generated considerable controversy and litigation:

Hebert v. Los Angeles Raiders and NFL (1991)

Plaintiff, Bobby Hebert, appeals from a judgment of dismissal of his action against the defendants, Los Angeles Raiders, and the National Football League (NFL).

The amended complaint alleged: Defendant NFL is an unincorporated association comprised of 28 professional football teams, each of which is a separate entity that operates a professional football franchise for profit in various cities across the United States. Defendant Raiders operates one of these franchises in Los Angeles under the team name Los Angeles Raiders. Plaintiff, a resident of California, has been a professional football player in the NFL since 1985, playing under contact to the New Orleans Saints (Saints), another NFL team. The NFL member teams constitute the only market in the United States for the services of major league professional football payers. Instead of engaging in free competition for players' services, the NFL, the Raiders, and other NFL member teams have combined and conspired to eliminate such competition among themselves through various agreements, including Plan B (hereinafter described), which prevents plaintiff from bargaining as a free agent and selling his services to the team for which he wishes to play.

The history of the NFL's anticompetitive restraints on players goes back to the "Rozelle Rule," adopted by NFL member teams in 1963 as an amendment to their constitution and bylaws. The Rozelle Rule provided that an NFL team desiring the services of a player whose contract had expired (veteran free agent) could not sign that player without paying some form of compensation to the player's former team. If the two teams could not agree on the compensation, Pete Rozelle, then commissioner of the NFL, would assess the compensation. The effect of the Rozelle Rule was to restrain competition among the NFL teams for players' services. It operated to restrict the players' freedom of movement by binding them to one team throughout their careers and denying them the right to sell their services in a free and open market. In 1976, the Rozelle Rule was held to constitute an unreasonable restraint of trade in violation of the Sherman Act, (*Mackey v. NFL*).

In 1977 and again in 1982, the NFL entered into collective bargaining agreement with the NFL Players Association (NFLPA). The agreements included the "First Refusal/Compensation" system whereby each NFL team could prohibit a veteran free agent from moving to another NFL team by exercising a right of first refusal and matching a competing team's offer to such a player. If the player's former team chose not to match the offer, it would receive substantial compensation from the new team in the form of one or more college draft choices. The 1982 collective bargaining agreement expired in 1987.

On February 1, 1989, despite the absence of a new collective bargaining agreement, the NFL and its member teams, acting unilaterally and without player approval, agreed to a new system of player restraints called Plan B. Under Plan B, the NFL, the Raiders and the other NFL teams agreed that each team had the right to "protect" 37 out of 46 players on an active player roster; these protected players continued to be subject to the anticompetitive first refusal/compensation system. The vast majority of players, including plaintiff, remain bound to their former teams under the Plan B first refusal/compensation system which eliminates the ability of players to obtain a competitive market value for their services by inhibiting or preventing bidding by NFL teams and also serves to restrict or eliminate the players' freedom of movement.

From February 1, 1986 to February 1, 1990, plaintiff was under contract to the Saints. Prior to the beginning of the 1990 NFL season plaintiff was ranked third by the NFL among active NFL quarterbacks. When plaintiff's contract expired (Feb. 1, 1990), he was designated "protected" by the Saints under Plan B. Accordingly, plaintiff had only a two-month period in which he could attempt to negotiate with another NFL team. Because of the anticompetitive restraints and effect of Plan B, plaintiff did not receive an offer from any NFL team during the two-month period and on April 1, 1990, when the period expired, plaintiff's ability to negotiate a contract with any team was completely foreclosed. Further, although plaintiff was no longer under contract to the Saints, the "rights" to plaintiff reverted to the Saints and he became their exclusive property for the 1990-1991 season. Thus, under Plan B, plaintiff had only two options: either play for the Saints on whatever terms they dictate or not play at all.

Beginning in January 1990, plaintiff had discussions with the Raiders about playing for them in the 1990 season and beyond. Plaintiff and his agent repeatedly were told by authorized representatives of the Raiders that the Raiders wanted to enter into a contract with plaintiff and would have done so but for the prohibitions contained in Plan B. At the time this action was filed (Oct. 1990), six weeks of the NFL regular season had elapsed, and plaintiff did not have a contract to play for any NFL team.

Plan B is a contract among the NFL, the Raiders, and the other NFL member teams which restrains plaintiff from engaging in his lawful profession, trade, or business in violation of California Constitution article I, section 1, and Business and Professions Code section 16600.

The amended complaint sought the following relief: (1) a declaration that the NFL's and the Raiders' participation in Plan B violates the constitution and section 16600 insofar as it restrains plaintiff from engaging in professional football; and (2) preliminary and permanent injunctions enjoining the NFL and the Raiders from participating in or enforcing Plan B.

Defendants demurred (seeking a dismissal for failure to state a claim) generally to the amended complaint on the ground the Commerce Clause of the federal Constitution precludes application of the provisions of California law relied upon by plaintiff to the player-team-league relationship of the NFL over plaintiffs opposition, the demurrer was sustained without leave to amend. Judgment was entered dismissing the amended complaint. This appeal followed.

In sustaining the demurrer to plaintiff's amended complaint, the trial court concluded that the present action is governed by *Partee v. San Diego Chargers Football Co.* wherein our Supreme Court held that the Commerce Clause precludes application of California's antitrust law to professional football.

In *Partee,* a professional football player who played for a team member of the NFL sued the team for damages alleging that the NFL's operating rules, including the Rozelle Rule, violated the Cartwright Act. In reversing judgment for plaintiff, the court noted that the NFL is engaged in interstate commerce and concluded that application of California's antitrust law to professional football would constitute an unreasonable burden on interstate commerce. In reaching this conclusion the court pointed to similarities between professional baseball's reserve system and the attributes of the NFL rules and practices challenged by plaintiff and quoted the following passage from *Flood v. Kuhn* which held that state antitrust laws are not applicable to professional baseball:

> Applying the foregoing test to the case before it, the *Partee* court stated: "Professional football is a nationwide business structured essentially the same as baseball. Professional football's teams are dependent upon the league playing schedule for competitive play, just as in baseball. The necessity of a nationwide league structure for the benefit of both teams and players for effective competition is evident, as is the need for a nationally uniform set of rules governing the league structure."

We agree that *Partee* is controlling and requires dismissal of plaintiff's amended complaint for failure to state a cause of action.

****

DECERTIFICATION OF THE UNION

After the loss in *Powell,* the players, guided by the union, voted to decertify the union. Decertification meant the players were no longer represented by the union. This move was not an expression of dissatisfaction with the union by the players, but was a clever legal strategy designed to eliminate the league's exemption from antitrust law. Management immediately changed insurance benefits for the players and lengthened the season.

In 1989, Freeman McNeil and several other players whose contracts with their current team had expired filed an antitrust action against the NFL. The suit alleged that Plan B violated the Sherman Act by restricting player movement and preventing players from negotiating new contracts on a competitive basis. The argument was that since there was no union representative, there could be no labor exemption from antitrust law. The McNeil case was consolidated with the remaining issues in the *Powell* case. The NFL claimed that the free agency rules were still exempt from antitrust law and, regardless, did not violate antitrust law. The trial court held that the appellate court's reasoning in *Powell* no longer applied because without a union representative there could be no "ongoing collective bargaining relationship." The suit could proceed and the NFL would not have the antitrust exemption as a defense (score for players).

The McNeil case went to a jury consisting of eight women, none of whom enjoyed professional football. The case received a lot of media attention as owners publicly complained about a group of housewives determining the fate of the NFL. The League argued that free agency would financially ruin many teams. That fear was well-founded. The jury found that Plan B had a substantially harmful effect on competition for player services.

In September of 1992, a jury in the *McNeil* case ruled in favor of 4 of the 8 players and awarded $1.6 million. The effect of the jury verdict went far beyond the individual players in the case. The jury found that Plan B was more restrictive than necessary and that players had suffered economic injury as a result of the system. The jury also found, however, that Plan B did help reinforce competitive balance in the NFL. Both sides claimed victory: the players because the verdict struck down Plan B, and the owners because the decision allowed a system that stopped short of unrestricted free agency. The parties were forced back to the bargaining table.

The players knew it would take time for the *McNeil* ruling to take effect. Ten players that remained unsigned at the time of the verdict immediately filed suit, *Jackson v. NFL* (1992), to avoid the restrictions of Plan B. The court granted the players an injunction prohibiting the enforcement of Plan B.

> Even if the court were to determine that the doctrine of collateral estoppel does not apply, the court nonetheless concludes, after hearing all of the evidence and arguments in the McNeil case, that plaintiffs demonstrate a substantial probability of success on the merits of their claims. See, e.g., *Smith v. Pro Football, Inc.,* (1978) (NFL draft violates Rule of Reason); *Mackey v. National Football League,* (1976) (Rozelle Rule found illegal under Rule of Reason), (1977); *Kapp v. National Football League,* (1974) (NFL draft and Rozelle Rule not justified by Rule of Reason), (1978) *Los Angeles Memorial Coliseum Comm'n v. National Football League,* (affirming jury verdict that NFL rule limiting franchise relocation was unreasonable), *North Ameri-*

can Soccer League v. National Football League, (overturning district court's decision and holding that NFL's cross-ownership rule violates Rule of Reason),(1982) *United States v. National Football League*, (1953) (striking down NFL rules limiting broadcast of games).

Based on the foregoing, the court concludes that this factor tips in favor of granting plaintiffs' motion for injunctive relief.

Before the court ruled, six of the ten players were released or traded. As to the remaining four players, the court agreed with their position and issued an order for a five (5) day period of non-enforcement. During the period, three of the four players signed contracts with other clubs, and the fourth was released to negotiate with other teams on his own. As a result, the case was dismissed as moot. It was apparent, however, that the players would prevail in court. The players could now bring about some meaningful changes.

After the *McNeil* and *Jackson* decisions, a class action suit, *White v. NFL,* was filed against the NFL on behalf of all players. The *White* case was never decided because a settlement was ultimately reached. The agreement provided for $115 million dollars for the players who had been affected by Plan B and for the NFLPA, which had immediately reconstituted as a union. More importantly, the parties agreed to a new CBA that included a form of free agency (big score for players).

At the time Plan B was implemented, the NFL owners also unilaterally decided to establish rules and pay regarding developmental squads. The owners agreed that each team would be permitted to retain 6 players on a roster for practice. The owners also decided that the salary for each player could not exceed $1,000 per week (The CBA executed in 1993 allowed for 5 players who had to be paid at least $3,333 per week). The players' union filed suit, *Brown v. Pro Football* (1996), alleging antitrust violations. One of the interesting arguments made on behalf of the players was that they were not like a typical union in that players were allowed to individually negotiate their particular salary. The trial court ruled that any labor exemption, which was the League's defense, terminated when the CBA expired, not when *impasse* was reached, as *Powell* had held. The trial court granted a judgment of $30 million to the players. The appellate court reversed and ruled that after *impasse* the League could unilaterally impose the rule, even though the developmental squads were not part of the previous CBA. The U.S. Supreme Court decided the case in June 1996. An excerpt of the Supreme Court's opinion in *Brown* is set forth below:

Brown v. Pro Football, Inc. (1996)

The question in this case arises at the intersection of the Nation's labor and antitrust laws. A group of professional football players brought this antitrust suit against football club owners. The club owners had bargained with the players' union over a wage issue until they reached impasse. The owners then had agreed among themselves (but not with the union) to implement the terms of their own last best bargaining offer. The question before us is whether federal labor laws shield such an agreement from antitrust attack. We believe that they do. This Court has previously found in the labor laws an implicit antitrust exemption that applies where needed to make the collective bargaining process work. Like the Court of Appeals, we conclude that this need makes the exemption applicable in this case.

We can state the relevant facts briefly. In 1987, a collective-bargaining agreement between the National Football League (NFL), a group of football clubs, and the NFL Players Association, a labor union, expired. The NFL and the Players Association began to negotiate a new contract. In March 1989, during the negotiations, the NFL adopted Resolution G-2, a plan that would permit each club to establish a "developmental squad" of up to six rookie or "first-year" players who, as free agents, had failed to secure a position on a regular player roster. Squad members would play in practice games and sometimes in regular games as substitutes for injured players. Resolution G-2 provided that the club owners would pay all squad members the same weekly salary.

The next month, April, the NFL presented the developmental squad plan to the Players Association. The NFL proposed a squad player salary of $1,000 per week. The Players Association disagreed. It insisted that the club owners give developmental squad players benefits and protections similar to those provided regular players, and that they leave individual squad members free to negotiate their own salaries.

Two months later, in June, negotiations on the issue of developmental squad salaries reached an impasse. The NFL then unilaterally implemented the developmental squad program by distributing to the clubs a uniform contract that embodied the terms of Resolution G-2 and the $1,000 proposed weekly salary. The League advised club owners that paying developmental squad players more or less than $1,000 per week would result in disciplinary action, including the loss of draft choices.

In May 1990, 235 developmental squad players brought this antitrust suit against the League and its member clubs. The players claimed that their employers' agreement to pay them a $1,000 weekly salary violated the Sherman Act. The Federal District Court denied the employers' claim of exemption from the antitrust laws; it permitted the case to reach the jury; and it subsequently entered judgment on a jury treble-damage award that exceeded $30 million. The NFL and its member clubs appealed.

The Court of Appeals (by a split 2-to-1 vote) reversed. The majority interpreted the labor laws as "waiv[ing] antitrust liability for restraints on competition imposed through the collective-bargaining process, so long as such restraints operate primarily in a labor market characterized by collective bargaining." The Court held, consequently, that the club owners were immune from antitrust liability. We granted certiorari to review that determination. Although we do not interpret the exemption as broadly as did the Appeals Court, we nonetheless find the exemption applicable, and we affirm that Court's immunity conclusion.

The immunity before us rests upon what this Court has called the "nonstatutory" labor exemption from the antitrust laws. The Court has implied this exemption from federal labor statutes, which set forth a national labor policy favoring free and private collective bargaining. The policy requires good-faith bargaining over wages, hours and working conditions, and delegates related rulemaking and interpretive authority to the National Labor Relations Board.

This implicit exemption reflects both history and logic. As a matter of logic, it would be difficult, if not impossible, to require groups of employers and employees to bargain together, but at the same time to forbid them to make among themselves or with each other any of the competition-restricting agreements potentially necessary to make the process work or its results mutually acceptable. Thus, the implicit exemption recognizes that, to give effect to federal labor laws and *policies* and to allow *meaningful* collective bargaining to take place, some restraints on competition imposed through the bargaining process must be shielded from antitrust sanctions.

The petitioners and their supporters concede, as they must, the legal existence of the exemption we have described. They also concede that, where its application is necessary to make the statutorily authorized collective-bargaining process work as Congress intended, the exemption must apply both to employers and to employees.

The antitrust exemption applies to the employer conduct at issue here, which took place during and immediately after a collective-bargaining negotiation; grew out of, and was a directly related to, the lawful operation of the bargaining process; involved a matter that the parties were required to negotiate collectively; and concerned only the parties to the collective-bargaining relationship. The Court's holding is not intended to insulate from antitrust review every joint imposition of terms by employers, for an employer agreement could be sufficiently distant in time and in circumstances from the bargaining process that a rule permitting antitrust intervention would not significantly interfere with that process.

****

The *Brown* opinion by the Supreme Court was a landmark decision on the non-statutory labor exemption and antitrust law. Essentially, the Supreme Court ruled that antitrust actions were generally not available as long as there was a collective bargaining relationship between the parties.

The issue in *Brown* was whether a multi-employer bargaining unit was shielded from antitrust liability by the non-statutory labor exemption when it unilaterally imposed a fixed weekly salary upon a group of employees after the collective bargaining process reached a point of *impasse*. The Court held that post-*impasse* restraints on competition lawfully imposed through collective bargaining were protected from antitrust challenges by the non-statutory exemption as long as they were reasonably part of their last good faith pre-*impasse* proposal.

The Court held that to allow an antitrust action by the developmental squad players would undercut the very nature and essence of the labor laws. In *Brown* the Court stated that an employer had 4 options at *impasse:*

1. maintain the status quo of the current or expired CBA
2. implement its last offer
3. lock out its workers and terminate business or hire replacement workers
4. negotiate individual interim agreements with the union

One of the dissenting Justices argued that the decision was wrong because professional football players, unlike other union employees, had the privilege of individually negotiating their salaries. As such, it is the employers, not the employees, who sought to implement a non-competitive uniform wage.

1993 COLLECTIVE BARGAINING AGREEMENT

The settlement from the *McNeil* case led to the 1993 CBA between players, represented by the recertified union and management. The 1993 agreement was hailed by both parties as ensuring labor peace in professional football for the next several years. The prediction was accurate. The CBA was a major accomplishment for both management and players in the NFL. The 1993 CBA's original expiration was 2000.

The 1993 CBA included significant changes in the relationship between the players and management that included a form of free agency, a salary cap, a rookie cap, minimum salaries, and reduction of the draft rounds. Some of the more-significant aspects of the current CBA are described below.

FREE AGENCY

There are different categories of free agency.

1. **Exclusive Rights Free Agent:** This designation was for a player whose contract expired at a time when he had less than three accrued seasons in the NFL. The player could market his services to other clubs if his team offered him a minimum salary tender on or before a designated day in February. If the tender was provided, the player could only sign with his current team, unless the tender was later withdrawn.

2. **Restricted Free Agent (RFA):** This status applied to a player whose contract expired when he had three accrued seasons, but less than four, in a capped year. The signing period for a RFA was generally from March 11 to April 21. If the player's current team made a *Qualifying Offer* it would obtain certain rights to the player. A *Qualifying Offer* entitled the current team to a right-of-first-refusal (ROFR), the right to match an offer from another team and retain the player. If the current team did not retain the player, the acquiring team would provide the current team with draft pick or picks as compensation. There were four levels of *Qualifying Offers* and each guaranteed different draft pick payment. In 2007, the low qualifying offer, which provided a draft pick in the round in which the relevant player was originally drafted, amounted to $850,000. The second round qualifying offer totaled $1.3 million, the first round qualifying offer equaled $1.85 million, and the highest qualifying offer, the first AND third round offer, was $2.35 million.

3. **Unrestricted Free Agent:** A player whose contract expired when he had accumulated at least four accrued seasons in a capped year was free to sign with any other club if he did so by a designated date, July 22 of the same year. If he did not sign elsewhere, his exclusive rights reverted to his old club after July 22, provided that the old club had given him a written tender in the required amount by June 1, offering to re-sign him for an additional year. An Unrestricted Free Agent would restrict signing elsewhere, however, if he was designated as a Franchise or Transition Player.

4. **Franchise and Transition Players.** Each team was allowed to designate one player with a Franchise, Exclusive Franchise or Transition player tag. These tags applied for one year and were generally used by teams to retain a player when a long-term contract agreement with the player could not be reached. July 15 was the deadline for teams to negotiate with players before they had to use one of these tags. Unlike many NFL player salary agreements, both of the one-year tag contracts were guaranteed once signed by the player.

A **Transition** designation required a team to offer the player the average of the top 10 salaries of the previous year at that player's position or a 20% salary increase, whichever was greater. The transition tag gave the team a first-right-of-refusal to match an offer given by another team. If the player got another offer the current team had 7 days to match the offer. If the current team failed to match the offer it lost all rights to the player and got no compensation.

A **Franchise** designation required a team to offer the player the average of the top 5 salaries at his position in the previous season, or a 20% salary increase, whichever was greater. A **Franchise** player could negotiate with other teams. If he received an offer, the current team could match the offer and keep the player or receive two first-round draft picks from the acquiring team as compensation.

An **Exclusive Franchise** designation required a team to offer a minimum of the average top 5 salaries of the player's position computed on the end of the restricted free agency signing period, or the average of the top 5 salaries at his position as of the end of last season, or a 20% increase in salary, whichever was greater. Other clubs could not negotiate with **Exclusive Franchise** players.

If a team wished to franchise a player for three consecutive seasons, the price in the third year became the average of the top five salaries at the highest paid position (generally quarterback), or a 20% salary increase, whichever was greater.

TEAM SALARY CAPS

The Salary Cap limited the total amount a team could pay for all salaries and bonuses. Originally, the cap was based on a formula determined by taking approximately 64% of Defined Gross Revenues (DGR) and dividing that sum by the number of teams in the league. DGR included gate receipts, broadcast revenue, some box seats receipts, and other sources, but did not include game-related concessions, parking, expansion franchise fees, and most luxury box income. The 2006 CBA expanded the revenue pool used for Salary Cap calculation to Total Revenue (TR) and adjusted the cap's percentage to 57.5%, which would increase to 58% in 2010. Incentives paid to players which were "likely to be earned" (LTBE) were included in the Salary Cap. Incentives "not likely to be earned" (NLTBE) were not included in the cap formula that year, but if paid were included the next year. The Salary Cap, expressed in millions below, grew steadily over the years.

1994 --$34.6
1995---$37.1
1996---$40.7
1997---$41.5
1998---$52.4

1999---$57.3
2000---$62.2
2001---$67.4
2002---$71.1
2003---$75.1
2004---$80.5
2005---$85.5
2006--$102
2007--$109
2008--$116 (approximate projection at the time of this writing)

The Salary Cap caused an adverse impact on many players. In order to comply with the cap or make room under the cap for the acquisition of other players, a number of veteran players have were released or forced to renegotiate their contracts for a lesser sum. Teams adjusted their personnel and compensation each year to comply with the cap. The process acquired its own term, "Caponomics."

CAP AVOIDANCE

The Salary Cap produced a considerable amount of effort and creative thinking by teams to find ways to avoid or minimize the effects of the rule. The most obvious method of minimizing the impact of the cap was through the proration of bonuses. For example, a $6 million signing bonus paid to a player on a 6-year contract would only count for $1 million on the cap each year, rather than $6 million in the year it was paid. Bonuses in 2005 and 2006 were allowed to be prorated for five years, while bonuses in 2007 were allowed to be prorated six years.

Many of the top draft choices or highly sought-after free agents do not, however, want to enter into long-term contracts. Contract terms that appear astonishing today may appear cheap five years from now. To avoid the problem, many players negotiated *voidable years* in their contracts. These provisions allowed a player the option of terminating the contract at an earlier date. For example, the last three years of the contract could be voided or set aside, allowing the player to test the market. If a player had this option and exercised it, the unamortized portion of the bonus was accelerated into the cap for that year. This approach allowed teams to delay, but not avoid, the effect of the Salary Cap.

ENTERING-PLAYER POOL — ROOKIE SALARY CAPS

Each year, the league set a total dollar figure that represented the maximum salary cap amount that could be spent on draft picks and undrafted free agents. This cap, however, varied with each team. The rookie allotment for the league in 2007 averaged $4.275 million per team, or about 3.9% of the Salary Cap. The NFLMC and NFLPA allocated a sum for each of the drafted players using a secretive formula not disclosed to the players, the clubs, or the public. Teams were not required to pay a drafted player a specific sum. Each team received a rookie allotment based on the sums assigned to the players that team drafted. Teams that held higher picks were allocated more dollars in the rookie pool. Early draft picks, of course, received signing bonuses that far exceeded the entering player pool allocation. Cap compliance was then achieved by prorating the signing bonus over the life of the contract.

MINIMUM PLAYER SALARY

The CBA had a formula for minimum salaries to players, which increased based on the amount of money in TR and on the number of years the player had been in the league. The minimum salaries from 2002 through 2007 are listed below:

($ in thousands)

CREDITED SEASONS	2002	2003	2004	2005	2006	2007
0	225	225	230	230	275	285
1	300	300	305	305	350	360
2	375	375	380	380	425	435
3	450	450	455	455	500	510
4–6	525	530	535	540	585	595
7–9	650	655	660	665	710	720
10+	750	755	760	765	810	820

As of 2002, a new system was implemented to make it less costly to retain older veteran players. Since the minimum salaries for older veterans were higher, the older veterans were often released from the team in favor of younger players for cap purposes. Under the new system, the Salary Cap count for a player with four or more Credited Seasons who signed a contract for the minimum salary with a bonus of $40,000 or less would be the same as the player with three Credited Seasons. That is, for cap purposes, the salaries of older veterans would be calculated the same as younger veterans.

MINIMUM TEAM SALARY

As of 2007, the Minimum Team Salary was 50% of TR. That is, each team had to spend at least that amount, divided by the 32 teams, on player salaries.

DRAFT

The draft was limited to 7 rounds. Rookies who were not drafted were essentially unrestricted free agents. The team with the No.1 overall pick had the right to negotiate and sign the first pick to a contract prior to the draft. Players taken with the first sixteen picks (the first half of the first round) could sign a contract up to six years long, while the other first round draftees could sign for a maximum of five years. Contracts for players in rounds 2-7 could not be longer than four years.

RENEGOTIATION

Rookies could not renegotiate their contracts in the two years. Veterans could renegotiate their contracts once at any time before expiration of the contract, but were prohibited from renegotiating again for the next 12 months.

CBA TERM

The CBA was extended through the 2013 league year. The last year of the agreement does not include the Salary Cap. In May 2008, the term was reduced to 2011 as a result of the opt-out discussed below.

TERMINATION PAY

The Termination Pay benefit contained in the CBA provided a partial guarantee of up to 50% of a player's "Paragraph 5 salary" for an eligible player who had completed his fourth or more credited season in the NFL. A player was eligible for termination pay if he was:

1. released after his club's first regular season game in September, and
2. he was on the club's active/inactive list on or after the club's first regular season game.

SEVERANCE PAY

Any player who was released after at least two credited seasons in the league was entitled to receive $10,000 for every year he played between 1993 and 1999, $12,500 for each season between 2000 and 2002, and $5,000 for each year played between 1989 and 1992 if he also had a credited season between 1993 and 1999.

CREDITED AND ACCRUED SEASONS

Credited Seasons -- A Credited Season was any season in which a player was on one of the following lists for at least three (3) regular season or post-season games: Active List, Inactive List, Injured Reserve List, or Physically Unable to Perform List. A player would also earn a Credited Season if he was released, injured, and paid the equivalent of at least three (3) game checks. Weeks on the Practice Squad would not count toward a credited season.

Earning Credited Seasons entitled a player to various benefits under the CBA. For instance, a player who had earned more than two (2) Credited Seasons in the NFL qualified to receive severance pay equal to $10,000 per Credited Season when he retired from the NFL. Also, a player with two (2) or more Credited Seasons was eligible to participate in the Second Career Savings Plan. A player with three (3) or more Credited Seasons was eligible to receive a pension starting at age 55.

Accrued Seasons -- An Accrued Season was a season during which a player had been on full pay status (Active, Inactive, or Injured Reserve List) for six (6) or more regular season games. However, a player who was on the Exempt Commissioner Permission List, the Reserve Physically Unable to Perform/Non-Football Injury List, or the Practice Squad for any of the six (6) qualifying games would not earn an Accrued Season, regardless of his pay status.

An accrued season entitled a player to advance through the free agency system. In a capped year, a player with four (4) or more Accrued Seasons became an unrestricted free agent once his contract expired (unless he was designated a franchise player). A player with three (3), but less than four (4), Accrued Seasons when his contract expired became a restricted free agent.

INJURY PROTECTION BENEFIT

A player who suffered an injury during the season that prevented him from being able to play in the last game or which required off-season surgery and continued to prevent him from playing football by the time of the pre-season physical examination of the following season, might be entitled to receive the Injury Protection Benefit under the 1993 CBA.

In order to qualify to receive the Injury Protection Benefit a player must have been under contract to an NFL club for the season after the season of injury and met the following criteria:

1. The Player must have been physically unable, because of a severe football injury, to participate in all or part of his club's last game of the season of injury as certified by the club physician following a physical examination after the last game; or the player must have undergone club-authorized surgery in the off-season following the season of injury, and;
2. The Player must have undergone whatever reasonable and customary rehabilitation treatment his club required of him during the off-season following the season of injury, and;
3. The Player must have failed the pre-season physical examination given by the club physician for the season following the season of injury because of such injury and have his contract terminated for the season following the season of injury.

A player who met the above criteria would receive an amount equal to 50% of his contract salary for the season following the season of injury, up to $200,000.

OTHER NFL TERMS USED IN THE CBA

a. **Active List**: For each regular season, the active list would be 45 players per club. These 45 players could dress each week for game day.
b. **Inactive List**: Eight players were inactive from each game including one quarterback. These players could not suit up; however, the quarterback could play if the other two active quarterbacks were hurt.

   c. **Practice Squad**: Each team could have five practice squad players. Each player was free to negotiate with another team during the year, but only from practice squad to active list, not to another practice squad.

   d. **Physically Unable to Perform (PUP)**: This term referred to a player that had a football-related injury from the previous season and was still unable to play due to the injury until the sixth week of the season. The team had to pay his salary.

   e. **Non-Football Injury**: An injury not related to football. Generally, the team was not obligated to pay the player during his disability.

   f. **Reporting Bonus**: A bonus paid to players for reporting to training camp. This payment reduced the temptation of players to hold out and demand a renegotiation.

   g. **Roster Bonus**: Compensation the player received if he made the team's roster. Generally a player was entitled to this bonus if he was on the team's active or playing roster for a certain number of games.

GATE RECEIPTS

For a number of years the visiting team received 40% of the gate receipts after a 15% deduction by the home team for maintenance. The 40% was now placed in a pool shared equally by all teams. This change was primarily made to accommodate divisional realignment concerns.

REVENUE SHARING

The major source of revenue for teams in the NFL is from television contracts. The television money is divided equally among the teams. This equal revenue sharing has been one of the most remarkable success stories of the NFL. The sharing approach has allowed "small-market" teams to compete financially with the high-revenue teams. But not all revenue is shared, such as luxury boxes and stadium naming rights. The result is that some teams are much richer than others, by as much as $100 million annually. To address the growing disparity the League expanded its revenue-sharing model. The top 15 revenue generating teams now contributed to a pool to be shared by the lower 17 teams. The pool was expected to amount to around $800 million for the duration of the contract. The plan was for the receiving teams to use this money for player salaries so that the poorer teams would be able to compete for the best talent.

STANDARD PLAYER CONTRACT (SPK)

Every player who agrees to play for an NFL team must sign a Standard Player Contract (SPK). Many players generally sign multiple one-year contracts. While a player is on the team, he is paid according to the terms of the contract. If a player is injured in the course of his work, the player is entitled to his full payment for that year as provided in the CBA. Based on the provisions in the CBA, not the contract, the player will generally be able to collect his salary during the next year, even if he is still injured.

Guaranteed contracts are becoming more common in the NFL, but they are still the exception. If the player's contract is not guaranteed, a team does not have to renew the contract for the second year. Note the following language in the SPK:

> If at any time, in the sole judgment of Club, Player's skill or performance has been unsatisfactory as compared with other players...then Club may terminate this contract. In addition, during the period any salary cap is in effect, this contract may be terminated if, in Club's opinion, Player is anticipated to make less of a contribution to Club's ability to compete than another player...

There are some exceptions, such as football-related injuries, but, basically, a team can hand a player his walking papers at any time, unless his contract is guaranteed.

COLLEGE DRAFT

A talented college football player cannot negotiate with multiple professional teams to determine who will make the best offer or to choose a team located in a city he prefers. The player will be subject to the draft and will *belong* to the team that selects him. If the team does not make an acceptable offer to the player, his only choice is to refuse to play. The player would have other options only if a competitive league existed or if he was talented enough to play in another sport.

From the teams' standpoint, the college draft provides the NFL with a reasonably fair method of dividing up the new talent. Most players coming out of college are not overly concerned about how the draft works or which team selects them. A player's major interest is whether or not he will be drafted and, if so, at what number and round. The draft slot determines the compensation that the athlete will receive.

Smith v. Pro Football (1978) was a successful antitrust challenge by a player against the NFL draft. James Smith was selected in the first round of the college football draft. He signed a one-year bonus contract for a total of $50,000—$22,000 in salary and $28,000 in bonuses. In the last game of the season, he suffered a career-ending injury. Smith was paid the balance on his contract. Two years later, he filed suit asserting that the college draft violated antitrust laws and prevented him from demanding more money as a rookie to play ball. The trial court found that the college draft did violate antitrust laws and awarded Smith $92,000. The appellate court upheld the ruling with respect to the draft being a violation of antitrust laws, but remanded the case for a new trial on damages. In *Kapp v. NFL* (1974), the court found the draft was patently unreasonable, because it established a perpetual boycott of prospective draftees. In *Zimmerman v. NFL* (1984), however, the court upheld the NFL draft because it was included in the CBA as part of the collective bargaining process.

As a freshman at Ohio State in 2002, Maurice Clarett was viewed by many as the top collegiate running back in the country. For disciplinary reasons, however, he was not allowed to play in 2003. Clarett decided to see if he could make it in the NFL. Few doubted that he could succeed on the football field, but there were serious legal hurdles that Clarett would have to overcome to join the ranks of the NFL.

For years, the NFL's rules provided that the draft was only open to athletes who had finished high school at least four years earlier. The rule was later modified to allow athletes to enter the draft after three years under a very liberal "hardship" exception. No player was allowed to participate in the draft, however, who had not been out of high school for at least three years. The NFL rule prohibited Clarett from entering the draft. Clarett chose to challenge the NFL's rule as an antitrust violation:

Clarett v. National Football League (February 2004)

Maurice Clarett's goal is to play in the National Football League next year. The only thing preventing him from achieving that goal is the League's rule limiting eligibility to players three seasons removed from their high school graduation. The question before the Court is whether this Rule violates the antitrust laws.

Clarett, a star freshman football player attending The Ohio State University, now in his sophomore year, challenges the Rule, claiming that he is ready, willing and able to play in the NFL and that his exclusion violates the antitrust laws. Clarett's challenge to the Rule raises serious questions arising at the intersection of labor law and antitrust law, not to mention the intersection of college football and professional football. Should Clarett's right to compete for a job in the NFL—the only serious pro football game in town—trump the NFL's right to categorically exclude a class of players that the League has decided is not yet ready to play?

The answer requires the Court to tackle a number of technical legal issues. The NFL defends itself by asserting three arguments: (1) the Rule is the result of a collective bargaining agreement between the NFL and the players union and is therefore immune from antitrust scrutiny; (2) Clarett has no standing under the antitrust laws to bring this suit; and (3) the Rule is reasonable.

While, ordinarily, the best offense is a good defense, none of *these* defenses hold the line. Because the Rule does not concern a mandatory subject of collective bargaining (wages, hours and conditions of employment), governs only non-employees, and did not clearly result from arm's length negotiations, it is not immune from antitrust scrutiny. Clarett has standing to sue because his injury flows from a policy that excludes all players in his position from selling their services to the only viable buyer -- the NFL. Finally, the NFL has not justified Clarett's exclusion by demonstrating that the Rule enhances competition. Indeed, Clarett has alleged the very type of injury -- a complete bar to entry into the market for his services -- that the antitrust laws are designed to prevent. It is axiomatic, in the words of Learned Hand, that the antitrust laws will not tolerate a contract "which unreasonably forbids any one to practice his calling."

Because the NFL cannot prevail on any of these defenses, the Rule must be sacked.

The NFL provides a number of justifications for the Rule, arguing that it protects at least four different classes of people. *First,* the NFL contends that the Rule protects the people it excludes because they "are not sufficiently mature, either physically or psychologically, to endure the rigors of professional football." *Second,* the Rule protects member clubs who might suffer financial adversity resulting from younger players' peculiar susceptibility to injury. *Third,* the Rule protects the League and its "entertainment product from the adverse consequences associated with such injuries." *Fourth,* the Rule protects young players who, if they declare but are not drafted, would lose their eligibility to play college football, or who might over-train or experiment with performance-enhancing drugs to speed their athletic development.

Clarett is suing the NFL under section 1 of the Sherman Antitrust Act and section 2 of the Clayton Act. He alleges that the Rule is an illegal restraint of trade because the teams have agreed to exclude a broad class of players from the NFL labor market, thereby constituting a "group boycott." In order to prevail on that claim, Clarett must demonstrate that he is entitled to judgment on the merits. However, he must first overcome the two affirmative defenses asserted by the NFL: (1) that the Rule is immune from the antitrust laws, and (2) that Clarett lacks standing to bring an antitrust claim.

A. The Nonstatutory Labor Exemption

The NFL argues that the Rule is immune from antitrust scrutiny based on what has come to be known as the "nonstatutory labor exemption." If the NFL is correct, the exemption provides a complete defense to Clarett's suit. Accordingly, I address the application of the nonstatutory labor exemption at the outset.

The Rule Does Not Address a Mandatory Subject of Collective Bargaining

The Rule provides that for college players seeking special eligibility, "at least three full college seasons [must] have elapsed since their high school graduation." Nowhere is there a reference to wages, hours, or conditions of employment. Indeed, the Rule makes a class of potential players *unemployable.* Wages, hours, or working conditions affect only those who are employed or eligible for employment.

The NFL argues that "if the draft itself is protected by the nonstatutory labor exemption, it follows *a fortiori* that rules governing eligibility for the draft . . . are also protected by the exemption." In support of this proposition, the NFL relies heavily on three recent Second Circuit cases all arising in the context of professional sports. However, each of those cases involve practices that affect wages, hours or working conditions.

In sum, none of the cases cited by the NFL involve job *eligibility.* The league provisions addressed in *Wood, Williams,* and *Caldwell* govern the terms by which those who *are drafted* are employed. The Rule, on the other hand, precludes players from entering the labor market altogether, and thus affects wages only in the sense that a player subject to the Rule will earn none. But the Rule itself, for the reasons just discussed, does not concern wages, hours, or conditions of employment and is therefore not covered by the nonstatutory labor exemption.

The Nonstatutory Labor Exemption Cannot Apply to Those Who Are Excluded from the Bargaining Unit

The exemption is also inapplicable because the Rule *only* affects players, like Clarett, who are complete strangers to the bargaining relationship. The labor laws cannot be used to shield anticompetitive agreements between employers and unions that affect only those outside of the bargaining unit. There is no dispute that collective bargaining agreements, and therefore the nonstatutory labor exemption, apply to both prospective and current employees. Newcomers to an industry may not object to provisions of collective bargaining agreements that speak to wages, hours, or conditions of employment on the grounds that they were not present for the bargaining sessions. "Newcomers in the industrial context routinely find themselves disadvantaged vis-a-vis those already hired .... that is [ ]a commonplace consequence of collective agreements." Indeed, the *Wood* court held that a player, once drafted, could not object to the league's salary structure on the grounds that he never consented to the collective bargaining agreement.

At the time an agreement is signed between the owners and the players' exclusive bargaining representative, all players within the bargaining unit and those who enter the bargaining unit during the life of the agreement are bound by its terms.

Clarett's situation is very different. He is not permitted to be drafted—allegedly because the NFL and the union agreed to exclude players in his class. But Clarett's eligibility was not the union's to trade away. Indeed, the Rule does not deal with the rights of *any* NFL players or draftees. That the nonstatutory exemption does not apply in such a case is simply the flip side of the rule that the exemption only applies to mandatory subjects of collective bargaining, those governing wages, hours, and working conditions. Employees who are hired after the collective bargaining agreement is negotiated are nonetheless bound by its terms because they step into the shoes of the players who did engage in collective bargaining. But those who are categorically denied eligibility for employment, even temporarily, cannot be bound by the terms of employment they cannot obtain. For this reason, too, the nonstatutory exemption does not apply.

The NFL Has Failed to Show that the Rule Arose from Arm's Length Negotiations

The nonstatutory exemption does not apply for a third reason: the NFL has failed to demonstrate that the Rule evolved from arm's-length negotiations between the NFLMC and the NFLPA. If there is any doubt on this issue, the NFL is not entitled to summary judgment on this defense.

While Clarett offers no *evidence* on the issue of arm's-length bargaining, he certainly highlights the NFL's absence of proof. Because the NFL has not demonstrated that the Rule evolved from this process, the NFL is not entitled to summary judgment based on the nonstatutory labor exemption.

Less Restrictive Alternatives to the Rule Exist

Nonetheless, even if a procompetitive justification for the Rule existed, summary judgment for Clarett would be appropriate because an alternative to the Rule exists that is less prejudicial to competition. The antitrust laws do not tolerate a policy that restrains trade -- even if there is some procompetitive benefit -- when a policy that results in less prejudice to competition would be equally effective.

For the reasons just explained, Clarett's motion for summary judgment is granted and the NFL's motions are denied. Because the Rule violates the antitrust laws, it cannot preclude Clarett's eligibility for the 2004 NFL draft. Accordingly, it is hereby ORDERED that Clarett is eligible to participate in the 2004 NFL draft.

****

The trial court ruled in Clarett's favor. The court cited three other cases with similar rules in professional leagues, all of which were found to be antitrust violations. In *Denver Rockets v. All Pro Management (Spencer Haywood)* (1971), the court struck down a 4-year rule imposed by the NBA. In *Boris v. U.S. Football League* (1984), the court found a similar rule invalid as it pertained to college football players, and in *Linseman v. World Hockey League* (1977), the court declared a hockey league rule that prohibited the drafting of a player younger than the age of 20 an illegal group boycott.

The *Clarett* decision received considerable criticism. Some writers expressed that the court had completely missed the mark as to the union's right to place restrictions on the entry to membership. The NFL filed a motion with the trial court requesting that the decision be stayed pending the appeal. The trial court denied the request. The NFL made the same request to the court of appeal. On April 19, just days before the 2004 draft, the appellate court issued a stay on the Clarett decision. The appellate court did not rule in favor of the NFL, but it did suspend the ruling in favor of Clarett, meaning Clarett would not be eligible for the draft. The appellate court based its ruling on its belief that the NFL would likely prevail in the matter. In addition, the NFL assured the appellate court that if the court ruled against the NFL, a supplemental draft would be conducted in order for Clarett to be drafted. The appellate court's order is below.

STAY GRANTED

We reserve decision on the merits of this appeal. A decision and opinion will follow. Appellant's motion for a stay pending the resolution of this appeal having been denied by the district court, appellant has moved before this Court for a stay pending the outcome of this appeal of the district court's opinion and order declaring appellee eligible to participate in the 2004 NFL draft. "Four criteria are relevant in considering whether to issue a stay of an order of a district court…pending appeal: the likelihood of success on the merits, irreparable injury if a stay is denied, substantial injury to the party opposing a stay if one is issued, and the public interest." *Mohammed v. Reno*. Appellant has demonstrated a likelihood of success on the merits. Any potential harm done to appellee by granting this motion to stay is sufficiently countermanded by the strength of the other factors weighing in appellant's favor. Appellant's agreement to hold a supplemental draft for appellee and all others similarly situated also mitigates any harm to the appellee in the event of his ultimately prevailing in this appeal. A stay is thus warranted to safeguard appellant from harm and ensure meaningful review of the issues presented by this appeal. Upon due consideration, it is hereby ORDERED that the appellant's motion for a stay pending the resolution of this appeal is GRANTED, effective immediately.

Clarett immediately filed a motion with the United States Supreme Court to have the stay lifted, but his request was denied. In May 2004 the appellate court formally rejected Clarrett's attempt to enter the NFL's draft and the Clarrett saga was over. In 2005 (when Clarett was finally eligible under the NFL rules), the Denver Broncos selected Clarett with the final pick of the 3rd round, but he was released during training camp.

NFL EUROPE

The NFL Europe, formerly the World League of American Football (WLAF), was a European football league sponsored by the NFL. The NFL's primary goal was to introduce American-style football to Europe with an eye toward expanding markets. The games were played in the spring and summer months. The league incurred substantial financial losses and the popularity of pro football did not catch on as was hoped. Each NFL team contributed about $350,000 every year to the league. In the past few years, there were calls from a number of owners to disband the venture, and in 2007, Commissioner Roger Goodell terminated the league for good. The NFL lost around $30 million a season on the League, and Goodell decided to look for other ways to market the NFL overseas. About 100 NFL players played in the League, including Kurt Warner (the 1999 and 2001 NFL MVP).

PLAYER CONDUCT POLICY

Roger Goodell succeeded the retiring Paul Tagliabue as the NFL Commissioner on September 1, 2006. At the time of the transition, the NFL was experiencing significant negative publicity following several players' off-the-field disciplinary and legal problems. For example, *nine* members of the Cincinnati Bengals had been arrested within the past year. Goodell made it instantly clear that such conduct would not be tolerated under his leadership, and he implemented a tough new "Player Conduct Policy" to help control off-field behavior and preserve the league's public image. Almost immediately, players like Adam "Pacman" Jones, Chris Henry, and Terry "Tank" Johnson received significant suspensions for off-the-field conduct. Some commentators criticized the harshness of these sentences, with Jones, in particular, being suspended for an entire season. It is also interesting to note that in the case of Jones, his suspension came down while his legal trials were still pending (that is, before he had been convicted of the crime). Commissioner Goodell had authority to take such action pursuant to the NFL CBA, but NFL disciplinary action taken prior to a legal finding of guilt could come under scrutiny in the future.

The most infamous off-field conduct that occurred in 2007 was the federal grand jury indictment of Michael Vick. In July 2007, Vick and three other men were charged with federal crimes stemming from their involvement in a sizable dog-fighting ring. This was not the first time Vick faced legal action for off-field conduct. In August, Vick agreed to a plea bargain in which he admitted financing the fighting ring and knowing key facts about the intricacies of the operation. A federal judge sentenced Vick to 23 months in jail, and in 2008, Vick faced a trial for related but separate charges under Virginia law (in the United States, federal and state criminal charges are distinct and may be brought independently). Immediately after Vick agreed to the federal plea bargain, the NFL suspended him indefinitely without pay, as a first-time offender under the Player Conduct Policy.

Vick's troubles did not end with the combined plea bargain/suspension; the Atlanta Falcons (Vick's team) also filed a claim through the league's arbitration system. The team's position was that Vick knew he was in violation of his contract when he signed a 10-year, $130 million deal in December 2004, and they sought the repayment of nearly $20 million in bonus money paid to Vick. The proceeding had significant financial implications for the Falcons because any ruling in their favor would be credited to their future salary cap calculations. On October 10, 2004, the arbitrator sided with the team and required Vick to reimburse the team for about $20 million. The NFLPA appealed the ruling and a federal judge in Minnesota (where all NFL CBA-related issues are litigated because original lawsuits were filed there in the early 1990s) reduced Vick's obligation to $3.75 million, due to a different interpretation of the CBA's language regarding how to classify certain bonus options. The decision certainly benefitted the troubled quarterback, though it also appears to have contributed to the NFL owners' decision to opt out of the CBA early. However, Vick still stood to lose millions of dollars in cancelled endorsement contracts due to his violation of those contracts' "morals clause ."

Vick's suspension came after he pled guilty, but what if Commissioner Goodell had suspended him *before* resolution of his legal issues? Some commentators have argued that the new Player Conduct Policy gives the Commissioner too much discretion to regulate off-field misconduct. Under the previous policy of Commissioner Goodell's predecessor, Paul Tagliabue, punishment was triggered only by a conviction or its equivalent; however, no such trigger was required under the new policy. What if Goodell issues a premature suspension and the player was later acquitted? This was not a hypothetical; in 1998, League officials suspended Green Bay Packers wide receiver James Lofton in relation to rape charges, but Lofton was later acquitted. The fact-dependent nature of criminal misconduct makes it very dangerous for the league to act before the legal system resolves the matter. The league does not have the competence or procedural safeguards to launch factual investigations that should be conducted by the courts, and even if it did, the courts are much better at making these determinations. Goodell cannot subpoena witnesses or force them to testify under oath, and he has no obligation to provide any of the constitutional protections enjoyed by criminal defendants.

Even more alarmingly, NFL Commissioner disciplinary authority cannot be appealed to a neutral arbitrator; instead, the player can only appeal to the Commissioner. In other words, the Commissioner enjoys the luxury of deciding whether or not his decision was fair and just.

2008 OPT-OUT OF CBA

The 1993 CBA has been repeatedly extended with modifications. The most recent negotiations in 2006 yielded an agreement that would expire in 2013, but in May 2008, the owners exercised an early opt-out that would end the agreement two years earlier. The reasons cited by the owners for the opt-out included: (1) high labor costs, (2) problems with the rookie pool, and (3) the league's inability because of court interpretations to recoup bonuses from players who later breach their contract. This last reason is directed primarily at the rulings in the cases of Ashley Lelie and Michael Vick.

The early opt-out means that the 2010 season would be uncapped, which favors the players. The CBA also provides, however, that in an uncapped year, a player must have 6 years in the league to obtain free agency status. The opt-out opens the possibility of a strike or lockout in 2011. NFLPA leader Gene Upshaw has repeatedly stressed that if the salary cap goes, the players will not give it back. Practically speaking, the owners' maneuver alters some of the rules governing cap amortization and moves up the timetable for negotiations on a new CBA. A work stoppage seems highly unlikely at present, but the situation certainly warrants monitoring.

CHAPTER 8

National Basketball Association (NBA)

The enormous growth of the NBA in the past decade has been nothing short of phenomenal. As recently as the 1980s, playoff games were sometimes shown on delayed telecasts, and several teams were on the verge of bankruptcy. The NBA television contracts are now valued in the billions and NBA franchise values have soared. In 1990, the Orlando Magic and the Minnesota Timberwolves each paid about $32.5 million as franchise fees. Just a few years later, the Toronto Raptors and the Vancouver Grizzlies each paid $125 million for their franchise. The league also enjoyed the good fortune of employing the most extraordinary and well-known athlete in the world—Michael Jordan. Thanks in large part to Jordan's immense popularity, the NBA became a global attraction.

Despite its success, or maybe because of it, the relationship between labor and management in the NBA became increasingly hostile during the 1990s. The chasm peaked in 1998, when management declared the third lockout of the past four years. But this lockout was unlike the others—it caused the cancellation of the first two months of the season. The 1998 season marked the first time the NBA missed games due to a labor dispute.

NBA LABOR HISTORY

The National Basketball Association's labor history is similar to the other major leagues. Unlike the NFL, the NHL, or MLB, however, the NBA had relative peace compared to the other leagues—until the lockout of 1998.

In 1976, the case of *Robertson v. NBA* resulted in a court-approved settlement agreement between the union and management. The agreement became known as the "Robertson Settlement Agreement" (RSA). The RSA included a modification of the college draft and the right of first-refusal. After the RSA was reached, the parties adopted a new CBA, which incorporated most of the RSA terms. The popularity of the NBA during this period paled in comparison with today's game. Many teams were on the brink of financial failure. At one point in the early '80s, a televised NBA playoff game was even interrupted for the showing of the movie *Old Yeller*.

According to management, the financial problems were due to the high salaries brought on by free agency and the right of first refusal that was created by the RSA. To address the situation, management unilaterally imposed a salary cap. The players filed suit, *Lanier v. NBA,* and the court ruled that the cap was unlawful. Because of financial pressures, however, the players agreed to modify the CBA to include a salary cap through the '86-'87 season. At the expiration of the '87 season, the players challenged the legality of the college draft, the right of first refusal and the salary cap on antitrust grounds. These provisions were upheld in *Bridgeman v. NBA* (1987).

1988 CBA SALARY CAP

The 1988 CBA salary cap provided for computation of the cap by multiplying the league's revenues, less player benefits, by 53% and then dividing that figure by the number of teams currently in the league. There were five basic exceptions to the salary cap and its application:

(1) A team was permitted to exceed the Salary Cap to the extent of its current contractual commitments;

(2) A team with a Team Salary at or over the Salary Cap could replace:

(i) A Restricted and Unrestricted Free Agent who elects not to re-sign a contract with that team at 100% of the Salary last paid to the player being replaced (salary slot); and

(ii) A retiree, a waived player, a holdout, or a player injured within 56 days of the first scheduled game at 50% of the Salary last paid to the player being replaced;

(3) A team with a Team Salary at or over the Salary Cap could enter into a one-year Player Contract with a College Draftee at the minimum player salary;

(4) A team could enter into any new Player Contract with any team Veteran without regard to Salary Cap limitations; (Larry Bird rule);

(5) A team at or over the Salary Cap could replace a player whose Player Contract has been assigned to another NBA Team.

The term "soft" was often used to describe the cap because of the number of exceptions, especially the "Larry Bird" rule, which allowed a team to spend any sum to retain its veteran players. As will be shown, however, *when* a contract is reached with a team's veteran players can have a dramatic impact on the Bird exception. The CBA prohibited the league, teams, or players from entering into any agreement designed to defeat the goal of the salary cap. Undisclosed agreements were expressly prohibited.

The 1988 CBA reduced the draft from 7 rounds to 2. The agreement also provided that a player became a *restricted* free agent after his initial contract expired. That is, the player would be subject to a first-right-of-refusal by his original team at the end of his rookie contract. The 1988 CBA expired in June of 1994. The players immediately challenged several aspects of the CBA, including the salary cap, in *NBA v. Williams.*

NBA v. Williams (1994)

The National Basketball Association (the "NBA") and the 27 teams (the "NBA Teams" or "Teams") that compete in the NBA commenced a declaratory action on June 17, 1994 against a class of NBA players as well as prospective NBA players, pursuant to 28 U.S.C. Sec. 2201. In particular, the NBA and the Teams seek a declaration that continued implementation of: (1) the college draft; (2) the right of first refusal; and (3) the salary cap does not violate federal antitrust laws. Alternatively, the NBA contends that these measures are not unreasonable restraints of trade and therefore do not violate the antitrust laws.

The same class of players who are defendants in the declaratory judgment claim, along with the National Basketball Players Association (the "NBPA") (collectively the "Players"), brought counterclaims alleging, in effect, that continuation of these policies are unreasonable restraints of trade not exempt from antitrust law and thereby violate the Sherman Act.

Background

This case is the fourth lawsuit initiated by either of the parties as a result of disputes that have arisen during collective bargaining negotiations. Indeed, I am convinced that this is a case where neither party cares about this litigation or the result thereof. Both are simply using the court as a bargaining chip in the collective bargaining process. Each is truly guilty of this practice. A recitation of the history of these lawsuits demonstrates this and puts this litigation in its proper context, i.e., a labor dispute that does not belong in litigation.

In 1970, the Players commenced a class action suit against the NBA in the federal district court for the Southern District of New York, challenging certain NBA imposed player restrictions on antitrust grounds. The NBA moved for summary judgment, arguing that the practices were shielded from antitrust laws by a labor exemption. The district court denied the NBA's motion on the ground that the exemption only shields unions and not employers. *Robertson v. National Basketball Ass'n.*, (1975).

In 1976, the parties in *Robertson* entered into, and the district court approved, a settlement agreement. This agreement effected a number of changes in the operation of the NBA, including modification of the college draft and institution of the right of first refusal. The settlement agreement provided that it would expire at the end of the 1986-1987 NBA season. In addition, it expressly provided that the Players had not waived their right to challenge in court any unilateral imposition of any rule, policy, practice or agreement by the NBA. When the Robertson settlement agreement was adopted in 1976, the Players and the NBA also entered into a multi-year collective bargaining agreement incorporating the substantive terms of the settlement agreement. The 1976 Collective Bargaining Agreement expired on June 1, 1979, and on October 10, 1980, the parties again entered into a multi-year collective bargaining agreement that expressly incorporated the terms of the Robertson settlement agreement, including the college draft and the right of first refusal.

The 1980 agreement expired on June 1, 1982. In 1983, the NBA sought for the first time to introduce the salary cap. The NBA contended that such a restriction was necessary because the majority of NBA teams were losing money, due in part, to rising player salaries and benefits. The players responded by filing a lawsuit challenging the legality of the salary cap. *Lanier v. National Basketball Ass'n.* A special master appointed to hear disputes under the Robertson settlement agreement determined that the salary cap would violate the terms of the settlement agreement and, therefore, could not be imposed without a modification of that agreement. The Players and the NBA entered into a Memorandum of Understanding that modified the expired 1980 Collective Bargaining Agreement to include a salary cap, and it continued in force through the end of the 1986-1987 season.

On June 8, 1987, the NBA and the Players entered into a Moratorium Agreement to facilitate negotiations, whereby the challenged practices would remain in effect but no new contracts would be signed. The Moratorium Agreement expired on October 1, 1987. The day the Moratorium Agreement expired, the Players commenced an action in the District of New Jersey, seeking a ruling that the college draft, the right of first refusal, and the salary cap violated the antitrust laws. *Bridgeman v. National Basketball Ass'n.*, (1987). The Players represented to the court that they would never agree to these restrictive practices. After a ruling on the labor exemption issue, discussed more fully below, the parties reached an agreement in principle, the final terms of which were memorialized in the 1988 Collective Bargaining Agreement. The 1988 Collective Bargaining Agreement continued the college draft, the right of first refusal and the salary cap.

The 1988 Collective Bargaining Agreement formally expired on June 23, 1994, the day following the last playoff game of the 1993-1994 NBA playing season. At a formal bargaining session, held in New York on April 7, 1994, the Players demanded that the three disputed employment practices be eliminated. In a position paper delivered to the NBA at that meeting, the Players expressly stated their view that the college draft, right of first refusal and the salary cap would "be subject to successful challenge under the antitrust laws." This position was reiterated at a second formal bargaining session, held on May 4, 1994.

On June 15, 1994, in a letter addressed to the NBA, the Players, while asserting that further negotiations would be futile, said that the Players would attend another meeting, but only in late June or mid-July. In that letter, the NBPA again threatened that the NBA's continuation of the employment conditions at issue would be "subject to scrutiny under the antitrust laws and ... are clearly in violation of those laws." At the preliminary injunction hearing on July 8, 1994, I informed the parties of my belief that this litigation was simply being used as a bargaining chip in the collective bargaining negotiations, and I advised them that the best course of action would be to resolve the dispute through negotiations. Apparently, the parties did attempt to negotiate, but such efforts were unsuccessful.

The College Draft

The college draft is held annually shortly after the NBA season concludes. It is a mechanism in which each team is allotted two selections. A team may exercise its selections or trade them to another team. The order of selection is generally determined by the records of the 27 Teams for the season immediately preceding the draft, i.e., the weaker teams select earlier. In the end, 54 prospective players are selected by the Teams. A player who is selected by a particular team may only negotiate with that team. Any team that negotiates with a player it did not select is severely penalized. Prospective players who are not drafted are free to negotiate with any NBA team.

The Right of First Refusal

Under the 1988 Collective Bargaining Agreement, the Teams maintain a right of first refusal over players who have played fewer than four seasons or who have not completed at least two contracts. When a player's contract expires, he is able to negotiate a new contract with any team. If a team has a right of first refusal over that player, however, it may match any offer another team makes. If there is a matching offer, the player may not sign with the new team, and his services are retained by his current team.

The Salary Cap

The salary cap is part of a complex player/owner revenue sharing arrangement in which the Players are guaranteed a percentage of the defined gross revenue of the team. This arrangement also operates as a ceiling on the total amount a team may spend on salaries for its players. As part of this arrangement, each team is also required to pay a minimum amount of salaries to its players. The salary cap may be exceeded by a team that wishes to pay a veteran player it currently employs. A team may not, however, exceed the salary cap to acquire a new player.

****

The Nonstatutory Labor Exemption

As a threshold matter, the NBA argues that antitrust law does not apply in this case because a collective bargaining relationship currently exists between the players and the NBA. In particular, the NBA contends that the nonstatutory labor exemption applies, and therefore, any antitrust claim the Players may seek must fail.

The dispute here arises because the 1988 Collective Bargaining Agreement has formally expired. The issue is whether antitrust immunity that existed while the Collective Bargaining Agreement was in effect continues after its formal expiration, and if so, for what length of time. I can find only four non-binding decisions addressing this precise issue. Unfortunately, each decision fashioned a different standard to apply.

The first case to address this issue was *Bridgeman v. National Basketball Ass'n.*, (1987). As noted in the factual summary in *Bridgeman*, the Players alleged that the continued effect of the college draft, the right of first refusal and the salary cap after the formal expiration of the 1983 Collective Bargaining Agreement violated federal antitrust laws. The NBA moved for summary judgment contending that the nonstatutory exemption immunized them from suit even though the 1983 Collective Bargaining Agreement had formally expired. Thus, the issue before the Bridgeman court was identical to the issue here.

The court refused to accept the Players' contention that antitrust immunity ends at the moment the collective bargaining agreement formally expires. The court noted that such a result would not be consistent with the National Labor Relations Act, 29 U.S.C. Sec. 151 et seq. (the "NLRA"). Id. Under the NLRA, the owners have an obligation, even after the collective bargaining agreement expires, to bargain fully and in good faith before altering a term or condition of employment that is a mandatory subject of collective bargaining. One can easily imagine the howls to be heard from the Players if the Teams unilaterally terminated medical coverage for themselves and their families at the formal expiration of the Collective Bargaining Agreement. It is for the good of our entire society that such is not the law. See 29 U.S.C. Sec. 158(a)(5). The *Bridgeman* court determined that the practical effect of this duty on employers is that the "terms and conditions of employment that are the subject of mandatory bargaining survive expiration of collective bargaining agreement."

The *Bridgeman* court also found the NBA's contention that antitrust immunity lasts indefinitely equally unavailing. In particular, the court reasoned that such a rule would discourage unions from entering into agreements, for fear of forever binding themselves with restraints that they could not subsequently attack in the courtroom. After considering the elements of the Mackey test, the issue turned on whether the disputed terms will likely become part of a subsequent collective bargaining agreement. Thus, the test that *Bridgeman* established was that antitrust immunity survives only as long as the employer continues to impose the restrictions unchanged, and reasonably believes that the challenged practice or a close variant of it will be incorporated in the next collective bargaining agreement.

In *Powell v. National Football League*, (1988), Judge Doty of the District Court of Minnesota addressed whether the NFL could continue to restrict player movement after the formal expiration of a collective bargaining agreement. Judge Doty agreed with Bridgeman to the extent that immunity does not cease with the formal expiration of the collective bargaining agreement, nor does it continue indefinitely. Judge Doty, however, held that the *Bridgeman* standard did not give proper regard for federal labor policy because it could encourage unions to be uncompromising while bargaining. Rather, Judge Doty adopted the so-called impasse standard to be the appropriate standard. Impasse was then defined as the point at which "there appears no realistic possibility that continuing discussions concerning the provision at issue would be fruitful." Thus, by "allowing a labor exemption to survive only until impasse, the law will not insulate a practice from antitrust liability, but will only delay enforcement of the substantive law until continued negotiations over the challenged provision become pointless."

Powell was reversed by the Court of Appeals for the Eighth Circuit in *Powell v. National Football League*, (1989), "*Powell II*." Specifically, *Powell II* held that the nonstatutory labor exemption extends beyond a mere impasse in negotiations and for as long as the labor relationship continues. The Eighth Circuit reasoned that once a collective bargaining relationship is established, federal labor policies become pre-eminent. As such, labor laws provide the opposing parties with sufficient tools to settle a dispute. For instance, employees may strike, employers may lock players out, and both parties may petition the National Labor Relations Board to prohibit unfair labor practices. Therefore, to provide the union with the ability to sue for treble damages under antitrust law "would ... improperly upset the careful balance established by Congress through the labor law."

The essence of *Powell II* is that once a collective bargaining arrangement is established and a valid and bona fide collective bargaining agreement is formed, federal labor law and its policies control. In other words, the disputes that arise from collective bargaining arrangements are labor disputes, and Congress has enacted laws that provide various remedies to these disputes. As the Eighth Circuit stated:

> The labor arena is one with well established rules which are intended to foster negotiated settlements rather than intervention by the courts. The League and the Players have accepted this "level playing field" as the basis for their often tempestuous relationship, and we believe that there is substantial justification for requiring the parties to continue to fight on it, so that bargaining and the exertion of economic force may be used to bring about legitimate compromise.

In sum, *Powell II* effectively held that antitrust immunity exists as long as a collective bargaining relationship exists and labor law remedies are available.

This reasoning mandates that the appropriate standard to apply is the *Powell II* standard. Antitrust immunity exists as long as a collective bargaining relationship exists. Accordingly, the NBA is granted the declaration it seeks; the continued implementation of these challenged measures by the NBA do not violate the antitrust laws as long as the collective bargaining relationship exists.

This does not mean that the Players are "stuck" with these provisions forever. Certainly, they can attempt to bargain these provisions away--including exerting economic pressure by means of a strike. Or, the Players may request decertification of the NBPA as a collective bargaining agent. I do not mean by this ruling to encourage the Players to decertify their union so that they may bring an antitrust claim. But, decertification is certainly an option the Players have. In fact, this is exactly what the National Football League Players Union did following *Powell II*. See *Powell v. National Football League*, (1991). Decertification, however, brings with it other consequences, namely the elimination of many federal labor remedies. In other words, the NBPA is a private actor with a variety of available choices. It is up to the Players to weigh the risks of all their actions. While I am not unconcerned that this decision may affect their decision to decertify, I simply note that the Players may not have it both ways. They may not avail themselves to the benefits of federal labor and antitrust law at the same time.

Even under a rule of reason analysis, however, it appears that the Players have failed to show that the alleged restraints of trade are on balance unreasonably anti-competitive. The pro-competitive effects of these practices, in particular the maintenance of competitive balance, may outweigh their restrictive consequences. Indeed, the Salary Cap seems to operate as a mechanism to distribute 53 per cent defined gross revenue to the Players. See *Mackey*, at 623 ("It may be that some reasonable restrictions relating to player transfers are necessary for the successful operation of the NFL. The protection of mutual interests of both the players and the clubs may indeed require this.")

For the foregoing reasons, the NBA and Teams' continued implementation of the college draft, right of first refusal, and the salary cap is hereby declared not to violate antitrust laws. This ruling mandates that the Players' counterclaims be denied. Parties are once again urged to pursue the only rational course for the resolution of their disputes--

--that is, a course of collective bargaining pursued by both sides in good faith. No court, no matter how highly situated, can replace this time honored manner of labor dispute resolution. Rather than clogging the courts with unnecessary litigation, the parties should pursue this course.

****

After the *Williams'* decision, the players and management agreed to maintain the status quo and to play the '94-'95 season under the terms of the old CBA. The parties also agreed not to engage in either a lockout or a strike. Management was primarily negotiating to make the "soft" cap "harder," similar to the NFL approach. The players were trying to do away with the restraints on free agency. As soon as the playoffs were over in '95, both sides were back at it. Eventually, a tentative six-year agreement was reached. The tentative agreement provided for the team salary cap to increase from $15.9 million to more than $23 million for the '95-'96 season. The cap was scheduled to gradually rise during the six-year term to $32.5 million in the last year of the CBA. The salary scale limited the pay of players selected in the first round of the draft to a maximum of 120% of the average pay of players drafted in the same position of the draft over the past seven years. Contracts for first round players could not exceed three years. Management the union leaders were in favor of the proposed CBA.

At this point, things got interesting. A number of players, led by Mr. Basketball himself, Michael Jordan, felt that the union could negotiate a better deal and were strongly opposed to the proposed CBA. Unable to get the CBA accepted, management imposed a lockout in July '95. The Jordan forces launched an unprecedented attempt to have the players vote to decertify the union. A lobbying effort that would have made any political party proud was waged by all three camps. Every NBA player received a video featuring "Air" Jordan and an eight-page letter urging the rejection of the CBA and the decertification of the union. The Jordan effort included a number of NBA stars, including Patrick Ewing and Reggie Miller. Union supporters included Clyde Drexler, Joe Dumars, Mark Price, Charles Barkley and Karl "the Mailman" Malone. Malone even threatened to leave the NBA and play in Europe if the union was decertified.

The vote in September '95 was heavily in favor of the union. After the vote, management and the union assumed they would be able to go forward with the CBA. The Jordan forces, however, were not finished. They forced a shakeup in union leadership. The new union leaders took the position that the union was bound by the terms it had agreed to in the proposed CBA, but that a new agreement could not be signed because there were still other terms that had to be negotiated. The NBA filed suit against some of the agents who were involved in the dispute and an unfair labor practice claim with the NLRB. Negotiations, growing increasingly bitter, continued. By July '96, one of the last issues to be worked out was the dispersal of $50 million in profit sharing from the NBA's television deal. After a very brief lockout, that issue was resolved and a new CBA was reached.

1996 COLLECTIVE
BARGAINING AGREEMENT

Some of the significant terms of the 1996 CBA included:

1. The salary cap for '96-97 was $24.3 million per team, increasing to at least $25.6 million in the following year. Most of the exceptions to the cap in the old CBA were retained, including the "Larry Bird rule." An injured player could be replaced by a player who was paid half the injured player's salary. The injury had to be diagnosed as one that would sideline a player the majority of the season. Each team was also given an extra $1 million slot that could be used for one or two players.

2. The minimum salary for veterans in '96-97 was $247,500; the minimum for rookies was $220,000.

3. The rookie pay scale was based on where the player was drafted. The player would receive a sum determined by the average pay of the draft slot for the last seven years. For example, the first year salary of Tim Duncan, the first pick in the '97 draft, was fairly well established before any contract negotiations began. Rookie contracts were limited to three years. After the three year expiration, the player could become an <u>unrestricted</u> free agent.

4. For veterans, the longest contract allowed was seven years with a maximum raise of 20% a season, with some exceptions.

5. Basketball Related Revenues (BRR), which are used to determine the salary cap, were expanded to include revenue from luxury suites, parking, concession, international television, and arena signage.

THE SALARY CAP AND THE
LARRY BIRD RULE

One of the ironies of salary caps in professional sports is that team owners fight vigorously for the limits in labor negotiations and then use every possible means to avoid the cap rules. The Miami Heat's signing of two players in August 1996, described by some writers as the "biggest mistake in NBA franchise history," is illustrative. The NBA's reaction to the contracts also demonstrated certain aspects of the Larry Bird exception.

Under the CBA rules in 1996, teams were prohibited from exceeding the salary cap. There were, however, a number of exceptions—notably the Larry Bird rule. The Bird rule allowed a team to exceed the cap by any amount to resign its own players. This is why the Chicago Bulls were able to pay Michael Jordan $30 million for the '95-'96 season, even though the salary cap was $24.3 million. But the timing of the contract, as the Miami Heat would learn, was critical. Although a team cap can be exceeded to resign its own players, that salary was factored in the cap with respect to the *later* signing of free agents.

Alonzo Mourning was a Miami Heat player. During a television interview after the '95-'96 season, he made a number of comments that indicated a deal, unannounced at the time, had been reached with Miami on his salary. It was later determined to be $112 million for seven years. Before Mourning actually signed, however, Miami signed free agent Juwan Howard to a seven-year, $98 million contract. After signing Howard, Miami announced that the team and Mourning had reached a contract. The League took the position, however, based on the television comments by Mourning, that the latter's contract was a "done deal" before Miami signed Howard. As a result of Mourning's contract, the League's position was that the Heat did not have cap room to sign Howard. The League voided the Howard contract. Miami initially sought arbitration on the NBA's ruling voiding the Howard contract, but later withdrew the objection. An adverse arbitration decision would have resulted in severe penalties to the team. Washington, Howard's original team, obtained permission to re-sign Howard with a $100 million-plus seven-year contract.

Miami's problems were not limited to Mourning. The Heat had also offered bonuses to Tim Hardaway and P. J. Brown. Miami's position was that the bonuses were "unlikely to be attained," which meant they would not be treated as salary for cap purposes that year. The league viewed the bonuses as "very easy" to achieve and therefore counted the bonuses toward the cap, which placed Miami even further over the cap line.

In October 2000, as a result of salary cap violations, NBA Commissioner David Stern handed down one of the most severe penalties ever levied in professional sports. The Minnesota Timberwolves were caught making secret salary agreements with Joe Smith. Stern voided Smith's current contract, resulting in Smith becoming a free agent. He also voided Smith's previous contract (thereby stripping him of his "Bird rights"), fined the Timberwolves $3.5 million, and took away the team's next five first round draft picks. The Commissioner made it clear that circumvention of the salary cap would not be tolerated.

THE 1998 LOCKOUT

The CBA executed in 1996 had a term of six years. But, the agreement also had a provision that allowed management to reopen talks if salaries exceeded 51.8% of BRI (Basketball Related Income). In 1998, the owners contended that salaries amounted to 57% of BRI. The union admitted the threshold of 51.8% had been exceeded, but disputed the 57% figure. Regardless, in the summer of 1998, the owners elected to reopen labor talks on the CBA.

According to the owners, the CBA had to be revised because the agreement was causing almost half the teams to lose money. Although the disparity was not nearly as great as it was in professional baseball, the NBA had become a league of "haves" and "have nots" regarding team income. The NBA, like the NFL and MLB, made equal distributions of national television income. The financial positions of the NBA teams varied, however, because revenue from gate receipts and local television contracts were not divided. In the 1996-97 season, the Chicago Bulls' payroll was more than $58 million, while the Vancouver Grizzlies total payroll was less than $19 million. Chicago's payroll was skewed by Michael Jordan's $30 million salary—which was $4.5 million more than the entire salary of the Utah Jazz. Jordan's salary, in fact, exceeded the total payroll of 21 teams.

The owners maintained that teams were losing money because player salaries were increasing faster than team incomes. They thought the salary escalation was due primarily to the early free agency rights of rookies. The 1996 CBA limited a rookie's first contract to three years and capped their salaries within a formula tied to past rookie contracts. The rookie cap provided a substantial benefit to the owners, but the rookie players became unrestricted free agents after three years. The result was that owners had to sign their rookies to exorbitant contracts in their second year or risk losing them to free agency one season later. The classic example was the $120 million contract given to Kevin Garnett in his second year. The owners wanted to change the CBA so that drafted players would not become free agents until after six years, and they wanted to do away with the Larry Bird exception.

The players expressed a willingness to modify the CBA in some respects, but were adamant that they would not accept changes to the rights of free agency or the Bird rule. Management declared a lockout. Initially, the lockout was not viewed with much alarm because it began in July, which left plenty of time to reach a settlement before the season started in November. Bargaining sessions were held and often abruptly ended with one or both parties walking out, claiming the other side was not serious about trying to reach a settlement. As the season approached, each side was painfully aware of how damaging the recent strike had been to baseball. But neither side would make substantial concessions, and the lockout extended into the season. For the first time in the league's history, a labor dispute cancelled games.

In the beginning, it appeared that the owners had the upper hand in the negotiations. The league had a provision in its television contract that required payments from the networks even if the games were canceled due to a labor problem, although the networks were entitled to recover the lost programming at the end of the contract term. Although owners would lose gate receipts and related revenue, the television contract ensured that teams would receive substantial income despite the lockout. The players, however, were not receiving any part of their paychecks.

In the early stages of the lockout, the players made an argument that could have dramatically changed the bargaining position of the parties. A large number of players were not free agents and had guaranteed contracts. The union claimed that these players were entitled to their salaries during the lockout. The union argued that the lockout was solely a decision of the owners. This was no small matter: the obligations, if owed, were estimated at around $800 million. Amazingly, the player contracts did not address the issue. The matter went to arbitration. The union was able to find one old player contract that had a specific provision that stated no salary payments were due in the event of a lockout. The union argued that the absence of this language in a contract meant a player was entitled to be paid. The union, however, lost the arbitration. If the union had won this decision, the lockout probably would have ended at a much earlier date and on terms more favorable to the players.

In many labor disputes, the parties often try to gain public sympathy for their side. Public support for one side or the other can assist the bargaining position of the favored party. This is especially true with professional sports. Despite their popularity, the players' attempt to gain public support was doomed from the start. While the players' extravagant salaries were common knowledge, the owners' books were private. This allowed the owners to at least *claim* they were losing money. Either way, sympathy for out-of-work millionaires was a stretch. Super agent David Falk organized a charity game with some players to raise funds for the impoverished athletes. The idea was a public relations nightmare and it was soon announced the proceeds would go to real charities. Late night television comedians had a field day with jokes and skits about the plight of the millionaire players. The players' effort to gain public support was a giant "air ball."

The players also had a problem with their negotiating strategy. NBA payrolls had developed into a two-class system. One category consisted of a few superstars on each team who were earning the bulk of the team's payroll. Many teams were paying up to 75% of their salary to two or three players. The salaries of the remaining players on each team were close to the minimum wage. Management exploited this chasm by offering more benefits for lower-salary players in return for greater restrictions on the earning power of the superstars. The union had the difficult task of trying to balance the rights of select marquee players and the remainder of its members. For acceptance, the CBA had to be approved by a majority of its members. Although the superstars had enormous influence, they still had only one vote.

A settlement was finally reached in January 1999, just in time for the league to package a modified 50-game season. The lockout had cost players and owners hundreds of millions of dollars. The work stoppage did not, however, seem to have the same lingering ill effects as the baseball strike. Michael Jordan's absence was an enormous loss to the game, but his retirement created a wide-open championship race that had been lacking during the Bulls' dominance.

The lockout was imposed by management, and the owners ultimately achieved some of the major constraints they were seeking. The media spin on the settlement was that management had beat the union. This description, however, is based more on the "winner-loser" mentality of the media and the public. Collective bargaining is not necessarily like a basketball game, with one winner and one loser. Both sides make concessions and gain advantages. Overall, the CBA did place some limits on what superstars could earn and it gave teams a longer hold on rookies. The bulk of NBA players, however, made significant gains.

1999 COLLECTIVE BARGAINING AGREEMENT

Some of the salient terms of the 1999 CBA were as follows:

1. Free Agency
   Drafted players were not eligible for free agency during their first four years. In the fifth year their team had a first right of refusal. The players were paid

according to a scale based on the salaries of previous players drafted in the same slot.

2. Percentage of Revenue Devoted to Salaries

   No fixed number in the first three years.

   53% in year 4; 56% in year 5; and 57% in year 6.

3. Maximum Salary:

   0-5 years—$9 million

   6-9 years—$11 million

   10 years or more—$14 million

4. Salary Cap Exceptions

   Middle class exception of $1.75 million in year 1. $2 million in year 2; $2.25 million in year 3; and the average salary in years 4-7.

   $1 million exception available in year 1; $1.1 mil in year 2; $1.2 mil in year 3; and a median salary exception in years 4-6 starting at about $1.7 mil.

5. Maximum Annual Raises

   12% for Bird players and 10% for others

6. Cost Certainty

   Escrow tax of 10% withheld from players salaries if percentage of income devoted to salaries exceeded 55% in years 4-7.

7. Minimum Salaries

   Rookies - $287,000

   1 year - $350,000

   2 years - $425,000

   3 years - $450,000

   4 years - $475,000

   5 years - $537,500

   6 years - $600,000

   7 years - $662,500

   8 years - $725,000

   9 years - $850,000

   10 years - $1 million

8. Revenue Sharing

   Basketball Related Income (BRI), including gate receipts, radio and television revenue, 40% of luxury box income, 40% of signage revenue, a pro-rata share of personal seat license income, and certain transactions. Not included in BRI were naming rights, income from theme stores, bars, and restaurants, 60% of luxury box, and 60% of signage revenue.

9. Salary Cap

   The NBA salary cap was set at slightly more than 48% of basketball-related income (BRI). In the 2000-01 season, the cap was $35.5 million and the minimum salary payroll was $26.6 million.

10. Luxury Tax

    If aggregate player salaries and benefits exceeded 61.1%, a luxury tax would be imposed. The provision required players to pay the league that part of their salaries that exceeded the limits.

11. Miscellaneous

    Opt-out clauses in the first 5 years of all contracts were not allowed. Sign and trade deals could only occur if the contract was for 3 years or more. Performance bonuses were limited to 25% of the value of the contract. The union's group licensing guarantee dropped to $20 million for the 1999 season and then rose to $25 million. Longer suspensions and higher fines for player misconduct were imposed. All players were subject to drug testing once per season. Marijuana and illegal steroids were added to the banned list of drugs.

12. Larry Bird Exception — Qualifying Veteran Free Agents
    TThis exception allowed teams to exceed the salary cap to resign their own free agents, up to the player's maximum salary. The player must have played for three seasons without being waived or changing teams as a free agent. If he was traded, the "Bird Rights" were traded with him, and his new team could use the Bird Exception to resign him. The Bird player could receive raises of up to 12.5%.

13. Early Bird Exception — Early Qualifying Veteran Free Agents
    This was a weaker form of the Larry Bird Exception. "Early Bird" status was achieved after just two seasons without being waived or changing teams as a free agent. Using this exception, a team could resign its own free agent for 175% of his previous season salary or the average player salary, whichever was greater. Early Bird contracts had to be for at least two seasons.

14. No Bird Exception — Non-Qualifying Veteran Free Agents
    This rule applied to veteran free agents who qualified for the above exceptions. A team could resign its own free agent in this category to a salary starting at 120% of his previous season salary or 120% of the minimum salary, whichever was greater, even if the player was over the cap. Raises were limited to 10% and contracts were limited to 6 years on this exception.

The rules of a CBA can sometimes have an affect outside of a league. The case below is an example.

Matter of Federation Internationale de Basketball

October 25, 2000

The principal question presented by this application is whether a provision of the private collective bargaining agreement between the National Basketball Association ("NBA") and the National Basketball Players Association ("NBPA"), which provides that the details of drug tests administered to NBA players shall remain confidential, should result in the denial of an application by Federation Internationale de Basketball ("FIBA") for discovery of test results administered to a former NBA player in order to defend itself in the German courts against a lawsuit brought by that player.

The collective bargaining agreements ("CBAs") between the NBA and the NBPA have contained an Anti-Drug Program since 1983. The current version of the program permits testing of players for drug use in limited circumstances and provides, among other things, for the expulsion from the league of those who test positive for so-called Drugs of Abuse. It provides also that the NBA and its affiliates "are prohibited from publicly disclosing information about the diagnosis, treatment, prognosis, test results, compliance, or the fact of participation of a player in the Program "except" as reasonably required in connection with the suspension or disqualification of a player."

On November 24, 1999, the NBA announced, as permitted by the CBA, "that Stanley Roberts of the Philadelphia 76ers had been expelled from the league because he tested positive for an amphetamine-based designer drug, a substance prohibited by the Anti-Drug Program agreed to by the NBA and the" NBPA.

Following his expulsion from the NBA, Roberts sought employment in Europe as a professional basketball player. As he allegedly was on the verge of signing a $500,000 per year contract to play for a team in Istanbul, FIBA — the rules of which authorize it to ban a player based on a positive drug test administered by the NBA — announced that Roberts was banned from FIBA competition worldwide for two years. Claiming that his prospective Turkish contract fell through as a result of the FIBA ban, Roberts pursued an internal appeals procedure before FIBA. When this proved fruitless, he sued FIBA in the District Court in Munich, Germany, and sought a preliminary injunction barring FIBA from barring him from FIBA competition. He argued, among other things, that he did not in fact violate the NBA's anti-drug rules, that FIBA in any event was not entitled to rely on the press announcement of the NBA test results, and in any case that the FIBA anti-drug policy is not enforceable as a matter of German law because it was not reflected in FIBA's Articles of Association.

In February 2000, the Munich court granted Roberts' application for a preliminary injunction. On October 20, 2000, FIBA moved by order to show cause for an order authorizing issuance of a subpoena commanding that the NBA produce documents relating to (1) Roberts' alleged violation of the NBA drug program (including documents relating to the positive drug test), and (2) any grievance instituted by Roberts under the CBA in connection with the alleged drug violation and the NBA's expulsion of Roberts.

Confidentiality

The NBA asserts that the information in question is confidential under the terms of the CBA between it and the players' association and therefore should not be disclosed. Indeed, it argues that the NBPA's willingness to agree to an anti-drug program in the future would be destroyed if this Court were to grant the requested relief. It goes so far as to contend that the NBA would be unable to maintain any anti-drug program at all if the absolute confidentiality of these test results were breached.

The NBA's position is unpersuasive, particularly in the circumstances of this case. Even if the mutual expectations of confidentiality implicit in the CBA were sufficient to defeat disclosure pursuant to compulsory process in a different situation, the NBA ignores the significance of the fact that it is Roberts — who has the only relevant privacy interest — who has put his compliance with the NBA program in issue by commencing litigation against FIBA in which he flatly denies any violation of the NBA program. Just as the attorney-client and other privileges are waived where the party entitled to confidentiality puts the substance of the privileged matter at issue, any privacy interest an NBA player or former player may have in the confidentiality of his own drug test results must yield where he voluntarily injects the accuracy or existence of those results into litigation brought by him.

The most basic point is that the CBA does not require that the fact of a positive drug test and expulsion be kept confidential. To the contrary, it explicitly authorizes publication of that information. All that is left, it appears, is the clinical detail about the nature of the test and the level of drugs found in the relevant bodily fluid. There simply is not a very great privacy interest in the details once the basic facts are known, as they are here.

In any case, the private interests of the NBA simply are not sufficient to warrant denial of this application on confidentiality grounds. The NBA's concern is only that the NBPA may resist inclusion of an anti-drug program in the next CBA. But the object of the law here is not to make the NBA's collective bargaining easier. Both sides have enormous stakes in reaching agreement on a future CBA. No doubt they will be able to do so, sooner or later.

FIBA's motion is granted in all respects. The NBA is directed to produce the documents described in the subpoena attached to applicant's moving papers forthwith.

****

FOUR-YEAR RULE

One issue which was not addressed in the 1999 CBA, but continued to stir controversy, was young players entering the NBA League before they finished, or even started, college. Entering the NBA draft before finishing college, once considered as a bold step, has now become common. The trend is fueled by the success of others who have made the leap. In each of the last few years, players who left college early, or skipped it altogether, have been some of the top draft choices. The incredible fame and wealth associated with NBA status are understandable temptations. In a recent draft 47 underclassmen declared for the draft that would take less than 60 players.

The NBA has received a considerable amount of criticism for *allowing* the young men to forego their education for the chance of making it in the League. From an economic standpoint it is hard to criticize players who want to play on an NBA team. But critics charge that most of the early draft entries fail. Moreover, NCAA rules state that upon entering the Draft, an athlete forfeits his college eligibility. Critics also argue that the early entry prevents the athlete from obtaining an education and hurts the college game. The criticism directed at the NBA is unfair for a number of reasons.

Major League Baseball has been drafting athletes directly from high school, or before they finish college, for years. Tiger Woods left college early to play professional golf. Professional tennis has had a number of teenagers competing for years. Yet there has been little criticism directed at these professional sports. Why makes college basketball players different?

The NCAA has discussed the matter with the NBA. The concern that allowing athletes to enter the draft early deprives young basketball players of obtaining an education is a suspect one. It is true that entering the League will cost a player his college eligibility, but this does not mean the athlete can not go to college if he wants to further his education. It only means he cannot have his college expenses paid for with an athletic scholarship. Furthermore, the scholarship is not wasted, since it will be awarded to another student-athlete who may not have attended college without the financial assistance.

The NCAA could, of course, change its rules to minimize the consequences of the decision to "go pro." Currently the NCAA rules prohibit a player who is selected in the draft, or who obtains an agent, from receiving a college scholarship. A simple change of the rules could allow players who do not get drafted to obtain or retain a scholarship. Such a move, however, would directly conflict with the NCAA's position on amateur status and is unlikely to ever be implemented. But the rule change seems like a reasonable adjustment, given the *concern* of the NCAA about the players' educational opportunity.

Aside from the fact that other sports use teenagers with little or no criticism, there are legal issues involved. Years ago the NBA had a four-year rule which prohibited players from entering the League until four years after their high school graduation. That rule was not changed by the League, but by the courts. In 1971 Spencer Haywood successfully challenged the NBA's 4-year rule in *Denver Rockets v. All Pro Management & Spencer Haywood*. The court stated:

> Section 2.05 of the by-laws of NBA provides as follows:
>
> A person who has not completed high school or who has completed high school but has not entered college, shall not be eligible to be drafted or to be a Player (in the NBA) until four years after he has been graduated or four years after his original high school class has been graduated, as the case may be, nor may the future services of any such person be negotiated or contracted for, or otherwise reserved. Similarly, a person who has entered college but is no longer enrolled, shall not be eligible to be drafted or to be a Player until the time when he would have first become eligible had he remained enrolled in college. Any negotiations or agreements with any such person during such period shall be null and void and shall confer no rights to the services of such person at any time thereafter.
>
> With respect to Haywood, Section 2.05 of the NBA by-laws, above quoted, has the effect of excluding him from the NBA until the commencement of the 1971-72 playing season. This provision prevents Haywood, a qualified professional basketball player, from contracting with any NBA team, even though he does not desire to, or may not be eligible to, attend college and even though he does not desire to, and is ineligible to, participate in collegiate athletics. There is a substantial probability, in light of all the evidence presented to this Court, that the effect of this provision is a group boycott on the part of the NBA and its teams against otherwise qualified players who come within the terms of said provision, and that it is an arbitrary and unreasonable restraint upon the rights of Haywood and other potential NBA players to contract to play for NBA teams until the happening of an event (i.e., the passage of four years from the graduation of a potential player's high school class) fixed by the NBA without the consent or agreement of such potential player.

There is a substantial probability, in light of all the evidence presented to this Court, that NBA by-law 2.05 constitutes a group boycott. But for the application of that by-law provision of NBA to Haywood, Haywood would be eligible to play for Seattle or any other NBA team at this time.

A professional basketball player has a very limited career.

Participating in professional basketball as a player against the best competition which the sport has to offer is as necessary to the mental and physical well being of Haywood as is breathing, eating and sleeping.

Unless NBA is enjoined from enforcing its by-laws and particularly its by-law No. 2.05, Haywood will be unable to continue to play professional basketball for Seattle and NBA will take retaliatory action against Seattle which may include the suspension or revocation of Seattle's franchise as a member team of NBA.

If Haywood is unable to continue to play professional basketball for Seattle, he will suffer irreparable injury in that a substantial part of his playing career will have been dissipated, his physical condition, skills and coordination will deteriorate from lack of high-level competition, his public acceptance as a super star will diminish to the detriment of his career, his self-esteem and his pride will have been injured and a great injustice will be perpetrated on him.

****

There is no question that the physical and emotional demands of the high-pressure lifestyle of the NBA is difficult at any age—even more so for someone still in his teens. But the same can be said for other sports such as baseball, tennis and golf, or even the movie or television business (where even pre-teenage children are involved on a regular basis). Young people make important decisions all the time. Is it fair to deny an 18 year old basketball player the right to play in the NBA simply because of his age? It is hard to argue with the success of LeBron James, who recently entered the NBA straight from high school, quickly became an All-Star, and led his Cleveland Cavaliers to the 2007 NBA Finals.

For a number of years, David Stern (the NBA Commissioner) has urged the adoption of a rule that would require a player to be at least 20-years old to enter the draft. The 20-year age limit would prevent a number of young players from entering the draft. But to be enforceable, the rule had to be included in the CBA, which meant getting the player's union to agree to the rule. The players have been historically opposed to the idea for a number of reasons, but in the 2005-06 CBA, the rule was finally modified to require a player to be at least 19 years of age and one year removed from high school to enter the draft. As a result, in 2006 star high school players Kevin Durant (University of Texas) and Greg Oden (Ohio State University) were forced to attend college for a single year before declaring for the NBA Draft. They were the first two players selected in the 2007 Draft.

2005 COLLECTIVE
BARGAINING AGREEMENT

The 2005-06 CBA was reached without a labor stoppage and with little fanfare. Highlights of the CBA are set forth below.

TERM:

The new CBA begins with the 2005-06 season and runs through the 2010-11 season. The NBA has the option to extend the CBA for the 2011-12 season.

LENGTH OF CONTRACTS:

The maximum length of a player contract has been decreased from 7 years for Bird players and 6 years for other players to 6 years for Bird players and 5 years for other players.

ESCROW LEVEL:

The escrow level will remain at 57%. This percentage will be guaranteed to the players so that if total player costs before deducting escrow monies from the players are less than 57% of BRI, the difference will be paid by the League to the players.

The maximum percentage of player salaries and benefits that can be withheld from the players for purposes of meeting the 57% escrow level will be 10% in year 1, 9% in years 2 – 5, and 8% in year 6. The previous escrow withholding was 10%.

TAX:

A team tax trigger will be set at 61% of BRI. (The previous CBA percentage was 63.3%). The tax will be in effect each season and will apply to any team with a payroll that exceeds the tax trigger. This 100% tax requires that a team pay the NBA a sum equal to the amount by which the team has overshot the trigger. The NBA establishes the tax trigger before each season based on a projection of BRI. For the 2005-06 season the tax trigger was set at $61.7 million.

SALARY CAP:

The salary cap for the 2005-06 season was $49.5 million, based on 49.5% of BRI. The new CBA provides that the salary cap will increase from 48% of BRI currently to 49.5% of BRI in 2005-06 and 51% of BRI for the remainder of the CBA. In the 2006-07 season the cap amounted to approximately $53 million and in 2007-08 it reached nearly $56 million. Despite the cap, some teams have salaries in excess of $100 million due to the cap exceptions.

ANNUAL INCREASES AND DECREASES:

The permissible year-to-year increases in multi-year player contracts are as follows: Bird and Early Bird Contracts may increase by up to 10.5% of year-1 salary (down form 12.5%). Other contracts may increase up to 8% of year-1 salary (down from 10%).

ROOKIE SCALE CONTRACTS:

Rookie Scale Contracts will provide for 2 guaranteed seasons with 2 separate one-year options in favor of the team for seasons 3 and 4. (In the previous CBA, Rookie Scale Contracts provided for 3 guaranteed seasons with a team option for year 4.) The first team option is exercisable following the end of the player's first season, and the second team option is exercisable following the end of the player's second season. A team that exercises both options will continue to have first refusal rights following the player's fourth season. Teams will still have the ability to pay 20% more or less than the scale amounts.

MAXIMUM PLAYER'S SALARIES:

In the first year of a new contract a player may receive the greater of 105% of the player's prior salary, or:

0-6 years of service:	25% of salary cap ($12 million in the first year)
7-9 years of service:	30% of salary cap ($14.4 million in the first year)
10 or more years of service:	35% of salary cap ($16.8 million in the first year)

The maximum player's salaries will continue to be based on 48.04% of BRI Salary Cap.

MINIMUM PLAYER'S SALARIES:

Not included, referred to in attached memorandum.

SALARY CAP EXCEPTIONS:

There are a number exceptions to the salary cap, some of which have already been discussed.

ROSTERS:

Each team is required to carry 12 players on its active list and at least 1 player on its inactive list. Players sent to the NBA Development League will continue to count on a team's inactive list.

RESTRICTIVE FREE AGENCY:

A team must exercise its options for the third and fourth season of a Rookie Scale Contract in order to have first refusal rights following year 4.

NBA DEVELOPMENT LEAGUE:

During a player's first two seasons in the League, his team will be permitted to assign him to a team in the NBADL. A player can be assigned to the NBADL up to three times per season. The player will continue to be paid his NBA salary and will continue to be included on his NBA team's roster (on the inactive list).

DRAFT ENTRY AGE:

Beginning in 2006, the age limit for entering the draft increased from 18 to 19 years of age. U.S. players must be at least one year removed from high school and 19 years of age (by the end of that calendar year) before entering the draft. An international player must turn 19 during the calendar year of the draft.

DRUG TESTING:

All players will be subjected to four random drug tests each season (during the period from October 1 through June 30). These tests will be for both recreational and performance-enhancing drugs. The penalties for testing positive for performance-enhancing drugs will be increased from suspensions of 5, 10 and 25 games for the first, second and any subsequent violation respectively, to 10 and 25 games suspensions for the first two violations, a 1-year suspension for the third violation, and disqualification from the league for a fourth violation.

NATIONAL BASKETBALL DEVELOPMENT LEAGUE (NBDL)

The National Basketball Development League (NBDL) was formed and is operated by the NBA as a minor league of sorts. The league started with eight teams, all located in the East. Attendance average was below 2,000 fans per game in the first year and dropped off in the following years. But the NBDL has survived, and now appears to have become a genuine farm club for the NBA. Initially an athlete had to be 21 years old to enter the League, but the age requirement has since been reduced to 18. The lower age level may encourage talented players who do not want to go to college to consider the NBDL.

National Hockey League (NHL)

CHAPTER 9

The National Hockey League (NHL) started in 1917 in Montreal, Canada. The League has a long history, but for many years it was confined to Canada and a few border states. By the early 1960s, the NHL had six teams, two in Canada and four in the U.S. In the last few decades the NHL has experienced enormous growth in numbers, territory, and value. There are now 30 teams in the League and all but six are in the U.S. Nine new franchises were awarded in the 1990s, and other suitors are in waiting. The value of NHL franchises continues to grow. The fees for the expansion franchises for Nashville, Atlanta, Columbus, and Minneapolis were each in the $80 million range and television revenues have been rising in some markets. The NHL is considered a major professional sports league along with the NFL, NBA, and MLB.

RESERVE CLAUSE HISTORY

As in the other professional leagues, the players in the NHL are subject to various reserve clause restraints. The following case is one of the earlier challenges by an NHL player to the reserve clause. The trial court ruled that the reserve clause was invalid. The court of appeal, however, reversed the decision and upheld the reserve clause. The decision also contains a dissenting judge's opinion.

Dale McCourt v. California Sports, Inc. & The Los Angeles Kings (1979)

Clearly, here, the restraint on trade (reserve clause) primarily affects the parties to the bargaining relationship. It is the hockey players themselves who are primarily affected by any restraint, reasonable or not. Second, the agreement concerning the reserve system involves, in a very real sense, the terms and conditions of employment of the hockey players both in form and in practical effect.

The issue, therefore, in our judgment, is narrowed to whether, upon the facts of this case, the agreement sought to be exempted was the product of bona fide arm's-length bargaining.

On May 4, 1976, the NHL and the NHLPA signed their first collective bargaining agreement retroactive from September 15, 1975. The collective bargaining agreement provides that paragraph 17 of the Standard Player's Contract and By-Law Section 9A are "fair and reasonable terms of employment."

We believe that, in holding that the reserve system had not been the subject of good faith, arm's-length bargaining, the trial court failed to recognize the well established principle that nothing in the labor law compels either party negotiating over mandatory subjects of collective bargaining to yield on its initial bargaining position. Good faith bargaining is all that is required. That the position of one party on an issue prevails unchanged does not mandate the conclusion that there was no collective bargaining over the issue.

Contrary to the trial judge's conclusion, the very facts relied upon by him in his opinion illustrate a classic case of collective bargaining in which the reserve system was a central issue. It is apparent from those very findings that the NHLPA used every form of negotiating pressure it could muster. It developed an alternate reserve system and secured tentative agreement from the owner and player representatives, only to have the proposal rejected by the players. It refused to attend a proposed meeting with the owners to discuss the reserve system further. It threatened to strike. It threatened to commence an antitrust suit and to recommend that the players not attend training camp.

For its part, the NHL, while not budging in its insistence upon By-Law Section 9A, at least in the absence of any satisfactory counter proposal by the players, yielded significantly on other issues. It agreed, as a price of By-Law Section 9A, to the inclusion in the collective bargaining agreement of a provision that the entire agreement could be voided if the NHL and the World Hockey Association should merge. The undisputed reason for this provision was player concern that with a merger of the two leagues, the reserve system would be rendered too onerous, because the players would, by the merger, lose the competitive advantage of threatening to move to the WHA. Likewise, the NHL team owners obtained a provision voiding the entire agreement should the reserve system be invalidated by the courts.

The trial court, while acknowledging that the new collective bargaining agreement contained significant new benefits to the players, held that they were not "directly related to collective bargaining on By-law 9A." This observation and the trial court's conclusion that "the NHLPA never bargained for By-law 9A in the first instance" typifies its approach. It is true that the NHLPA did not "bargain for" By-Law Section 9A; it bargained "against" it, vigorously. That the trial judge concluded the benefits in the new contract were wrung from management by threat of an antitrust suit to void the By-Law merely demonstrates that the benefits were bargained for in connection with the reserve system, although he opined that the threat of a suit was a more effective bargaining tool than the threat of a strike. And while we agree with the trial judge that inclusion of language in the collective bargaining agreement that the reserve system provisions were "fair and reasonable" would not immunize it from antitrust attack, it is manifest from the entire facts found by the court that there was no collusion between management and the players association.

From the express findings of the trial court, fully supported by the record, it is apparent that the inclusion of the reserve system in the collective bargaining agreement was the product of good faith, arm's length bargaining, and that, what the trial court saw as a failure to negotiate, was in fact simply the failure to succeed, after the most intensive negotiations, in keeping an unwanted provision out of the contract. This failure was a part of and not apart from the collective bargaining process, a process which achieved its ultimate objective of an agreement accepted by the parties.

Injunction vacated.

EDWARDS, CHIEF JUDGE, dissenting.

I respectfully dissent. My basic disagreement with the majority opinion is planted on the proposition that if sports clubs organized for profit are to be exempted from the antitrust laws, this should be accomplished by statutory amendment, in accordance with the Constitution of the United States. Any such amendment would necessarily follow extensive hearings on the possible implications of the exemption, not only on organized sports, but also on the whole of the American economy, a process not available to the Judicial Branch.

The essence of the restriction on competition involved in this case is an agreement between all National Hockey League clubs not to hire any hockey player who has become a free agent (by refusing reemployment contract terms offered by his previous club) without undertaking to "equalize" the loss to his former club by agreed on or arbitrated transfer of players or cash.

The restriction, by its terms, is upon the NHL constituent clubs. Its impact, however, is clearly upon star hockey players. Clause 9A.6 obviously diminishes the hockey star's bargaining power, both with his previous employer and any prospective employer. It also may require any player who is transferred under the equalization clause to live in a city and play for a club against his professional (or private) best interests.

The legal question posed by this case is whether an association of employers may in the organized sports industry (here it is hockey) gain exemption from the antitrust laws for an agreement among themselves to restrict otherwise free competition in employment of hockey players by imposing their employer-devised agreement upon a union representing that class of employees through use of economic inducement or compulsion. Before we give judicial sanction to such a practice as consistent with the antitrust and labor-management laws of this country, we should take a long, hard look at the implications for sections of the national economy other than organized sports.

Superstars, whose services are at a high premium, can be found in many areas of industry and commerce other than the world of sports. Is there any distinction to be drawn between Clause 9A and similar restrictions in, for example, the field of dress manufacturing for the services of highly talented designers, or in the metalworking industries for the services of highly talented engineers, designers, or die shop leaders, or the entertainment field for highly talented personnel, or in the publishing field for highly talented writers?

Such a restriction on freedom of competition (and human freedom in choice of employment) in the interest of promotion or maintenance of business profits, has a distinctly predatory ring.

Appellants' defense of 9A is cast principally in public policy argument. It runs: Star players like McCourt produce the victories and championships for the club. They also attract the paying customers and generate profits. When star players are monopolized by one club, that club gains profits at the expense of all other clubs in the league. When the star players are distributed somewhat evenly throughout the league, team competition is enhanced and the well-being of the league as a whole is protected. The result is beneficial to the league and to the league's sports-minded public.

The point of this dissent is not to disagree with this public policy argument. Congress, which adopted the antitrust laws in the first instance, may choose to exempt nationally organized sports leagues from the antitrust laws by allowing carefully devised controls over player contracts designed to prevent league imbalance. My problem is that I cannot find any rationale for this court's devising such a policy which is 1) consistent with the antitrust statutes, or 2) which could be limited to the field of sports, or 3) which is supported by decisions on antitrust issues in the United States Supreme Court.

Until this case, I do not know of any instance where profit-making businesses have succeeded in justifying a cartel arrangement which suits their purposes by dint of securing that arrangement's introduction a collective bargaining agreement and thus acquiring the right of the "labor union exemption." The majority's approval of this arrangement in this case in fact stands the labor union exemption squarely on its head.

****

The labor history of the NHL has been similar to the other leagues. The NHL has had three labor stoppages, all between 1992 and 2005. The first was a strike by the players in 1992 that only lasted 10 days. The strike was followed by a lockout in 1994-95. As a result of the lockout the 84 game-season was reduced to 48 games. The next lockout of 2004, however, proved to be the most costly.

1990 LABOR PROBLEMS

Like other leagues, some teams in the NHL in the 1990s were suffering financially. The NHL's problems, however, were more pronounced than other leagues. In the mid-'90s the League had one franchise, the Pittsburgh Penguins, file for bankruptcy. Even more troubling were reports that at least half of the teams were losing money each year. One franchise declaring bankruptcy is embarrassing, but several clubs on the brink of insolvency could destroy the League.

As in the NBA, NHL management blamed the poor financial condition of teams on escalating player salaries. The blame-the-players approach is to be expected from management, but in the NHL there was evidence to back it up. The NHL was paying about 75% of League revenue to player salaries -- the highest percentage of all four major leagues. The owners in the NHL, like their counterparts in other leagues, are apparently unable to control their own salaries and must rely on restrictions in the CBA.

In 1998, the CBA in place was extended through 2004. The CBA prevented a strike or lockout, but the differences between management and the union was growing. As early as 1998 both sides began preparing for labor problems at the expiration of the CBA in 2004. Management reportedly had each team contribute $10 million to raise a "war chest" of $300 million in anticipation of a work stoppage. The union took similar action. As 2004 approached, labor negotiations became more contentious with little, if any, progress between the parties.

The union conceded that some adjustments were needed to address the revenue and cost problems but claimed that management was grossly exaggerating the League's losses. Each side put forth numerous proposals as to how the CBA should be changed to address the economic issues. One issue was the focal point -- management wanted "cost certainty," which the union derided as a euphemism for a "salary cap." The union was adamant that it would not accept a cap.

The players' recognition of a revenue problem was demonstrated when the union proposed an unprecedented one-time roll-back of 5% on players' salaries. The large gap between the parties was illustrated by management's counter-offer of a 24% roll-back.

2005 LOCK OUT

In September 2005, with no agreement in sight, management declared a lockout. Negotiations continued, but management's insistence on a salary cap initially appeared to be a deal-breaker. The union eventually relented and agreed to a cap of $52 million per team. Management countered with a proposed cap of $40 million. The union responded with an offer to accept a cap of $49 million and management countered with a cap of $42.5 million. Ultimately the gap could not be bridged and in February 2005 management officially canceled the remainder of the season. The cancellation was the first time a major sports league lost an entire season to a labor dispute. For the first time since 1919, when there was a flu epidemic, there would be no Stanley Cup Championship in the NHL.

The lockout lasted 310 days—the longest labor stoppage in professional sports in U.S. history. In July 2005, the parties reached an agreement on a new CBA. The new CBA features a salary cap, $39 million in the first year.

2005 COLLECTIVE
BARGAINING AGREEMENT

The term of the CBA is six years. The union has the option to extend the agreement for one year and may reopen the agreement following year 4 (2008-09). The new CBA has major changes to the economic system of the League. Total player cost of the 30 clubs cannot exceed 54% of League-wide revenue. The percentage is linked to future revenue and could rise to as much as 57% if League revenue exceeds $2.7 billion.

No club payroll for the 2005-06 season can be less than $21.5 million and no payroll can exceed $39 million including salaries and bonuses. Each player's current contract will include a substantial % reduction each year for the duration of the contract. The following are some other changes in the CBA.

Entry Level Salary: The entry-level salary limit is $850,000 for 2005-06 draftees and will rise to $925,000 by 2011.

Draft: The draft has been reduced from 9 rounds to 7.

Minimum Salary: The minimum salary has been increased from $185,000 to $450,000 in 2005-06 and will escalate to $500,000 in the final two years of the agreement.

Olympics: NHL players may participate in the Olympic winter games in 2006.

Renegotiations: Player contracts may not be renegotiated.

Two-Way Arbitration: Eligibility rules for players' salary arbitration were modified and clubs will now have the ability to elect salary arbitration for eligible players.

Drug Policy: The CBA includes a first time drug program with respect to performance-enhancing substances. Each player is subject to two "no notice" tests per year. A first positive test will result in a mandatory 20-game suspension without pay to the player. A second positive test will trigger a 60-game suspension. A third positive carries a permanent suspension penalty, but the player is eligible for reinstatement after two years.

Free Agency: Players in the NHL, like those in the other leagues, are classified into various categories. The classifications are referred to as a "Group" and are based on a number of factors, including age, years in the NHL, and, to some extent, years in professional hockey (other leagues). A player is placed in one of six Groups, Group I through Group VI, depending on his qualifications. The player's Group status determines his rights with respect to a number of issues, including free agency and compensation rights. The Group classification of the player is primarily established by the player's age and years in the League. The criteria for the Group classification of players is complex and lengthy. Parts of the system are as follows:

Rookies are generally placed in Group I and subject to the reserve system and compensation limits. The duration of the Group I status is based on the player's age at the time of his first contract. A player who signs his first contract at ages 18-21 remains a Group I player for three years; the period is two years if the player was 22-23 years of age when he signed his first contract and one year if he was 24. A player 25 and older is not subject to the entry level system and compensation limits.

Group II players are generally those who are no longer Group I players. Group II players become restricted free agents after the expiration of their Group II contract. Group III includes any player 31 years of age, who has four or more accrued seasons in the League, is a Group III player and qualifies for unrestricted free agency.

Group IV players are those who have never signed a Player Contract and who have met the conditions of a "defected player." A defected player refers to players who were under contract with other leagues. There are several ways a Group IV player can become a free agent.

Group V players include most players who have 10 years of professional experience, including in the minor leagues, provided the player has not previously elected to become an unrestricted free agent.

Group VI players are those who are 25 years of age and have completed 3 or more years of professional seasons. A Group VI player becomes a free agent at the expiration of his contract.

The following case illustrates the ongoing struggle between the players and the union with management over free agency status.

National Hockey League Players' Association and Aquino, Plaintiffs-Appellees, v. Plymouth Whalers Hockey Club et al., Defendants-Appellants. April, 2003

Plaintiff-appellee, National Hockey League Players' Association (NHLPA), brought this action alleging that the Ontario Hockey League (OHL) and all of its member teams conspired with the National Hockey League (NHL) to violate Section 1 of the Sherman Antitrust Act. NHLPA sought declaratory judgment and injunctive relief on behalf of the hockey players it represents. The district court issued a preliminary injunction. This court stayed the preliminary injunction. Defendants-appellants, OHL and its member teams, appeal the district court's grant of the preliminary injunction. For the reasons set forth below, we reverse the district court's grant of the preliminary injunction.

The NHLPA, an unincorporated labor association organized under the laws of Ontario, is the exclusive collective bargaining representative for all current and future NHL hockey players. The OHL is one of three amateur hockey leagues that comprise the Canadian Hockey League (CHL). The OHL consists of twenty teams whose players range in age from sixteen to twenty. While the vast majority of the OHL clubs are located within Ontario, Canada, two of the teams are located in Michigan, and one team is located in Pennsylvania. According to appellees, the OHL is a major source of players for the NHL, and various financial and other agreements exist between the two organizations.

The OHL eligibility rules provide that each team may have only three twenty-year-old players, typically referred to as "overage" players. In addition to limiting the number of overage players, the OHL adopted a rule in August of 2000 under which any overage player signed by an OHL team must have been on a Canadian Hockey Association (CHA) or USA Hockey Player's Registration Certificate the previous season. This rule, commonly referred to as the Van Ryn Rule (also referred to as "the Rule"), effectively prevents OHL teams from signing any twenty-year-old United States college hockey players because the National Collegiate Athletic Association (NCAA) does not allow individuals holding a CHA or USA Hockey Player's Registration Certificate to play hockey at an NCAA school.

Background on the Van Ryn Rule:. Mike Van Ryn is a former University of Michigan hockey player. Van Ryn was drafted by the New Jersey Devils, an NHL hockey team, while still a student at Michigan. In June 1998, the Devils acquired the exclusive rights to negotiate with and sign Van Ryn. Van Ryn played hockey for Michigan during the 1998-99 season. After that season, Van Ryn decided to explore his options to become a professional hockey player. Van Ryn took advantage of the OHL rule in effect at that time, which allowed clubs to sign overage players regardless of where they had played the previous season, and he signed with the Sarnia Sting. Pursuant to the Collective Bargaining Agreement (CBA) between the NHL and the NHLPA, if New Jersey did not sign Van Ryn by June 1, 2000, he would become a free agent. Therefore, by signing with the Sting, Van Ryn believed that he would become an unrestricted free agent, which would have allowed him to sign with any NHL team. New Jersey, however, declared that Van Ryn's decision to play for the Sting rendered him a "defected" player under the CBA, thereby preventing him from becoming an unrestricted free agent. The NHLPA filed a grievance on Van Ryn's behalf challenging New Jersey's position and the NHLPA prevailed. Van Ryn then signed with the St. Louis Blues, another NHL team, and received higher compensation than the Devils offered him. Shortly thereafter, the OHL teams agreed to the new Van Ryn Rule, effectively barring twenty-year-old United States college players from playing in the OHL.

Anthony Aquino (a plaintiff in this case) is a twenty-year-old hockey player who has been affected by the Van Ryn Rule. At age sixteen, Aquino, a Canadian citizen, was drafted by an OHL team, the Owen Sound Attack. Instead of playing for the Attack, Aquino chose to attend Merrimack College in Massachusetts. Aquino began playing hockey at Merrimack during the 1999-2000 season and played for three seasons. In June 2001, Aquino was drafted by the Dallas Stars, an NHL hockey team. During the 2001-02 season, the Attack traded its rights to Aquino to the Oshawa Generals, another OHL team. While attending Merrimack College, Aquino was placed on the Generals' "protected list," which prevented Aquino from negotiating or signing with any other team in the CHL.

Aquino decided against returning to Merrimack for a fourth season. After deciding not to return to Merrimack, Aquino believed that he had two options for working toward a career in the NHL. Aquino could attempt to sign with and play for the team that drafted him, the Stars. Signing with the Stars, however, would result in his becoming a restricted agent with that team for the next eleven years. In the alternative, Aquino could play in the CHL, most likely for the Generals, an OHL team, for one year as an overage player, which would allow him to become a free agent in 2003. The Van Ryn Rule, however, currently prevents Aquino from playing for the Generals.

After recognizing that the court must determine whether the Van Ryn Rule amounts to an unreasonable restraint of trade in violation of *Section 1* of *the Sherman Act* under either a *per se* analysis or a rule of reason analysis, the district court applied a *per se* analysis because it found that the Van Ryn Rule constitutes a group boycott.

Because nearly every contract that binds parties to an agreed course of conduct "is a restraint of trade" of some sort, the Supreme Court has limited the restrictions contained in *Section 1* to bar only "unreasonable restraints of trade." In order to establish their antitrust claim, appellees must prove that appellants (1) participated in an agreement that (2) unreasonably restrained trade in the relevant market. The district court found, and the parties do not contest, that appellants have entered into an agreement via their adoption of the Van Ryn Rule. Appellants, however, contest the district court's finding that the Van Ryn Rule is an unreasonable restraint of trade.

The Supreme Court has stated that the *per se* rule is a "demanding" standard that should be applied only in clear cut cases. Therefore, "courts consistently have analyzed challenged conduct under the rule of reason when dealing with an industry in which some horizontal restraints are necessary for the availability of a product" such as sports leagues. Moreover, the Supreme Court has recognized that in cases involving industries "in which horizontal restraints on competition are essential if the product is to be available at all," the rule of reason analysis should apply.

Under the rule of reason appellees have the initial burden of demonstrating significant anticompetitive effects within the relevant product and geographic markets. The term 'relevant market' encompasses notions of geography as well as product use, quality, and description.

While appellees have established that the Van Ryn Rule might result in significant personal injury to Aquino, appellees have failed to present evidence of an injury to a definable market. The antitrust laws were enacted for "the protection of *competition,* not *competitors.*" Therefore, appellees have failed to establish that the Van Ryn Rule has a significant anticompetitive effect on a relevant market. For all the reasons set forth above, we reverse the district court's grant of a preliminary injunction and remand for further proceedings consistent with this opinion.

****

Professional Franchises

The previous chapters on the professional leagues focused on the relationship between owners and players in the leagues. This chapter will focus on non-player issues in the professional leagues, including conflicts between and among the owners and the leagues. A brief description of other professional leagues is also provided.

SPORTS FACILITIES

For years, owners of professional franchises gave little thought to the facility available to them in their host city. In the latter part of the 1980s, however, a major shift in thinking developed on this issue, especially in the NFL and MLB. Owners began demanding state-of-the-art facilities, and for the most part their demands have been met. Since 1986 there has been an unprecedented construction boom in professional sports facilities throughout the United States. Over seventy percent (70%) of the four major league teams now play in stadiums or arenas that have been built or had major renovations since the late 1980s. And the stadium boom is far from over—nearly half of the nation's professional sports teams are playing in or awaiting the completion of new stadiums or arenas. Billions of dollars of projects are currently under construction or in the planning stages. The use of public funds for these facilities has been hotly debated in communities across the country and in Congress.

FRANCHISE FREE AGENCY

The relationship between a professional franchise and its host community is often viewed, at least by fans, as a marriage that is expected to last forever. Communities generally have great pride in their teams. Franchises in turn make a considerable effort to bond with their fans. Like some marriages, however, despite the best intentions, the relationship between the team and community may not last.

Franchise stability has been maintained for the most part in Major League Baseball. The Montreal Expos were recently relocated to Washington, D.C., and became the Nationals. Before that move the last franchise relocation in baseball was in 1972, when the Washington Senators moved to Texas and became the Rangers. In order to move a franchise, an owner must receive permission from the League, which is obtained by a vote of the other owners. An inability to obtain approval and the lack of an antitrust claim regarding the rules has stymied relocations in baseball.

The NBA has experienced some team relocations, but the number and consequences have been minimal. However, new owner Clay Bennett's recent attempt to relocate the Seattle Supersonics to Oklahoma City could alter this trend. Franchise movement in the NHL has been more disruptive. Four teams have changed their locations in the past several years. Interestingly, the migration has been from Canada to the United States.

The NFL has received the greatest impact from franchise movement. From 1970 through 1990, several teams in the NFL moved to other venues. The relocations usually caused an uproar in the community losing the franchise, but the overall situation was manageable until the 1990s. In the early 1990s an epidemic of actual and threatened franchise relocations erupted. The rash of relocations was an assault on the stability of the League, and the problem became so paramount that a phrase was coined to describe the trend—"franchise free agency."

In 1995, three NFL teams relocated over the objections of the League. The Los Angeles Rams went to St. Louis, the restless Los Angeles Raiders migrated back to Oakland, and the Cleveland Browns moved to Baltimore. In the same year the Houston Oilers announced they would move to Tennessee for the following season and several more teams were discussing -- or outright threatening -- to relocate unless their host cities constructed new stadiums or made improvements to the existing facilities. NFL franchises had previously relocated without League approval, but never before had the number and nature of the moves been so disruptive to the League.

The Cleveland Browns' move to Baltimore created the greatest reaction. Unlike most relocating teams, which are motivated in part by low attendance at games, the Cleveland Browns consistently had sell-out crowds. The Cleveland fans were as loyal (some might say rabid) as any in the League. The Cleveland move sent shock waves throughout the League and to every host city. If it could happen to Cleveland, it could occur to any city.

Numerous lawsuits were filed to prevent the Browns' relocation. The Browns' move caused such an uproar that the NFL intervened and brokered a settlement among the parties. The settlement included an unprecedented commitment by the League to place another franchise in Cleveland by 1999 and a loan from the NFL to assist Cleveland in building a new stadium facility. The agreement also provided that Cleveland would retain the right to the "Browns" name and the team colors.

What has caused franchises with longstanding ties to their communities to suddenly uproot and abandon their devoted fans for unfamiliar locations? Why is it that Los Angeles, the second largest market in this country, has not had an NFL franchise for years? To answer these questions it is necessary to review the legal and economic forces at work.

LEGAL ISSUES

In the 1980s, the Los Angeles Coliseum was without a professional franchise tenant. The Coliseum made an offer to Al Davis, owner of the then Oakland Raiders, to lease the facility to the Raiders. Davis liked the proposal and, as required by League rules, applied for permission to relocate. The other team owners, however, would not approve Davis' request. The Coliseum and the Raiders sued the NFL and the other owners. The suit alleged that the NFL's relocation rules were a violation of antitrust law. After years of litigation, the court ruled in favor of the Coliseum and the Raiders. The Raiders were allowed to move and the League had to pay millions of dollars in damages and legal fees.

Within a month after the *Raiders* decision, the owner of the Baltimore Colts packed up his team (in the middle of the night) and moved to Indianapolis. The Colts did not even seek the League's permission. The decision in the *Raiders* case made it clear that restrictions on relocations could be enforceable if written properly. The NFL changed the rules accordingly after the *Raiders* decision. The League made no effort, however, to challenge the Colts' move. Even though every NFL owner had agreed to be bound by the League's rules, the prevailing attitude after the *Raiders* case was that franchise owners could relocate at their own discretion.

ECONOMIC FACTORS

The *Raiders* decision explains how teams are able to legally move despite the contrary wishes of the League. The *Raiders* case does not, however, provide the motive for team relocations. Why do teams relocate? For the same reason that drives most other business decision -- MONEY.

In 1961 the NFL adopted a new business approach. In previous years, each team was on its own to negotiate television contracts. No single contract would be negotiated by the League on behalf of all teams. Furthermore, all television revenue would be shared equally by each team. Gate receipts would be divided so that the home team would retain 60% and the visitor 40% after a standard 15% deduction by the home team for maintenance. The concept was intended to increase television revenue and to provide financial parity among the teams. The strategy was an enormous success. Television revenues increased dramatically and small market teams, like the Green Bay Packers, were able to compete financially for top players. As of 2002, the visiting teams' share of gate receipts for pre-season and regular season games were pooled and shared equally among all teams.

In the last decade, however, revenue problems began to develop. Income from parking, concessions, some club seats and luxury boxes are not shared. Some franchise owners have favorable stadium leases which provide them with substantial revenue from these non-shared sources. The number and quality of luxury boxes, which can provide enormous revenue, varies considerably among NFL stadiums. In addition, a few franchises, like the Dallas Cowboys, own their stadium facility. Texas Stadium, the home of the Cowboys, has 280 luxury suites and generates millions in unshared revenue for the Cowboy franchise each year. Some skyboxes rent for as much as $350,000 per year and are leased for ten year terms. The Washington Redskins have 208 "executive suites" that will generate about $15 million per year and total stadium revenue is in the range of $52 million. Washington's stadium revenue is several times larger than the amount earned by many other teams. This inequality carries on to the playing field, as the teams with the best stadiums are in a better position financially to acquire the best players or coaches.

ACQUIRING A FRANCHISE — THE STADIUM GAME

Franchise owners who are on the low end of the non-shared revenue curve argue they must consider relocating to more profitable facilities to stay competitive. Adding to the problem is the fact that there are a number of communities without franchises that are determined to achieve professional league status. These communities do whatever they can to induce unhappy franchises to their cities. The inducements include building state-of-the-art facilities and offering generous lease terms. The competition to keep or acquire professional franchises is a major factor in the construction boom for stadiums and arenas.

A professional franchise is viewed as a tremendous source of pride for most communities. The conventional wisdom has been that a professional team provides a considerable economic benefit to the area. Cleveland was prepared to argue in court, in its attempt to keep the Browns franchise, that the team contributed to the economic welfare of the Cleveland area and that it provided intangible benefits such as an increased sense of community pride. Practically every major city that does not have a professional franchise has made attempts to obtain a team.

One method of obtaining a franchise is to have the league grant an expansion team to the city. A few years ago two new franchises, Jacksonville and Carolina, had to each pay $140 million to enter the League. The new teams were, however, only allowed to receive half of the allotted television revenues for the first three years, which amounts to another $70 million in costs. New franchises today are expected to cost around $500 million. These astonishing values are directly attributable to the limited number of NFL franchises, a simple case of supply and demand. NFL franchises, despite their enormous values, will always be very difficult to obtain. Granting a franchise is a business, not sports, decision.

Some franchises are granted without this traditional business evaluation. For many years New Orleans tried unsuccessfully to obtain an NFL franchise. During this period Louisiana had two of the most powerful men in Congress, Senator Russell Long and Representative Hale Boggs. At the time Congress was looking into the NFL to determine if its operations constituted a violation of antitrust law. Congress eventually dropped the investigation and, by coincidence, New Orleans obtained an NFL franchise. Absent these unusual circumstances, it takes an enormous amount of lobbying, patience and financial strength to convince the NFL to grant a new franchise to a community.

The more common method used by cities to obtain a franchise is to lure an existing team away from its location. The offer from the new city generally includes a promise to provide a new or recently refurbished stadium with favorable lease terms. The bidding by the new city to attract the franchise generally forces the existing host city to make offers to keep the team at home. The franchise has the enviable bargaining position to play each bidder against the other to "sweeten the pot." Even if the franchise does not really intend to move, it can use the interest from other communities to obtain concessions from its host city. The threat of relocation has become a common practice by franchise owners.

Public officials are often reluctant to spend enormous sums on facilities that are viewed by many as playgrounds for wealthy owners and players. The same officials, however, do not want to be blamed for letting their beloved team leave the community. Local and state governing bodies have had to increasingly struggle with this dilemma. One suggested idea to counter this situation is to require each league to be divided into two separate competing leagues. This change would help reverse the bargaining power of the communities and force the franchises to compete against each other for the use of public facilities.

Some communities are so determined to acquire a professional franchise that they have built expensive stadiums with nothing but the hope that they could attract a professional team. Tampa built a baseball stadium that was empty for years. The Tampa stadium was, however, ideal relocation leverage for baseball teams seeking to extract concessions from their host community. St. Louis built a football stadium even though it did not have an NFL team. The attitude of communities who feel they must have a professional franchise, no matter what the cost, is, "if we build it, they will come." The high stakes gamble paid off for St. Louis and Tampa. Tampa was eventually able to acquire a new MLB franchise and St. Louis attracted an existing NFL team.

The St. Louis acquisition is telling. St. Louis, which lost an NFL franchise years ago to Phoenix, made the Rams, who were in Los Angeles, an offer the Rams "could not refuse." The city, county and State of Missouri incurred about $262 million in debt to build the Rams the 70,000-seat Trans World Dome. (The cost will amount to about $700 million with interest). The Rams were given $20 million for relocation costs and the use of a $10 million practice facility. The (St. Louis) Rams have a 30-year stadium lease with annual rent of just $250,000, the fifth-lowest rate in the NFL. The Rams will receive 100% of the revenues from the stadium's 100 luxury suites, 6,250 club seats and concessions. The team gets $4.5 million of the first $6 million in stadium advertising and the $1.3 million a year paid by Trans World for stadium naming rights.

At the time of the Rams' move, the NFL rules required a vote of 23 of the 30 owners. The initial request for approval by the Rams to relocate to St. Louis was rejected. The League was then put on notice, however, that antitrust actions would be filed by the Rams *and* the Attorney General of Missouri for damages in excess of $1 billion. The owners reconsidered and granted the Rams' request to move to St. Louis.

After the St. Louis deal with the Rams was finalized, a consultant involved in the process was reported to have stated, "this will be the best stadium deal ever in the NFL, except for the next one." The prophesy appears to be correct. Financial packages even greater than that offered by St. Louis have been given to the Baltimore Ravens and the Seattle Seahawks. The new Cleveland franchise has a stadium deal that will make the franchise one of the most valued in professional sports. The Baltimore Ravens' stadium cost $200 million and was built with mostly public funds. The team pays no rent, but does pay operating and maintenance costs of about $3.5 million per year and is responsible for a 10% city admissions tax. The Ravens share of Personal Seat Licenses, however, is close to $70 million. The team keeps all the revenue from luxury boxes, premium seats, concessions and advertising in the stadium. The Ravens even receive 50% of all revenue produced at the stadium from non-football events. These incredibly favorable lease terms are now the standard in the industry.

EFFORTS TO RESTRICT RELOCATION

The relocation frenzy has been a two-edged sword for the NFL. Relocations, or the threat of moving, has produced a huge windfall for the League. The teams get new facilities with lavish suites that produce substantial revenues. The teams pay little or no construction costs or rental payments.

Relocation does, however, come at a cost. One obvious downside is the bad feelings and publicity in the abandoned community. A more significant financial consideration, however, occurs when a team leaves a large television market to enter a smaller one. The bulk of the NFL's revenue comes from its contracts with the television networks. Los Angeles is the second largest television market in the country, but has not had an NFL team for the past several years. The Rams left the Los Angeles market for the lucrative stadium deal in St. Louis. The League is currently negotiating a new franchise for Los Angeles, no doubt with some urging from the networks.

The NFL's recognition of the problem of teams going to smaller television markets for stadium deals was apparent in negotiations with the New England Patriots. For years the Patriots attempted to get public funds from the Massachusetts legislature to improve its facilities, but without success. The state of Connecticut saw an opportunity to gain an NFL franchise and made the team a very appealing stadium proposal. The team's owner tentatively accepted Connecticut's offer. The move would have taken the NFL team from a television market ranked sixth (6th) in the country to one that was not even in the top twenty five (25). The NFL stepped in and provided financial assistance to insure that New England would get the improvements it had been seeking. Connecticut was left waiting at the altar.

The relocations have disrupted communities and alienated fans – fans who also happen to be voters. As a result, the problem drew the attention of Congress. A number of bills have been introduced in Congress to restrict the ability of a professional franchise to relocate. One bill was entitled, "Give Fans a Chance Act of 1997." The law, if passed, would have required a team to give a community an advance notice of at least 180 days before relocation. During this period a local government could try to find a new buyer for the team who would keep the team in its present location. The franchise would have to consider the new offer. In addition, the league would be required to hold a hearing as to the need for relocating. The public would be entitled to speak at the hearing. The bill would also require the league to require that certain criteria be met before the team is allowed to move. Congress also considered granting the NFL an antitrust exemption in order to strengthen the League's ability to enforce relocation rules. The laws did not pass, but may have put pressure on the League to curtail the relocations. The host communities have also gotten wiser. Many of the leases on the new stadiums have provisions that require the franchise to pay substantial damages if the team vacates the stadium before the expiration of the lease.

TEAM CONTRACTION

Although Major League Baseball has not experienced the same relocation problem as the NFL (largely because of the antitrust exemption), the League did encounter a strong public backlash when it announced that contraction, or elimination, of some teams was being considered. One of the teams on the hit list was the Minnesota Twins. Immediately after the League's announcement was made public the Metropolitan Sports Facility Commission filed suit against the Twins and MLB. The suit sought to enforce the Twins' lease agreement and to prohibit MLB from interfering with the contract between the Twins and the Metrodome, the Twins' home field. The court ruled that the Twins had to honor the lease and play their home games in 2002 at the Metrodome.

The reasoning of the court in the Twins case is significant. In a typical commercial lease dispute a court awards monetary damages. But the court went to great lengths to explain that professional baseball was different from a private enterprise in that it involved a public interest. The court found that the welfare, prestige and commerce of the people of Minnesota would suffer irreparable harm if the Twins did not play their home games as scheduled. The fact that the lease did not require the Twins to pay rent supported the court's position that the agreement was not a typical commercial lease.

A similar decision recognizing the "public interest" of professional sports was reached in separate cases involving the New York Jets and the New York Yankees where the teams were ordered to play their home games at a certain stadium.

STADIUM FINANCING

Modern sports facilities and favorable rights with respect to the use and revenue derived from them have become the key factor for franchise owners to gain a financial advantage over their competitors. Where do the funds come from to pay for these facilities?

Historically, when a city had both professional football and baseball teams, one stadium served both teams. A multipurpose facility is no longer acceptable to most franchises. Each franchise now wants a stadium designed for its particular sport and expects to be the primary tenant.

A "state of the art" stadium for a professional football or baseball franchise can cost in the $300 million range. In general, owners cannot, or will not, provide the costs for construction. Unless the facility is shared by a professional baseball team, the utilization of a football stadium is about 12 games per year, which limits opportunities to generate revenue from the facility.

Traditionally, the money to construct arenas and stadiums has come from public funds, usually in the form of tax-free bonds issued by the local governmental body. The city or county issues bonds that pay a relatively low rate of interest. The bonds are attractive to investors, however, because the interest earned on municipal bonds is tax free. The bond obligations are paid with public funds.

There are, however, market limits on the amount of bonds that a city can issue and to the taxes it collects to pay the bonds. Opponents of publicly-financed stadiums (and there are many) argue that bond money should be used for traditional, and more important, government projects, such as roads, schools, police protection and other priorities.

Franchise owners usually get considerable control over the stadium and keep the revenue generated from tickets, parking, and concessions. Some studies suggest that cities get very little economic return on the huge investment made on sports facilities. The players, with their high salaries, do not necessarily live on a permanent basis in the city. Most of the jobs created by a franchise are part-time or seasonal and provide only entry-level pay. There is evidence that the money generated from a franchise is, for the most part, simply money shifted from another sector of the local economy. That is, the ticket and concession money generated from the games are the same funds that would have been spent on movies and clothes without the stadium. Historically, few disputed that hosting a Super Bowl provided an enormous economic boost for the fortunate community. Recent studies, however, indicate that many locales, particularly places with vibrant tourism in February (when the Super Bowl is played) such as Miami, may reap little to no benefit from the event. Money given to hotels does not remain in the local area but instead usually flows to the headquarters of national or international hotel chains. And if people tend to visit a destination during the winter in most years, the Super Bowl may only yield different and not necessarily additional patrons. Finally, cities often expend large sums of money in preparation for the Super Bowl.

There are studies which reflect that federal taxpayers subsidize millions of dollars in financing stadiums and get little or no benefit. Since 1990, billions of public dollars have been used to construct or refurbish sports facilities. Some congressmen have described tax-free bond financing for stadiums as a housing program for multi-millionaire owners and players. A bill was introduced in Congress, the Stop Tax-Exempt Arena Debt Issuance Act of 1996, to prevent tax-exempt financing of professional sports facilities. The bill did not pass.

Throughout the country, voters are being asked to approve new taxes that will be used for the renovation or construction of professional athletic facilities. The campaigns for and against the stadium proposals have been heated and the results mixed. Cincinnati approved a plan to fund construction of new facilities. Pittsburgh voters initially rejected stadium taxes, but later approved modified proposals. Houston approved a plan to build a new baseball stadium, but refused to accept a demand by the NFL's Oilers for a new taxpayer-financed stadium. Houston's rejection resulted in the loss of the Oilers franchise. A few years later Houston agreed to build a new facility to acquire a new NFL franchise, the Texans. In 1997 San Francisco voters narrowly approved a tax for stadium renovations which were viewed necessary to keep the NFL's 49ers in the city. Seattle residents rejected a tax in 1996, by 1,000 votes out of 500,000, to build a new stadium for MLB's Seattle Mariners. A later measure was, however, approved by the legislature for two stadiums, one for the Mariners and one for the NFL's Seahawks. Illinois agreed to contribute $432 million in cost to upgrade Soldier Field, the home of the NFL's Chicago Bears.

Some states have drawn the line and refuse to commit tax dollars to professional facilities. Minnesota voters have refused to approve tax proposals for new stadiums. San Francisco voters rejected a tax proposal in 1996 that was to be used to replace Candlestick Park despite threats that the MLB's Giants would leave San Francisco if the vote failed. In December 2001 the New York Mayor announced a plan to spend $800 million of tax dollars to build two stadiums with retractable roofs for the New York Yankees and the New York Mets. A new administration later put a stop to the plans.

A few franchises have demonstrated that new facilities can be built without public money. MLB's San Francisco Giants built a new stadium with private financing. The stadium cost of over $300 million was offset somewhat by a naming rights deal with PAC Bell, charter seat sales and corporate sponsorships. The NFL's New England Patriots and the Washington Redskins have also built their new venues with private funding.

ALTERNATIVE FINANCING SOURCES

As opposition to the use of public funds for professional facilities mounts, alternative sources of financing are being sought. A device to raise part of the funds for stadium construction or improvements is the Private Seat License (PSL). Although they are not called PSLs, choice seats to football or basketball games at many universities cannot be obtained unless the purchaser makes a generous contribution to the athletic department. The PSL is simply a charge for the "right" to buy season tickets. PSLs have received a lot of criticism, but they were essential in putting Charlotte on the professional sports map. Charlotte raised almost $150 million for Ericsson Stadium through the sale of PSLs. PSLs were also a critical part of the financial packages offered by St. Louis and Oakland to construct or improve stadium facilities. St. Louis sold 46,000 PSLs at prices ranging from $250 to $4,000 each and raised $70 million to help pay for the Rams move. Cleveland also used PSLs to obtains funds for the new stadium.

Another possible source of funding for the construction of the expensive facilities needed for professional sports is the corporate sector. Large companies have the financial strength to provide the revenue needed for the construction of a multi-million dollar facility. These companies are also in a position to benefit from such an investment. Business entities are well aware of the enormous marketing benefits associated with sports. In addition to their traditional advertisements, companies are now routinely serving as the sponsors of sporting events. Corporate sponsorship of tennis and golf tournaments and college football bowl games are as common as half-time and time outs during games.

A recent trend is to have a sports facility named in association with a corporate sponsor. The sale of naming rights has become a hot and valuable commodity. Corporations are paying millions for the privilege of having their name on a facility. Almost one-third of the professional stadiums and arenas in the U.S. now have corporate names. More are sure to come.

A largely untapped source of funds for stadium construction is public stock offerings. A few professional teams have sold shares publicly, but the offerings were to finance the team's operations, not to build a facility. With the exception of the Green Bay Packers, the NFL does not allow public ownership of a franchise. The Packers have a unique ownership structure. The team is actually a non-profit corporation publicly owned by about 1,898 shareholders and managed by a 45-member unpaid board of directors. The owners receive no dividends and the team shares are worth exactly the same value as when they were issued 46 years ago. MLB recently changed its rules to allow publicly held corporations to own a minority interest in a team. The Cleveland Indians wasted no time in offering stock in the team. The stock brought in an estimated $64 million. The sale was structured, however, so that the owner's control of the team was not diluted. Public ownership of professional franchises will probably increase over the next decade. The need for funds to construct facilities will be a factor in the trend.

FRANCHISE OWNERSHIP

Trying to purchase a professional franchise can be a very contentious and frustrating endeavor. The acquisition is not simply a function of having a willing seller and sufficient funds for the purchase of the team. Frank Morsani's attempt to acquire a Major League Baseball team illustrates the difficulties.

In 1984 Frank Morsani and a group of Tampa investors reached an agreement to purchase 51% of the stock of a Major League Baseball team, the Minnesota Twins, from owners Griffith and Haynes for $24 million. A condition of the agreement was that Morsani first purchase the 42.14% interest in the team held by Murphy. Morsani reached an agreement to purchase Murphy's interest for $11.5 million. The sale was also conditioned on approval by Major League owners as provided in League rules. Apparently several team owners, who would later become defendants in Morsani's lawsuit, maneuvered to have Griffith and Haynes sell their interest to Pohlad, who became the owner of the Twins. The same owners urged Morsani to cooperate with Pohlad's attempt to acquire the remaining interest in the Twins. Morsani initially refused, but was told neither he nor the Tampa area would ever acquire a Major League team if he failed to comply with the request. Morsani capitulated in exchange for "the promise of another team" in the future.

Four years later Morsani and his group reached an agreement to purchase the controlling interest in the Texas Rangers and to move them to Florida. Morsani alleged the same persons again prevented the sale. Morsani withheld filing a legal action on the promise that his group would have a team by 1993. Later, a Major League team was given to Florida, but the franchise went to Wayne Huizenga, not Morsani. Finally, another franchise was awarded, the Tampa Bay Devil Rays, which began playing in 1998. Unfortunately, the Devil Rays franchise was also not awarded to Morsani. Morsani filed suit, *Morsani v. Major League*, (1995), asserting a *state* antitrust violation and a tortious interference-with-contract theory. The trial court dismissed both actions. The appellate court reversed the trial court on both claims and ruled that Morsani was entitled to a trial.

Morsani v. Major League Baseball (1995)

The complaint alleges that in 1982, Morsani attended the major league baseball winter meetings, expressed his desire to purchase a major league baseball team and sought advice from various defendants concerning the team's purchase and relocation to the Tampa Bay area. Upon the defendants' advice, TBBG was formed. Various defendants told the plaintiffs that they would support and approve the sale of the Minnesota Twins, Inc., to them if they would secure a site to build a major league baseball stadium in the Tampa Bay area. At an expense in excess of $2 million, the plaintiffs secured a long-term lease with the Tampa Sports Authority for the construction of a baseball stadium and entered into negotiations with the shareholders of Minnesota Twins, Inc., for the purchase of their stock.

In 1984, the owners of 51% of the stock of Minnesota Twins, Inc., Calvin Griffith and Thelma Griffith-Haynes, agreed to sell their controlling interest to the plaintiffs for approximately $24 million on condition that they first buy H. Gabriel Murphy's 42.14% minority interest in the corporation. The plaintiffs then negotiated and entered into a fully-executed written contract with Murphy for the purchase of his interest, at a purchase price of $11.5 million. The contract provided that its closing was conditioned upon prior approval by the owners of other American League teams, as the Constitution of the American League required, and any other approvals which might validly be required. Thereafter, with full knowledge of these agreements, various defendants conspired together and used improper means to prevent the plaintiffs from consummating their purchase. They caused Griffith and Griffith-Haynes to sell their 51% interest to Carl Pohlad. They also demanded that the plaintiffs assign their contract with Murphy to Pohlad, and that Murphy consent to the assignment. At the time this assignment was demanded, the value of the minority interest purchased by the plaintiffs had increased from $11.5 million to $25 million.

The plaintiffs balked at the demand and sought payment for the $13.5 million increase in value of the contract, as well as reimbursement of the $2 million previously expended, as a condition to assigning the contract to Pohlad. The relevant defendants then threatened the plaintiffs. These threats were that plaintiffs would never own an interest in a major league baseball team, and that there would never be a major league baseball team in the Tampa Bay area, unless the plaintiffs assigned the contract as demanded and accepted only $250,000.00 for the assignment, and, further, that they agree to forbear pursuing any legal remedies for the additional $15 million plus in damages in exchange for obtaining an ownership interest in another major league baseball team in time to begin the 1993 season. In exchange for the promise of another team, the plaintiffs assigned their contract to Pohlad.

The complaint also alleged that in 1988, several defendants informed the plaintiffs that they would support and approve the sale of the Texas Rangers, Ltd. to the plaintiffs. The plaintiffs then reached an agreement with Eddie Gaylord for the purchase of his 33% interest in the partnership, and entered into a written contract with Eddie Chiles for the purchase of his 58% controlling interest in the partnership. Thereafter, with full knowledge of these agreements, various defendants conspired together and used improper means to prevent the plaintiffs from consummating their purchase. They caused both Gaylord and Chiles to breach their agreements with the plaintiffs in favor of a Texas investor. They then, again, threatened the plaintiffs that they would never own an interest in a major league baseball team, and that there would never be a major league baseball team in the Tampa Bay area, unless the plaintiffs agreed to forbear pursuing any legal remedies in exchange for obtaining an ownership interest in another major league baseball team in time to begin the 1993 season. In exchange for the renewed and continuing promise of another team, the plaintiffs once again withheld their claims.

Some of the defendants informed the plaintiffs in 1988 that, consistent with the prior promises made to obtain their forbearance, the plaintiffs would be awarded an expansion team in time to begin the 1993 season. Thereafter, various defendants conspired together and used improper means to prevent the plaintiffs from obtaining the promised team. In 1989, they interfered with the plaintiffs' advantageous business relationships by demanding that one of the investors in TBBG relinquish his interest as a condition of obtaining the team, and thereby reduced the corporation's financial viability. The defendants then prohibited the plaintiffs from obtaining any additional financial backing from persons or entities not located in the Tampa Bay area, including Sam Walton. These interferences reduced the financial viability of the plaintiffs well below that of a competitor group led by H. Wayne Huizenga, and effectively eliminated the plaintiffs from contention for the promised expansion team which began the 1993 season as The Florida Marlins in Miami.

To establish the tort of interference with a contractual or business relationship, the plaintiff must allege and prove (1) the existence of a business relationship under which the plaintiff has legal rights, (2) an intentional and unjustified interference with that relationship by the defendant and (3) damage to the plaintiff as a result of the breach of the business relationship.

[I]t is clear that the privilege to interfere in a contract because of a financial interest is not unlimited. The better view is that it is necessary for the interfering party to have a financial interest in the business of the third party which is in the nature of an investment in order to justify the interference. ... Furthermore, a privilege to interfere with a third party's conduct does not include the purposeful causing of a breach of contract.

Where there is a qualified privilege to interfere with a business relationship, the privilege carries with it the obligation to employ means that are not improper. We conclude, therefore, that Counts I, II and III state a cause of action for tortious interference with advantageous contractual and business relationships and reverse their dismissal.

Turning to the antitrust claim, the defendants, relying on the United States Supreme Court decisions supporting baseball's exemption from antitrust laws, argued that these cases exempt from the antitrust laws the entire business of baseball. The trial judge thoroughly reviewed those cases and a more recent case pertinent to the antitrust cause of action, *Piazza v. Major League Baseball*. In *Piazza*, Judge Padova concluded that the precedential value of the trilogy of Supreme Court decisions regarding baseball's exemption is limited to the reserve system. Although the trial judge here found Judge Padova's decision well-reasoned, he ultimately concluded that he was bound by the decision in *Butterworth v. National League* of Professional Baseball Clubs which granted a petition to set aside the state's civil investigative demands pursuant to state antitrust law. On appeal, the Florida Supreme Court answered in the negative the following question: Does the antitrust exemption for baseball recognized by the United States Supreme Court in Federal Base Ball Club of Baltimore ... and its progeny exempt all decisions involving the sale and location of baseball franchises from federal and Florida antitrust law?

The trial judge below did not have the benefit of the Florida Supreme Court's decision which reversed the appellate court and held that federal and state antitrust laws applied to decisions involving sales and locations of baseball franchises, and that the antitrust exemption for baseball extended only to the reserve system.

****

Piazza v. Major League Baseball (1993) involved an unsuccessful attempt by investors to purchase the San Francisco Giants and relocate the team to St. Petersburg, Florida. When the effort failed the investors sued claiming defamation and antitrust violations. The trial court analyzed the history of baseball's antitrust exemption and concluded it was limited to the reserve clause. The case settled and was therefore never reviewed by an appellate court.

Major League Baseball v. Crist (2001) was the product of MLB's attempt to eliminate one or more teams from the league that were viewed as unprofitable. One of the Florida teams was a prime target for elimination. In an attempt to stop the action, Florida's Attorney General (AG) started an investigation to determine if MLB was violating antitrust law. MLB filed suit in Florida and asserted the antitrust exemption to prevent the investigation. The trial court agreed with MLB and enjoined the AG's action. Florida appealed the decision. The appellate court expressed some misgivings about the antitrust exemption, but deferred to the previous Supreme Court decisions and affirmed the trial court.

In 1994, the owners of the NBA's Minnesota Timberwolves, Minnesota Professional Basketball Limited Partnership (MPBLP), signed an agreement to sell the Timberwolves to Top Rank of Louisiana, Inc. The agreement provided for the relocation of the franchise to New Orleans. The attempt to sell the team produced immediate suits and countersuits by the various parties.

The agreement to sell was executed on June 5. On June 15, the NBA filed suit in federal court against MPBLP to prevent the sale and relocation. The NBA argued that the complex process of schedules for the '94-'95 season was almost complete and that the relocation would cause scheduling problems and irreparable damages. Other concerns may have motivated the NBA to block the sale, but the scheduling problem was a good issue to raise with respect to a possible antitrust challenge. The next day, the federal court granted the NBA a temporary injunction preventing the sale and relocation until the NBA's hearing on a preliminary injunction could be heard.

On June 21, MPBLP filed a cross-claim against Top Rank, again in federal court, seeking damages from Top Rank for its failure to secure NBA approval and its failure to complete the transaction. On June 24, Top Rank filed suit against MPBLP for breach of contract and against the NBA for contract interference. This suit was filed in a Louisiana state court. On June 28, the Louisiana state court issued a temporary restraining order preventing the NBA and its teams from finalizing the '94-'95 schedule.

On July 1, the federal court granted the NBA a preliminary injunction prohibiting MPBLP from selling or relocating the franchise. The federal court also issued an order enjoining the Louisiana court from conducting further proceedings in the suit. On July 14, the Louisiana court, relying on the federal Anti-Injunction Act (28 USC 2283) issued its own injunction to prevent the NBA from finalizing its schedule. On July 19, the federal court issued an injunction against the Louisiana court and ordered that the Louisiana court not issue any other orders in the case. Top Rank appealed the July 1 and July 19 orders of the federal court, but both decisions were upheld on appeal.

NBA V. MINNESOTA
TIMBERWOLVES (1994)

In these consolidated appeals, Top Rank of Louisiana, Inc. (Top Rank) challenges two district court orders granting preliminary injunctive relief to the National Basketball Association (NBA) in Top Rank's legal dispute with the Minnesota Professional Basketball Limited Partnership (MPBLP) and NBA over ownership and relocation of the Minnesota Timberwolves professional basketball team (Timberwolves). Essentially, the challenged orders keep the Timberwolves in Minnesota for the 1994-95 NBA season, relieve the NBA from enforcement of a state court preliminary injunction barring the season, stay proceedings in state court litigation brought by Top Rank against the MPBLP and NBA, and prohibit the federal court parties from participating in the state court litigation. We affirm in part, reverse in part, and remand for further proceedings.

In March 1994, the NBA began the lengthy process of scheduling the 1994-95 NBA season. The NBA needed to finalize the schedule by mid-July so the NBA's member teams could publicize playing dates, sell tickets, arrange radio and television contracts, make travel arrangements, and finish the many other necessary season preparations. On June 5, 1994, over two months into the scheduling process, the MPBLP, owner of the Timberwolves, signed an agreement to sell the Timberwolves to Top Rank. The agreement provided that Top Rank would relocate the team from Minnesota to New Orleans, Louisiana. Because the MPBLP and Timberwolves were members of the NBA, the agreement conditioned the sale and relocation on the NBA Board of Governors' approval.

On June 15, a committee of the NBA Board of Governors met with Top Rank to consider approving the agreement. At the meeting, Top Rank refused to disclose the source of several millions of dollars it planned to use to buy the Timberwolves. Based on the nondisclosure, the committee determined Top Rank's financial support was inadequate and voted to recommend that the NBA's full Board of Governors reject the agreement.

Within hours of the committee's vote, the NBA brought a lawsuit against the MPBLP and Top Rank in federal district court in Minnesota seeking a declaration that NBA permission was required before the Timberwolves could be sold or relocated. Because the NBA's nearly finalized 1994-95 season schedule was based on the Timberwolves' presence in Minnesota, the NBA also asked the court for a temporary restraining order and a preliminary injunction preventing the MPBLP and Top Rank from closing the sale and moving the team without the NBA's approval. In support of its requests, the NBA showed that it was too late in the scheduling process to move the Timberwolves without jeopardizing the upcoming 1994-95 basketball season. On June 16, the court ordered the MPBLP not to close the sale or move the team until the court ruled on the NBA's request for a restraining order.

Nearly a week later, on June 21, the full NBA Board of Governors adopted the committee's recommendation and rejected the agreement. That same day, the MPBLP terminated the agreement and filed a cross-claim against Top Rank in the district court. The MPBLP sought a declaration that it had rightfully terminated the agreement, and breach of contract damages for Top Rank's failure to secure NBA approval as the agreement required. On June 23, the district court temporarily restrained the MPBLP from closing the sale or moving the team until the court considered the NBA's request for a preliminary injunction.

On June 24, Top Rank filed a state court lawsuit against the MPBLP and NBA in Louisiana. Top Rank sought specific performance or damages from the MPBLP for breach of the agreement, and damages from the NBA for interference with the agreement. On June 28, the state court issued a ten-day temporary restraining order preventing the NBA and all its member teams from finalizing the 1994-95 NBA season schedule.

On July 1, the district court granted the NBA's request for preliminary injunctive relief. The district court's order enjoined the MPBLP from selling the team to Top Rank or moving the team to New Orleans until the entry of a court order stating otherwise, the entry of final judgment, or June 15, 1995, whichever occurred first. The district court also enjoined the state court from conducting further proceedings in Top Rank's lawsuit and relieved the NBA from the state court's temporary restraining order, which expired by its own terms on July 8.

Relying on the Anti-Injunction Act, the state court rejected the district court's order and, on July 14, entered its own preliminary injunction preventing the NBA from preparing a schedule for the 1994-95 season. On July 19, the district court enjoined enforcement of the state court's preliminary injunction, barred future orders by the state court, prohibited the parties to the federal action from participating in Top Rank's lawsuit, and outlined stiff contempt sanctions for disobedience. Top Rank appeals both the district court's July 1 and July 19 orders.

Top Rank does not challenge the district court's finding that the NBA would suffer irreparable harm unless the Timberwolves remained in Minnesota for the 1994-95 season. Instead, Top Rank contends the district court should not have enjoined the sale to Top Rank without also enjoining the MPBLP from negotiating with other buyers who might move the team and inflict the same harm on the NBA. Although we agree with Top Rank that an injunction absolutely prohibiting the MPBLP from selling the team to any buyer might have provided greater protection to the NBA, the sale to Top Rank was the only threat identified in the NBA's motion, and neither the NBA nor Top Rank ever requested a broader injunction. The district court's failure to order more protection than the parties requested is not an abuse of discretion.

In a related vein, Top Rank complains the district court underestimated the injury that the preliminary injunction would cause Top Rank. Top Rank asserts it has been severely injured because the district court did not prevent the MPBLP from selling the Timberwolves to other buyers. Top Rank's brief alleges the Timberwolves franchise "is about to be sold to another potential purchaser," and thus Top Rank's interests are in great jeopardy. Contrary to Top Rank's assertion, any injury Top Rank suffers from the MPBLP's negotiations with other buyers is not the result of the district court's orders, but of Top Rank's own failure to request an injunction preventing the negotiations. Having failed to seek preliminary relief, Top Rank cannot complain the district court should have protected Top Rank's interests on the court's own initiative. Further, Top Rank does not explain why its injury is not compensable. Given the district court's uncontested finding that Top Rank can be made whole with money damages, the court did not abuse its discretion in concluding the second Dataphase factor weighed in favor of keeping the Timberwolves in Minnesota.

Top Rank also argues the district court misjudged Top Rank's chances of prevailing on the merits of its dispute with the MPBLP. Top Rank theorizes that despite the NBA Board of Governors' initial rejection of the agreement, the MPBLP prematurely terminated the agreement and, in this way, denied Top Rank any opportunity to cure the NBA's rejection before the agreement's closing date. Thus, Top Rank contends it is likely to prevail on its claim to enforce the agreement against the MPBLP. Top Rank's argument is misplaced. The relevant consideration is whether the NBA, the party seeking the preliminary relief, is likely to prevail on its claim that NBA approval is required before the Timberwolves can be sold to Top Rank. Top Rank does not challenge the district court's assessment that the NBA was likely to succeed on its claim because "the closure of the [agreement is] in some fashion contingent on the NBA's approval."

****

The four major leagues each have rules that prohibit the sale of a franchise without league approval. Each league does a background check on potential purchasers before approval is granted. The leagues are extremely cautious about who they allow into their elite group. The investigation is very broad and includes such matters as criminal or gambling activity. One of the more important aspects of the review is the determination of whether the buyer has the financial resources to run a professional team. Without sound financial backing a team--and the league--will suffer. The NFL recently rejected the attempt by a wealthy suitor to buy the Minnesota Vikings' franchise. The initial proposal appeared acceptable. After further investigation, however, the League rejected the application.

The investigation of potential owners is supposed to be extensive. In 1997 the NHL's process, however, failed. John Spano was approved to buy the NHL Islanders from John Pickett. The purchase of the team and cable rights involved about $150 million. Immediately after the sale Spano was exposed as a con man. His checks were no good and he was unable to even pay property taxes on his home. In a short period of time, however, he was able to charge almost $250,000 to the team for meals, private jet service and hotels. The ownership of the team was eventually returned to Pickett. Spano was charged with criminal bank fraud.

SINGLE ENTITY — MAJOR LEAGUE SOCCER

Soccer is the most popular team sport in the world. The attention devoted to the World Cup has been compared to having a Super Bowl every day for three weeks. Examples of Cup mania were demonstrated during the 1998 event: over 4 million phone calls from Great Britain alone were made in one hour to acquire the last 160,000 tickets, the Italian Parliament revamped its schedule in order to watch the home team play and over 10,000 workers in Sao Paulo left their jobs without permission to watch a match--the workers were not punished.

The game, however, has never dominated in the United States as it has in the rest of the world. An attempt to establish a national professional team in the 1980s failed after a few years. Although the professional league attempt was unsuccessful, participation in the sport continued to grow. Soccer is projected by many observers to be the leading team sport for market growth. Interest in soccer was boosted in 1994 when the United States served as host to The World Cup, soccer's premier event.

The United States hosted the Women's World Cup in 1999 that drew crowds of 60,000 to 70,000 at many of the games. As a result of the strong support, a professional U.S. women's soccer league was created. Unfortunately, the league could not survive and was disbanded.

Major League Soccer (MLS): MLS is sanctioned by the United States Soccer Federation (USSF), which is in turn a member of the Confederation of North, Central American and Caribbean Association of Football (CONCACAF), one of six world regional organizations under the umbrella of the Federation Internationale de Football Association (FIFA). The national organizations are responsible for organizing national teams to play in events such as the Olympics and the World Cup. Although MLS falls under the sanction of the USSF, it is an entirely separate entity.

Major League Soccer (MLS) for men began play with 10 teams in 1996. The results were encouraging. MLS officials had anticipated an average draw of 12,000 fans at the games. As the first season ended, however, the attendance average was 19,000. Another major accomplishment in 1996 was total fan attendance in excess of two million. The All-Star game for the '96 season was a sell-out at the New York Giants Stadium. The League did, however, experience a drop in attendance during the second year of play. In the third year MLS experienced what is common to the other major sports leagues, some locations did very well at the gate, while others did poorly. Although the League is still losing money, it has some television contracts which are vital to its survival. There is hope that the decision by phenom Freddy Adu to join the league, rather than play for one of the other teams in the world, will enhance the respect of the league. Adu, at the age of 14, was hailed as the next Pele.

The MLS's regular season runs from April through September with the Championship Game in October. The League recruits some of the best and most well-known players in the world which has helped increase fan interest. In the first season, each team could not have more than four foreign players on the field at a time. The number was expanded to five for the '97 season. In the first year the minimum salary in the League was $24,000 and the maximum was $175,000. The maximum salary for 1997 was increased to $192,500.

The structure of MLS is unlike that of the other major professional leagues. MLS is set up as a single entity. The League, not the individual teams, drafts the players, assigns the players to the clubs and sets the salaries. The primary goal of the single entity arrangement is an attempt to insulate the League from antitrust suits by players. Section 1 of the Sherman Act prohibits two or more persons from contracting to restrain trade. One person (or one entity) cannot violate section 1 of the law. Several players filed a suit, *Fraser v. Major League Soccer,* against the League claiming the salary restraints were a violation of antitrust laws. The suit claimed that the League was not a single entity and that each team should be recognized as a competitor to the other teams as the courts have found in the other sports leagues. The MLS players had not formed a union and therefore there was no collective bargaining relationship and non-statutory exemption to protect the League from an antitrust claim. The trial court in *Fraser* upheld the League's single entity position. Although the appellate court did not specifically agree with the trial court on the single entity argument, the decision was upheld.

Fraser v. Major League Soccer, L.L.C. (2002)

Professional soccer players sued Major League Soccer, LLC ("MLS"), nine independent operator/investors in MLS, and the United States Soccer Federation, Inc. ("USSF"), alleging violations of Sherman Act sections 1 and 2, 15 U.S.C. §§ 1-2, and Clayton Act section 7, and seeking injunctive relief and monetary damages. The district court granted summary judgment for defendants on the section 1 and Clayton Act counts. After a twelve-week long trial on the section 2 count, the jury returned a special verdict leading to judgment in favor of defendants. Players now appeal the disposition of all three counts. We begin with a statement of the background facts.

I. Background Facts

Despite professional soccer's popularity abroad, the sport has achieved only limited success in this country. Several minor leagues have operated here (four such leagues exist today), but before the formation of MLS, only one other U.S. professional league--the North American Soccer League ("NASL")--had ever obtained Division I, or top-tier, status. Launched in 1968, the NASL achieved some success before folding in 1985; MLS attributes the NASL's demise in part to wide disparities in the financial resources of the league's independently owned teams and a lack of centralized control.

MLS has, to say the least, a unique structure, even for a sports league. MLS retains significant centralized control over both league and individual team operations. MLS owns all of the teams that play in the league (a total of 12 prior to the start of 2002), as well as all intellectual property rights, tickets, supplied equipment, and broadcast rights. MLS sets the teams' schedules; negotiates all stadium leases and assumes all related liabilities; pays the salaries of referees and other league personnel; and supplies certain equipment.

At issue in this case is MLS's control over player employment. MLS has the "sole responsibility for negotiating and entering into agreements with, and for compensating, Players." In a nutshell, MLS recruits the players, negotiates their salaries, pays them from league funds, and, to a large extent, determines where each of them will play. For example, to balance talent among teams, it decides, with the non-binding input of team operators, where certain of the league's "marquee" players will play.

However, MLS has also relinquished some control over team operations to certain investors. MLS contracts with these investors to operate nine of the league's teams (the league runs the other three). These investors are referred to as operator/ investors and are the co-defendants in this action. Each operator/investor has the "exclusive right and obligation to provide Management Services for a Team within its Home Territory" and is given some leeway in running the team and reaping the potential benefits therefrom.

The league began official play in 1996. The following February of 1997, eight named players sued MLS, the USSF, and the operator/investors under various antitrust theories. In count I, the players claimed MLS and its operator/investors violated Sherman Act section 1 by agreeing not to compete for player services. In count III, the players claimed MLS monopolized or attempted to monopolize, or combined or conspired with the USSF to monopolize, the market for the services of Division I professional soccer players in the U.S., in violation of Sherman Act section 2, by preventing any other entity from being sanctioned as a Division I professional soccer league in the United States or otherwise competing against MLS. In count IV, the players claimed that the combination of assets of the operator/investors in MLS substantially lessened competition and tended to create monopoly in violation of Clayton Act section 7.

****

Sherman Act Section 1

Some have urged that sports leagues in general be treated as single entities-- individual sports teams, after all, must collaborate to produce a product. However, this approach has not been adopted in this circuit and we must work with the framework of existing circuit law. Single entity status for ordinarily organized leagues has been rejected in several other circuits as well.

Even so, the district court concluded that under *Copperweld Corp. v. Independence Tube Corp.*, (1984), MLS and its operator/investors were uniquely integrated and did comprise a single entity. *Copperweld* established that a parent and its wholly owned subsidiary are not subject to attack under section 1 for agreements between them. They are treated for section 1 purposes as a single economic actor. But what the Supreme Court has never decided is how far *Copperweld* applies to more complex entities and arrangements that involve a high degree of corporate and economic integration but less than that existing in *Cooperweld* itself.

While MLS defends the district court's single entity ruling, players say that this view is form over substance and the substance is simply a conspiracy among *de facto* team owners to fix player salaries, which they claim to be a *per se* violation of the antitrust laws. We disagree completely with this latter characterization. We also find that the case for applying single entity status to MLS and its operator/investors has not been established but that in this case the jury verdict makes a remand on the section 1 claim unnecessary.

If ordinary investors decided to set up a company that would own and manage all of the teams in a league, it is hard to see why this arrangement would fall outside *Copperweld's* safe harbor. Certainly the potential for competition within the firm is not enough: after all, a railroad could in theory provide alternative routes between the same cities and a grocery could locate competing branches of its chain quite near one another; yet no law requires competition within a company. It is common practice, but hardly essential, that the teams in a sports league have independent owner/managers.

Further, MLS is manifestly more than an arrangement for individual operator/investors by which they can cap player salaries. In many ways, MLS does resemble an ordinary company: it owns substantial assets (teams, player contracts, stadium rights, intellectual property) critical to the performance of the league; a substantial portion of generated revenues belongs to it and is to be shared conventionally with both operator/investors and passive investors. And the fact that MLS was structured with the aim of achieving results that might not otherwise be possible does not automatically condemn it.

The rejection of the *per se* rule is straightforward. Although players portray MLS as a sham for horizontal price fixing, the extent of real economic integration is obvious. Further, MLS and its investors did not compete previously; the arrangement was formed as a risky venture against a background of prior failure and the outcome has been to add new opportunities for players—a Division 1 soccer league in the United States—and to raise salaries for soccer players here above existing levels.

We thus have every reason to think that if the section 1 claim had not been dismissed on summary judgment it would have been presented at trial with the same market analysis alleged in the complaint. It follows that had the district court allowed the section 1 claim, it too would have been defeated by the jury's finding that the market alleged in the complaint had not been proved. Accordingly, any error in dismissing the claim based on a single entity theory was harmless so long as the jury verdict stands, a matter we address in the next section. The outcome, as the plaintiffs shaped their own case, would have been the same.

****

Individual Sports–Nascar, Golf & Olympics

The term "individual sports" is somewhat misleading. Rare is the athlete who does not rely on others for support. For example, a NASCAR driver's performance is directly related to the assistance provided by his pit crew and other personnel who communicate strategy during a race. This chapter, however, addresses sports that involve individual competitors rather than teams.

Sports such as golf, tennis, auto racing, track and field, and mixed martial arts have generated ever-increasing revenues, spectator interest, and (as a result) legal attention over the past few years. Individual sports pose some novel challenges to the business and legal sides of sports than team sports, but there is also overlap between the two. For example, are golfers or race drivers considered to be independent contractors or employees of administrative bodies such as the Professional Golfers Association (PGA Tour) or NASCAR? To what extent does antitrust and labor law govern these associations, given the absence (or presence) of collective bargaining? Are sports agents for individual sports subject to a different set of rules than those who bargain with teams? And perhaps most importantly, should courts attempt to govern these individual sports, or should they allow the sport's governing body to interpret its own rules? This chapter will focus primarily on issues and concepts that are novel to individual sports and their participants.

NASCAR

The National Association of Stock Car Auto Racing (NASCAR) was founded in 1947 by Bill France as an organization to govern organized stock car racing. Over the past fifty years, NASCAR has become the primary governing body of motorsports in the United States. The popularity of NASCAR has sky-rocketed, and today it holds the second-highest television ratings of any professional sport in the United States, behind pro football. NASCAR held 17 of the top 20 attended sporting events in the country, fans spend around $3 billion annually on licensed products, more Fortune 500 companies sponsor NASCAR than any other sport, and races are televised in around 150 countries worldwide.

POINT SYSTEM

NASCAR sanctions various regional and national racing series, but its most popular is the "NASCAR Sprint Cup Series." The Sprint Cup consists of 36 races over 10 months, with varying amounts of prize money available in each race. To win the cup, a driver must earn more points than any other driver during the season. Points are awarded based on a driver's "finishing position" in the race – the first place driver receives the highest number of points, and the last place driver receives the fewest. Generally 43 drivers start each race, and the winning driver receives 185 points. There is a 15-point differential between the first- and second-place driver, a 5-point differential between each of the second-to fifth-place drivers, a 4-point differential between each of the sixth- to tenth-place drivers, and a 3-point differential between the eleventh- to forty third-place drivers. The last-place (43rd) driver receives 34 points.

In 2004, NASCAR made changes to the point system's structure as a means of increasing popularity towards the end of the season. The "Chase for the Championship" now begins after the first 26 races, with the top ten drivers in points and any other driver within 400 points of the leader earning a berth in the Chase. In 2007, the "400 point" rule was eliminated, and currently the top 12 drivers in points now qualify for the Chase. These 12 drivers have their point totals re-set to 5,000, and each driver receives a 10-point bonus for each victory during the first 26 races.

The Sprint Cup offers a variety of bonus points to its drivers beyond the points awarded for finishing positions. There are 5-point bonuses available in each race for leading at least one lap and for leading the most laps (so the maximum point total for a driver in a single race is 195). There is also a parallel "owner point system," and a car owner earns points whenever his car is in a race regardless of the driver. These points help the owner's racing team obtain more qualifying entries in NASCAR races. The 2007 winner of the Sprint Cup was Jimmie Johnson.

COURT REVIEW OF NASCAR DECISIONS

To participate in NASCAR events, a racing team must pay a licensing fee to NASCAR and become a member of the organization; however, membership does not entitle the racing team to participate in the decision-making process. As a result, there have been multiple court cases where NASCAR participants challenge the results of a race. The following is one such case:

Crouch v. Nascar(1988)

This case arises out of a 100 lap NASCAR-sanctioned stock car race that took place at Catamount Speedway in Vermont on August 11, 1985. Two incidents took place during the course of this race that gave rise to the controversy between the parties. The first incident occurred at the beginning of the race, when there was a restart because of an accident involving the LaJoie car. During this restart, the LaJoie car remained in the pit area behind the start/finish line. As the other cars on the track approached the start/finish line at the beginning of the second lap, the LaJoie car crossed the start/finish line in the pit area and then entered the track with the rest of the cars. Gordon Nielsen, the official scorer of the race, ruled that LaJoie could not receive credit for laps completed until he had first crossed the start/finish line on the track, rather than in the pits. LaJoie contends that Nielsen's decision was wrong because it was contrary to NASCAR scoring procedures used throughout the rest of the country, and that his car was scored throughout the race with one lap less than it would otherwise have been given because of Nielsen's erroneous ruling.

The second incident occurred during laps 68-71. During lap 68, a yellow caution flag was displayed to the drivers because of another accident. Under Rule 12-4(a) of NASCAR's rulebook, "[a]fter cars receive [the] yellow flag at the start and finish line, all cars must hold [their] position until either the green flag is again displayed, or the red flag which would automatically stop the race [is displayed]." According to Thomas Curley, the local NASCAR track official, LaJoie improperly passed several cars after the yellow flag was displayed, in violation of Rule 12-4(a). LaJoie contends that if the local officials had made the correct decision with respect to the first incident, then he would have been positioned on the lap 68 restart ahead of the vehicles that he passed under the yellow flag. He thus believed that he had a right to pass the cars because of Nielsen's scoring error during laps 1 and 2.

There is a dispute between the parties as to what happened next. Curley asserts that a black flag was displayed to the LaJoie car for four consecutive laps, although Bob Johnson, LaJoie's crew chief, maintains that he saw the black flag only once. Under Rule 12-6 of the rulebook, a driver is to report to the NASCAR official at the pit immediately after a black flag is displayed to him or her. Rule 12-6 also provides that after a car has been black-flagged for three consecutive laps, "scoring on [the] car involved will be discontinued until [a] pit stop has been made and [the] car is released by a NASCAR official to resume racing." Curley maintains that after the LaJoie car failed to obey the black flag on the third lap, he told Nielsen to stop scoring the LaJoie car and informed Johnson either directly or indirectly that scoring had been stopped on the LaJoie car. Johnson and LaJoie deny that they were ever told that their car had been disqualified or that scoring on their car had been stopped. No black flag with a white cross was displayed to LaJoie, although Rule 12-6 provides that such a flag is to be displayed to inform a driver that scoring of his or her car has been discontinued. Despite Curley's instruction to Nielsen to stop scoring the LaJoie car as of lap 71, Nielsen continued to record the LaJoie car on the scoring tapes.

The national NASCAR officials then reviewed the materials concerning the race. As one official noted in his affidavit, the referral from Curley was "the kind of request which we are frequently asked and routinely answer as part of the administration of NASCAR sponsored events." J. App. at 46. Based upon the materials presented, NASCAR decided that upon correction of the scoring errors that had been made, LaJoie should be declared the winner of the race. In addition, NASCAR officials concluded that LaJoie had violated the black flag rule, and that a penalty should be imposed for this violation. They thus issued a penalty notice to LaJoie pursuant to Rule 13-2 and fined him $1,200.

Plaintiffs then brought this action in court alleging that the lap 1-2 decision and the lap 68-71 alleged disqualification dealt with "race procedure" decisions of local NASCAR officials that could not be reviewed by NASCAR headquarters under Section 11 of the rulebook. Rule 11-1 provides that "[d]ecisions of NASCAR officials assigned to an event with respect to the interpretation of the NASCAR Rules, as they may pertain to race procedure, shall be final and there shall be no appeal or protest thereof." Under this rule, race procedure decisions "include, but are not necessarily limited to, the line up of the cars, the start of the race, the control of the cars, the election to stop or delay a race, the positioning of cars on re-starts, and the assessment of lap and time penalties." NASCAR moved to dismiss or for summary judgment on the ground that its official decisions are not subject to judicial review. NASCAR contended that its decisions were not reviewable under Rule 9-2, which provides that "[b]y submitting his entry application and/or taking part in any activity relating to the event, a competitor agrees to abide by the decisions of those officials relating to the event, and agrees that such decisions are non-appealable and non-[litigable] except as provided in Section 13 and 14 of this Rulebook [which provide for an internal review and appeal process]."

Discussion

The threshold issue that we must resolve is the proper standard for judicial review of NASCAR's interpretation of its own rules. Our decision in *Koszela v. National Association of Stock Car Auto Racing, Inc. (1981),* provides some guidance. In that case, we considered claims that NASCAR misapplied its rules in determining the rightful winner of two races and that its decisions regarding the two races were arbitrary and clearly erroneous. We first reasoned that the principle of judicial noninterference set forth in the law of voluntary associations was not strictly applicable, noting that NASCAR was a for-profit company that completely dominated the field of stock car racing and that its members have no rights whatsoever with respect to the internal governance of the organization. We added, however, that a reviewing court is not free to reexamine the correctness of the official track decisions in question because NASCAR's rules "do not provide for any administrative appeal, much less judicial review, of official decisions." We also noted that the only provision granting a competitor the right to challenge occurrences at the track is the protest mechanism, and that "this provision is not intended to be a device by which disappointed competitors may challenge an official's interpretation of the rules or the application of the rules to the facts." We accordingly refused to reexamine the correctness of the official track decisions in question.

In the instant case, the district court cited *Koszela,* and concluded that because of the considerations discussed in that case it was "precluded from reviewing the official decisions of NASCAR officials with respect to the Catamount race." It added that "[t]o allow competitors to challenge the assessment of lap and time penalties or the timing and scoring of laps would result in the same type of protracted disputes that the finality rule is meant to prevent. ... By according final weight to the official NASCAR track decisions, this court avoids placing itself in the position of 'super-referee.' "

The court also concluded, however, that the considerations that preclude review of the correctness of the official track decisions do not necessarily prevent the review of the procedures used to implement these decisions. The court added that "[w]hile courts may be hesitant to unnecessarily interject themselves into the private affairs of an association, where the association enforces its rules in a manner that is unreasonable or arbitrary courts may intervene." In applying this standard, the court did not defer to NASCAR's judgment that under its rules, the disputed actions of the local track officials did not constitute the imposition of a lap or time penalty, or to NASCAR's decision that disqualification is not a race procedure decision. Rather, the court apparently believed that under its adopted standard, it was appropriate to undertake a *de novo* review of the NASCAR rules in order to determine whether the national NASCAR officials had acted unreasonably or arbitrarily by reviewing the local track officials' decisions.

The court's decision in *Charles O. Finley & Co. v. Kuhn, cert. den (1978)*, also is relevant. In that case, the court concluded that a waiver of recourse to the courts that was signed by the major league baseball clubs was valid, noting that such a waiver coincides with the common law standard disallowing court interference. The court added that there are exceptions to this general rule of nonreviewability of the actions of private associations, however, "1) where the rules, regulations or judgments of the association are in contravention to the laws of the land or in disregard of the charter or bylaws of the association and 2) where the association had failed to follow the basic rudiments of due process of law."

In the instant case, Crouch and Wright are not claiming that they were deprived of any procedural safeguards or that their due process rights were violated, however. Rather, the crux of their complaint is that NASCAR improperly provided LaJoie with a procedural safeguard, *i.e.,* review of the local track officials' decisions by the NASCAR headquarters. In fact, LaJoie maintains that if the district court correctly held that the local track officials' actions constituted a disqualification, then he was entitled to be informed of the disqualification and to have the disqualification decision reviewed by NASCAR headquarters pursuant to Section 13 of the rulebook. Section 13 provides that all violations of NASCAR rules are to be reported in writing to the NASCAR Vice President for Competition, and that this Vice President can review these reported violations. We therefore do not believe that the cases discussing the occasional need for a court to intervene in the internal affairs of an association because of the lack of adequate safeguards support the district court's decision.

Although here there was no allegation of inadequate procedural protections, the district court still thought that it was appropriate to conduct its own analysis of NASCAR's interpretation of its procedural rules. Moreover, despite the court's recognition that NASCAR possesses considerable stock car racing expertise upon which it may rely in interpreting its own rules, the court apparently did not give much weight to that expertise in reaching its decision that NASCAR acted unreasonably by overturning a race procedure decision made by a local track official. Rather, the court evidently felt that in order to determine whether NASCAR acted unreasonably or arbitrarily, it should itself delve into NASCAR's rulebook and decide *de novo* whether the lap 68-71 incident involved a disqualification, and whether a disqualification constitutes a lap and time penalty and is therefore a nonreviewable race procedure decision.

We believe the district court erred in making this inquiry. As the Seventh Circuit noted when rejecting the argument that the Commissioner of Baseball's actions were "procedurally unfair," certain standards, such as "the best interests of baseball, [and] the interests of the morale of the players and the honor of the game ... are not necessarily familiar to courts and obviously require some expertise in their application." The court accordingly proclaimed that the judiciary should not be professional baseball's "umpire and governor." We believe that federal courts are equally unfamiliar with standards such as "race procedure decision" and "lap and time penalty," and thus should decline the plaintiffs' invitation to become the "super-scorer" for stock car racing disputes. Furthermore, there is no contention that NASCAR acted "in disregard of [its] charter or bylaws." Rather, plaintiffs-appellees contend essentially that NASCAR misinterpreted its own internal regulations. Accordingly, we conclude that the district court should have deferred to NASCAR's interpretation of its own rules in the absence of an allegation that NASCAR acted in bad faith or in violation of any local, state or federal laws. We believe that adopting any lower standard for reviewing an organization's interpretation of its own procedural rules would create too great a danger that courts will become mired down in what has been called the "dismal swamp"—the area of a group's activity concerning which only the group can speak competently. Indeed, the district court's admitted confusion about the proper interpretation of NASCAR Rule 13-5 is one illustration of how perilously close the court came to the edge of the swamp under its adopted standard of review. As we acknowledged in *Koszela*, "[u]ltimately, the solution for unauthorized or improper officiating lies not in individual challenges seeking to undo what has been done, but rather in pressure brought upon the officials in charge by drivers, owners, fans, and even NASCAR to improve the caliber of [NASCAR's supervision of races]."

In this case, there was no allegation that the officials at NASCAR headquarters were acting in bad faith or unlawfully in examining the lap 68-71 incident. The affidavit of James Hunter, NASCAR's Vice President for Administration, states that he believed that local officials were "uncertain whether the issues presented were scoring or race procedure questions, and, accordingly, asked NASCAR to make that determination, among others." The affidavit also stated that NASCAR frequently received this type of request. In a second affidavit, Hunter added that "[t]he decision by NASCAR to place Mr. LaJoie in first place was made in good faith, without knowledge of any disqualification, and in an attempt to interpret and apply the NASCAR rules to a difficult situation created by a wrong scoring decision at the outset of the race." In their amended complaint, plaintiffs did not allege that NASCAR acted in bad faith or illegally. Indeed, the district court implicitly acknowledged that the national officials acted in good faith. Specifically, the court noted that the national officials believed that the local officials' decision to penalize LaJoie in connection with the lap 68-71 incident resulted in part from the scoring error the local officials made in connection with the lap 1-2 incident. The national officials therefore thought that it was appropriate to correct both decisions. Moreover, as we noted in *Koszela*, it is common practice to refer race procedure questions to the national NASCAR office. We thus believe that the district court should have deferred to NASCAR's interpretation of its own rules, under which NASCAR had the authority to review and decide the disputed issues.

****

Under *Crouch,* NASCAR (and other sport governing bodies) have considerable leeway to interpret their own rules. Is this good or bad? Should courts be more willing to get involved?

SPONSORSHIP CONFLICT

When Nextel in 2004 became the title sponsor of what is now called the Sprint Cup (because of a 2005 merger between Nextel and Sprint), NASCAR agreed to prohibit other telecommunication companies from acquiring car sponsorships as part of the exclusivity arrangement. To protect certain drivers and crews from losing funding, the parties agreed to grandfather in existing primary sponsors Cingular and Alltel. The nature of this exception became disputed, however, when in 2007 the now-merged Cingular AT&T implemented plans to drop the "Cingular" from the company name and proceed forward as simply "AT&T."

To complete the name change, the company wanted to convert its "Cingular" car into an "AT&T" car under the exception NASCAR granted in 2004. NASCAR objected to this proposal on grounds that it had specifically made an exception for a Cingular car and had not granted the company a transferrable and universal exemption from the Nextel exclusivity agreement. The district court examining the case scrutinized the language of the "Driver and Car Owner Agreement" between NASCAR, Richard Childress Racing (RCR), and the driver of RCR's Cingular #31 car, Jeff Burton. The opinion refers to that agreement as the "RCR Agreement" and to plaintiff AT&T's agreement (through Cingular) with RCR as the "Sponsorship Agreement."

At&T Mobility Llc V. Nascar (2007)

Plaintiff's contractual right to feature its current brand and logo on the # 31 Car is found in plaintiff's Sponsorship Agreement with RCR. The Sponsorship Agreement between RCR and plaintiff gives "Cingular" the right, "in accordance with its status as Primary Sponsor" to designate the "Cingular marks" appearing on the car. The agreement further defines "Cingular" as a company, not a brand - i.e., as "Cingular Wireless LLC" which is the company now known as AT&T Mobility LLC and is the plaintiff here. In view of the fact that Cingular Wireless LLC has changed its name and adopted the AT&T logo and brand, the Court concludes that, insofar as the Sponsorship Agreement between RCR and plaintiff gives plaintiff as a company the right as primary sponsor to designate the marks that appear on the # 31 Car, that agreement authorizes plaintiff to designate its current name (AT&T) and logo (the AT&T globe) to be featured on the car.

As explained above, the RCR Agreement provides that, "[n]otwithstanding" the exclusivity afforded Sprint Nextel "NASCAR and Nextel will allow any and all existing product licensing relationships in the Category to continue through the current term of their agreement." RCR The Addendum to the Agreement further provides: "To the extent that [RCR] has a licensing agreement which is part of

[a] sponsorship agreement [RCR] shall have the right to continue to license such products so long as such sponsorship relationship continues."

The Court concludes that NASCAR's refusal to permit plaintiff to feature its current logo and brand on the # 31 Car likely violates these provisions. Plaintiff's "product licensing relationship" with RCR necessarily encompasses the right to display its current brand and logo on the # 31 Car; without that, the value of the license it has obtained from RCR would be greatly diminished. By permitting plaintiff's "relationship" with RCR to continue despite Sprint Nextel's exclusivity, the RCR Agreement & Addendum necessarily protect plaintiff's right to have its current brand and logo featured on the car. By interfering with that right and not allowing plaintiff to specify the marks that are to be placed on the # 31 Car, NASCAR is likely in breach of the RCR Agreement & Addendum.

NASCAR contends that its commitment to grandfather plaintiff's sponsorship rights is confined to plaintiff's use of the "Cingular" brand and logo. NASCAR argues that on its face, the RCR Agreement & Addendum do not give RCR the right to display anything other than the Cingular brand on the # 31 Car. The text of the RCR Agreement & Addendum, however, includes two limitations on plaintiff's grandfathered sponsorship rights, neither of which suggests that plaintiff would be confined to the "Cingular" brand or logo on the # 31 Car. From the face of the contract, the restrictions are as follows: "the sponsor shall not increase its brand position on the vehicle" and "if such sponsor fails to renew with undersigned Team, Driver/Team shall not sign a subsequent sponsorship or licensing agreement in the Category." If NASCAR had intended to restrict the logos and branding on the # 31 Car, it could have included such limitations in clear and unambiguous language. The absence of any reference to such a limitation on the brand or logo for the # 31 Car in the RCR Agreement & Addendum refutes NASCAR's claim that its grandfathering commitment was confined to plaintiff's use of the "Cingular" logo and brand.

Construction of a contract is a question of law for the Court based on the intent of the parties set forth in the contract. If the Court decides that the language of a contract is clear and unambiguous, the Court simply enforces the contract according to its clear terms. The Court looks to the contract alone for its meaning. Although NASCAR makes several arguments based on conversations and documents that followed the RCR Agreement & Addendum which purportedly explain the contract language and the restrictions on branding, the Court need not look to this evidence to determine the parties' intent because the RCR Agreement & Addendum are clear and unambiguous. The restriction on branding and logos is absent.

NASCAR also contends that the terms of its Rule Book give NASCAR discretion to reject any car design for any reason, and thus that NASCAR's determinations as to paint schemes could never give rise to a claim under the RCR Agreement & Addendum. The RCR Agreement itself, however, incorporates the Rule Book by reference. The Addendum to the RCR Agreement states that its grandfathering provisions apply "[t]o the extent that RCR has a sponsorship . . . which precludes [RCR] from complying with the [RCR Agreement]." Therefore, the Addendum provides that notwithstanding the body of the RCR Agreement including the Rule Book reference, plaintiff as a pre-existing sponsor is grandfathered in as long as it does not increase its brand position on the car or change teams. To the extent the discretion contemplated in NASCAR's Rule Book conflicts with NASCAR's commitment to grandfather plaintiff's sponsorship rights, the language in the grandfather clause of the Addendum thus makes clear that the grandfathering commitment trumps.

In light of the above, the Court concludes that plaintiff has demonstrated a substantial likelihood of success on the merits of its breach of contract claim as an intended third party beneficiary of the RCR Agreement & Addendum.

****

Unfortunately for AT&T, the appellate court overturned the decision on a narrow ruling that concluded AT&T did not have standing to bring the lawsuit because its role in the RCR Agreement did not meet the "third party beneficiary" standing requirement. Consequently, AT&T was procedurally barred from winning, despite any potential substantive merits. To settle the dispute without further litigation, the two parties compromised in an agreement by which AT&T will remain Burton's primary sponsor through 2008 (when its Sponsorship Agreement expires) and then quietly leave the Sprint Cup.

GOLF—PGA TOUR

The most well-known PGA Tour court case involves Casey Martin's eligibility to play on the tour. Martin suffers from Klippel-Trenauney-Weber syndrome, a condition that causes his calf muscles and the bones in his right leg to gradually deteriorate. He was a considerably talented golfer and was aided, in no small part, because the sport typically allows players to ride around the course in a golf cart, rather than walk.

Martin played golf for Stanford University and showed enough promise that in 1997 he decided to try professional golf in spite of his physical condition. However, the PGA Tour rules did not allow its participants to ride carts during tournaments. Martin was allowed to use a cart for the PGA Tour Qualifying Event after a court issued a preliminary injunction forbidding the PGA from enforcing the "no cart" rule against him. Martin failed to qualify for the PGA Tour but did secure a spot on the Nike Tour (a lower-level tour operated by the PGA). After he won the season's first tournament, he went to court to try and win a permanent ruling allowing him to use a cart during official PGA play. The case involved disability law, and a major problem for Martin (similar to NCAA athletes) was that he did not qualify as an "employee" of the PGA Tour (and thus could not claim rights under Title I of the Americans With Disabilities Act (ADA)).

The first issue in the case was whether the PGA Tour was a "private club or establishment." If so, the PGA would be exempt from Title III of the ADA governing discrimination in places of public accommodation, and Martin would lose before the case ever went to trial. But if the PGA was not a private club, then the case could proceed.

The trial court found that the PGA Tour was a "commercial enterprise" and thus subject to Title III of the ADA. The PGA's position was that allowing an individual not to walk the course for any reason would "fundamentally alter" the nature of the competition because it might give the player a competitive advantage. The judge disagreed, pointing out that Martin would still have to walk over a mile during an 18-hole round and that the fatigue he suffered as a result of his condition was "undeniably greater" than that his healthy competitors would suffer from walking the course. The trial judge therefore concluded that allowing Martin to walk would not fundamentally alter the nature of the PGA Tour, and entered a permanent injunction in favor of Martin.

The Court of Appeals agreed with the lower judge's assessment, and Martin's claim eventually rose all the way to the Supreme Court of the United States. Portions of the decision are excerpted below:

Pga Tour, Inc. V. Martin (2001)

When Martin turned pro and entered petitioner's Q-School, the hard card permitted him to use a cart during his successful progress through the first two stages. He made a request, supported by detailed medical records, for permission to use a golf cart during the third stage. Petitioner refused to review those records or to waive its walking rule for the third stage. Martin therefore filed this action. A preliminary injunction entered by the District Court made it possible for him to use a cart in the final stage of the Q-School and as a competitor in the NIKE TOUR and PGA TOUR. Although not bound by the injunction, and despite its support for petitioner's position in this litigation, the USGA voluntarily granted Martin a similar waiver in events that it sponsors, including the U.S. Open.

It seems apparent, from both the general rule and the comprehensive definition of "public accommodation," that petitioner's golf tours and their qualifying rounds fit comfortably within the coverage of Title III, and Martin within its protection. The events occur on "golf course[s]," a type of place specifically identified by the Act as a public accommodation. In addition, at all relevant times, petitioner "leases" and "operates" golf courses to conduct its Q-School and tours. As a lessor and operator of golf courses, then, petitioner must not discriminate against any "individual" in the "full and equal enjoyment of the goods, services, facilities, privileges, advantages, or accommodations" of those courses. *Ibid.* Certainly, among the "privileges" offered by petitioner on the courses are those of competing in the Q-School and playing in the tours; indeed, the former is a privilege for which thousands of individuals from the general public pay, and the latter is one for which they vie. Martin, of course, is one of those individuals. It would therefore appear that Title III of the ADA, by its plain terms, prohibits petitioner from denying Martin equal access to its tours on the basis of his disability.

Petitioner argues otherwise. To be clear about its position, it does not assert (as it did in the District Court) that it is a private club altogether exempt from Title III's coverage. In fact, petitioner admits that its tournaments are conducted at places of public accommodation. Nor does petitioner contend (as it did in both the District Court and the Court of Appeals) that the competitors' area "behind the ropes" is not a public accommodation, notwithstanding the status of the rest of the golf course.

Rather, petitioner reframes the coverage issue by arguing that the competing golfers are not members of the class protected by Title III of the ADA.

According to petitioner, Title III is concerned with discrimination against "clients and customers" seeking to obtain "goods and services" at places of public accommodation, whereas it is Title I that protects persons who work at such places. As the argument goes, petitioner operates not a "golf course" during its tournaments but a "place of exhibition or entertainment," and a professional golfer such as Martin, like an actor in a theater production, is a provider rather than a consumer of the entertainment that petitioner sells to the public. Martin therefore cannot bring a claim under Title III because he is not one of the " ' *clients or customers* of the covered public accommodation.' " Rather, Martin's claim of discrimination is "job-related" and could only be brought under Title I-but that Title does not apply because he is an independent contractor (as the District Court found) rather than an employee.

We need not decide whether petitioner's construction of the statute is correct, because petitioner's argument falters even on its own terms. If Title III's protected class were limited to "clients or customers," it would be entirely appropriate to classify the golfers who pay petitioner $3,000 for the chance to compete in the Q-School and, if successful, in the subsequent tour events, as petitioner's clients or customers. In our view, petitioner's tournaments (whether situated at a "golf course" or at a "place of exhibition or entertainment") simultaneously offer at least two "privileges" to the public—that of watching the golf competition and that of competing in it. Although the latter is more difficult and more expensive to obtain than the former, it is nonetheless a privilege that petitioner makes available to members of the general public. In consideration of the entry fee, any golfer with the requisite letters of recommendation acquires the opportunity to qualify for and compete in petitioner's tours. Additionally, any golfer who succeeds in the open qualifying rounds for a tournament may play in the event. That petitioner identifies one set of clients or customers that it serves (spectators at tournaments) does not preclude it from having another set (players in tournaments) against whom it may not discriminate. It would be inconsistent with the literal text of the statute as well as its expansive purpose to read Title III's coverage, even given petitioner's suggested limitation, any less broadly.

Petitioner does not contest that a golf cart is a reasonable modification that is necessary if Martin is to play in its tournaments. Martin's claim thus differs from one that might be asserted by players with less serious afflictions that make walking the course uncomfortable or difficult, but not beyond their capacity. In such cases, an accommodation might be reasonable but not necessary. In this case, however, the narrow dispute is whether allowing Martin to use a golf cart, despite the walking requirement that applies to the PGA TOUR, the NIKE TOUR, and the third stage of the Q-School, is a modification that would "fundamentally alter the nature" of those events.

In theory, a modification of petitioner's golf tournaments might constitute a fundamental alteration in two different ways. It might alter such an essential aspect of the game of golf that it would be unacceptable even if it affected all competitors equally; changing the diameter of the hole from three to six inches might be such a modification. Alternatively, a less significant change that has only a peripheral impact on the game itself might nevertheless give a disabled player, in addition to access to the competition as required by Title III, an advantage over others and, for that reason, fundamentally alter the character of the competition. We are not persuaded that a waiver of the walking rule for Martin would work a fundamental alteration in either sense.

As an initial matter, we observe that the use of carts is not itself inconsistent with the fundamental character of the game of golf. From early on, the essence of the game has been shot-making—using clubs to cause a ball to progress from the teeing ground to a hole some distance away with as few strokes as possible. That essential aspect of the game is still reflected in the very first of the Rules of Golf, which declares: "The Game of Golf consists in playing a ball from the teeing ground into the hole by a stroke or successive strokes in accordance with the rules." Rule 1-1, Rules of Golf, App. 104 (italics in original). Over the years, there have been many changes in the players' equipment, in golf course design, in the Rules of Golf, and in the method of transporting clubs from hole to hole. Originally, so few clubs were used that each player could carry them without a bag. Then came golf bags, caddies, carts that were pulled by hand, and eventually motorized carts that carried players as well as clubs. "Golf carts started appearing with increasing regularity on American golf courses in the 1950's. Today they are everywhere. And they are encouraged. For one thing, they often speed up play, and for another, they are great revenue producers." There is nothing in the Rules of Golf that either forbids the use of carts, or penalizes a player for using a cart. That set of rules, as we have observed, is widely accepted in both the amateur and professional golf world as the rules of the game. The walking rule that is contained in petitioner's hard cards, based on an optional condition buried in an appendix to the Rules of Golf, is not an essential attribute of the game itself.

Petitioner, however, distinguishes the game of golf as it is generally played from the game that it sponsors in the PGA TOUR, NIKE TOUR, and (at least recently) the last stage of the Q-School—golf at the "highest level." According to petitioner, "[t]he goal of the highest-level competitive athletics is to assess and compare the performance of different competitors, a task that is meaningful only if the competitors are subject to identical substantive rules." The waiver of any possibly "outcome-affecting" rule for a contestant would violate this principle and therefore, in petitioner's view, fundamentally alter the nature of the highest level athletic event. The walking rule is one such rule, petitioner submits, because its purpose is "to inject the element of fatigue into the skill of shot-making," and thus its effect may be the critical loss of a stroke. As a consequence, the reasonable modification Martin seeks would fundamentally alter the nature of petitioner's highest level tournaments even if he were the only person in the world who has both the talent to compete in those elite events and a disability sufficiently serious that he cannot do so without using a cart.

The force of petitioner's argument is, first of all, mitigated by the fact that golf is a game in which it is impossible to guarantee that all competitors will play under exactly the same conditions or that an individual's ability will be the sole determinant of the outcome. For example, changes in the weather may produce harder greens and more head winds for the tournament leader than for his closest pursuers. A lucky bounce may save a shot or two. Whether such happenstance events are more or less probable than the likelihood that a golfer afflicted with Klippel-Trenaunay-Weber Syndrome would one day qualify for the NIKE TOUR and PGA TOUR, they at least demonstrate that pure chance may have a greater impact on the outcome of elite golf tournaments than the fatigue resulting from the enforcement of the walking rule.

Even if we accept the factual predicate for petitioner's argument—that the walking rule is "outcome affecting" because fatigue may adversely affect performance—its legal position is fatally flawed. Petitioner's refusal to consider Martin's personal circumstances in deciding whether to accommodate his disability runs counter to the clear language and purpose of the ADA. As previously stated, the ADA was enacted to eliminate discrimination against "individuals" with disabilities, 42 U. S. C. §12101(b)(1), and to that end Title III of the Act requires without exception that any "policies, practices, or procedures" of a public accommodation be reasonably modified for disabled "individuals" as necessary to afford access unless doing so would fundamentally alter what is offered, §12182(b)(2)(A)(ii). To comply with this command, an individualized inquiry must be made to determine whether a specific modification for a particular person's disability would be reasonable under the circumstances as well as necessary for that person, and yet at the same time not work a fundamental alteration.

To be sure, the waiver of an essential rule of competition for anyone would fundamentally alter the nature of petitioner's tournaments. As we have demonstrated, however, the walking rule is at best peripheral to the nature of petitioner's athletic events, and thus it might be waived in individual cases without working a fundamental alteration. Therefore, petitioner's claim that all the substantive rules for its "highest-level" competitions are sacrosanct and cannot be modified under any circumstances is effectively a contention that it is exempt from Title III's reasonable modification requirement. But that provision carves out no exemption for elite athletics, and given Title III's coverage not only of places of "exhibition or entertainment" but also of "golf course[s]," 42 U. S. C. §§12181(7)(C), (L), its application to petitioner's tournaments cannot be said to be unintended or unexpected, see §§12101(a)(1), (5). Even if it were, "the fact that a statute can be applied in situations not expressly anticipated by Congress does not demonstrate ambiguity. It demonstrates breadth."

Under the ADA's basic requirement that the need of a disabled person be evaluated on an individual basis, we have no doubt that allowing Martin to use a golf cart would not fundamentally alter the nature of petitioner's tournaments. As we have discussed, the purpose of the walking rule is to subject players to fatigue, which in turn may influence the outcome of tournaments. Even if the rule does serve that purpose, it is an uncontested finding of the District Court that Martin "easily endures greater fatigue even with a cart than his able-bodied competitors do by walking." 994 F. Supp., at 1252. The purpose of the walking rule is therefore not compromised in the slightest by allowing Martin to use a cart. A modification that provides an exception to a peripheral tournament rule without impairing its purpose cannot be said to "fundamentally alter" the tournament. What it can be said to do, on the other hand, is to allow Martin the chance to qualify for and compete in the athletic events petitioner offers to those members of the public who have the skill and desire to enter. That is exactly what the ADA requires. As a result, Martin's request for a waiver of the walking rule should have been granted.

The ADA admittedly imposes some administrative burdens on the operators of places of public accommodation that could be avoided by strictly adhering to general rules and policies that are entirely fair with respect to the able-bodied but that may indiscriminately preclude access by qualified persons with disabilities. But surely, in a case of this kind, Congress intended that an entity like the PGA not only give individualized attention to the handful of requests that it might receive from talented but disabled athletes for a modification or waiver of a rule to allow them access to the competition, but also carefully weigh the purpose, as well as the letter, of the rule before determining that no accommodation would be tolerable.

The judgment of the Court of Appeals is affirmed.

****

Is this the right decision? Does the ability to ride in a cart give a player an unfair advantage over his competitors who must walk? Which approach is correct: *Crouch* (which let NASCAR interpret its rules) or *Martin* (which overruled the PGA's interpretation of its rules)? Is there a difference between the two cases?

THE OLYMPICS

Although the Olympics has team sports it also has individual competitors and governing issues similar to the individual sports addressed above. The Olympics have an extraordinarily complex governing structure, and naturally the tension between the legal system and the governing body's role in policing and interpreting its own regulations is perhaps most evident here. The International Olympic Committee (IOC) controls the Olympic Games, and it in turn allows each nation's Olympic committee to determine which athletes will compete. The United States' committee (USOC) oversees matters relating to participation in the Olympics and other international contests.

In addition, most Olympic sports have their own governing bodies which conduct world championships and establish eligibility rules. The IOC has also given these international federations the responsibility for determining and enforcing Olympic eligibility requirements for their particular sport. These international sport federations also contain individual national federations – the relationship between the two is similar to that between the IOC and the respective national Olympic committees. The complicated delegation of authority between all of these organizations makes it difficult for courts to decide how and when to intervene in disputes involving international sports.

The most infamous Olympic episode in recent history occurred in 1994, when figure skater Nancy Kerrigan was assaulted right before the U.S. Figure Skating Championships that would determine which American skaters would participate in the 1994 Olympics. Kerrigan did not skate in the event, and competitor Tonya Harding won the championship and a spot on the team. Because her leg would presumably heal before the Olympics, Kerrigan was also selected for the team.

It was then discovered that the assault on Kerrigan had been arranged by Harding's recently-divorced husband, although Harding denied any personal knowledge or participation in the attack. Criminal investigation of Harding ensued, and the U.S. Figure Skating Association (USFSA) convened a panel to investigate the incident. The panel charged Harding with involvement in the conspiracy, and under USFSA rules Harding was entitled to a hearing in front of the panel and a later arbitration. Because the proceedings would not be completed until after the 1994 Olympic Games, the USOC scheduled its own hearing to determine whether Harding could participate in the Games. However, Harding sought a court order prohibiting the USOC action, and the USOC subsequently dropped its hearing and allowed Harding to skate in the Olympics. She finished eighth and Kerrigan won a silver medal.

After completion of the Olympics, Harding agreed to a plea bargain and resigned from the USFSA and competitive skating generally. The USFSA went forward with its hearing, and although Harding chose not to appear, the panel found that Harding had prior knowledge of Kerrigan's attack and thus violated the USFSA Code of Ethics. Harding was stripped of her 1994 U.S. Figure Skating title, permanently banned from the USFSA, and the matter was closed.

STEROIDS

Steroid use (or "doping") has become an increasingly important issue for international sports. In October 1990, sprinter Harold "Butch" Reynolds received a 2-year suspension from the International Amateur Athletic Federation (IAAF) following a positive test for anabolic steroids. This suspension would have kept Reynolds out of the 1992 Olympic Games, and he brought a federal suit arguing that the test results were erroneous. The judge said that Reynolds must first use the athletic system's administrative process. An arbitration hearing under the U.S. Olympic Committee's procedures found that the suspension was improper on the grounds that two separate tests taken by Reynolds appeared to be from different people. The IAAF refused to accept the ruling and ordered a separate hearing which eventually found Reynolds guilty.

The U.S. Olympic trials were to be held in a matter of weeks, and Reynolds returned to court. Even though the IAAF failed to show up, the court found that it had jurisdiction over the organization and entered a preliminary injunction allowing Reynolds to participate in the Olympic trials. He qualified as an alternate in the 4x400 relay, but the USOC refused to allow him to travel with the team because of the IAAF's refusal to allow him to participate in the Olympics. Reynolds did not attend the Olympics.

More recently, U.S. track and field star Marion Jones was connected with the highly publized BALCO steroid investigation. Jones, who won five gold medals, pled guilty in October 2007 to lying to the federal BALCO investigators by denying the use of performance-enhancing drugs. Upon her admission, the U.S. Anti-Doping Agency ordered Jones to forfeit all awards dating back to 2000. In addition, the IOC formally stripped Jones of all five Olympic medals. In January 2008, a district judge sentenced Jones to six months in prison, 200 hours of community service, and two years' probation for perjury.

OSCAR PISTORIUS: CHEETAHS A CHEATER?

The International Association of Athletics Federations (IAAF) voted unanimously in January of 2008 to ban the "Cheetah prosthetic" in competitions organized under IAAF Rules. This decision effectively precluded double-amputee Oscar Pistorius of South Africa from competing in the 2008 Beijing Olympics. The 21-year-old Pistorius, who uses the J-shaped carbon fiber blades as artificial legs, had reached within a second of the required qualifying time for the 400 meter and applied for eligibility in the upcoming Olympic games.

The IAAF concluded from its research that the Cheetah amounted to a "technical aid" not allowed in able-bodied competition because the prosthetic confers a 30% mechanical advantage to the user by creating less vertical movement and by using energy more efficiently than a natural ankle. Thus Pistorius could run with the blades at the same speed as an able-bodied athlete while consuming less energy. Were the IAAF's decision subject to American anti-discrimination laws, it is interesting to consider how it would fair in light of the Casey Martin precedent.

However, Pistorius appealed to the Court for the Arbitration of Sports, which in May of 2008 overruled the IAAF decision because it determined that the IAAF had not proved "that the biomechanical effects of using this particular prosthetic device gives Oscar Pistorius an advantage over athletes not using the device." Because he has not yet posted a time sufficiently fast to qualify, Pistorius likely will not achieve a top three finish in the Beijing games. Despite criticism from the International Paralympic Committee and other organizations, the IAAF will apparently limit its inquiries in this field to biomechanics, at least as indicated by the rulings on the Cheetah.

Swimmers wearing the one-piece fully body LZR Racer have accounted for 36 of the 40 world records broken since it was introduced. Does this technology provide an unfair advantage? Does it matter if any swimmer can wear the suit?

Part III

College Athletics and the NCAA

Collegiate sports are in many respects different from the professional leagues previously discussed. The view of college athletics as a mere extracurricular school activity is, however, no longer realistic. Intercollegiate sports are a major source of entertainment to the public and are as much, if not more so, a part of this country's culture as professional sports. Intercollegiate sports involve thousands of participants and employees, millions of fans and billions of dollars. *Forbes* valued Notre Dame's football program at over $90 million in 2006 (including the subsidies the team pays to the athletic department to fund other sports). The state of Georgia expected that hosting the 2007 Final Four in Atlanta would bring $61 million to the state. Analysts estimated businesses across the country would in total suffer $1.2 billion in lost productivity from the 2007 March Madness. College athletics is Big Business.

Athletic departments must, in many ways, be run like a business and produce income to operate. Despite the popularity and large revenues generated by college sports, most athletic departments are not profitable. The growing emphasis on producing winning teams, especially in the potential money-making sports, has as much to do with economics as school spirit. A successful football or basketball program can earn a program hundreds of thousands, if not millions, of dollars. Revenue, however, does not come free. Most athletic departments incur large expenses and therefore a losing program—on the field and in the books—can drown a school in debt. Generating revenue is the number one priority for many athletic departments.

NATIONAL COLLEGIATE ATHLETIC ASSOCIATION (NCAA)

It is impossible to discuss intercollegiate athletics without focusing on the role of the National Collegiate Athletic Association (NCAA). The NCAA is a private unincorporated organization that began in the early 1900's. The private, as opposed to public, nature of the NCAA is noteworthy. The United States Supreme Court ruled in *Tarkanian v. NCAA* that the NCAA is not a "state actor" with respect to constitutional due process requirements.

The NCAA's initial purpose was to reform the rules of football to make the game less dangerous. Initially, the NCAA limited itself to rule-making aspects of the sports. By 1921, the organization was sponsoring athletic events. Today, the NCAA is essentially the proprietor of intercollegiate athletics and oversees 88 championships in 23 sports. Other countries in the world do not combine athletics with education. The unique approach in the U.S. further reflects the significant role of the NCAA in collegiate sports.

MEMBERSHIP AND DIVISIONS

A school that is accredited by a recognized academic agency and which meets NCAA athletic standards can join the association. The NCAA currently has about 1,000 members. Membership is divided into three divisions: Division I, Division II, and Division III. Division I schools that have football programs were previously divided into Division I-A and Division I-AA as to their football programs. The NCAA recently changed the description of the football programs in Division I. The football programs that were formerly identified as Division I-A are now referred to as the Football Bowl Subdivision. Division I-AA schools are in the Football Championship Subdivision.

A school's NCAA classification is determined by a number of factors set by the NCAA. The factors include how much money is spent on scholarships, the number of scholarships and sports offered, the level of competition and attendance. For example, a Division I-A school must offer at least 16 sports, male and female combined. A set number of the regular season football games must be played at home against Division I-A teams and certain attendance figures must be met. The school must sponsor at least one male and female sport per season. The requirements for a Division I-AA are somewhat less. A Division II school must sponsor at least five male and female sports. Division III schools must also offer five male and female sports, and three of each must be team sports. Division III schools cannot offer athletic scholarships, but can provide scholarships based on need.

NCAA AND COLLEGIATE SPORTS REVENUE

No aspect of the NCAA operation draws more attention than its annual Division I basketball tournament, often referred to as "March Madness." The basketball extravaganza is one of the more phenomenal sporting events in the country. The tournament has become such an attraction that many companies experience a drop in productivity during the games because employees are concentrating on the games. For a few weeks tournament games are played in front of over 750,000 fans in arenas throughout the country. Millions more watch the games on television. And it is the television contract, an 11-year-$6 billion deal, that is the crown jewel of revenue for the NCAA and its members. About $400 million is distributed to the conferences each year. Some of the money is paid to schools based on the number of sports offered and how many athletes are on scholarship. A portion of the proceeds are paid to conferences based on the performance of their teams in the tournament. A conference is awarded a "unit" for each win in the tournament by a team in the conference and the payments are made over a six-year period. No units are awarded, however, for the championship game. The tournament revenue provides a major source of funding for many schools.

Schools or conferences with successful football and basketball programs earn huge sums from ticket sales and television rights during the regular season. In addition, the football Bowl Championship Series (BCS) provides a substantial revenue source for the teams and conferences that are chosen to play. Although the NCAA sanctions football bowl games, it does not control or receive the revenue. The money is paid directly to the school or conferences that participate. A conference that has a team in a BCS game can anticipate receipts in the range of $11 million to $13 million dollars.

The revenues generated by the NCAA and the colleges have a downside. The money earned is in stark contrast to the amateur status of the college athlete as required by the NCAA. In addition, the NCAA's revenue raises the problem of deciding how the money should be divided among the schools. Should the NCAA's revenue go only to teams that are involved in the contests, to every team in the respective conference or to every NCAA member? What formula should be used to determine the distribution? Should the schools spend the money received from the NCAA only on the sport that earned it, or on all sports? Should some of the funds be used for academic programs?

The financial rewards can lead to litigation between schools. In 2002 the University of Georgia filed suit against Tulane for breach of contract. The schools had an agreement to play three football games, two were scheduled to be played in Athens, Georgia, in 2002 and 2003 and one at the Louisiana Superdome in 2008. Tulane was to receive $450,000 for each game in Athens and Georgia was to be paid $400,000 for the game in the Superdome. Tulane backed out of the agreement. Georgia's suit alleged that Tulane claimed it had to get out of the games because its conference rules were changed from a seven to eight conference game schedule. The suit alleged the claims by Tulane were false and that the real reason the games were cancelled was to allow Tulane to earn more money by playing games against Texas, one of which was played in September 2002. The case eventually settled.

The BCS revenue is considered to be one of the reasons some schools have changed their conference affiliation. Miami University in Florida is a perennial football powerhouse and it regularly appears in the BCS. Miami, Syracuse and Boston College decided they wanted to leave the Big East and join the Atlantic Coast Conference. The threat resulted in lawsuits and counter suits between Miami and the Big East conference and some of its members. Some of the Big East schools claimed they made substantial financial investments in their athletic programs based on the assurance that Miami would remain in the Big East Conference. In particular, Connecticut spent $90 million on stadium improvements for its newly created football program.

Due to the enormous popularity of college sports, and the free or relatively inexpensive labor provided by the athletes, the public's perception is that athletic programs are profitable. The average revenue in Division I schools continues to rise. The growth rate, however, is misleading. First, the growth in revenue is limited to a small group of elite programs. Second, the accounting involved is subject to question. Most schools include some form of institutional subsidies in their revenue figures. In reality, most athletic departments, including Division I programs, operate at a loss. The primary reason is escalating costs. At the January 2001 NCAA Convention, the President of the NCAA, Cedric Dempsey, announced that the more than 970 NCAA members of the NCAA brought in over $3 billion in revenues in the previous year—but spent $4.1 billion in the same period.

NCAA's Regulatory Role

The NCAA regulates almost every aspect of intercollegiate sports among its members. In its effort to maintain the integrity of college sports, the NCAA has established a vast body of rules and regulations. The scope of NCAA regulation has become extremely broad and complex. Complete compliance is difficult even for the most well intended school. The regulations include rules of the games and the eligibility and conduct of players, coaches and institutions. In order to participate in intercollegiate athletic events, member schools and athletes must comply with NCAA rules.

The role and duty the NCAA has undertaken is formidable and is a constant source of controversy. Not a season goes by without a report of alleged violations by an athlete or institution of NCAA rules. Information about misconduct will prompt an investigation by the NCAA. When the NCAA determines its rules have been violated, an array of sanctions may be imposed which range from minor restrictions to the "death penalty." The latter pertains to an order for the institution to abandon a sport for a period of time and has only been imposed on one school. Sanctions can include prohibitions on television appearances, post-season play, scholarship restrictions and forfeiture of games. Unfortunately, athletes who were not involved in the violations, or not even enrolled at the school at the time, often bear the brunt of the penalties.

The NCAA is constantly being challenged with respect to its regulations. Although the disputes cover a wide range of issues, they generally concern the treatment of the student-athlete. The NCAA has the Student-Athlete Advisory Committee (SAAC) which is a student organization within the NCAA that serves to provide the perspective of the student-athlete. But, the SAAC has only an advisory role and has been criticized as ineffectual. In the last few years two student groups were formed to put more pressure on the NCAA to enact changes on behalf of student-athletes.

In the 1999-2000 basketball season the Student Basketball Committee (SBC) was formed with the support of the National Association of Basketball Coaches (NABC). The SBC consisted of about 48 collegiate basketball players, including some of the top players in the country. The SBC was created primarily in response to what was viewed as the unfair treatment by the NCAA of some collegiate basketball players, particularly with respect to the players or their parents receiving prep school tuition payments. The SBC challenged the suspensions and called for changes in the NCAA rules. The SBC became inactive, however, when the players in the association finished their collegiate careers.

In January 2001 the Collegiant Athlete Coalition (CAC) was formed by current and former student-athletes. Chapters were organized at a several schools in the west. The mission of CAC was to improve conditions for the student-athlete and focused on goals such as securing healthy coverage for all sports related injuries including those that occur in voluntary activities, year-round health insurance, an increase in life insurance policies, and an increase in monthly stipends. CAC stated it had no interest in advocating a strike to achieve its goal. CAC was supported, however, by the U.S. Steelworkers union. What impact, if any, CAC may have remains to be seen.

Can student-athletes form a union pursuant to labor law? Section 7 of the NLRA grants employees the right to organize. The law requires that the employer-employee relationship be engaged in interstate commerce. Based on previous court decisions the interstate commerce element would easily be met. The real issue is whether student-athletes would be recognized as "employees." The NLRB has found that graduate assistants at New York University could form a bargaining unit. The school argued that the payments made to the assistants was financial aid and was not compensation for work. The school also maintained that the services performed were primarily educational. The NLRB, however, found that NYU paid and controlled the assistants and therefore they were employees.

The courts that have previously addressed the issue have uniformly held that student-athletes are not employees. Recognition of student-athletes as employees and allowing them to organize into a union would likely bring about enormous changes in collegiate athletics. Given the importance college sports have in our culture the courts will be reluctant to recognize student-athletes as employees. That recognition would allow student-athletes to form a union and reshape college athletics.

NCAA Amateur Status

One NCAA rule which has caused considerable controversy is the requirement of "amateur" status of the college athlete. The regulation involves a number of factors, but three aspects are central to the rule:

1. A student will lose his amateur status if he receives any type of compensation for participating in that sport (unless permitted by the NCAA).
2. A student will lose his eligibility if he announces he is available for the professional draft (unless permitted by the NCAA).
3. A student will lose his eligibility if he retains an agent for representation with respect to a professional contract for that sport. (No exceptions.)

A professional athlete in one sport may represent a member institution in a different sport. However, the student-athlete cannot receive institutional financial assistance in the second sport unless the student-athlete:

(a) Is no longer involved in professional athletics,
(b) Is not receiving any remuneration from a professional sports organization, and
(c) Has no active contractual relationship with any professional athletics team. However, an individual may remain bound by an option clause in a professional sports contract that requires assignment to a particular team if the student-athlete's professional career is resumed.

A student-athlete may inquire of a professional sports organization about eligibility for a professional-league player draft or request information about the individual's market value without affecting his or her amateur status. But the student will lose his amateur status if he asks to be placed on the draft list or the supplemental draft list of a professional league in that sport, (exceptions for basketball) even though:

(a) He asks that his name be withdrawn from the draft prior to the actual draft,

(b) His name remains on the list but he is not drafted;

(c) He is drafted but does not sign an agreement with any professional team;

A student-athlete or his legal guardian or the institution's professional sports counseling panel may enter into negotiations with a professional sports organization without the loss of the student's amateur status. A student who retains an agent, orally or in writing, shall lose his amateur status for that particular sport. An agency contract not specifically limited in writing to a sport shall be deemed applicable to all sports and the student shall be ineligible to participate in any sport. Merely signing an unenforceable contract for representation can preclude a student from amateur sports.

Securing advice from a lawyer concerning a proposed professional sports contract shall not be considered contracting for representation by an agent under this rule, unless the lawyer also represents the student-athlete in negotiations for such a contract.

PAYING ATHLETES

The wisdom of the NCAA's position with respect to the amateur status of college athletes has been the subject of considerable debate. The issue has come under increasing scrutiny as revenues from college sports reach staggering proportions.

An ongoing dispute which has intensified over the years is whether student-athletes should be paid for their services. The argument is that the athletes' skill, work, and sacrifice generate huge sums of money for the schools and coaches. The athletes, however, are not allowed to reap any financial benefit from their labor other than their scholarship benefits. In addition, until recently student-athletes were prohibited by NCAA rules from working to earn money during the school term.

Some states are starting to take steps to bring about change within the NCAA. The Nebraska legislature recently considered paying additional money to Nebraska football players. It was reported that from 1994 to 2003 the football teams for the University of Nebraska generated about $155 million dollars in revenue, but during that same period only $14 million had been spent on football scholarships. Colorado, Texas, and Oklahoma were also considering measures that would increase compensation to some student-athletes. Aside from the NCAA rules, however, any attempt to compensate some male athletes would likely conflict with Title IX, a topic discussed in a later chapter. One consideration, among many, is to allow student-athletes to collect frequent flyer miles for their traveling to athletic events.

In California a law was proposed that would require state universities to provide an extra stipend of $2,400 for necessary travel, out-of-season medical care and clothing. The law would have allowed a student to transfer to another college without sitting out another year if the head coach departed. The most radical part of the law, however, would have allowed a student to sign with an agent without losing his eligibility. The law, which did not pass, would have put the California schools in direct conflict with NCAA regulations.

One of the pressing problems related to the rules of amateur status is the acceptance by student-athletes of money or gifts from sports agents or their associates. Some observers have suggested that 75% of the student-athletes who have the potential of being drafted in the NFL or NBA accept gifts from agents, or their associates, during their college eligibility. Those in support of paying athletes argue that the payment would reduce, if not eliminate, the athletes temptation to yield to agents bearing gifts. Another view is that the athlete who, while still eligible for college athletics, accepts money from an agent is generally motivated by desire, not need. There is a question as to whether some additional living allowance will serve as a deterrence to a student-athlete who wants to obtain additional benefits.

The enormous problem of agents paying student-athletes caused the NCAA to re-evaluate its position. In response to the problem, the NCAA changed its rules to allow student-athletes to work in the off-season during the school year and earn up to the value of the cost of attendance at the institution in which they are enrolled. In order to be eligible, a student must have been at the school for one academic year. This change was hailed by many as a greater recognition of the students' interest by the NCAA. Opponents of the change are fearful the rule will be abused and that the cost of monitoring the athletes will be substantial. Regardless, there is a question as to how much time a student-athlete has during the "off-season" to maintain a job.

The NCAA also recently considered, but rejected, a proposal to allow select athletes, who might consider turning professional before the exhaustion of their college eligibility, to obtain loans. Athletes projected to go high in the NFL and NBA draft are, however, allowed to purchase insurance to provide for a financial recovery in the event of a career-ending injury. The insurance coverage is generally limited to about 65% of the guaranteed income during the first three years of a contract for the particular league. The NCAA rule on insurance is also available to women who qualify for the WNBA draft.

The argument that student-athletes are financially exploited has merit. Putting aside the NCAA rules, however, the payment of student-athletes is fraught with problems. Would the payment be made only to athletes on sports that generate surplus revenue such as football and basketball? Should the payment be conditioned on that sport making a profit? The latter would bring about some interesting accounting questions such as rent for the stadium or arena. Should revenue from the profit-making sports continue to be used to fund other sports? Should all players receive the same pay or should the payment be based on the skill of the player as in the professional leagues? How much should be paid to the athlete? Should the payment be based on the player's performance each week or guaranteed even if the player performs poorly? Would the promise to pay be for one season or for four-year periods? The argument about paying players has broad appeal and momentum, but may create more problems than it solves. Regardless, the debate is far from over.

The NCAA rules on amateurism are also having a severe impact on athletes who were previously unaffected. Americans who compete in the Olympics and win gold medals can now receive financial awards. Few would argue that the money is not well earned. The swimmers from the 1996 U.S. team who still had college eligibility, however, were unable to accept the payment of about $65,000 without giving up their right to compete at the collegiate level. This choice was particularly hard on the swimmers because, unlike many other sports, there are few opportunities to earn money as a professional in the sport after finishing college. The women's gold medal soccer team had the same choice, accepting the money meant giving up any remaining college eligibility. The women's gymnastics team had to make a similar decision regarding the lucrative and popular post-Olympic tours. The unfortunate dilemma faced by Olympic athletes may put additional pressure on the NCAA to modify its position on amateurism.

ENDORSEMENTS AND PROMOTIONAL ACTIVITIES

The NCAA generally prohibits a student-athlete from advertising or promoting a product or service and from appearing on a radio or television show if it is related to athletic ability or prestige. These rules have also been applied in some questionable situations.

Harold Dennis was the sole survivor of a bus crash which killed 27 people and left Dennis with horrible burns. Dennis overcame his injuries and succeeded in becoming a walk-on player for the Kentucky football team. His recovery was so impressive that he was offered a television-movie contract for his story. The NCAA ruled the agreement was a violation and suspended Dennis from playing. To retain his eligibility, Dennis was forced to rescind the contract.

Dan Kreft was a basketball player for Northwestern majoring in electrical engineering. His school and curriculum are highly regarded academically. Kreft created a home page on the World Wide Web and updated it with his personal and perceptive thoughts on his academic and athletic experiences. His web site was so popular it drew the attention of a national publication, *Sports Illustrated*. The magazine asked Kreft to place his writings in their publication. Kreft agreed to have his material published for free. The NCAA ruled that if Kreft wrote a byline story he would be promoting a commercial entity which would constitute improper exploitation of his status as an athlete and a violation of NCAA rules. There was no dispute that the magazine's interest in Kreft was due to his ability with words, not a basketball. The NCAA, however, held firm. *Sports Illustrated* wrote a response to the NCAA's position which questioned the rationale of a rule which bars college students, who happen to be athletes, from writing in a national magazine.

Another example of how absurd the NCAA rules had become was demonstrated when the NCAA notified the *Tallahassee Democrat* newspaper that it was jeopardizing the eligibility of players at Florida, Florida St. and Florida A&M in its 5-year tradition of publishing diary entries written and submitted by players on the teams. No compensation was paid to the players, but the NCAA found that the publication was used as a promotion in the sale of the paper. Of course, the same reasoning could apply to interviews, stories, photographs or videos of players regularly used by the news media or sports publications.

In the spring of 1996, the NCAA made a controversial ruling in the case of Darnell Autrey. Autrey was a Northwestern football player who, in his sophomore year, was a Heisman Trophy contender. Autrey was also a serious theater student. Autrey was offered a part in a movie to be filmed in Italy. The arrangement called for payment of Autrey's expenses, but no compensation. The NCAA initially held that Autrey's appearance would violate its rules and threatened penalties that ranged from a one-game suspension to losing his remaining two years of eligibility. Autrey filed suit against the NCAA and argued that the NCAA's position conflicted with its own FUNDAMENTAL POLICY as stated in part

> The competitive athletics programs of member institutions are designed to be a vital part of the educational system. A basic purpose of this Association is to maintain intercollegiate athletics as an integral part of the educational program and the athlete as an integral part of the student body.
>
> The time required of student-athletes for participation in intercollegiate athletics shall be regulated to minimize interference with their opportunities for acquiring a quality education in a manner consistent with that afforded the general student body.

The court granted an injunction in Autrey's favor. In the opinion the judge suggested that the NCAA come to its senses and recognize the folly of its position. The NCAA threatened to appeal. After further review the NCAA acknowledged conflicting rules which seem to allow a student to appear in a television production, but not films. The NCAA further noted that Autrey was a theater major and his role was not related to his athletic ability. The NCAA agreed to waive the rule and Autrey was allowed to accept the movie role.

As a result of considerable criticism it received with respect to the above situations, the NCAA changed its by-laws that allows student-athletes to appear in film and television roles and write articles for newspapers and magazines and to be paid the going rate for such work. The NCAA now allows a student-athlete to appear on a radio or television program or engage in writing projects related to their athletic ability provided no endorsement is made or compensation is received.

One of the highlights of the 1998 Winter Olympics was the U.S. women's victory and gold medal in hockey. The popularity of the achievement was demonstrated when the team was chosen to be featured on one of sports most recognized mediums—the Wheaties cereal box. Unfortunately, 15 of the team's 20 members had to decline this once-in-a-life-time opportunity. The 15 women were members of their college hockey teams with remaining eligibility. Their appearance on the Wheaties box would have violated NCAA regulations and resulted in a forfeiture of their remaining college eligibility. Shame on the NCAA.

Jeremy Bloom was a high school state champion football player, track star and an exceptional skier. He was also a good student who finished high school with a 3.4 GPA. The University of Colorado ("CU") offered him a football scholarship, but he chose to defer enrollment to pursue his dreams of competing in the Olympics. For a time Bloom was the reigning World Cup champion in freestyle mogul skiing. He represented the United States in the 2002 Olympic Winter Games. His athletic ability as a skier, personality, and good looks earned him endorsement contracts with Dynastar, Oakley, and Under Armour, a modeling contract from Tommy Hilfiger, and opportunities with MTV, Nickelodeon, and others. These endorsement contracts provided funds to enable Bloom to train for the Olympic competition—which is the custom in that sport. The entertainment opportunities also fit with his major in communications and his desire to have a career in television and movies.

Bloom wanted to continue competing in football and train for the 2006 Olympics. Bloom estimated that the latter would require over $75,000 a year in expenses. In order to avoid the NCAA's prohibition on endorsement money Bloom requested a waiver and proposed creating a trust that the NCAA or the U.S. Olympic Committee would administer. The NCAA refused his request. Bloom filed suit against the NCAA, but he also discontinued his endorsement contracts which allowed him to play football for CU in 2002 and 2003. In January 2004 Bloom decided to accept endorsement money in order to pursue his skiing career.

Bloom's lawsuit against the NCAA was a breach-of-contract action. He sought an injunction against the NCAA with respect to its rules pertaining to endorsement contracts. Although he was not a direct party to the contract between the NCAA and CU, Bloom argued that the agreement was created for the benefit of students like him. The courts agreed that as a student-athlete Bloom did have standing to file suit against the NCAA as a third-party-beneficiary of the contract between the NCAA and CU.

Bloom argued that the endorsement money was due to his ability as a skier, which is not a college sport, and had nothing to do with his football skills. Bloom further argued that the NCAA allows athletes to play professional sports, for example baseball, and play another collegiate sport, such as football. The NCAA argued that Bloom's endorsement contracts were due in part because of his status as a multi-sport athlete. The trial and appellate courts found that it was unlikely Bloom would succeed at a trial on the merits and refused to grant him a preliminary injunction. Bloom continued the fight, but eventually lost the case.

The Bloom decision provoked the Colorado legislature to pass a resolution stating that Bloom should be allowed to play football at CU and accept endorsement money to fund his training for the Olympics. The legislators cited the example of John Elway, who played college football at Stanford while under contract with a professional baseball team.

UNDERCLASSMEN — PROFESSIONAL DRAFT

The NCAA has strict rules regarding a student-athlete who seeks to be drafted before his college eligibility has expired. In the past a student lost his remaining college eligibility in a sport if he entered the draft. In 1994, the NCAA changed the rules with respect to underclassmen basketball players. Students who declared their desire to enter the NBA draft were allowed to renounce the declaration within 30 days of the draft and retain their college eligibility. The player could not however, sign a contract with an agent or receive compensation without losing his eligibility. In 1998 the rule was modified again to require a player to withdraw at a time before the draft to retain his eligibility. Additionally, if a player with remaining eligibility declares himself available for the NBA draft, but is not drafted, the player preserves his college eligibility as long as he did not retain an agent.

Football players are treated differently than basketball players regarding the draft declaration. If an underclassman football player elects to be considered in the draft he looses his college eligibility regardless of whether he changes his mind or is not even drafted. After the 2001 season, Donte Stallworth, a receiver with another year of eligibility, announced he would enter the NFL draft. Immediately after his announcement he changed his mind and asked the NCAA to reinstate his eligibility. The request was denied.

Why are football players treated differently? To accommodate college football coaches. The coaches feel they need to know who will leave the team well in advance of recruiting deadlines. The NCAA considered, but rejected, a change that would allow a football player to declare for the draft and retain his eligibility if he withdrew the declaration within 72 hours of the deadline for the draft.

An argument can be made that football and basketball players should have the right to not only enter the draft, but to be drafted and then allowed a period of time to decide if they want to retain their college eligibility. Opponents, and there are many, claim allowing players to test their status in the professional drafts would create havoc for coaches. The problems that might arise, however, are probably exaggerated. The number of underclassmen who will be drafted by the NFL or NBA is small. In addition, the potential disruption that might occur would exist at all schools. Finally, the purpose of the NCAA and its regulations, supposedly, is to serve the best interest of the student-athlete. The rules forcing an underclassman to forfeit his college eligibility in order to determine his draft status appears to be driven by motives other than what is in the best interest of the student-athlete.

The NCAA rule allows an underclassman to enter the NBA draft and return to school with his eligibility. However, the NBA draft rules may lead to some unintended consequences. The NBA rules limit the initial salary payments of a player taken in the draft. If an underclassman declares for the draft, but is not drafted, he can return to his college and play. That same player may also be considered a free agent according to NBA rules. That is, any NBA team could attempt to bid for his services without concern for the above limit. This bidding could occur at any time, including during his remaining college career. This may be an unlikely scenario, but it is a possibility.

The consequences of ineligibility as a result of the draft declaration should not be underestimated. In 1989, the NFL had a rule, referred to as a "hardship exemption," which allowed underclassmen to enter the draft. About 25 underclassmen took advantage of the exemption. In the following year, due in part to legal necessity, the draft was opened to anyone who had been out of high school for at least 3 years. During the next four years about 200 more underclassmen entered the NFL draft. Of the total, about 150 or so made the roster of a NFL team. Consider the fate of the others. These players no longer had the scholarship for the free education or the opportunity to play and display their talent for next year's draft. Except for the truly exceptional athlete, an early draft declaration is a risky decision.

Braxston Banks declared for the NFL draft and retained an agent in 1989 with one year of eligibility remaining at Notre Dame. He was not drafted and attempted to return and play his final year. Notre Dame took the position that he was ineligible due to the NCAA rules. Banks sued the NCAA, not Notre Dame, asserting the rules violated antitrust laws. The trial court found there was no antitrust violations and dismissed the case. The appellate court upheld the decision and stated:

> The no-agent and no-draft rules are vital and must work in conjunction with other eligibility requirements to preserve the amateur status of college athletics, and prevent the sports agents from further intruding into the collegiate educational system.

Consider the above statement and recall that the NCAA rules permit college athletes to become "professionals" in one sport and retain their amateur status in others. *Gaines v. NCAA* was another case in which an underclassman, Gaines, a scholarship player for Vanderbilt, submitted his name for the NFL draft and retained an agent after his junior year. After Gaines was not selected by any team in the draft he petitioned the NCAA for another year of eligibility. The NCAA denied his request and Gaines filed suit alleging the rule was a violation of section 2 of the antitrust law, that is, it was an unlawful exercise of monopoly power by the NCAA. In upholding the NCAA's decision the court stated:

> As a result of NCAA Rules 12.1.1(f), 12.2.4.2, and 12.3.1, Gaines is now ineligible to complete his fourth year of eligibility as a football player at Vanderbilt. Rule 12.1.1(f) provides that an athlete loses his amateur status when he enters a professional draft or enters into an agreement with an agent to negotiate a professional contract. Rule 12.2.4.2 commonly known as the "no-draft" rule, makes a player ineligible for participation in a particular intercollegiate sport when he or she asks to be placed on the draft list or supplemental draft list of a professional league in that sport. Rule 12.3.1 commonly known as the "no-agent" rule, makes any player ineligible for participation in any future intercollegiate sport in which the player agrees, orally or in writing, to be represented by an agent for the purposes of marketing the player's abilities in the sport. This Rule applies even if the player receives no money or financial benefit of any kind from the agent, even if the agent is a family member or a close family friend, and even if the agent has not charged and agrees not to charge the player any fee. ...
>
> This Court is convinced that the NCAA Rules benefit both players and the public by regulating college football so as to preserve its amateur appeal. Moreover, this regulation by the NCAA in fact makes a better "product" available by maintaining the educational underpinnings of college football and preserving the stability and integrity of college football programs. Therefore, Gaines cannot succeed on the merits of his Sec. 2 claim because the NCAA has shown legitimate business justifications for the Rules at issue.
>
> It seems obvious to this Court that rules which are justified by legitimate business reasons necessarily cannot be deemed "unreasonably exclusionary" or "anticompetitive." Thus, the legitimate business reasons of the NCAA justifying enforcement of the eligibility Rules negate any attempt by Gaines to show the second element of a Sec. 2 claim—willful maintenance of monopoly power. Consequently, regardless of whether the NCAA justifications are viewed as a defense to a Sec. 2 challenge or rather as proof contradicting an assertion of willful monopolization, they necessitate a ruling by this Court in favor of the Defendants at this preliminary injunction stage of the proceeding.

The NFL Advisory Committee was established to give underclassmen an idea as to how they may fare in the draft. The Committee is comprised of team executives. When they receive the name of an athlete considering a move to the professional level they review the player's potential and report to the NFL Clearinghouse. The League compiles a consensus on the player and notifies the player of the result. The response by the Committee is by no means a guarantee. Underclassmen have been informed they would go high in the draft only to discover, after their declaration, that the opinion of the Committee is often way off the mark.

Underclassmen in baseball and hockey do not face the same problem regarding draft declarations. These players are drafted without their participation. Neither the drafting of the player nor contract discussions will render them ineligible. If a contract is reached, or if an agent represents the player, however, eligibility will be lost.

The NCAA rules allow a student-athlete to obtain advice regarding a professional contract from an advisor, such as an attorney, without losing his eligibility. The athlete can discuss with and receive recommendations from the advisor regarding an offer from a professional team. The athlete must pay the advisor an appropriate rate for his services. Utilization of an advisor, rather than an agent, should be considered by athletes who want to retain their collegiate eligibility if a satisfactory contract is not reached. If the advisor communicates with the team, however, he will be construed as an agent and the athlete will become ineligible. In addition, once a contract is agreed upon, the athlete will no longer be eligible for intercollegiate competition in that sport.

As a result of mounting criticism the NCAA is under pressure to adjust to the changing times. In January 2000 Division II schools passed a series of rule changes that allow a prospective student-athlete the chance, before his college enrollment, to be drafted by a professional sports team, enter into a professional sports contract, receive compensation for competition, participate on a professional sports team and accept prize money for competition without jeopardizing their college eligibility. The athlete is required to spend a full year at the college, referred to as a "year in residence" without competing in athletics and forfeits a year of eligibility for each year he participated in professional sports. Division I schools considered, but did not pass, a rule allowing an athlete who was considered a likely first-round draft choice in men's basketball, women's basketball or baseball or a third-round or higher choice in football or hockey to obtain a $20,000 loan and disability insurance that would be paid for by the NCAA.

ACADEMIC RULES

For many years the NCAA did not involve itself with the academic admission requirements for student-athletes. In the early 1960s, the NCAA adopted a standard that was based on a formula of high school records and test scores. Enter Robert Parrish, considered one of the top high school basketball players in the country in 1972. Parish would later become a prominent player with the NBA's World Champion Boston Celtics and teammate of the legendary Larry Bird. Parrish did very poorly on the ACT test and was not recruited by most schools who determined he would not be eligible. Centenary College, a small school in Shreveport, however, thought otherwise and granted Parrish a scholarship. After an investigation the NCAA concluded that Parrish was ineligible to play. Parrish and Centenary disagreed. Parish took the NCAA to court, *Parish v. NCAA*, seeking an injunction to prevent the enforcement of the rule. Parrish alleged that the NCAA rule violated his constitutional rights. The trial and appellate court ruled in favor of the NCAA. While the case was slowly going through the courts, however, Parrish continued to play and in 1973 the NCAA changed the rule.

The new rule by the NCAA required an athlete to have a 2.0 GPA in high school. A decade later the NCAA adopted the infamous Proposition 48. Proposition 48 received a lot of criticism as being discriminatory against minorities. Proposition 48 required at least a 2.0 GPA in a core course curriculum and a minimum SAT score of 700 or an ACT score of 15. Initially Proposition 48 allowed "Partial Qualifiers," that is, students who met one, but not both, of the above requirements, the right to receive the athletic scholarship, but they were not allowed to play for the first year (or thereafter without sufficient progress). In the late 1980s, the NCAA adopted Proposition 42, which prohibited financial aid to Partial Qualifiers. Although not as well known as 48, Proposition 42 drew even greater adverse reaction, especially from the Black Coaches Association (BCA). The NCAA then went to Proposition 26 which allowed Partial Qualifiers to receive non-athletic, need-based financial aid.

The NCAA then adopted a sliding scale approach with respect to standardized test scores and grade point average (GPA). For example, a 900 SAT (21-ACT) and a 2.00 GPA was acceptable as was a 700 SAT (17-ACT) and a 2.5 GPA. The definition of a Partial Qualifier was changed to require a sliding scale on both SAT and the GPA. A student had to score above 600 on the SAT and have above a 2.0 GPA to attain Partial Qualifier status. Partial Qualifiers were able to receive athletic scholarships and practice, but not play, with the teams in their freshmen year.

Cureton v. NCAA is a case that was filed by two students challenging the NCAA's academic rules. The students who filed the suit each had excellent grades in high school, but failed to achieve the minimum requirements on the SAT test. The suit alleged the standardized tests recognized by the NCAA discriminated against African Americans in violation of Title VI of the Civil Rights Act of 1964. Standardized tests have been part of the NCAA's Division I initial eligibility requirements since 1986 when Proposition 48 became effective. The plaintiffs claimed that the use of the tests as an absolute standard exceeded the practice by most universities. In fact, about 240 colleges did not require submission of standardized test scores for admission. There are some reports, based on GPAs in high school and college, that standardized tests are not absolute indicators of academic success and a number of critics have charged the tests are a poor method of determining whether students are qualified for college. In 1999 the trial court ruled in favor of the plaintiffs. The court ruled that the NCAA's sponsorship of its National Youth Sports Program resulted in the receipt of federal funds and the application of Title IX. In addition, the court found that member schools who receive federal funds had ceded their authority to the NCAA to run their athletic programs.

The NCAA filed an appeal and the decision was reversed. The appellate court ruled that the NCAA did not directly receive federal funding and was not subject to Title VI of the 1964 Civil Rights Act that forbids discrimination on the basis of race, color, or national origin. Several suits similar to the *Cureton* case have been filed against the NCAA. As a result, the weight given to the standardized test scores has been reduced.

Another problem facing the NCAA is its rule that pertains to the "core curriculum" a student-athlete is required to meet in high school. The NCAA requires that a student-athlete must successfully complete a certain number of "core courses" in English, math and science. The original number of core courses was 11 and was later increased to 13. For students entering after August 2005 the number of core courses required will be 14 and for those entering after August 2008 the number will rise to 16. Whether a school's course fits within the "core" criteria proved problematic. Many of the NCAA "consultants" who were responsible for determining whether a course met the definition of a "core" course had no training whatsoever for the task. Decisions were often made based solely on the name of the course without any knowledge about the course contents. In one case the NCAA ruled that Kenny Thomas, a basketball player for the University of New Mexico, was academically ineligible. The NCAA's position was that a course taken by Thomas in the 9th grade was not a "core" course. Thomas filed suit and obtained an injunction which allowed him to play in the 1995-1996 season. The case was eventually settled.

Major reforms that were recently enacted will put more pressure on schools to emphasize academics in their athletic programs. Starting in 2006 schools will be penalized if their athletes' classroom performance does not meet certain standards regarding graduation rates. Athletes will be required to complete 20% of their degree requirements each year to remain eligible. Failure to comply with the requirements can subject the schools to the loss of scholarships and post-season eligibility.

There is the argument that the NCAA's zeal to enforce academic standards on athletes has gone too far and that student-athletes should not be required to perform at a higher academic standard than the rest of the student population. There are situations, however, which raise the question of whether the NCAA, or the schools and conferences, are doing enough on the issue of academic integrity. Although not as common as in years past, there remain student-athletes majoring in "college eligibility." Some school curriculums consist of courses on fly-fishing, walking and AIDS-awareness. It should come as no surprise that some college sports programs have a graduation rate of 20%. One must remain aware, however, that student-athletes who transfer to a different institution or enter a professional draft count against the graduation rate.

In 2005 the NCAA began evaluating schools, individual programs and student-athletes according to the Academic Progress Rate (APR). The APR is designed to track eligibility and retention of scholarship athletes. Each semester a school may receive a points for scholarship athletes who remain eligible and for athletes who stay in school or graduate. The points are put into a formula and used to supplement the Graduation Success Rate (GSR). If a program does not meet minimum standards penalties can be imposed, including the loss of scholarships.

A lot of college competition involves considerable travel. Many of the sports, for example basketball, compete in the middle of the week. The NCAA's basketball tournament, a source of enormous revenue for the association and its members, extends the season even further. The travel, mid-week games and tournament play requires the student-athletes to miss a number of classes. Does the NCAA really believe that a student-athlete involved in the NCAA basketball tournament can focus on class responsibilities?

It is somewhat ironic that student-athletes are not allowed course credit on the subject they are learning the most about while at college—their sport. Students not only earn credit but often major in subjects such as music, dance, acting and journalism. Aside from the development of their physical skills, student-athletes spend an enormous amount of time learning mental aspects of their sport including proper techniques, training, safety, and complex offensive and defensive schemes. But for some reason, any suggestion to give course credit for this intense and rigorous instruction is met with ridicule.

COLLEGE TRANSFERS

Once a student enrolls in a college, NCAA rules prohibit a representative of another college from contacting that student without permission from the current school. Without such permission, financial aid cannot be provided to a transferee until at least one year has passed. Even with permission from the first institution, the basic rule is that a transfer student is ineligible to compete in football and basketball until after a full academic year, and in some cases two years, in residence at the new institution. There are a number of exceptions to this rule. But, the rule does raise questions in view of the fact that the NCAA rules also require that athletic scholarships be granted for only one-year terms. Coaches do not forfeit their eligibility when they change schools, why should student-athletes? Many individuals choose a particular academic institution because they feel their prospective coach will best cater to their interests or prepare them for a professional athletic career. These students are somewhat abandoned when a coach departs for greener pastures because the student, unlike the coach, must forfeit an entire year of eligibility if they feel a transfer is necessary. For example, Rich Rodriguez in late 2007 accepted the head coaching position of Michigan's football team and simply moved his operations and "spread offense" over from West Virginia. Because his 6-foot-7 frame would not fit well in Rodriguez's new system, quarterback Ryan Mallet, who attended Michigan to play for the now retired Lloyd Carr, chose to transfer to Arkansas and suffer a lost year of eligibility. Should Mallet have to pay for Carr's retirement and the university's hiring of a coach whose practices largely contradict Mallet's expectations?

FIVE-YEAR/10-SEMESTER RULE

The NCAA rules provide:

> A student-athlete shall complete his or her seasons of participation within five calendar years from the beginning of the semester or quarter in which the student-athlete first registered for ... college. (Exemptions are made for military service, pregnancy and interruptions due to Olympic activities.

Mike Jones' senior year as a football player for the University of Southwestern Louisiana (USL) involved a fight with the NCAA over the interpretation of the 5-year rule. Jones was declared ineligible by the NCAA early in the 1996 season after he requested a third year of football eligibility at USL. Jones attended Polk Community College in Florida for two years, but was not a student-athlete. He was red-shirted in 1993 at USL and punted for the Cajuns in 1994 and '95. Because of the NCAA's position, Jones filed suit, *Jones v. NCAA* (1996) seeking a ruling that he was eligible to play. The trial and appellate court ruled in Jones' favor in August. The NCAA took the matter to the Louisiana Supreme Court in September and won a decision, placing Jones on the sidelines for USL's next five games. Significantly, however, the Supreme Court stated the following:

> Courts should not interfere with the internal affairs of a private association *except* in cases when the affairs and proceedings have not been conducted fairly and honestly, or in the cases of fraud, lack of jurisdiction, the invasion of property or pecuniary rights, or when the action complained of is capricious, arbitrary, or unjustly discriminatory.

The Supreme Court remanded the matter back to the district court. The trial judge again ruled in favor of Jones finding:

> The Court finds the entire appeals process to be arbitrary and capricious as to this plaintiff because he has no standing to appeal a decision by the NCAA which directly affects him. Instead, he must rely on the University to advance his rights, should they choose to do so. The Court finds such a system affecting such important individual rights to be patently unfair.
>
> The Court further finds that the plaintiff has proven he will suffer irreparable injury if this injunction is not issued because he only has the opportunity to play four more football games this season at USL, and that his failure to continue to play will greatly decrease his opportunity to become a professional football player with its monetary advantages. Accordingly, this Court reissues the original preliminary injunction in the form and substance rendered by the Court on August 29th, 1996.

DRUG TESTING

One of the more controversial areas with respect to the regulation of an athlete's conduct pertains to drug testing. Few would dispute that preventing athletes from using drugs, be they recreational or performance-enhancing, is a notable goal. Drug testing does, however, involve an intrusion on an individual's constitutional and privacy rights. There have been a number of court challenges by athletes with respect to drug testing. The court decisions are not uniform, but the trend is clearly to permit testing if appropriately conducted.

In the following case, the trial and appellate courts ruled that the NCAA's drug testing procedure was a violation of the student-athlete's right to privacy. The California Supreme Court, however, reversed and upheld the NCAA's testing.

Hill v. NCAA

The question presented by this case concerns the method used by the NCAA to monitor athletes as they provide urine samples. A tested athlete's urination is directly observed by an NCAA official of the same sex as the athlete who stands some five to seven feet away. Even the diminished expectations of privacy in a locker room setting do not necessarily include direct and intentional observation of excretory functions. Plaintiffs had a reasonable expectation of privacy under the circumstances; their privacy interest was impacted by the NCAA's conduct. The NCAA was therefore required to justify its use of direct monitoring of urination.

In support of direct monitoring, the NCAA introduced substantial evidence that urine samples can be altered or substituted in order to avoid positive findings and that athletes had actually attempted to do so. The NCAA's interest in preserving the integrity of intercollegiate athletic competition requires not just testing, but effective and accurate testing of unaltered and uncontaminated samples. If direct monitoring is necessary to accomplish accurate testing, the NCAA is entitled to use it.

There may indeed be less intrusive alternatives to direct monitoring that could nonetheless fully satisfy the tester's objective of insuring a valid sample. Because we are limited to the record before us, we necessarily leave any further consideration of less intrusive alternatives to direct monitoring initially to the judgment and discretion of the NCAA, and then to future litigation, if any.

The National Collegiate Athletic Association (NCAA) sponsors and regulates intercollegiate athletic competition throughout the United States. Under the NCAA's drug testing program, randomly selected college student-athletes competing in postseason championships and football bowl games are required to provide samples of their urine under closely monitored conditions. Urine samples are chemically analyzed for proscribed substances. Athletes testing "positive" are subject to disqualification.

By its nature, sports competition demands highly disciplined physical activity conducted in accordance with a special set of social norms. Unlike the general population, student-athletes undergo frequent physical examinations, reveal their bodily and medical conditions to coaches and trainers, and often dress and undress in same-sex locker rooms. In so doing, they normally and reasonably forgo a measure of their privacy in exchange for the personal and professional benefits of extracurricular athletics.

A student-athlete's already diminished expectation of privacy is outweighed by the NCAA's legitimate regulatory objectives in conducting testing for proscribed drugs. As a sponsor and regulator of sporting events, the NCAA has self-evident interests in ensuring fair and vigorous competition, as well as protecting the health and safety of student-athletes. These interests justify a set of drug testing rules reasonably calculated to achieve drug-free athletic competition. The NCAA's rules contain elements designed to accomplish this purpose, including: (1) advance notice to athletes of testing procedures and written consent to testing; (2) random selection of athletes actually engaged in competition; (3) monitored collection of a sample of a selected athlete's urine in order to avoid substitution or contamination; and (4) chain of custody, limited disclosure, and other procedures designed to safeguard the confidentiality of the testing process and its outcome. As formulated, the NCAA's regulations do not offend the legitimate privacy interests of student-athletes.

For these reasons the NCAA's drug testing program does not violate plaintiffs' state constitutional right to privacy. We will therefore reverse the judgment of the Court of Appeal and direct entry of final judgment in favor of the NCAA.

Dissenting Opinion

The superior court expressly found that the "amount of drug abuse by student-athletes in the United States is insignificant to virtually nonexistent." "The minimal evidence of drug use is almost entirely limited to anabolic steroid use by certain football players. ..." That means, of course, that there was no significant drug abuse to be deterred by any drug testing program to be established by the NCAA. The superior court impliedly found that the NCAA was, or should have been, aware of the foregoing when it established its drug testing program: The NCAA "voted to adopt the program. The reports upon which the NCAA relied were introduced here. They do not support the action taken." Because there was no significant drug abuse to be deterred before any NCAA drug testing program was established, the absence of such abuse cannot be attributed to the NCAA drug testing program that was later established. Ante hoc, ergo non propter hoc.

Is visually monitored urine collection actually required? The superior court found that it was not. It could not have been clearer on the point: "Direct monitoring of an athlete urinating is not necessary to ensure a valid sample." And again: "It is not necessary to scrutinize the athletes while urinating." The finding was squarely based on the testimony of Ronald Heitzinger, one of the NCAA's expert witnesses. Heitzinger stated that he had heard of a collection device "which is basically a beaker or some kind of receptacle into which the urine sample is placed which contains a thermometer so that you can detect whether or not someone is using their own urine as opposed to trying to cheat [with] someone else's urine[.]" Indeed, he admitted that he himself had "develop[ed] a method for checking [a] urine sample that did not require actually monitoring the person giving urine. ..."

Today, the majority take away from Stanford student-athletes—and all other Californians—the right of privacy guaranteed by the California Constitution. At the same time, they grant to the NCAA—and any other intruding party—a "right of publicity" based on nothing more than their own views of "good" and "bad" "policy."

The NCAA is now free to use in California the weapons it had chosen for its "war on drugs." "What better way to show that" it "is serious about its 'war on drugs' than to subject" student-athletes "to this invasion of their privacy and affront to their dignity? To be sure, there is only a slight chance that it will prevent some serious ... harm resulting from" student-athlete "drug use, but it will show to the world that" it "is 'clean,' and-most important of all—will demonstrate" its "determination ... to eliminate this scourge of our society! I think it obvious that this justification is unacceptable; that the impairment of individual liberties cannot be the means of making a point; that symbolism, even symbolism for [a] worthy ... cause ... cannot" justify an abridgment of the right of privacy.

****

A growing problem with drug testing is the use of various dietary or vitamin supplements by student-athletes. Many of the supplements will cause a positive test result. The students who fail the test often argue that they were assured by the sales person that the supplement was not illegal. What the students do not realize, however, is that just because it is legal does not rule out that it contains an NCAA banned substance. Students who have pleaded ignorance after failing a drug test because of a dietary substance are rarely successful in overturning their positive tests results.

ANTITRUST ACTIONS

NCAA rules have been challenged in court as a violation of antitrust laws. Most decisions have been in favor of the NCAA, but some courts have found the NCAA rules to be illegal. The courts generally apply antitrust law to the NCAA's commercial rules which relate to marketing and selling of NCAA events. The courts have been reluctant, however, to apply antitrust law to the NCAA rules that pertain to academic and amateur standards of athletes.

A successful antitrust claim against the NCAA involved restrictions on televised games. The trial and appellate courts found the NCAA's 1982-85 Football Television Plan violated antitrust law because the rules restricted the number of games a member institution could televise. The decision impacted networks, producers, syndicators, advertisers, the NCAA, and its member institutions. The Supreme Court upheld the trial and appellate court decision that the Plan was an antitrust violation. The Supreme Court rejected the stringent *per se* illegal test, however, as the basis for its decision.

NCAA v. Board Of Regents (1984)

Individual competitors lose their freedom to compete. Price is higher and output lower than they would otherwise be, and both are unresponsive to consumer preference. A restraint that has the effect of reducing the importance of consumer preference in setting price and output is not consistent with this fundamental goal of antitrust law. Restrictions on price and output are the paradigmatic examples of restraints of trade that the Sherman Act was intended to prohibit. At the same time, the television plan eliminates competitors from the market, since only those broadcasters able to bid on television rights covering the entire NCAA can compete. Thus, as the District Court found, many telecasts that would occur in a competitive market are foreclosed by the NCAA's plan. ...

It inexorably follows that if college football broadcasters be defined as a separate market—and we are convinced they are—then the NCAA's complete control over those broadcasters provides a solid basis for the District Court's conclusion that the NCAA possesses market power with respect to those broadcasts. "When a product is controlled by one interest, without substitutes available in the market, there is monopoly power. ..."

Thus, the NCAA television plan on its face constitutes a restraint upon the operation of free market, and the findings of the District Court establish that it has operated to raise price and reduce output. Under the Rule of Reason, these hallmarks of anticompetitive behavior place upon petitioner a heavy burden of establishing an affirmative defense which competitively justifies this apparent deviation from the operations of a free market.

The NCAA plays a critical role in the maintenance of a revered tradition of amateurism in college sports. There can be no question but that it needs ample latitude to play that role, or that the preservation of the student-athlete in higher education adds richness and diversity to intercollegiate athletics and is entirely consistent with the goals of the Sherman Act. But consistent with the Sherman Act, the role of the NCAA must be to *preserve* a tradition that might otherwise die; rules that restrict output are hardly consistent with this role. Today we hold only that the record supports the District Court's conclusion that by curtailing output and blunting the ability of member institutions to respond to consumer preference, the NCAA has restricted rather than enhanced the place of intercollegiate athletics in the Nation's life. Accordingly, the judgment of the Court of Appeals is affirmed.

****

In the *Board of Regents* case the trial court defined the relevant market as "live college football television." The trial court found that the NCAA had almost absolute control over the supply of college football for television and it characterized the NCAA as a "classic cartel." The trial court found no evidence that college football on television adversely effected gate attendance and that the NCAA regulation regarding recruitment and amateurism standards could adequately address any problem of competitive balance. The Court of Appeal labeled the NCAA television plan "illegal *per se* price fixing." The Court of Appeal held that even if it was not a *per se* violation, the alleged procompetitive justifications did not offset the anticompetitive effects on price and output, so the television plan was illegal even under the rule of reason standard. The Supreme Court recognized that league sports require competitor cooperation on a number of rules and regulations and that the NCAA plays a critical role in the maintenance of amateurism in college sports. The Supreme Court, however, concluded that the NCAA violated federal anti-trust laws by "curtailing output and blunting the ability of member institutions to respond to consumer preference."

After the NCAA's television plan was defeated, the Division 1-A and 1-AA member institutions adopted three binding principles for the 1984 season that included the following:

1. There shall be no televising of collegiate football games on Friday nights, and any afternoon football televising on that day of the week must be completed by 7 p.m. local time in each location in which the program is received.

2. No member institution shall be obligated to televise any of its games, at home or away. No member institution may make any arrangements for live or de-

layed televising of any game without the prior consent of its opponent institution.

3. The gross rights fee paid for each 1984 national telecast or cablecast shall be subject to an assessment of 4 percent to be paid to the NCAA by the home institution. The assessment will be used to fund the costs of the NCAA postgraduate scholarship program and football-related NCAA services. A "national telecast" is defined as a football game televised or cablecast s i - multaneously to at least 20 million homes in at least 30 states, or televised or cablecast to 50 percent of U.S. television homes as reported by the 1984 Edition/No 52 of Television and Cable Factbook and all updates to that publication issued prior to August.

The Sports Broadcast Act of 1961, 15 U.S.C. Sec. 1291-1295, provides for an antitrust liability exemption for the pooled sale of telecasting rights for professional football, baseball, basketball, and hockey leagues. The Act does not apply to intercollegiate athletics. The Act does protect college and high school football in that it requires the blacking out of professional football telecasts on Friday evenings and Saturdays from the second Friday in September to the second Saturday in December within 75 miles of the game site of any college or high school game scheduled to be played on such a date, 15 U.S.C. Sec. 1293.

A major antitrust action against the NCAA involved an NCAA rule to limit the amount of compensation received by certain coaches, referred to as "restricted earnings coaches." The NCAA rule permitted college basketball teams to have one head coach, two full time coaches and one part-time assistant. The latter could earn no more than $12,000 in salary and $4,000 in basketball-related outside income, such as summer camps. The NCAA's reasoning to put a (low) ceiling on what a part-time assistant coach could earn, but not regulate at all the salaries of the other coaches, who may earn several hundred thousand dollars per year, is described below. A class action antitrust suit was filed on behalf of affected basketball coaches challenging the restricted earning rule in *Law v. NCAA*. The court ruled in favor of the affected coaches and the rule has been set aside. A similar suit was filed on behalf of baseball coaches, *Schreiber v. NCAA* and a third suit on behalf of other coaches. All parties agreed to be bound by the decision in the *Law* case.

Law v. NCAA (1995)

This matter comes before the Court on Plaintiffs' Motion for Summary Judgment on the Issue of Liability. Plaintiffs in this suit allege that the Division I members of the National Collegiate Athletic Association ("NCAA"), in violation of the Sherman Antitrust Act, 15 U.S.C. Sec. 1 (the "Sherman Act"), have conspired to limit the maximum compensation they will pay to one category of basketball coaches, the "restricted earnings coaches." Defendant argues that the agreement at issue here--NCAA Bylaw 11.02.3, adopted in January 1991—does not restrict plaintiffs' potential compensation; defendant further argues that in any case, Bylaw

11.02.3 does not violate the Sherman Act because the restriction is justified under the circumstances presented. Therefore, defendant maintains that the agreement embodied in Bylaw 11.02.3 is not an unreasonable restraint of trade. Plaintiffs move for summary judgment, asserting that there is no dispute about the existence or the terms of the restriction, that the restriction on its face is an impermissible restraint of trade, and that the NCAA can thus demonstrate no set of facts that would allow the restriction to pass muster under the Sherman Act.

I. Background

The NCAA is an association of over 800 colleges and universities engaged in intercollegiate athletic competition. Its members are divided into Division I, Division II and Division III schools, depending on the number of sports offered at the school, its philosophy towards athletics and athletic scholarships, the number of participants in its athletic programs, the level of attendance at athletic events, the size of the school's facilities and a number of other factors. NCAA Division I basketball programs are generally of a higher stature and have more visibility than Division II and III basketball programs. The NCAA has approximately 300 Division I schools. Each Division I member of the NCAA hires and employs its own basketball coaches.

In 1989, the NCAA established a Cost Reduction Committee, charged with the task of formulating recommendations to NCAA members for reducing costs in intercollegiate athletics without compromising access of student-athletes to higher education or disturbing the competitive balance of the NCAA. At that time, many NCAA member institutions perceived difficulties in meeting costs associated with the maintenance of intercollegiate athletic programs. For example, many NCAA institutions were reducing the number of sports they offered as a means of controlling the overall cost of their athletic programs. In addition, because of troubles in managing their overall athletic budgets, some NCAA schools found themselves in noncompliance with Title IX requirements regarding women's athletics. Financial problems notwithstanding, many NCAA institutions meanwhile felt pressure to maintain, or even increase, spending on recruiting talented players and coaches and on other aspects of their sports programs in order to stay athletically competitive with rival schools. In defendant's words, they experienced pressure to "keep up with the Joneses." The NCAA formed the Cost Reduction Committee in response to what some viewed as a catastrophic cost spiral which, if not controlled, would eventually cause the complete demise of intercollegiate athletics.

Every four years, the NCAA commissions the "Raiborn Report," an analysis of financial trends and relationships in intercollegiate athletics prepared by Mitchell H. Raiborn, a professor of accounting at Bradley University. The Cost Reduction Committee used the 1986 Raiborn Report (covering the period 1981-85) to map out its task of reducing costs in intercollegiate athletics. According to the 1986 Raiborn Report, personnel, scholarships and travel comprised the largest items in the athletic budgets of member institutions, and the majority of institutions across the country were running deficit football and basketball programs. The 1986 Raiborn Report found that in 1985, forty-two percent of NCAA Division I schools reported deficits averaging $824,000 in their overall athletic program budgets. Regarding overall athletic department expenses, the report noted:

The percentage increase in average expenses between 1978 and 1985 exceeds 100 percent for all institutions except [member institutions in Division III that do not have football programs]. ... Average 1985 [Division I] expenses of $4,609,000 are 286 percent of the 1973 average, which indicates a 186 percent increase since 1973. The long-run trend analysis ... indicates a significant percentage increase in the average expenses of each responding group.

According to the 1986 Raiborn Report, fifty-one percent of the responding Division I institutions incurred expenses exceeding revenues in their basketball programs in 1985, sustaining an average deficit of $145,000.

Early in its discussions, the Cost Reduction Committee identified five areas in which cost reduction could be achieved: financial aid, recruiting, staffing policies, competitive policies and ancillary support services. The Committee identified personnel as the largest expense in intercollegiate athletic programs and determined that costs could be reduced by curtailing football and basketball staffs and by limiting personnel in other sports as well. The Cost Reduction Committee directed its subcommittee on personnel limitations to consider, in particular, the coaching categories in football and basketball for graduate assistants, volunteers and part-time coaches.

As a result of its deliberations, the Cost Reduction Committee proposed legislation (collectively, the "Restricted Earnings Coach Rule"), which limited the number of coaches in all Division I sports and required institutions to designate one of their coaches in every sport other than football a "restricted earnings coach." In Division I men's basketball, the limit set for coaching staffs was three head or assistant coaches and one restricted earnings coach. The Restricted Earnings Coach Rule also required that restricted earnings coaches' compensation be limited to $12,000 during the academic year and $4,000 during the summer months. The Cost Reduction Committee determined that these figures approximated the cost of out-of-state tuition at public institutions and average tuition at private institutions, and was thus roughly equivalent to the salaries previously paid to graduate assistant coaches. Under the rule, restricted earnings coaches may receive additional compensation for performing duties for another department of the institution during either the summer or the academic year, provided that (1) such compensation is commensurate with that received by others performing the same or similar assignments, (2) the ratio of compensation received for coaching duties and any other duties is directly proportionate to the amount of time devoted to the two areas of assignment, and (3) the individual is qualified for and performing the duties outside the athletic department for which the individual is compensated. The Division I members of the NCAA voted in January 1991 to adopt the Restricted Earnings Coach Rule effective August 1, 1992.

The limitations set forth in the Restricted Earnings Coach Rule reflect an effort by the Cost Reduction Committee, in its own words, to "establish a 'restricted earnings' category that will encourage the development of new coaches while more effectively limiting compensation to such coaches." In addition, the chairman of the Committee told NCAA members in January 1990 that the goal of the Cost Reduction

Committee was to "cut costs and save money" and that "the basic premise that we need to create legislation to save us from ourselves has overwhelming support."

The Restricted Earnings Coach Rule does not attempt to limit what member institutions spend on their basketball programs, except as to salaries of restricted earnings coaches. It does not prevent member institutions from increasing expenditures on other aspects of their athletic programs as they implement the cost reduction measures involving restricted earnings coaches. The Cost Reduction Committee did not recommend and the NCAA did not adopt any measure limiting salaries or compensation paid to other employees in athletic departments, such as head or assistant coaches.

The Restricted Earnings Coach Rule is binding on all Division I members and all restricted earnings coaches. All plaintiffs are or were employed as restricted earnings basketball coaches at NCAA Division I institutions, and their compensation as restricted earnings coaches thus is subject to and governed by the Restricted Earnings Coach Rule.

D. Effects of the Restricted Earnings Coach Rule

The NCAA first argues that the Restricted Earnings Coach Rule has no anticompetitive effect because restricted earnings coaches may avoid the restraining effect of the rule by obtaining coaching positions with high school teams, non-NCAA college teams, NCAA Division II or III teams, overseas teams or, in fact, by obtaining other employment not related to their coaching duties. At best, this argument amounts to an assertion that because Division I restricted earnings coach positions represent such a small portion of the market, the NCAA has no market power in this arena and thus its restraint can have no adverse competitive impact.

This argument by the NCAA is wholly unconvincing. The absence of proof of market power does not foreclose a finding of anticompetitive behavior under the Sherman Act. In fact, where there is an agreement not to compete in terms of price, " 'no elaborate industry analysis is required to demonstrate the anticompetitive character of such an agreement.' " Id. (quoting *National Soc'y of Professional Engineers v. United States*, (1978)). Where a restraint runs counter to the Sherman Act's requirement that price be responsive to consumer preference, proof of market power is unnecessary because such an agreement's anticompetitive character is evident.

The NCAA acknowledges that before the rule was enacted, some restricted earnings coaches were paid $60,000 to $70,000—apparently because the schools that employed them believed their services were worth that amount. Controlling such responses to consumer preference was in fact the very objective which the NCAA sought to achieve in enacting the rule. Because the Restricted Earnings Coach Rule specifically prohibits the free operation of a market responsive to demand and is thus inconsistent with the Sherman Act's mandates, it is not necessary for the Court to undertake an extensive market analysis to determine that the rule has had an anticompetitive effect on the market for coaching services.

The NCAA next argues that its regulation may even be procompetitive because, if the NCAA does not collapse as a result of its skyrocketing costs, it will be able to continue providing the product of college basketball and there will thus continue to be jobs available in the market for basketball coaches. For all its alarming rhetoric, however, the NCAA has offered no compelling evidence that its member institutions are on the brink of financial disaster or that the de minimus effect which reducing the salaries of the lowest paid member of each school's coaching staff by a few thousand dollars would pull them back from the abyss. Moreover, even if the situation of intercollegiate athletics was every bit as dire as the NCAA makes it out to be in resisting the coaches' challenge to the Restricted Earnings Coach Rule, the NCAA's argument--that the regulation is procompetitive because it will help the NCAA schools stay in the black so that they can continue providing intercollegiate athletics at all—cannot succeed.

The market for coaching services is different from the market for intercollegiate sports. In the market for coaching services, coaches are the producers and schools are the consumers, whereas in the market for intercollegiate sports, the schools become the producers and the public the consumers. Procompetitive justifications for price-fixing must apply to the same market in which the restraint is found, not to some other market. If price-fixing buyers were allowed to justify their actions by claiming procompetitive benefits in the product market, they would almost always be able to do so by arguing that the restraint was designed to reduce their costs and thereby make them collectively more competitive sellers. To permit such a justification would be to give businesses a blanket exemption from the antitrust laws and a practically limitless license to engage in horizontal price-fixing aimed at suppliers. This license the Court will not issue—even in the unique context of intercollegiate athletics.

E. NCAA Justifications for the Restricted Earnings Coach Rule

Because the Restricted Earnings Coach Rule constitutes a restraint on the operation of a free market, and because the uncontroverted facts demonstrate that its effect has been to stabilize and, in some cases, depress prices in the market for coaching services, the rule of reason next places on the NCAA a "heavy burden of establishing an affirmative defense which competitively justifies" this infringement on the Sherman Act's protected domain.

The NCAA attempts to carry its burden by emphasizing the importance of maintaining a level playing field in the sports arena, retaining and fostering the spirit of amateurism which is one of college athletics' defining characteristics, and protecting NCAA member institutions from self-imposed, ruinous cost increases.

The NCAA has not cleared the first of these two hurdles. As noted previously, the NCAA has offered no evidence that the Restricted Earnings Coach Rule furthers its stated objectives at all. The NCAA's stated objectives are to level the playing field to obtain competitive equity, to provide for an entry-level coaching position and to cut costs. The NCAA has submitted no evidence to this Court that requiring schools to pay their fourth-ranked basketball coaches all the same low salary levels the playing field in any significant way, especially when there is no limit on how disparately the three more senior coaches may be paid by competitor schools. Similarly, the NCAA has presented no evidence that the restricted earnings coach positions are now more likely to be filled by young or inexperienced coaches than they were when salaries were competitive. Nor has the NCAA offered any evidence that the Restricted Earnings Coach Rule really achieves an overall reduction in costs; as stipulated by the parties, nothing in the Restricted Earnings Coach Rule prevents NCAA schools from spending money saved (if any) from fixing the restricted earnings coach's salary on some other aspect of their basketball programs, such as increasing the head coach's salary. Because the NCAA has failed to meet its burden of establishing that the Restricted Earnings Coach Rule actually promotes a legitimate, procompetitive objective, it is unnecessary for plaintiffs to demonstrate that the Restricted Earnings Coach Rule is the least restrictive alternative available to the NCAA to achieve its stated goals or that comparable benefits could be achieved through viable, less restrictive means.

Because the Restricted Earnings Coach Rule is a restraint of trade as prohibited by the Sherman Act, the NCAA bears a heavy burden in this case to establish that the restraint enhances competition or, in other words, promotes a legitimate, procompetitive goal. On this record, the Court finds that the NCAA has not met this weighty burden and that plaintiffs are entitled to judgment as a matter of law on the issue of liability.

IT IS THEREFORE ORDERED that Plaintiffs' Motion for Summary Judgment on the Issue of Liability be and hereby is sustained.

****

The appellate court upheld the trial court's decision that the restricted earnings rule was a violation of antitrust law. That is, the NCAA was liable to the coaches. The case went back to the trial court on the issue of damages. In May, 1998 a jury rendered a verdict for a little over $22 million dollars. The award included $11.2 million for men's basketball coaches, $1.6 million for baseball coaches and $9.5 million for other coaches. Under antitrust law damages are trebled—the judgment was $67 million plus attorney fees of about $10 million. The NCAA appealed the damage award. The case was finally settled for $54.5 million.

The NCAA suffered another major legal setback in the recent case of *Smith v. NCAA*. The case involved a challenge to the NCAA's Bylaw 14.1.8.2. The rule prohibits a student-athlete from playing at a postgraduate school other than the institution from which the student earned her undergraduate degree. Ms. Smith alleged the rule was a violation of antitrust and Title IX law. The trial court dismissed both claims. The appellate court agreed on the antitrust claim, but also found that Smith was entitled to proceed on the Title IX action. The appellate court's opinion indicated that the NCAA's receipt of funds from member institutions, who in turn receive federal funds, would render the NCAA subject to the Title IX.

The U.S. Supreme Court reversed the *Smith* decision and ruled that the NCAA was not a recipient of federal funds merely because it members, who pay dues to the NCAA, receive federal funds. This was a major victory for the NCAA. The Supreme Court went further, however, and held that the plaintiff could try to show that the NCAA receives federal funds by virtue of it management of a youth sports program. The Supreme Court also said the NCAA could come under the law if it is shown that the schools have assigned their authority to run programs to the NCAA. Within weeks of the Supreme Court's decision, a trial court held in *Cureton v. NCAA* that the NCAA was in fact subject to Title IX and other federal laws for the two reasons described by the Supreme Court. As stated earlier, the *Cureton* decision was, however, reversed on appeal.

The NCAA faced another antitrust challenge in connection with its "two in four" rule for participation in preseason men's basketball tournaments. The rule restricts each Division I team to two exempt tournaments in a four-year period and only one in a season. A tournament can result in as many as four games, but only one game is counted against a team played in an exempt tournament. (Teams are limited to the number of games they can play in a season.) In *Worldwide Basketball & Sports Tours v. NCAA (2003)* the trial court found that the rule violated section 1 of the Sherman Act and issued an injunction prohibiting the enforcement of the rule. The NCAA appealed. The appellate court issued a stay on the injunction. That is, the court held that the rule would remain in force pending the appeal.

In 1998 the Bowl Championship Series (BCS) was formed. The BCS includes the conferences with all of the traditional football powerhouses and Notre Dame and the four major bowls, the Rose, Sugar, Orange and Fiesta. The BCS ranks teams according to a formula that involves subjective polls, computer rankings, schedule strength and team record. The complications and factors that influence the rankings are mind-boggling. The championship game between the number one and two team was rotated each year among the four bowls. The structure of the BCS made it possible, but much more difficult, for a team that is not in one of the member conferences to get invited to one of the BCS games. The revenues that are received from participation in the BCS are substantial. The conferences that are at a disadvantage have repeatedly threatened to challenge the BCS as an antitrust violation. As a result of the criticism, the BCS added a fifth bowl to the formula.

In 2004, Andy Carroll, a former University of Washington football player, filed an antitrust action against the NCAA. Carroll's suit claims the NCAA's rules limiting the number of scholarships that may be awarded in football to 85 is a violation of antitrust law. Carroll alleges he was led to believe that he would probably get a scholarship when he was a "walk-on" member of the team. He claims he was later advised that because of the rule the school would not be able to offer him a scholarship. Carroll's suit is seeking class-action status.

NCAA AND DUE PROCESS — THE TARKANIAN SAGA

A case with enormous legal implications involved a challenge against the NCAA by Jerry "the Shark" Tarkanian, who, at the time, was the basketball coach for the University of Nevada Los Angeles (UNLV). Tarkanian's suit against the NCAA went to the U.S. Supreme Court on a constitutional question as to the NCAA's obligation to provide due process rights to Tarkanian.

When Tarkanian first arrived at UNLV, the school was already under investigation for alleged NCAA violations. It wasn't long, however, before the NCAA alleged Tarkanian himself had broken the rules. Specifically, the NCAA accused Tarkanian of improperly paying for an athlete's flight home and of arranging a grade for a player. Tarkanian and UNLV conducted their own investigation which cleared Tarkanian and produced affidavits to support their findings. The dispute notched up considerably when the NCAA accused Tarkanian of inducing witnesses to fabricate evidence. The NCAA conducted a hearing and presented their evidence which consisted of NCAA investigators testifying as to what others had told them about the violations. This type of evidence is generally considered hearsay and inadmissible in court. Tarkanian was not allowed to question or cross examine his accusers nor was he allowed to call his own witnesses. The NCAA concluded Tarkanian had violated NCAA rules and put UNLV on probation. The NCAA also required UNLV to suspend Tarkanian. Tarkanian held a tenured position at the school that entitled him to certain rights with respect to his job with UNLV. Tarkanian took the matter to the Nevada state courts asserting the NCAA hearing was conducted in a manner that violated his constitutional rights to due process. The Nevada courts agreed and issued injunctions prohibiting UNLV from suspending the coach. The NCAA took an appeal that was eventually heard by the U.S. Supreme Court. The Supreme Court ruled that the NCAA was not a "state actor" and therefore did not have to comply with due process rights in its dealings with Tarkanian.

In its opinion, the U.S. Supreme Court stated:

> Finally, Tarkanian argues that the power of the NCAA is so great that the UNLV had no practical alternative to compliance with the demand. We are not all sure this is true, but even if we assume that a private monopolist can impose its will on a state agency by a threatened refusal to deal with it, it does not follow that such a private party is therefore acting under color of state law.

Although Tarkanian lost that round of the case against the NCAA, he continued to fight the organization for over 20 years. In 1998 he received a $2.5 million settlement.

Based on the *Tarkanian* decision it would appear that the NCAA can conduct a hearing in any manner it desires and require member schools to comply with its orders regardless of the fairness. This could put the schools in a "Catch 22" situation. If they enforce sanctions imposed by the NCAA in a manner which did not provide the accused due process they may violate an individual's constitutional rights. If they refuse to comply with the NCAA order the school may face serious sanctions from the NCAA.

The *Tarkanian* case is significant, but its impact should not be overstated. First, in response to criticism which arose after the Tarkanian affair, the NCAA implemented changes that provide for some due process safeguards for those accused of infractions. In addition, NCAA rules must have some rational basis. No court, for example, would uphold an NCAA rule that prohibited left-handed students from participating in college athletics. Finally, regardless of the NCAA's status, schools are required in disciplinary proceedings to provide certain constitutional due process rights to students and staff. Failure to do so could result in a court order against the school preventing the disciplinary action. It is unlikely that the NCAA would sanction a school for complying with a court order.

Women's Sports

It is indecent that the spectators should be exposed to the risk of seeing the body of women being smashed before their very eyes.
BARON PIERRE DE COUBERTIN, founder of the modern Olympics, circa 1896

Participation in sports has historically been viewed as an activity primarily for males. Most sports require speed, physical strength, and endurance. Males have, in general, possessed an advantage over females in those aspects. Our culture has deep-rooted expectations that males, at a very early age, will participate in sports. In the past, the same expectations have not existed for females. In 1900 only five countries sent a total of 19 women to the Olympics in Paris. The women competed only in tennis and golf. The United States did not send female athletes to the Olympics until 1920 and the female competition was limited to diving, swimming, and tennis. Women from the U.S. did not participate in Olympic track events until 1928. In the 1996 Olympics 169 of the 197 countries sent women athletes to compete. Of the 10,800 participants in the 1996 Olympics, 3,800 of them were women.

Enormous changes with respect to female participation in sports have occurred in the past two decades. In 1972 one in twenty-seven girls in the U.S. participated in high school sports. In 1998 the ratio had climbed to one in three. The value of NCAA scholarships to females went from $100,000 in 1972 to $180 million in 1996. In the 1996-97 school years, of the 328,000 students participating in college sports, 128,000 were women.

The public's interest in female sports has increased dramatically. Some of the most watched and talked about events in the Olympics involve women's competition. The Olympic games also now enable some female athletes to enjoy financial rewards for their effort. Winners of gold medals in women's basketball and swimming are entitled to monetary awards.

At the collegiate level, soccer, volleyball, softball, golf, tennis, track, lacrosse, crew, and basketball are now well-recognized sports for women. In the 1995-1996 season, women's college basketball drew over 5 million fans, which was almost three times the attendance that existed in 1982. National television coverage of women's college basketball games continues to grow. Television exposure will likely increase the interest in the women's games and generate revenue for their programs. Shortly after the University of Connecticut won its first women's national title the school signed a $2.28 million television contract with a local station for coverage of its games.

On the professional level, female ice skaters have done very well financially. Professional golf and tennis for women is well established, although the pay lags behind that of men's tournaments. Top female basketball players no longer have to go to Europe to play professional ball. Although the American Basketball League (AFL) folded after only a couple of seasons, the Women's National Basketball Association (WNBA) appears stable; in 2006 the franchises were valued at an average of approximately $10 million.

No sporting event in women's sports, however, has had the impact of the U.S. Women's Soccer team. The U.S. team won the inaugural women's soccer World Cup in 1991. But, the event was held in China and few people in this country knew, or cared, about the victory. By 1996, however, when the U.S. women won the Olympic gold, it was clear that women's soccer in this country was real. Everyone loves a winner and especially a world champion. The fact that soccer is considered to be the most popular in the world and one in which the U.S. men get little respect, made the success even more significant.

No one, however, not even the U.S. team's strongest supporters, anticipated the success of the World Cup games in the U.S. in the summer of 1999. The organizers were hoping to sell about 350,000 tickets, but many in the industry felt that was optimistic. As it turned out, over 600,000 tickets were sold. The championship game between the U.S. and China had 90,000 fans in the Rose Bowl and millions more all over the world watching on television. The U.S. World Cup victory is being compared with other seminal moments in sports history—regardless of gender. The incredible success of the event added enormous support to the movement to start a women's professional soccer league, which unfortunately failed.

TITLE IX

The recent growth of women's sports is due in large part to the legal system. Specific laws and court decisions have played a vital role in the new opportunities for women. No law has had as great an impact as the 1972 Education Amendments to the Civil Rights Act of 1964, commonly referred to as Title IX.

The debate over Title IX has focused on the opportunity for girls to participate in sports. Sports activity was not, however, the reason Title IX was initially enacted. In the early years of the 1960s many state universities openly admitted that female student enrollment was intentionally limited. No such restrictions applied to male students. During this period some public colleges turned away thousands of female applicants without rejecting a single male. Some university brochures proclaimed that female admission was limited to women who were specially qualified. Quotas at some medical and law schools allowed the acceptance of only 5% to 10% female applicants. Disclosure of this overt discrimination prompted some in Congress, in particular female members, to push for a law that would prohibit such treatment. A law, Title IX, was passed to prohibit the gender discrimination.

As a result of Title IX, female participation in sports in the 1970s and early 1980s experienced tremendous growth. In 1984, however, the U.S Supreme Court ruled in the case of *Grove City College v. Bell* that the law only applied to the specific program receiving the funds. Few collegiate athletic departments received federal funds and were, therefore, according to *Grove City*, exempt from the law. Congress, however, later enacted the Civil Rights Restoration Act of 1987 reversing *Grove City*. The Act made it was clear that the law applied to collegiate athletic departments. In 1992, the U.S. Supreme Court ruled in *Franklin v. Gwinnett County Public Schools* that private damage claims were available to those injured by violations of the act. The combination of the congressional action and the court's ruling made athletic departments throughout the country an easy target for Title IX actions. Colleges were suddenly under enormous pressure to make radical changes with respect to their gender approach to athletics.

EDUCATIONAL AMENDMENTS OF 1972 — TITLE IX (20 U.S.C. SEC. 1681 SEX)

(a) **Prohibition against discrimination; exceptions**—No person in the United States shall, on the basis of sex, be excluded from participation in, be denied the benefits of, or be subjected to discrimination under any education program or activity receiving Federal financial assistance except. ...

(b) **Preferential or disparate treatment because of imbalance in participation or receipt of Federal benefits; statistical evidence of imbalance**—Nothing contained in subsection (a) of this section shall be interpreted to require any educational institution to grant preferential or disparate treatment to the members of one sex on account of an imbalance which may exist with respect to the total number or percentage of persons of that sex participating in or receiving the benefits of any federally supported program or activity, in comparison with the total number or percentage of persons of that sex in any community, State, section, or other area: *Provided*, That this subsection shall not be construed to prevent the consideration in any hearing or proceeding under this chapter of statistical evidence tending to show that such an imbalance exists with respect to the participation in, or receipt of, the benefits of, any such program or activity by the members of one sex.

ACCOMPANYING EDUCATION DEPARTMENT REGULATIONS:

34 CFR SEC. 106.41. ATHLETICS.

(a) *General.* No person shall, on the basis of sex, be excluded from participation in, be denied the benefits of, be treated differently from another person, or otherwise be discriminated against in any interscholastic, intercollegiate, club or intramural athletics offered by a recipient, and no recipient shall provide any such athletics separately on such basis.

(b) *Separate Team.* Notwithstanding the requirements of paragraph (a) of this section, a recipient may operate or sponsor separate teams for members of each sex where selection for such teams is based upon competitive skill or the activity involved is a contact sport. However, where a recipient operates or sponsors a team in a particular sport for members of one sex but operates or sponsors no such team for members of the other sex, and athletic opportunities for members of that sex have previously been limited, members of the excluded sex must be allowed to try out for the team offered unless the sport involved is a contact sport. For the purposes of this part, contact sports include boxing, wrestling, rugby, ice hockey, football, basketball and other sports the purpose or major activity of which involves bodily contact.

(c) *Equal opportunity*. A recipient which operates or sponsors interscholastic, intercollegiate, club or intramural athletics shall provide equal athletic opportunity for members of both sexes. In determining whether equal opportunities are available the Director will consider, among other factors:

(1) Whether the selection of sports and levels of competition effectively accommodate the interests and abilities of members of both sexes;
(2) The provision of equipment and supplies;
(3) Scheduling of games and practice time;
(4) Travel and per diem allowance;
(5) Opportunity to receive coaching and academic tutoring;
(6) Assignment and compensation of coaches and tutors;
(7) Provision of locker rooms, practice and competitive facilities;
(8) Provision of medical and training facilities and services;
(9) Provision of housing and dining facilities and services;
(10) Publicity—Unequal aggregate expenditures for members of each sex or unequal expenditures for male and female teams if a recipient operates or sponsors separate teams will not constitute noncompliance with this section, but the Assistant Secretary may consider the failure to provide necessary funds for teams of one sex in assessing equality of opportunity for members of each sex.

From 1987 to 1997, over 150 Division I schools added women's soccer to their athletic programs. Male sports programs, however, continue to dominate. In 1995 male athletes outnumbered female athletes by a 2 to 1 margin in Division I programs and male athletes received $354 million in scholarships compared to $212 received by female athletes in 1995-96 according to a study by the Women's Sports Foundation. There are reasons, however, to believe that the increase in male athletes at the collegiate level over the past several years is misleading. Some of the increase in male sports participation is due to the fact that a number of additional schools have joined the NCAA in the past few years.

Title IX only applies to institutions that receive federal funds. All public and most private schools fall into this category. Professional teams, which are privately owned and operated, are generally not within the ambit of the law.

Compliance with Title IX, at the present time, can be achieved in one of three ways:

1. The school can provide athletic participation opportunities to female student-athletes in numbers substantially proportionate to their enrollment in the overall student population. This is referred to as the "proportionality" test and is the criteria that most courts are applying.
2. The school can demonstrate a history and continued effort of program expansion for female student-athletes. To meet this burden the school would have to show it is responding to the developing athletic interests and abilities of the members of the underrepresented gender.
3. The school can demonstrate that current athletic programs effectively accommodate the interests and abilities of the school's female student-athletes. That is, the interests and abilities of the underrepresented gender nevertheless have been fully and effectively accommodated by the present athletics program.

The Office for Civil Rights (OCR) of the Department of Education is in charge of enforcing Title IX. There are two methods for enforcement:

1. A complaint may be made which will be reviewed by OCR.
2. An individual can file suit without going through the administrative procedure.

In either case, the OCR attempts to conduct an investigation within 90 days of a complaint. If violations are found, the school is given an opportunity to bring its programs into compliance. If the school fails to comply, federal funds may be terminated.

As a generalization, Title IX does not require separate teams for the sexes, but permits separate teams in two situations: 1) contact sports; and 2) sports in which selection for the team is based on competitive skill.

The expansion of women's teams that began in the 1970s began to take a financial toll on schools. The budget constraints eventually led to the elimination of some sports programs, male and female, at a number of institutions. Although the law is clear that compliance with any one of the three criteria would suffice, the courts have focused almost exclusively on the "proportionality" test. Any school that had eliminated a women's sport or that had not aggressively added women's programs could not use the second test, that is, a "history" of program expansion in defense of a Title IX suit. The third test, "accommodation," was vague. By default, the courts latched onto the "proportionality" criteria.

In *Pederson v. LSU*, the court found the proportionality test was inappropriate to determine Title IX compliance. The court reasoned that the proportionality test assumes that men and women on all campuses are equally interested and able to participate in collegiate sports. Although LSU was held to have violated Title IX, the court's decision not to rely solely on the proportionality appeared to be a major break for schools. The *Pederson* decision, however, was not followed by other courts.

In *Neal v. Board of Trustees of California State University*, a federal court ruled the school could not reduce the number of members of its wrestling program even if its intent was to reach proportionality among the male and female athletes. The court concluded that to exclude some men wrestlers on the basis of their gender would result in a failure to accommodate the interest of male and female athletes in violation of Title IX. In *Boucher v. Syracuse University* the court found that the school was in compliance pursuant to the "history" of program expansion. Although no new female sports' programs had been created in recent years, the school was able to show an increase in scholarships, facilities, coaching staff and support services for female sports. *Pederson, Neal* and *Boucher*, are, however, the exceptions. Most Title IX cases have been decided against the schools on the basis of the proportionality test.

Dropping or cutting back on men's sports to comply with Title IX has caused a considerable amount of controversy. In *Kelly v. U. of Illinois*, a group of male swimmers from the University filed suit after the school's swimming team was eliminated in order for the school to comply with Title IX. The swimmers argued that they were being subjected to unlawful reverse discrimination. The court upheld the school's action. There has been a number of calls for legislation to clarify that Title IX should not be used to destroy existing men's sports.

There is probably not a college in this country with an athletic program that has not undergone major changes in an attempt to comply with Title IX. Several successful lawsuits have been filed against colleges, including LSU and Auburn, asserting that the schools' policies regarding athletic activities were in violation of the law. A seven-year legal battle between Colgate University and its women's ice hockey athletes was ended with an agreement by the school to elevate the women's hockey team to varsity status.

Title IX actions are not limited to colleges. A number of suits have been filed against secondary schools. In *Hoover v. Emikeljohn*, a 16 year old girl challenged her high school's rule preventing her from playing on the boy's junior varsity soccer team. The school's rule was allegedly based on the medical risk to females. The school did not have a female soccer team. The court ruled in the girl's favor. What if the school only had a girl's soccer program, would a boy be able to join the team? Does it matter what the high school athletic association rules provide? In *Clark v. Arizona*, a group of boys sued when they were barred from playing on their school's volleyball team which was limited to girls. The boys lost.

Michigan High School Athletic Association (MHSAA) was found in violation of Title IX because of its unequal scheduling of girls' athletic seasons in *CFE v. MHSAA*. Some of the girls' sports were scheduled during non-traditional seasons which limited their ability to play against other high schools and to be noticed by college scouts. The court felt this conduct resulted in discrimination in multiple ways. It reduced the female athletes' ability to obtain athletic scholarships. Furthermore, the court found that the scheduling was done to accommodate boys' sports. The court held that the MHSAA was subject to Title IX because member schools ceded authority over athletics to the Association and the Association collected gate money that would have otherwise gone to the public schools.

In 1996 there were over 1,000 girls wrestling at the high school level in 24 states. Most of the girls have no league of their own and matches between their own sex are rare. In Texas, the private organization governing wrestling, the Texas Interscholastic Wrestling Association, refused to sanction matches with girls and the officials refused to referee matches not sanctioned. The Association stated its position was based on concern for injuries to the girls and sexual harassment claims. A lawsuit seeking an injunction against the Association was filed on behalf of the female wrestlers. The court ruled that the Association was a private organization and was not required to sanction the matches with female wrestlers.

The Title IX case that has drawn the most attention is *Cohen v. Brown University*. The dispute in *Cohen* began with female students complaining that the school had stopped funding their gymnastics and volleyball teams in order to gain funds for the buy-out of a football coach's contract. Brown had also terminated men's golf and water polo. The budgets of the women's teams eliminated were about four times larger than the budgets of the men's teams that were cut. The money saved from cutting the men's programs was about $16,000, but the women's programs eliminated amounted to $62,000.

In 1992, a class action suit was filed on behalf of the females at Brown. In March 1995, the trial court found Brown in violation of Title IX and ordered compliance. In the fall of '96, an appellate court, in an opinion of over 100 pages, upheld the trial court decision. The appellate court rejected Brown's argument that it should be able to offer fewer athletic opportunities for women than men because women were not as interested. The appellate court did reverse the trial court's decision ordering women's gymnastics, fencing, skiing and water polo to be upgraded to full varsity status. Brown stated it wanted to drop men's programs to come into compliance and the appellate court ruled Brown should be given the opportunity to do that and develop a new plan for compliance.

Cohen v. Brown University (1993)

In this watershed case, defendants-appellant Brown University appeals from the district court's issuance of a preliminary injunction ordering Brown to reinstate its women's gymnastics and volleyball programs to full intercollegiate varsity status pending the resolution of a Title IX claim. After mapping Title IX's rugged legal terrain and cutting a passable swath through the factual thicket that overspreads the parties' arguments, we affirm.

I. Brown Athletics: An Overview

College athletics, particularly in the realm of football and basketball, has traditionally occupied a prominent role in American sports and American society. For college students, athletics offers an opportunity to develop leadership skills, learn teamwork, build self-confidence, and perfect self-discipline. In addition, for many student-athletes, physical skills are a passport to college admissions and scholarships, allowing them to attend otherwise inaccessible schools. These opportunities, and the lessons learned on the playing fields, are invaluable in attaining career and life successes in and out of professional sports.

The highway of opportunity runs in both directions. Not only student-athletes, but universities, too, benefit from the magic of intercollegiate sports. Successful teams generate television revenues and gate receipts which often fund significant percentages of a university's overall athletic program, offering students the opportunity to partake of sports that are not financially self-sustaining. Even those institutions whose teams do not fill the grandstands of cavernous stadiums or attract national television exposure benefit from increased student and alumni cohesion and the support it engenders. Thus, universities nurture the legends, great or small, inhering in their athletic past, polishing the hardware that adorns field-house trophy cases and reliving heroic exploits in the pages of alumni magazines.

In these terms, Brown will never be confused with Notre Dame or the more muscular members of the Big Ten. Although its football team did play in the 1916 Rose Bowl and its men's basketball team won the Ivy League championship as recently as 1986, Brown's athletic program has only occasionally achieved national prominence or, for that matter, enjoyed sustained success. Moreover, at Brown, as at most schools, women are a relatively inconspicuous part of the storied athletic past. Historically, colleges limited athletics to the male sphere, leaving those few women's teams that sprouted to scrounge for resources.

The absence of women's athletics at Brown was, until 1970, a consequence of the absence of women in the school; Brown sponsored a women's college—Pembroke—but did not itself admit women. In 1971, Brown subsumed Pembroke. Brown promptly upgraded Pembroke's rather primitive athletic offerings so that by 1977 there were fourteen women's varsity teams. In subsequent years, Brown added only one distaff team: winter track. Hence, in the 1991-92 academic year, Brown fielded fifteen women's varsity teams—one fewer than the number of men's varsity teams.

II. The Plaintiff Class

In the spring of 1991, Brown announced that it, like many other schools, was in a financial bind, and that, as a belt-tightening measure, it planned to drop four sports from its intercollegiate varsity athletic roster: women's volleyball and gymnastics, men's golf and water polo. The University permitted the teams to continue playing as "intercollegiate clubs," a status that allowed them to compete against varsity teams from other colleges, but cut off financial subsidies and support services routinely available to varsity teams (e.g., salaried coaches, access to prime facilities, preferred practice time, medical trainers, clerical assistance, office support, admission preferences, and the like). Brown estimated that eliminating these four varsity teams would save $77,813 per annum, broken down as follows: women's volleyball, $37,127; women's gymnastics, $24,901; men's water polo, $9,250; men's golf, $6,545.

Before the cuts, Brown athletics offered an aggregate of 328 varsity slots for female athletes and 566 varsity slots for male athletes. Thus, women had 36.7% of the athletic opportunities and men 63.3%. Abolishing the four varsity teams took substantially more dollars from the women's athletic budget than from the men's budget, but did not materially affect the athletic opportunity ratios; women retained 36.6% of the opportunities and men 63.4%. At that time (and for a number of years prior thereto), Brown's student body comprised approximately 52% men and 48% women.

Following Brown's announcement of the cutbacks, disappointed members of the women's volleyball and gymnastics teams brought suit. They proceeded on an implied cause of action under Title IX, 20 U.S.C. Secs. 1681-1688 (1988). The plaintiffs charged that Brown's athletic arrangements violated Title IX's ban on gender-based discrimination, a violation that was allegedly exacerbated by Brown's decision to devalue the two women's programs without first making sufficient reductions in men's activities or, in the alternative, adding other women's teams to compensate for the loss.

On plaintiffs' motion, the district court certified a class of "all present and future Brown University women students and potential students who participate, seek to participate, and/or are deterred from participating in intercollegiate athletics funded by Brown." And, after hearing fourteen days of testimony from twenty witnesses, the judge granted a preliminary injunction requiring Brown to reinstate the two women's teams pending the outcome of a full trial on the merits. We stayed execution of the order and expedited Brown's appeal.

III. Title IX and Collegiate Athletics

Title IX prohibits gender-based discrimination by educational institutions receiving federal financial support--in practice, the vast majority of all accredited colleges and universities. The statute sketches wide policy lines, leaving the details to regulating agencies.

A. Scope of Title IX.

At its inception, the broad prescriptive language of Title IX caused considerable consternation in the academic world. The academy's anxiety chiefly centered around identifying which individual programs, particularly in terms of athletics, might come within the scope of the discrimination provision, and, relatedly, how the government would determine compliance. The gridiron fueled these concerns: for many schools, the men's football budget far exceeded that of any other sport, and men's athletics as a whole received the lion's share of dedicated resources—a share that, typically, was vastly disproportionate to the percentage of men in the student body.

B. Statutory Framework.

Title IX, like the Restoration Act, does not explicitly treat college athletics. Rather, the statute's heart is a broad prohibition of gender-based discrimination in all programmatic aspects of educational institutions:

No person in the United States shall, on the basis of sex, be excluded from participation in, be denied the benefits of, or be subjected to discrimination under any education program or activity receiving Federal financial assistance. …

20 U.S.C. Sec. 1681(a) (1988). After listing a number of exempt organizations, section 1681 makes clear that, while Title IX prohibits discrimination, it does not mandate strict numerical equality between the gender balance of a college's athletic program and the gender balance of its student body. Thus, section 1681(a) shall not be interpreted to require any educational institution to grant preferential or disparate treatment to the

members of one sex on account of an imbalance which may exist with respect to the total number or percentage of persons of that sex participating in or receiving the benefits of any federally supported program or activity, in comparison with the total number or percentage of persons of that sex in any community, State, section, or other area: *Provided,* that this subsection shall not be construed to prevent the consideration in any hearing or proceeding under this chapter of statistical evidence tending to show that such an imbalance exists with respect to the participation in, or receipt of the benefits of, any such program or activity by the members of one sex.

20 U.S.C. Sec. 1681(b) (1988). Put another way, a court assessing Title IX compliance may not find a violation *solely* because there is a disparity between the gender composition of an educational institution's student constituency, on the one hand, and its athletic programs, on the other hand.

That is not to say, however, that evidence of such a disparity is irrelevant. Quite the contrary: under the proviso contained in section 1681(b), a Title IX plaintiff in an athletic discrimination suit must accompany statistical evidence of disparate impact with some further evidence of discrimination, such as unmet need amongst the members of the disadvantaged gender.

1. The Regulations. DED's regulations begin by detailing Title IX's application to college athletics. The regulations also recognize, however, that an athletic program may consist of gender-segregated teams as long as one of two conditions is met: either the sport in which the team competes is a contact sport or the institution offers comparable teams in the sport to both genders. See 34 C.F.R. Sec. 106.41(b).

Finally, whether teams are segregated by sex or not, the school must provide gender-blind equality of opportunity to its student body. The regulations offer a non-exclusive compendium of ten factors which OCR will consider in assessing compliance with this mandate:

(1) Whether the selection of sports and levels of competition effectively accommodate the interests and abilities of members of both sexes;
(2) The provision of equipment and supplies;
(3) Scheduling of games and practice time;
(4) Travel and per diem allowance;
(5) Opportunity to receive coaching and academic tutoring;
(6) Assignment and compensation of coaches and tutors;
(7) Provision of locker rooms, practice and competitive facilities;
(8) Provision of medical and training facilities and services;
(9) Provision of housing and dining facilities and services;
(10) Publicity.

34 C.F.R. Sec. 106.41(c) (1992). The district court rested its preliminary injunction on the first of these ten areas of inquiry: Brown's failure effectively to accommodate the interests and abilities of female students in the selection and level of sports.

It seems unlikely, even in this day and age, that the athletic establishments of many coeducational universities reflect the gender balance of their student bodies. Similarly, the recent boom in Title IX suits suggests that, in an era of fiscal austerity, few universities are prone to expand athletic opportunities. It is not surprising, then, that schools more often than not attempt to manage the rigors of Title IX by satisfying the interests and abilities of the underrepresented gender, that is, by meeting the third benchmark of the accommodation test. Yet, this benchmark sets a high standard: it demands not merely some accommodation, but full and effective accommodation. If there is sufficient interest and ability among members of the statistically underrepresented gender, not slaked by existing programs, an institution necessarily fails this prong of the test.

Brown argues that DED's Policy Interpretation, construed as we have just outlined, goes so far afield that it countervails the enabling legislation. Brown suggests that, to the extent students' interests in athletics are disproportionate by gender, colleges should be allowed to meet those interests incompletely as long as the school's response is in direct proportion to the comparative levels of interest. Put bluntly, Brown reads the "full" out of the duty to accommodate "fully and effectively." It argues instead that an institution satisfactorily accommodates female athletes if it allocates athletic opportunities to women in accordance with the ratio of interested and able women to interested and able men, regardless of the number of unserved women or the percentage of the student body that they comprise.

Because this is mountainous terrain, an example may serve to clarify the distinction between Brown's proposal and our understanding of the law. Suppose a university (Oooh U.) has a student body consisting of 1,000 men and 1,000 women, a one to one ratio. If 500 men and 250 women are able and interested athletes, the ratio of interested men to interested women is two to one. Brown takes the position that both the actual gender composition of the student body and whether there is unmet interest among the underrepresented gender are irrelevant; in order to satisfy the third benchmark, Oooh U. must only provide athletic opportunities in line with the two to one interested athlete ratio, say, 100 slots for men and 50 slots for women. Under this view, the interest of 200 women would be unmet--but there would be no Title IX violation.

We think that Brown's perception of the Title IX universe is myopic. The fact that the overrepresented gender is less than fully accommodated will not, in and of itself, excuse a shortfall in the provision of opportunities for the underrepresented gender. Rather, the law requires that, in the absence of continuing program expansion (benchmark two), schools either meet benchmark one by providing athletic opportunities in proportion to the gender composition of the student body (in Oooh U.'s case, a roughly equal number of slots for men and women, as the student body is equally divided), or meet benchmark three by fully accommodating interested athletes among the underrepresented sex (providing, at Oooh U., 250 slots for women).

Brown assumes that full and effective accommodation disadvantages male athletes. While it might well be that more men than women at Brown are currently interested in sports, Brown points to no evidence in the record that men are any more likely to engage in athletics than women, absent socialization and disparate opportunities. In the absence of any proof supporting Brown's claim, and in view of congressional and administrative urging that women, given the opportunity, will naturally participate in athletics in numbers equal to men, we do not find that the regulation, when read in the common-sense manner that its language suggests, offends the Fifth Amendment.

This case aptly illustrates the point. Brown earnestly professes that it has done no more than slash women's and men's athletics by approximately the same degree, and, indeed, the raw numbers lend partial credence to that characterization. But, Brown's claim overlooks the shortcomings that plagued its program before it took blade in hand.

If a school, like Brown, eschews the first two benchmarks of the accommodation test, electing to stray from substantial proportionality and failing to march uninterruptedly in the direction of equal athletic opportunity, it must comply with the third benchmark. To do so, the school must fully and effectively accommodate the underrepresented gender's interests and abilities, even if that requires it to give the underrepresented gender (in this case, women) what amounts to a larger slice of a shrinking athletic-opportunity pie.

****

The appellate court in *Brown* was obviously influenced by its appreciation of the positive impact accomplished by Title IX. In another portion of the opinion the court noted:

> One need look no further than the impressive performance of our country's women athletes in the 1996 Olympic Summer Games to see that Title IX has had a dramatic and positive impact on the capabilities of our women athletes, particularly in team sports.

Brown appealed to the United States Supreme Court, but writs were denied. Critics of the *Brown* decision, and there were many, argued that the ruling requires that women be given opportunities, at the expense of men, even if men are more interested in participating in sports. There was evidence that in Brown's intramural programs, which has no limits on participation, men outnumbered women by a margin of 8 to 1.

There is considerable concern that based on the *Brown* decision and the application of the proportionality test, a school's athletic program will have to match the undergraduate student population male-to-female ratio. The problem is compounded by the fact that the majority of students at many schools are female.

The irony of the *Brown* case is that the school was a leader in providing opportunities in sports to females. From 1972 to 1978 Brown added women's teams in basketball, crew, cross-country, field hockey, gymnastics, lacrosse, soccer, softball, squash, swimming, track and field, and volleyball. If Brown had spread the progress over 20 years rather than doing it earlier it may have been able to comply with Title IX by the second test, that is, by demonstrating a history of expanding women's programs.

The litigation in the early 1990s focused primarily on the issue of participation rates. The emphasis now seems to be shifting to scholarships. In order to compete as a Division I school the NCAA requires a minimum of six male varsity sports. The NCAA also mandates a maximum number of scholarships for each team, male and female. Some sports are classified as "head-count" sports and others are "equivalency" sports. An athlete in a head-count sport must receive a full scholarship. Scholarships in an equivalency sport can be divided among two or more students. Women's head-count sports include basketball (15 scholarships), gymnastics (12 scholarships), volleyball (12 scholarships) and tennis (8 scholarships) for a total of 47 scholarships. Head-count sports for men include only football (85) and basketball (13). Those two male sports consume ninety-eight (98) scholarships. Equivalency sport scholarships are very limited. Soccer and field hockey, for example, are each entitled to twelve scholarships.

Many proponents of Title IX argue that the root of the compliance problem is with football. A college football team has 85 athletes on scholarship and a large number of walk-ons. Based on these numbers, colleges with football teams may be required to field two or three more women's teams than men to comply with Title IX. Each school in the Southeastern Conference (SEC) has adopted a gender-equity plan that requires the schools to have two more women's sports than available to men. To offset the football numbers some schools have started a program in crew for females, a sport that demands a large number of members. Some schools are offering crew scholarships to healthy young women who have never participated in the sport.

It is easy to single out football, which consumes such a large number of players and scholarships, as the culprit in the proportionality problem. But, many football programs, unlike other sports, are self-supporting. In addition, a number of football programs generate revenues that are used to fund women's sports.

Few people dispute that Title IX has brought about long overdue changes in attitudes and opportunities for females in sports. But, there is a growing concern that as a result of court rulings on Title IX actions, men's sports, in particular Olympic events such as gymnastics, swimming and wrestling are on the verge of extinction at the collegiate level. From 1982 to the late 1990s about ninety-nine (99) colleges had eliminated wrestling and 64 had eliminated men's swimming. Men's gymnastics shrunk from 133 teams in 1975 to 32 in 1997. Even Title IX's most ardent supporters admit that the law was never intended to cause these unfortunate results.

In his first term President Bush indicated support for Title IX but he also spoke of opposition to the "strict proportionality" test that has become so divisive. That criticism along with the inclusion of a statement regarding Title IX in the Republican Party's 2000 platform fueled the belief that the Bush administration would enact changes in Title IX. The consensus was that the law itself did not need to be changed. The focus was on the regulations as drafted by the OCR that administers the law. No changes, however, were implemented.

For various reasons collegiate wrestling programs are often one of the male sports eliminated by schools as a means of complying the Title IX. The National Wrestling Coaches Association (NWCA) filed suit against the U.S. Department of Education over the impact of Title IX. The suit, *National Wrestling Coaches Assn. v. Dept. of Education* did not challenge Title IX itself. The NWCA's complaint was directed at the Department's enforcement regulations, particularly the proportionality rule. The suit asserted that approximately two hundred male college teams had been cut to comply with Title IX and that the enforcement policy had resulted in reverse discrimination. The court ruled that the association lacked standing to sue and that no evidence was submitted to support the claim that changing the 3-prong test would have resulted in the reinstatement of any teams that had been dropped. The Court of Appeal upheld the trial court's ruling and stated the following:

> The direct causes of appellants' asserted injuries – loss of collegiate-level wrestling opportunities for male student-athletes – are the independent decisions of educational institutions that choose to eliminate or reduce the size of men's wrestling teams.

JACKSON V. BIRMINGHAM BOARD OF EDUCATION

Title IX's protection was expanded by the U.S. Supreme Court in 2005 in *Jackson v. Birmingham Board of Education.* The facts of the case had all the ingredients of a Hollywood movie—the little guy trying to do the right thing and taking on the powerful system—and ultimately winning.

Roderick Jackson did not set out to be a champion of Title IX. Jackson was a coach of a girls' basketball team at a public high school. He complained to the school that his girls' team was receiving less funding than the boys' team. Mr. Jackson began receiving negative work evaluations and was eventually removed from his position.

Mr. Jackson used his meager finances to hire a lawyer and filed a suit that alleged his removal was in violation of Title IX. The trial court dismissed the complaint and held that Title IX's private cause of action did not include retaliation claims. Mr. Jackson was unable to continuing paying legal fees, but he filed an appeal on his own. The appellate court affirmed the trial court's dismissal of the case.

Mr. Jackson's tenacity and the appeal of his argument got the attention of the National Women's Law Center. The Center stepped in and provided Mr. Jackson with highly experienced legal counsel—for free. An application to the U.S. Supreme Court to hear the case was made. The U.S. Supreme Court not only agreed to review the case it ultimately ruled in Mr. Jackson's favor, albeit in a 5-4 decision. The U.S. Supreme Court stated:

> Retaliation against a person because that person has complained of sex discrimination is another form of intentional sex discrimination encompassed by Title IX's private cause of action. Retaliation is, by definition, an intentional act. It is a form of 'discrimination' because the complainant is being subjected to differential treatment. ... Moreover, retaliation is discrimination 'on the basis of sex' because it is an intentional response to the nature of the complaint: an allegation of sex discrimination. We conclude that when a funding recipient retaliates against a person *because* he complains of sex discrimination, this constitutes intentional 'discrimination' 'on the basis of sex,' in violation of Title IX. ... If recipients were permitted to retaliate freely, individuals who witness discrimination would be loathe to report it, and all manner of Title IX violation might go unremedied as a result.

EMPLOYMENT OPPORTUNITIES

Title IX has provided enormous opportunities for female athletes. The same cannot be said with respect to employment opportunities in sports for women. In 1972, when Title IX was enacted, over 90% of women's teams were coached by females, but by 1978, that percentage had dropped to 58%. The drop is apparently due in part to the increase in the number of job opportunities with female teams created because of Title IX that were filled by men.

There is no dispute that men have traditionally held most jobs in sports. In 1997 there were only three women who were commissioners of Division I athletic conferences in the United States out of 26 conferences. In 1996 the Women's Sports Foundation found that men made up nearly 75% of college coaches for men's and women's sports combined, and that 45% of head coaches for women's teams were held by men.

There are encouraging signs with respect to female employment in sports. Tennessee's highly successful basketball coach, Pat Summitt, led the way with a significant salary package. Female coaches at a number of other schools have witnessed their status and salary enhanced. A few women are athletic directors at Division I schools. Male coaches for female teams are common, but the reverse is rare. However, in 1996 the Anchorage Alaska college basketball team hired Jody Hensen as an assistant basketball coach. Ms. Hensen is one of the few women hired to coach a men's team at the college level; Kerri McTieran at Kingsboro Community College in Brooklyn and Bernadette Locke-Mattox, who was at Kentucky from 1991-94, are two others who broke the male-only barrier. Although these examples are nominal, it is a start. Not very long ago, hiring a female in such a male dominated position would have been out of the question.

Laws other than Title IX generally used by females in the sports employment context include employment discrimination laws such as Title VII and the Equal Pay Act, 29 USC Sec. 206(d)(1). These laws provide that no employer, subject to the Act, shall discriminate between employees based on race, religion ... or sex.

The female basketball coach of Howard University won an award in the trial court in excess of one million dollars against the school based on Title IX and the Equal Pay Act. The female coach was being paid $44,000 and the salary of the male coach of the men's team was $78,000. But, the female basketball coach at the University of Southern California (USC) lost a similar case. USC was able to show that the male coach had more duties and much more experience and was therefore entitled to a higher salary than his female counterpart.

Harker v. Utica College of Syracuse (1995) was a suit filed by the former female women's basketball coach against Utica College. Ms. Harker alleged that her termination was a violation of Title VII, Title IX and the Equal Pay Act. The court found that the plaintiff was not terminated because of her sex or her complaints to the school about alleged violations of Title IX, but because of poor evaluations she received from her own players. A bill was introduced in the Tennessee legislature that would have required equal base pay for all coaches and athletic directors at Tennessee's colleges and universities. The Equal Employment Opportunity Commission (EEOC) has issued rules, which if followed by the courts, will make it much harder to pay male coaches more than females.

Ortiz-Del Valle v. NBA was a sex employment discrimination suit. The female plaintiff claimed she was denied the opportunity to work as a game official for the NBA because of her sex. The jury rendered a staggering $7.85 million award which was reduced to about $300,000 on appeal.

Colleges and secondary schools seeking to hire coaches for female teams generally try to place a female in that position. Some men have won substantial awards in court when they were not hired even though they were more qualified than the female that was given the position. Geraldine Furh, however, won a substantial award against Hazel Park High School in Michigan when she proved that she was more qualified to coach the boys team than the male coach who was hired.

An older case regarding female employment in the sports world was *Ludtke v. Kuhne*, (1978). Then Commissioner of Major League Baseball, Bowie Kuhne, announced that female reporters would not be allowed in the clubhouse to interview players immediately after the game. Ms. Ludtke, who was a writer for *Sports Illustrated*, filed suit seeking to enjoin enforcement of the rule. Ms. Ludtke wanted the right to enter the clubhouse of Yankee Stadium during the 1977 World Series between the Yankees and the Dodgers. The Court found that the rule interfered with Ms. Ludtke's right to pursue her profession as a sports writer and was a violation of her constitutional rights and granted the injunction. Yankee Stadium was owned by the city of New York and was being leased to the Yankees; the tax dollar involvement may not have been essential for the decision, but it was mentioned by the court.

Although not related to employment, a California case involving the right of a woman to participate in a sport received national attention. Mary Ann Warfield was an avid golfer and club champion. She received a club membership to the Peninsula Golf & Country Club in a divorce settlement. The Club asserted a male-only rule for members and barred her from exercising membership rights. The lower courts ruled against her, but the California Supreme Court reversed and held that the Club's action was a violation of the state's civil rights law.

WOMEN'S NATIONAL BASKETBALL ASSOCIATION (WNBA)

For years women who excelled in college basketball had two choices regarding the sport upon graduation. They could go to Europe where women's professional basketball thrives—and pays well—or give up the game. The U.S. was not the land of opportunity. Times have changed. Much of the credit goes to Title IX. For a brief period the U.S. had two professional women's basketball leagues. The American Basketball League (ABL) started its first season in 1996 and the WNBA started in 1997.

The ABL operated under a single entity approach similar to Major League Soccer. That is, the league, not the teams, contracted with the players, assigned the players to teams and set the salaries. The ABL was able to sign some of the top collegiate and Olympic players at salaries that ranged from $40,000 to $150,000. Some of the players were given rights to acquire ownership interests in the teams and were able to earn more through endorsement arrangements. The ABL played a 40-game schedule during the regular basketball season and prohibited its players from playing with other teams during the off-season.

The WNBA is owned and backed by the National Basketball Association (NBA) and has substantial television contracts. The League's 28-game season is, however, in the summer. There was some question as to whether the summer schedule would attract fans, but attendance exceeded expectations in the first season. The total attendance figures dropped somewhat, however, during the third season.

Previous attempts in women's professional basketball were unsuccessful. Interest in women's sports, however, has increased dramatically in the past decade.

The conventional wisdom was that the market would support one, but not two, leagues. In 1998, during the season, the ABL stopped play and filed for bankruptcy. The WNBA has survived and although it is not drawing the numbers it would like, it appears that the League will remain in play for some time.

Part IV

Intellectual Property

Major sporting events are well-established cultural institutions. The Super Bowl, the World Series, the NBA Finals, the Stanley Cup, NASCAR races, college football bowl games, the NCAA basketball tournament and the College World Series have become *de facto* holidays for a large number of people in this country. The impact is global in the case of the Olympics and soccer's World Cup. Thousands are drawn to stadiums and arenas and millions more gather around their television sets to watch the contests or visit sport web sites for updates. The tremendous appeal and following of sports provides an ideal marketing tool for advertisers.

The value to companies from an association with sporting events, teams and athletes is staggering. Networks pay billions of dollars to broadcast games. Manufacturers pay millions to place team logos or colors on their products. Athletes like Shaquille O'Neal, Tiger Woods and Venus Williams can often earn more from endorsements than from competing in their sport. In a phrase, "sports sell."

The rights described above are generally referred to as intellectual property. Intellectual property includes trademarks, copyrights and patents. The right to benefit from the use of one's name or likeness is usually referred to as the right-of-publicity and, in the context of this material, will be also be treated as intellectual property. This chapter will discuss some of the intellectual property issues and other forms of corporate sponsorship in the world of sports.

LICENSES AND ENDORSEMENTS

Intellectual property rights in sports are often transferred, for a fee, to another party. The owners of the right, for example, a league, team or athlete, can grant another the privilege of using the right in specified ways. The authorization usually is in the form of a license or endorsement.

A license is permission granted by an owner of intellectual property to another party to use the property in an agreed upon manner. The right could include the use of a trademark on clothing, the right to broadcast an event or to use the name or likeness of an athlete in a commercial.

An endorsement of a commercial product or service is a public statement of preference for, and recommendation of, that product or service by a person or entity. According to the Federal Trade Commission (FTC) an endorsement can be a celebrity endorsement such as Coke's commercials with Michael Jordan. There is also an expert endorsement, for example Tiger Woods' use of a particular golf club. The standard of accuracy is higher in the expert endorsement, but in each case the athlete should actually use the product. The owner of Callaway golf clubs has long complained that many professional golfers who endorse other companies are actually using Callaway clubs in tournaments. The PGA now inspects and records the contents of each golfer's bag before play and participants are prohibited from using clubs not included on their official list.

TRADEMARKS

Marks have been used to identify property for thousands of years. In ancient Egypt cattle were branded to identify their owners, and stonecutters marked their structures to record their work. Over 500 years ago England required its sword makers to place an identifying mark on their weapons. These customs were the early forms of commercial marks.

All marks include words or symbols, or a combination of the two. Marks may also include shapes, colors, sounds, and movements. Almost anything that distinguishes someone's goods or services from others may qualify as a protectable mark. The different legal classifications of marks are the following:

TRADEMARK: This is a mark to identify goods with the manufacturer such as Nike's shoes, Wilson's footballs, Lexus' cars, or McDonalds' burgers.

SERVICE MARK: This is to identify a service, such as the sports agency IMG or McDonalds' food service.

TRADE DRESS: Trade dress usually includes a trademark and the entire package of the product or service. Trade dress may include McDonalds' "golden arches," the shape of a coke bottle or the color scheme of a football team.

TRADE NAME: This identifies the business itself, such as General Motors or the NFL.

CERTIFICATION MARK: This mark is to certify compliance with standards, like the Good Housekeeping seal of approval.

COLLECTIVE MARK: This is to indicate membership in a group like the Boy Scouts.

APPLICABLE LAW

Companies often spend a considerable amount of time and money acquiring and developing intellectual property rights. Although intangible, intellectual property rights are prized assets. Consider the phenomenal value of the names or marks of the Olympics, Nike, NASCAR, NFL, NBA, PGA, ABC and the NCAA. Like all other valuable property these rights must be protected from other parties who may try to exploit the marks without authorization. Intellectual property laws are designed to establish who has rights to a mark and to provide remedies for infringement.

The most important trademark law is the Federal Trademark Act (15 U.S.C. 1125) which is often referred to as the Lanham Act. The Act is designed to prevent non-owners from exploiting the goodwill or recognition of an existing mark. The Act provides for registration of trademarks and service marks. It also creates a federal cause of action of infringement of federally registered marks. Federal registration provides rights throughout the United States and creates a presumption that the mark is valid and being properly used as a trademark. After five years of continuous use, the registration can become incontestable which eliminates numerous grounds for cancellation and other defenses. A trademark registration is valid for 10 years and can be renewed indefinitely, provided it is in actual use in interstate commerce. The law creates a separate remedy to stop the unauthorized use of a mark and to compensate the owner for infringement. Section 43(a) applies even if the mark is not registered and also protects trade names that cannot be federally registered.

Most states also have trademark registration laws that provide exclusive rights within the state. Even without state registration users of a mark can seek relief under other remedies. The actions are usually based on common law remedies or unfair competition laws. Common law remedies and unfair competition rights do not extend beyond the actual geographic or field of use.

Probably the most recognized mark in sports is the Olympic name and its symbol. In 1978 Congress passed the Amateur Sports Act (36 U.S.C. 371) which recognized the United States Olympic Committee (USOC) as the governing body of Olympic events in this country. The Act also gave the USOC the right to control the promotional or commercial use of the five-ring Olympic symbol and Olympic related terms or phrases. The 1998 amendments to the Act expanded the list of marks exclusively conferred upon the USOC for use in the United States to include those affiliated with the Paralympic Games and the Pan-American Games.

The USOC is very aggressive in going after anyone who tries to use the Olympic symbol or name to promote its business. Generally the USOC will start with a "cease and desist" letter to the offender. If that does not work, court action will immediately follow and the USOC is usually successful.

In *USOC v. American Media,* however, the court ruled that a magazine's title, *Olympics USA,* was not a violation of the rights provided to the USOC under the Amateur Sports Act. The court did allow the USOC to amend its pleadings to state a claim under the Lanham Act. *U.S. Olympic Com. V. MEOB & America's Team Properties,* (2003) was another rare defeat for the USOC. MEOB registered for trademark the name "America's Team." The USOC immediately challenged MEOB's right to the name. MEOB transferred the rights to a newly created company, America's Team Properties, who took on the fight against the USOC. The court found that the USOC did not own the rights and ruled in favor of America's Team Properties.

In order to obtain relief in a trademark action a plaintiff must establish three elements:

(1) Distinctive: A mark must be distinctive to have protection under the law. Courts generally classify marks as fanciful, arbitrary, suggestive, descriptive, and generic. Arbitrary or fanciful marks bear no relationship to the product or service and are the strongest because they are the most distinctive. NIKE is an example of an arbitrary mark as is APPLE—for computers. Suggestive or descriptive terms suggest a quality about the product or service and can be trademarked, but not as easily as arbitrary marks. Generic terms are common descriptive words. It is very difficult to obtain a trademark on a generic term. A television station was denied the right to a trademark on the name, "sports channel." The court ruled the words were generic and not subject to ownership. One television sports program had a segment called, "the play of the day" and another station had "the replay of the day." Both spots highlight an exciting sports play made that day. Do they have exclusive rights to use these phrases for commercial purposes?

Some words may not be distinctive, but may acquire trademark status through "secondary meaning." That is, the words have taken on a second meaning because of the public's association of the words with a product or event. The Boston Marathon and *Monday Night Football* are examples of descriptive or generic terms that have acquired a secondary meaning in the public. Does ABC own the rights to the phrase, "Wide World of Sports?"

(2) Ownership: Ownership in a mark is achieved pursuant to use and registration as set forth in the law. The plaintiff must establish that the ownership provides priority protection in the market at issue.

(3) Likelihood of Confusion: In most cases the plaintiff will have to prove that the defendant's use of the mark is causing confusion among consumers. That is, the public is associating the defendant's product with the plaintiff's mark. Or, the defendant's use of a similar symbol is diminishing the value of the plaintiff's mark.

In considering the likelihood of confusion, courts generally consider the following factors: (1) the strength of the plaintiff's mark; (2) the similarity between the marks; (3) the similarity of the products or services; (4) actual confusion among consumers; and (5) the sophistication of the buyers. The courts may also consider the plaintiff's investment and treatment of its mark, the methods by which the products are advertised, the geographical distribution of the products and the similarity in appearance of the products.

The most common type of trademark infringement involves "passing off" of unlicensed goods. Billions of dollars in revenue are lost each year from the sale of counterfeit or "knockoff" goods. Major sporting events are prime targets. Unlicensed merchandise with the name, logo, or colors of the contest, team, or players are often sold near the event. The individuals selling the items know they are infringing on the property rights of others and have no intention of paying a licensing fee to the owners of the mark. These "pirates" usually appear suddenly, make quick sales—often out of the trunk of a car, and disappear. Counterfeit goods such as caps, tee-shirts and jerseys, are also sold on a larger scale through merchants who may or may not be aware of the origin of the merchandise. It is estimated that for certain golf clubs, there are more counterfeit than authentic products on the market.

In the following case, various universities joined together to sue Smack apparel, which was selling a variety of college football T-shirts in school colors and with slogans such as "Bourbon Street or Bust" (highlighting the "OU"), "Show us your beads" (same highlighting), "Beat Oklahoma," and "Sweet as Sugar," referencing to the 2004 Sugar Bowl between Louisiana State University and Oklahoma University. Additionally, Smack marketed T-shirts depicting the locales of Ohio State University and Southern California University and announcing each place as home of the X-time national champions (seven and eight, respectively). Each shirt used one or more school colors and featured a "Smack" logo; some added the scores of football games in which the universities competed.

Board of Supervisors v. Smack Apparel Col.

I. BACKGROUND

Plaintiffs Louisiana State University (LSU), the University of Oklahoma (OU), Ohio State University (OSU), and the University of Southern California (USC), along with their licensing agent, Collegiate Licensing Company (CLC), have sued defendant Smack Apparel Company and its principal, Wayne Curtiss, under the Lanham Act and related state statutes.

The universities each own trademark registrations for both their names and their commonly used initials. Additionally, over a century ago each university adopted a particular color combination as its school colors (purple and gold for LSU, crimson and creme for OU, scarlet and gray for OSU, and cardinal and gold for USC). The universities have spent millions of dollars over the years in marketing and promoting items bearing their initials and school colors. Plaintiffs generally allege that defendants have engaged in unfair competition by selling shirts bearing the distinctive two colors used by the universities, along with other symbols which identify the universities. . .

II. ANALYSIS

Section 43(a) of the Lanham Act, codified at 15 U.S.C. §1125(a), prohibits the use in commerce of "any word, term, name, symbol, or device, or any combination thereof, or any false designation of origin, false or misleading description of fact, or false or misleading representation of fact" which is "likely to cause confusion, or cause mistake, or to deceive as to the affiliation, connection, or association of such person with another person, or as to the origin, sponsorship, or approval of his or her goods, services, or commercial activities.". . .

1. Secondary meaning.

Plaintiffs describe their marks as "color schemes in the context of merchandise that makes reference to the Plaintiff Universities or their accomplishments and is directed to their fans and other interested consumers." There is no question that a color scheme may be protectible as a trademark if it "identifies and distinguishes a particular brand (and thus indicates its "source")." In *Wal-Mart Stores, Inc. v. Samara Bros., Inc.,* the Supreme Court made clear that under *Qualitex,* color is not protectible without proof of secondary meaning.

Accordingly, plaintiffs must demonstrate that their color schemes, logos, and designs on shirts referring to them or their accomplishments have attained "secondary meaning," which is a shorthand for denoting that "in the minds of the public, the primary significance of a [mark] is to identify the source of the product and not the product itself." To acquire a secondary meaning in the minds of the buying public, a labeled product, when shown to a prospective customer, must prompt the reaction, "That is the product I want because I know that all products with that label come from a single source and have the same level of quality." In other words, the article must proclaim its identity of source and quality, and not serve simply to stimulate further enquiry about it. ... The Fifth Circuit has adopted a seven factor test for establishing secondary meaning:

That a particular mark or trade dress has acquired secondary meaning can be proven by a consideration of the following evidence: (1) length and manner of the use of the mark or trade dress, (2) volume of sales, (3) amount and manner of advertising, (4) nature of use of the mark or trade dress in newspapers and magazines, (5) consumer-survey evidence, (6) direct consumer testimony, and (7) the defendant's intent in copying the trade dress. While each of these types of evidence alone may not prove secondary meaning, in combination they may indicate that consumers consider the mark or trade dress to be an indicator of source. In considering this evidence, the focus is on how it demonstrates that the meaning of the mark or trade dress has been altered in the minds of consumers. Under this test, "the burden of proof rests at all times with the plaintiff, and '[a] high degree of proof is necessary to establish secondary meaning for a descriptive term.'"

The court finds that plaintiffs have established secondary meaning in their particular color schemes, logos, and designs. It is undisputed that the universities have used their color combinations for a lengthy period of time. The universities market scores of items bearing their color schemes, logos, and designs, and sales of these items exceed tens of millions of dollars. The universities advertise items with their school colors in almost every conceivable manner, and the record contains ample evidence that the universities' school colors have been referenced numerous times in magazines and newspapers. The universities have even used the colors to refer to themselves, *i.e.,* LSU sometimes refers to itself as the "Purple and Gold." Defendants admit that they selected the color schemes, logos, and designs for their shirts in order to refer to the universities and call them to the mind of the consumer, although defendants deny that they intended to confuse the public into thinking the universities manufactured Smack's shirts. ... Applying the Fifth Circuit's test for secondary meaning, the court concludes that there are no genuine issues of disputed material fact, and plaintiffs' color schemes, logos and designs have achieved secondary meaning. . .

2. Likelihood of confusion.

Plaintiffs must demonstrate that the use of its mark by defendant "is likely to cause confusion among consumers as to the source, affiliation, or sponsorship" of defendants' "products or services. A 'likelihood of confusion' means that confusion is not just possible, but probable." ...

In assessing whether use of a mark creates a likelihood of confusion as to affiliation or endorsement, we consider the "digits of confusion," a list of factors that tend to prove or to disprove that consumer confusion is likely. Those factors are: (1) the type of mark allegedly infringed; (2) the similarity between the two marks; (3) the similarity of the products or services; (4) the identity of retail outlets and purchasers; (5) the identity of the advertising media used; (6) the defendant's intent; and (7) any evidence of actual confusion.

The digits are a flexible and nonexhaustive list. They do not apply mechanically to every case and can serve only as guides, not as an exact calculus. Additionally, in _Sunbeam Products, Inc. v. West Bend Co.,_ the court added an eighth digit: the degree of care employed by consumers. "No one factor is dispositive, and a finding of a likelihood of confusion does not even require a positive finding on a majority of these 'digits of confusion.'" . . .

The first digit of confusion, the type of the mark, "refers to the strength of the mark." "The stronger the mark, the greater the protection it receives because the greater the likelihood that consumers will confuse the junior user's use with that to the senior user." ... As detailed above, the universities' color schemes, logos, and designs are extremely strong marks that have been used for decades and have acquired secondary meaning in the context of reference to the plaintiffs' universities or their accomplishments, which are directed to their fans and other interested consumers.
. .

The second digit of confusion, similarity of the marks, is determined by comparing the marks. ... The marks at issue are virtually identical: Smack's shirts bear the same color schemes and similar logos and designs as those of the plaintiffs, and their shirts each bear logos and designs leaving no doubt that they refer to the plaintiff universities. There are instances where consumers have connected Smack's shirts to the universities, believing there to be some affiliation or sponsorship.

Under the third digit of confusion, similarity of products or services, "the greater the similarity between products and services, the greater the likelihood of confusion." Even if products are not directly competing, a likelihood of confusion may exist because consumers may be confused as to the sponsorship, affiliation, or connection between the parties' products. It is undisputed that both Smack and the universities market shirts bearing the same color schemes, logos, and designs. Smack argues that its products differ from those authorized by the universities because, in addition to the respective colors, they include irreverent phrases or slang comments. This argument runs afoul of the principle that a trademark provides protection for one's investment in good will. "The creation of value in a trademark requires 'the expenditure of great effort, skill and ability' and a competitor should not be permitted to take a 'free ride' on the trademark owner's good will and reputation." Clearly, "[t]hose who invest time, money and energy in the development of good will and a favorable reputation [should] be allowed to reap the advantages of their investment." Smack's use of irreverent phrases or slang comments misuses the plaintiffs' reputation and good will, which is embodied in their trademarks. Smack may not trade upon or exploit the universities' reputation and goodwill.

The fourth digit of confusion requires analyzing the identity of retail outlets and purchasers. "Dissimilarities between the retail outlets 'lessen the possibility of confusion, mistake, or deception.'" The record reflects that some of Smack's shirts are sold through its own internet website but that others are sold in booths and kiosks set up by retailers near stadiums on the days on which the respective university plaintiffs play football. Smack's shirts also are sold in retail outlets alongside those of the plaintiffs. There is no dissimilarity between retail outlets.

The fifth digit of confusion is the identity of the advertising media used ... Smack admits that it participates in the same trade shows as plaintiffs, and advertises and markets its shirts for sales at those shows. Smack's use of the universities' color schemes, logos, and designs through the advertising of its shirts at the same or similar venues as those used by the universities creates a likelihood of confusion.

The sixth digit of confusion is intent to confuse customers. Although defendants do not admit they intended to deceive consumers as to the source of their shirts, they admit that they "used school colors and 'other indicia' with the intent of identifying the university plaintiffs as the subject of the message expressed in the shirt design." This factor weighs in favor of likelihood of confusion because defendants used the color schemes, logos, and designs of the plaintiffs with "an intent" to "rely upon the drawing power" in enticing fans of the particular universities to purchase their shirts.

The seventh digit, actual confusion, tests whether defendants have used plaintiffs' trademarks, and the public has identified the marks as those of the plaintiffs. The only evidence of actual confusion in this case is survey evidence presented by the plaintiffs. This evidence, however, is hotly contested and unnecessary. It has long been held that actual confusion need not be proved. Rather, a showing of a likelihood of confusion is sufficient.

A likelihood of confusion, the eighth digit, weighs in favor of the plaintiffs. "Confusion is more likely ... if the products in question are 'impulse' items or are inexpensive." The products at issue in this case are relatively inexpensive shirts, which are not purchased with a high degree of care. The court concludes plaintiffs have established likelihood of confusion.

4. Fair use.

Smack argues that even if the universities' color schemes, logos, and designs are entitled to trademark protection, its use thereof is a nominative fair use ... [A] "nominative fair use" occurs when a junior trademark user employs "another's trademark to identify, not the defendant's goods or services, but the plaintiff's goods or services. This is not an infringement so long as there is no likelihood of confusion." The court concludes that the nominative fair use defense is not applicable because plaintiffs have demonstrated a likelihood of confusion. [The court granted summary judgment to the plaintiff universities and thus forced Smack to either obtain official licensing rights or discontinue the activities described herein.]

****

Many trademark cases do not involve deliberate attempts to sell counterfeit goods, but are genuine disputes over the use marks at issue. In 1996, *Sports Illustrated*, the national magazine, filed suit against a bar in Baton Rouge, Louisiana, named "Sports Illustrated," citing unfair competition. The suit accused the bar of attracting customers by association with the magazine's name. Although the bar owner may have tried to take advantage of the magazine's popularity, it is unlikely customers mistakenly believed there was an association between the bar and the publication. Prior to the suit, however, there were news reports of two students who almost died from alcohol consumption at the bar. The magazine probably feared adverse publicity from that type of activity. The case was settled and the bar changed its name to "Sports."

An interesting trademark issue was raised in a case brought by three of this country's most famous golf courses, Pinehurst, Pebble Beach, and Harbour Town. They filed suit against Tour 18, a golf course development that prides itself in "copying" famous golf holes. The court ruled Tour 18 could keep the holes it copied from the Pebble Beach and Pinehurst courses. The court found, however, that Tour 18's replica of Harbour Town's famous red and white lighthouse on hole 18 was an improper infringement. According to the court, this duplication weakened the lighthouse's propensity to bring Harbour Town to a golfer's minds when they encounter the trade dress of the lighthouse hole.

Another trademark case involving golf courses was *Champions Golf Club, Inc.,* (Champions) v. *The Champions Golf Club, Inc.* Champions Golf Club, the plaintiff, was started in Houston in 1959 by two players who had achieved championship playing status. Their course has hosted a number of top golf events. In 1985 another course was opened in Lexington, Kentucky and was named "The Champions Golf Club." The developers of the Kentucky course claimed the name was in reference to the championship caliber of Kentucky basketball and the area's thoroughbred horses. The Houston club registered its name in 1978 with Texas and the Kentucky course registered its state trademark in 1986. In 1989 the Houston club requested the Kentucky course change its name. The request was denied. In 1990 the Houston club obtained a federal trademark registration and filed suit against the Kentucky course. The trial court found no consumer confusion and ruled in favor of the Kentucky course. The court of appeal reversed and sent the matter back to the trial court. A settlement was reached that prohibited the Kentucky club from the using the name "Champions" and the singular term "Champion" unless it is combined with another term.

The NFL Oakland Raiders filed suit against the NFL for trademark infringement. The Raiders claimed they had a California registered trademark for a logo that included a pirate with an eye patch and cross-swords. The NFL had approved a skull and cross-sword logo for the Carolina Panthers and a new black and silver shield mark for the Tampa Bay Buccaneers. The Raiders' complaint alleged the NFL's action was a violation of its marks.

ESPN filed a suit to stop College Sports Production Network (CSPN) from using CSPN as its moniker claiming the name is deceptively similar to ESPN and would result in confusion. CSPN had planed to be the first network to feature college sports exclusively. After the suit was filed CSPN changed its name.

Two major sports institutions had a trademark battle over the use of a "star" symbol. The NFL's Dallas Cowboys and the shoe company Converse both use a five pointed star as a logo. Dallas has used the symbol since 1960, but Converse started using the star on its shoes as early as 1916. Although a star symbol is generic, there was little doubt that each logo had acquired a secondary meaning in the eyes of the public. Whether the public confuses the football team with the shoe company is another question.

A number of trademark issues in sports arise from simple phrases that were made with little or no thought to describe an event or activity. The slogan sticks and becomes popular and therefore valuable. But, who owns the rights?

Hanford Dixon and Frank Minifield were defensive backs for the Cleveland Browns years ago. They coined the phrase, "Dawg Pound" to describe the rabid, (pun intended) fans who sat in a certain area of the Cleveland stadium. The name stuck and became very popular—and marketable. The NFL, ever watchful for such matters, obtained a trademark on the term. The NFL concedes that Dixon and Minifield came up with the slogan, but was not willing to share the royalties. A similar issue arose in 1998 with the Atlanta Falcons. A fan started using the term "dirty birds" in various ways in support of the team. The popularity of the phrase took off, due in part to the Falcons' surprising march to the Super Bowl. The enterprising fan began selling merchandise with the slogan. Just as business was getting ready to take-off, however, the young merchant received a "cease and desist" letter from the Falcons and the NFL, who claimed they had obtained ownership of the phrase.

The Kentucky High School Athletic Association, KHSAA, is the owner of the slogan, "Sweet Sixteen" and "Sweet 16." The KHSAA has used the term since 1988 and has the mark registered. The KHSAA agreed to let the NCAA use the phrase in connection with its college basketball tournament. What about the phrase, "Final Four?"

A number of colleges stage huge pep rallies at midnight for the first practice of basketball season. The custom has become so established that it has acquired a name, "Midnight Madness." In 1999, however, an attorney sent letters to over 350 colleges warning them that his client owns the trademark to the phrase.

Some disputes do not involve the use of an exact phrase or mark, but arise because the defendant's work is deceptively similar to the plaintiff's mark. For years the Pittsburgh Steelers had an ongoing battle against the Pittsburgh Brewery on trademark issues. The Steelers had to file suit against the Brewery which was marketing its Iron City beer as "Blitzburg Beer." The beer cans had a black and gold color scheme with images of the Steelers' four Super Bowl rings.

The following case is an example of an entrepreneur who attempted to take advantage of a football program to market beer.

University of Georgia v. Laite (1985)

Laite, a Macon, Georgia, wholesaler of novelty beers, began marketing "Battlin' Bulldog Beer." The beer was sold in red-and-black cans bearing the portrayal of an English bulldog wearing a red sweater emblazoned with a black "G." The bulldog had bloodshot eyes, a football tucked under its right "arm," and a frothy beer stein in its left "hand."

Laite hoped that the "Battlin' Bulldog" would pile up yardage and score big points in the always-competitive alcoholic beverage market. Unfortunately, however, the pug-faced pooch was thrown for a loss by the University of Georgia Athletic Association, Inc. ("UGAA"), which obtained preliminary and permanent injunctive relief in federal district court based on the "likelihood of confusion" between the "Battlin' Bulldog" and the "University of Georgia Bulldog." Laite now cries "foul," arguing that (1) the "University of Georgia Bulldog" is not a valid trade or service mark worthy of protection, (2) the district court used the wrong factors in comparing the "Battlin' Bulldog" with the "University of Georgia Bulldog," and (3) the court's conclusion that the sale of "Battlin' Bulldog Beer" created a "likelihood of confusion" is clearly erroneous. After viewing a "replay" of the proceedings below, we conclude that no error was committed and affirm the judgment of the district court in all respects.

The University of Georgia's athletic teams have long used the nickname, "Bulldogs." In 1981, UGAA registered with the State of Georgia certain service marks incorporating the word "bulldog" or the portrayal of an English bulldog. One such service mark depicts an English bulldog wearing a sweater with a "G" emblazoned on it. ...

As the district court pointed out, it is the combination of similar design elements, rather than any individual element, that compels the conclusion that the two bulldogs are similar. Had the cans of "Battlin' Bulldog Beer" been printed in different colors, or had the "Battlin' Bulldog" worn a different monogram on its sweater, we might have a different case. Instead, the cans are red and black, the colors of the University of Georgia, and the "Battlin' Bulldog" wears the letter "G." To be sure, the "Battlin Bulldog" is not an exact reproduction of the "University of Georgia Bulldog." Nevertheless, we find the differences between the two so minor as to be legally, if not factually, nonexistent.

The defendant's intent likewise is apparent from the record. The record establishes that the Royal Brewing Company of New Orleans, Louisiana, the brewer of "Battlin' Bulldog Beer," wrote to several southeastern colleges, including the University of Georgia, seeking permission to use the colleges' symbols on cans of beer (Royal Brewing Company apparently contacted Georgia Tech University—"Ramblin' Wreck Beer," the University of Kentucky—"Fighting Wildcats Beer," and Louisiana State University—"Fighting Tigers Beer." Although the record does not reveal whether Royal Brewing Company contacted any other schools, one shudders to think of such possible concoctions as "Deacon Beer" - Wake Forest University—or "Quaker Beer"—the University of Pennsylvania). Furthermore, Laite candidly admitted in the court below, and at oral argument in this court, that "Battlin' Bulldog Beer" was intended to capitalize on the popularity of the University of Georgia football program (This, of course, is why the "Battlin' Bulldog" carries a football under one "arm.") In short, there can be no doubt that Laite hoped to sell "Battlin' Bulldog Beer" not because the beer tastes great (nor is there any evidence in the record that "Battlin' Bulldog Beer" is, to borrow the words of a well-known commercial, "less filling"), but because the cans would catch the attention of University of Georgia football fans. ...

... The fact that many other colleges, junior colleges, and high schools use an English bulldog as a symbol does not significantly diminish the strength of UGSA's mark, since almost all of the other schools (1) are geographically remote, (2) use a different color scheme, or (3) have names that begin with a letter other than "G." The remaining schools are so few in number and small in size that they pose no real threat to the strength of UGAA's mark ...

Laite also argues that no confusion could result from the sale of "Battlin' Bulldog Beer" because the cans contain the disclaimer, "Not associated with the University of Georgia." We reject this argument for two reasons. First, the disclaimer is relatively inconspicuous on the individual cans, and practically invisible when the cans are grouped together into six-packs. Second, in the Boston Pro. Hockey case we dismissed a similar argument, stating:

> The exact duplication of the symbol and the sale as the team's emblem satisfying the confusion requirement of the law, words which indicate it was not authorized by the trademark owner are insufficient to remedy the illegal confusion. Only a prohibition of the unauthorized use will sufficiently remedy the wrong.

The injunction is upheld.

****

The following are extracts from two older cases which demonstrate the appeal of the Dallas Cowboys franchise, including its cheerleaders, and how others attempted to exploit the popularity of the brand. In both cases, the Cowboys won injunctions to stop the described activity.

Dallas Cowboys Cheerleaders Inc. v. Scoreboard Posters (1979)

In 1977 five members of the Cowboys Cheerleaders posed for a poster to be distributed commercially. The poster shows the five Cowboys Cheerleaders dressed in their official cheerleading outfits in front of a glittering backdrop, with the words "Dallas Cowboys Cheerleaders'," appearing in large script at the bottom of the poster. As of December 1978, over three quarter of a million copies of the poster had been sold at an average retail price of $2.50 apiece. The poster is copyrighted.

The Texas Cowgirls are a group of former Dallas Cowboys Cheerleaders. Five members of the Texas Cowgirls posed for a poster mimicking the Cowboys Cheerleaders poster. The five women in the Cowgirls poster wear uniforms nearly identical to the official Cowboys Cheerleaders uniforms, they are positioned in a formation like that of the women in the Cowboys Cheerleaders poster, they are in front of a similar backdrop, and at the bottom of Cowgirls poster there is written in large script: The Ex-Dallas Cheerleaders." In the Texas Cowgirls version of the poster, however, the halter tops of the cheerleading uniforms are unbuttoned, leaving the women in the poster with exposed breasts. This poster was offered for public sale. Orders had been placed and a magazine featuring photographs of naked women had published a picture of the poster.

****

Dallas Cowboys v. Pussycat Cinema, Ltd. (1979)

Plaintiff in this trademark infringement action is Dallas Cowboys Cheerleaders, Inc., a wholly owned subsidiary of the Dallas Cowboys Football Club, Inc. Plaintiff employs thirty-six women who perform dance and cheerleading routines at Dallas Cowboys football games. The cheerleaders have appeared frequently on television programs and make commercial appearances at such public events as sporting goods shows and shopping center openings. In addition, plaintiff licenses others to manufacture and distribute posters, calendars, T-shirts, and the like depicting Dallas Cowboys Cheerleaders in their uniforms. These products have enjoyed nationwide commercial success, due largely to the national exposure the Dallas Cowboys Cheerleaders have received through the news and entertainment media. Moreover, plaintiff has expended large amounts of money to acquaint the public with its uniformed cheerleaders and earns substantial revenue from their commercial appearances.

At all the football games and public events where plaintiff's cheerleaders appear and on all commercial items depicting the cheerleaders, the women are clad in plaintiffs' distinctive uniform. The familiar outfit consists of white vinyl boots, white shorts, a white belt decorated with blue stars, a blue bolero blouse, and a white vest decorated with three blue stars on each side of the front and a white fringe around the bottom. In this action plaintiff asserts that it has a trademark in its uniform and that defendants have infringed and diluted that trademark in advertising and exhibiting "Debbie Does Dallas."

Pussycat Cinema, Ltd., is a New York corporation which owns a movie theatre in New York City; Zafarano is the corporation's sole stockholder. In November 1978 the Pussycat Cinema began to show "Debbie Does Dallas," a gross and revolting sex film whose plot, to the extent that there is one, involves a cheerleader at a fictional high school, Debbie, who has been selected to become a "Texas Cowgirl." In order to raise enough money to send Debbie, and eventually the entire squad, to Dallas, the cheerleaders perform sexual services for a fee. The movie consists largely of a series of scenes graphically depicting the sexual escapades of the "actors." In the movie's final scene Debbie dons a uniform strikingly similar to that worn by the Dallas Cowboys Cheerleaders and for approximately twelve minutes of film footage engages in various sex acts while clad or partially clad in the uniform. Defendants advertised the movie with marquee posters depicting Debbie in the allegedly infringing uniform and containing such captions as "Starring Ex Dallas Cowgirl Cheerleader Bambi Woods" and "You'll do more than cheer for this X Dallas Cheerleader." (Bambi Woods, the woman who played the role of Debbie, is not now and never has been a Dallas Cowboys Cheerleader).

Defendant asserts that the Lanham Act requires confusion as to the origin of the film, and they contend that no reasonable person would believe that the film originated with plaintiff. Appellants read the confusion requirement too narrowly. In order to be confused, a consumer need not believe that the owner of the mark actually produced the item and placed it on the market. The public's belief that the mark's owner sponsored or otherwise approved the use of the trademark satisfies the confusion requirement. In the instant case, the uniform depicted in "Debbie Does Dallas" unquestionably brings to mind the Dallas Cowboys Cheerleaders. Indeed, it is hard to believe that anyone who had seen defendants' sexually depraved film could ever thereafter disassociate it from plaintiff's cheerleaders. This association results in confusion which has "a tendency to impugn [plaintiff's services] and injure plaintiff's business reputation ... "

****

REVERSE CONFUSION

The problem of confusion between similar marks is generally central to a trademark infringement case. Typically, the senior user of the mark is a larger and more dominant producer. The junior user is a smaller company trying to exploit the name recognition of the larger-senior user. The consumer may buy the *junior* product because of the mistaken belief of the association with the established brand. There are, however, situations where the established mark of a smaller, less-known, company is copied or adopted by a larger company. This is referred to as *reverse confusion*.

The Harlem Wizards, a professional basketball team that toured the U.S. and abroad for 35 years, filed a franchise infringement suit to prevent the NBA's Washington team from adopting its name. The Washington franchise was called the *Bullets*, but decided this name was inappropriate and changed it to Wizards. The Harlem team sought an injunction to prohibit the NBA team from using the name. In a 1997 decision, *Harlem Wizards Entertainment v. NBA Properties*, the court found that although both entities were engaged in professional basketball, the different nature of the teams would prevent confusion and ruled the NBA team could use the name.

Las Vegas Diamondbacks v. Arizona Diamondbacks was a case filed by an amateur softball team to enjoin the Arizona Major League Baseball franchise from using the *Diamondback* name. The softball Diamondbacks had used the name for several years prior to the formation of the new MLB franchise. The court held that to prevail the softball Diamondbacks would have to show it had a "protectable interest" in the name and that consumer confusion would result in both teams using the same name. The court ruled against the softball team on both counts. The softball team was, at least, able to continue to use the name.

Beloit College in Wisconsin has a Division III football team nicknamed the *Buccaneers*. The NFL sent Beloit a stern letter demanding that the team abandon its 20 year use of the team logo because of its similarity to the NFL's Tampa Bay Buccaneers. The NFL letter suggested there may be fan confusion. Beloit refused and challenged the Tampa team to settle the matter on the field. Tampa declined the challenge and the NFL's demands were silenced.

A small company that had registered the right to the term *Dream Team* long before the NBA began using the phrase settled a suit with the NBA for an undisclosed sum. The settlement transferred all rights in the name to the NBA.

PARODY

Unauthorized use of a trademark or publicity rights may be allowed if the use is viewed as a parody of the mark or its owner. Cardtoons is a company that manufactured and marketed satirical baseball cards. The MLBPA brought suit to stop the sale of the cards claiming it infringed on a player's right to publicity and copyright laws. The back of each card contained the following disclosure: "Cardtoons baseball is a parody and is NOT licensed by Major League Baseball Properties or Major League Baseball Players Association." The appellate court upheld the trial court's rule that the parody was protected by the First amendment. The appellate court also found that the cards were designed to amuse, not confuse, consumers and therefore did not infringe upon MLBPA's property rights under the trademark law.

The following case also involves a parody of the slogan, "Just Do It" made popular by another sports' giant--Nike.

Nike, Inc. v. "Just Did It" Enterprises (1992)

Background

Plaintiff Nike, Inc. ("Nike") filed this suit against defendant Michael Stanard ("Stanard") alleging trademark infringement, unfair competition, trademark dilution, and deceptive trade practices arising out of defendants' manufacture and sale of T-shirts and sweatshirts bearing the logo "MIKE," displayed in the same typeset and along with a reproduction of the Swoosh stripe for which Nike has been granted trademark protection. Moreover, Nike contends that defendants' use of the tradename "Just Did It" Enterprises constitutes infringement on Nike's slogan "Just Do It."

Nike seeks an order that defendants have infringed its exclusive rights in the trademark NIKE, the Swoosh stripe design, the NIKE and Swoosh design combination, and the trademark slogan "Just Do It." Nike seeks a permanent injunction enjoining defendants from further use of the NIKE, Swoosh stripe, and "Just Do It" trademarks. Nike also seeks the following relief: 1) an order pursuant to Sec. 36 of the Federal Trademark Act, 15 U.S.C. Sec. 1118 requiring defendants to deliver for destruction all infringing articles, 2) an order pursuant to Sec. 35(b) of the Federal Trademark Act, 15 U.S.C. Sec. 1117(b), requiring defendants to account for and pay Nike for all profits they have realized from the infringing activity, and 3) an order requiring defendants to costs of this action and reasonable attorneys' fees, in accordance with Sec. 35 of the Federal Trademark Act, 15 U.S.C. Sec. 1117.

Although it is not registered, the slogan "Just Do It" is also entitled to trademark protection. An unregistered mark is still entitled to trademark protection where its use is inherently distinctive as applied to the goods on which it is used, or where its use has acquired secondary meaning in the marketplace. Although Stanard is correct in arguing that "Just Do It" is a common phrase used in the English language, Nike's use of the phrase in association with apparel makes it distinctive and arbitrary so that it is entitled to trademark protection. Moreover, Nike's extensive use of the phrase in conjunction with its promotion of its products has given it significant public recognition. Therefore, we conclude as a matter of law that Nike has established the validity of the marks in question.

We find that there is a significant likelihood of confusion resulting from Stanard's use of a mark similar to Nike's. A comparison of plaintiff's and defendant's marks reveals that they are virtually identical. In fact, the only difference between the marks is that Stanard has substituted an "M" for the "N," thus using the word "MIKE" rather than "NIKE ." Even Stanard himself admitted in his deposition that from a distance, the two marks could not be distinguished.

Moreover, both parties sell T-shirts and sweatshirts. Both parties' merchandise is offered to the general public, although Stanard has limited his offering to persons named "Mike ." However, people named "Mike" are part of the consumer market which purchases Nike products. Moreover, 44 of the 123 orders which Stanard received were from persons with names other than Mike. (Stanard Deposition). Additionally, purchasers of defendant's goods are not likely to exercise a particularly high degree of care in purchasing them.

Evidence has been submitted which indicates that Stanard intended to pass off his merchandise as that of Nike. In addition to constructive notice of Nike's trademark rights by virtue of Sec. 22 of the Federal Trademark Act, 15 U.S.C. Sec. 1072, Stanard admits to having actual knowledge of Nike's trademark rights as well as a desire to benefit from Nike's advertising and promotion. When asked at his deposition whether someone reading his T-shirt from across the room may think that it says NIKE, Stanard responded. "That's the whole point."

The final factor for consideration in evaluating likelihood of confusion is actual confusion. However, evidence of actual confusion is not required for likelihood of confusion to be established. Here, while Nike has not submitted any evidence of actual confusion, even Stanard has admitted that actual confusion could occur if his products were viewed from a distance. Moreover, given that our evaluation of the other six factors tilts towards Nike's position, we find that Nike has sufficiently demonstrated likelihood of confusion and has demonstrated trademark infringement.

However, Stanard argues that his work is entitled to protection under the First Amendment as a parody. In support of his parody argument, Stanard cites several cases where seemingly infringing activity was protected under the First Amendment as a parody. Parody is not a defense to trademark infringement, but rather it is another factor to be considered in determining the likelihood of confusion. In addition, a defendant's parody argument will be disregarded where the purpose of the similarity between the marks is to capitalize on the popularity of the famous mark for the defendant's commercial use.

In Mutual of Omaha the defendant designed a logo displaying the words "Mutant of Omaha" and featuring a war-bonneted, emaciated human face. This design was placed on T-shirts in conjunction with the phrase "Nuclear Holocaust Insurance." The reverse side of the T-shirts read, "When the world's in ashes, we'll have you covered." Defendant also designed a shirt reading "Mutant of Omaha's Wild Kingdom," featuring a one-eyed tiger. Plaintiff Mutual of Omaha, whose primary business is selling insurance, filed a lawsuit claiming that defendant's design infringed on their trademark, which featured the words "Mutual of Omaha" and an Indian headdress. In finding that defendant's logo constituted trademark infringement, the court rejected defendant's claim of parody, finding that defendant's logo did not create a clear distinction as to the source of the message and did not dispel the likelihood of confusion, like an appropriate parody would.

Similarly, in Hard Rock Cafe Licensing Corp. v Pacific Graphics, Inc., defendant designed heat transfers for T-shirts bearing the logo "Hard Rain Cafe ." Defendant claimed that this was a parody, in attempt to poke fun at the constant rain in Seattle. However, the court rejected defendant's parody argument, finding that the logo designs were so similar that consumer confusion was likely.

The only case cited by defendants which bears a striking similarity to the facts in this case is *Jordache Enterprises v. Hogg Wyld, Ltd.* There, defendants created and sold designer jeans bearing the name "Lardache" and featuring a pig's head as the logo. Plaintiff, a well-known maker of designer jeans, including a line of clothing for large-sized women, claimed that defendants' product infringed upon their name "Jordache" and logo of a horse's head. The court found that the logos were sufficiently different to limit consumer confusion. The court found that while Jordache's mark was refined and subtle, presenting an image of "class," the Lardache mark and pig was brash, brightly colored, and conveyed a "cute, humorous" image.

We find that the circumstances presented in this case are more akin to those in Mutual of Omaha and Hard Rock, and find that defendants' use of the MIKE logo and Swoosh stripe creates a likelihood of confusion so as to constitute infringement and unfair competition. We therefore find that Nike will succeed on its infringement claims.

Because we find that Nike prevails on the merits, that Nike will suffer irreparable harm should an injunction not be granted, and that the balancing of harms tips decidedly in favor of Nike, we grant a permanent injunction preventing defendants from infringing on any Nike trademark in any manner. We also order Stanard to deliver any remaining merchandise, advertisement, or any other material bearing the MIKE logo, pursuant to Sec. 36 of the Federal Trademark Act, 15 U.S.C. Sec. 1118. Since Stanard has stated under oath that he did not make a profit, we will not require an accounting pursuant to Sec. 35(b) of the Federal Trademark Act, 15 U.S.C. Sec. 1117(b).

****

Mr. Stanard is apparently a gusty fellow. He not only took on the Nike giant, but refused to roll over even after the trial court loss. Probably to the surprise of Nike, he appealed.

Nike, Inc. v. "Just Did It" Enterprises (1993)

Stanard is an award-winning commercial artist whose works include, among others, the trademark "Louisville Slugger," printed on its baseball bats. As a summer project, he and his daughter decided to market his first name, Mike, as a takeoff on the NIKE logos. They named the enterprise JUST DID IT. Stanard marketed t-shirts and sweatshirts ($19.95 to $39.95) to the general public with the given or first name of Michael, focusing on the northern suburbs of Chicago. He also mailed brochures to college athletes and celebrities named Michael. Approximately two-thirds of those purchasing his shirts were named "Mike." Stanard asserts that the other one-third probably bought a t-shirt for a friend, relative or loved one named "Mike." Although JUST DID IT Enterprises mailed over 1,400 brochures, the project lost money.

Only one letter separates MIKE from NIKE. Even Stanard admits that a person might not notice the difference between the two from across the room. In fact, Stanard admitted that his "whole point" was to give someone viewing from a distance the impression that the shirt actually read NIKE. In essence, Stanard believes that the word play (such as his own personal logo of STANARD with the background of the Standard Oil trademark) is humorous and deserves First Amendment protection as a fair use of trademarks. He sees this whole matter as a "joke on Nike's image which has become a social phenomenon," a "trick upon the perception of the viewer," and his own "personal pun." The district court disagreed. Although the record contains no mention that anyone ever actually confused the two designs, the court concluded as a matter of law that MIKE and NIKE were too similar and likely to confuse consumers. The court granted Nike's motion for summary judgment and this appeal followed.

Trademarks consist of words or symbols that identify and distinguish goods for the benefit of consumers. 15 U.S.C. Sec. 1127. Manufacturers and merchants invest a great deal in trademarks for the good will of their businesses. Obviously they hope the public at large identifies their trademarks. When businesses seek the national spotlight, part of the territory includes accepting a certain amount of ridicule. The First Amendment, which protects individuals from laws infringing free expression, allows such ridicule in the form of parody. Webster defines parody as "a writing in which the language and style of an author or work is closely imitated for comic effect or in ridicule. ..."

But parodies have a legal hurdle to overcome. Federal law prohibits copies or imitations that confuse consumers. This protects trademarks as a form of intellectual property and guards against confusion, deception or mistake by the consuming public.

We agree with the district court that parody is not an affirmative defense but an additional factor in the analysis.

[T]he keystone of parody is imitation. It is hard to imagine, for example, a successful parody of Time magazine that did not reproduce Time's trademarked red border. A parody must convey two simultaneous—and contradictory—messages: that it is the original, but also that it is not the original and is instead a parody. To the extent that it does only the former but not the latter, it is not only a poor parody but also vulnerable under trademark law, since the customer will be confused.

In the end, we must simply ask whether a retail customer buying a shirt from JUST DID IT Enterprises with the name MIKE on a swoosh design would likely believe that it is "in some way related to, or connected or affiliated with, or sponsored by," the plaintiff NIKE. Thus, customer "confusion" need not be restricted to a mistake regarding the source of the goods; the court should also consider whether the customer would believe that the trademark owner sponsored, endorsed or was otherwise affiliated with the product. Likelihood of confusion is frequently a disputed issue upon which reasonable minds may differ.

Stanard has forthrightly proclaimed his knowledge of Nike's marks and his attempt to create a parody of them. Some observers may not think his creation is funny. That does not much matter. What matters is whether the "Mike" shirts confused the consuming public into thinking that they were a Nike product. Based on the facts of record, this court cannot conclude that confusion reigns unless the plaintiff presents undisputed facts showing that it is entitled to relief as a matter of law. Thus, we must analyze several factors relevant to the likelihood of confusion.

Similarity of Trademarks

The marks are no doubt similar; save one letter they are identical. Obviously if a humorist wished to parody NIKE, using a variation of the name or swoosh design would necessitate some identification of the original. Stanard certainly accomplished that. The parties do not dispute that only one letter separates MIKE from NIKE and that a person could not tell the difference between the two from across the room. The parties do dispute whether NIKE and MIKE would be pronounced the same.

Stanard argues that a customer interested in purchasing a T-shirt or sweatshirt covered with the word NIKE and its swoosh design is not interested only in the quality of the merchandise but also in associating with a major sportswear company. NIKE is not merely a brand name printed on a tab at the back of the collar, but a statement about the person wearing it to those viewing the item. Thus, whether it connotes a parody depends in large part on whether the public would actually read the T-shirt or sweatshirt in question. That a person cannot tell the difference between the two from across the room matters little. We are dealing here with customer confusion when choosing to purchase, or not purchase, the items, not public confusion at viewing them from afar.

The district court did not compare the slogan JUST DO IT with the name of Stanard's enterprise, JUST DID IT, and the parties only briefly address the matter. We believe in the context of this case, however, the comparison is important. Stanard does not sell his shirts off the rack at stores. His was a mail-order business. To purchase a shirt, the customer had to make a check payable to JUST DID IT Enterprises. Not so with Nike. There is no evidence in the record that Nike sells shirts through the mail, or whether consumers can purchase products directly from Nike or must rather go through a dealer. Nike asserts JUST DO IT is its slogan, not the name of the business to which customers make checks payable in order to receive Nike products. Certainly Nike would not have us compare the similarity of MIKE and NIKE on actual shirts, because the customer never sees the actual MIKE shirt until after purchasing it. Thus, in order for a customer to be confused in this case, he must see MIKE as similar to NIKE, and continue to be confused while making a check out to JUST DID IT Enterprises.

After examining the size of the word MIKE and the mail-order form used for customer purchasing, we cannot conclude, as did the district court, that as a matter of law the parody and trademark are so similar as to confuse the consumer. Yes, they are similar; but similarity alone does not end the inquiry. A jury could find that MIKE and NIKE, in text, meaning, and pronunciation, are not so similar as to confuse consumers, especially when making the decision to purchase or not to purchase. A jury could also find that ordering a shirt from JUST DID IT Enterprises would not confuse a consumer, considering that Nike uses JUST DO IT only as its slogan.

Similarity of Products and Concurrent Uses

Our next inquiry concerns the similarity of the products upon which MIKE and NIKE attach. Where the goods are in close competition, trademarks need not be as similar in order to find an infringement. The parties have not disputed that Stanard has manufactured and marketed its parody on the same types of items that Nike sells. The district court was thus correct in concluding that as a matter of law Nike's trademark and Stanard's parody dealt with similar products, used for similar purposes.

Marketing Channels

Nike obviously markets its products to the general public. The parties dispute, however, the effect of Stanard's distribution. Stanard asserts that he marketed the clothing only to that part of the general public with the given or first name of Michael. Although the parties do not dispute that two-thirds of the purchasers were named "Mike," they dispute whether the other one-third bought a shirt for a friend, relative or loved one named "Mike." The district court did not specifically rule on this issue. The court simply observed that people named Mike were part of a consumer market.

Trademark Strength

The stronger the trademark the greater protection received from the courts. This factor can also include the likelihood of expansion of the product lines. The parties do not dispute the validity of Nike's trademarks, nor their strength. We agree with the district court's conclusions that Nike's trademarks are widely recognized and deserve protection.

Actual Confusion

Proof that a trademark parody actually confuses consumers provides substantial evidence in proving likelihood of confusion. Stanard asserted the names of many individuals who were not confused by the parody. Nike responded with no evidence of actual confusion. While actual confusion is not essential to show likelihood of confusion, Nike still must demonstrate why a customer could conclude Stanard's shirt was a Nike product. Nike has not done this, leaving an open question where a jury could conclude that Stanard's trademark parody would not likely confuse a purchaser.

Intent of the Parodist

An intent on the part of Stanard to palm off his products as those of another would raise an inference that the consumer would likely be confused. An intent to parody, however, raises the opposite inference. Given the parody defense, the question is whether the intent was to confuse or amuse.

No one likes to be the butt of a joke, not even a trademark. But the requirement of trademark law is that a likely confusion of source, sponsorship or affiliation must be proven, which is not the same thing as a "right" not to be made fun of.

The district court concluded that Stanard intended to pass off his merchandise as that of Nike. The court noted that Stanard had actual and constructive notice of Nike's trademarks, desired to benefit from Nike's advertising and promotion, and that someone from across the room would think that NIKE and MIKE were identical. These factors do not support the court's conclusion. The district court rested on Stanard's statement that to be initially tricked at first glance from across the room was "the whole point." But a jury could surely conclude that any initial confusion ends with a closer look, when the observer "gets it."

Parodies do not exist by mere happen-stance. Actual knowledge of the trademark by the presenter as well as the observer or consumer is virtually required. When determining whether Stanard intended to amuse or confuse, it matters not whether he benefited from Nike's advertising and promotions. Nor is it relevant how he expected to promote his parody. Advertising and promotion are valid considerations when examining marketing channels (see Part C, supra), but not for determining his intent. We have already rejected any "across the room" test for intent to confuse a consumer, especially since Stanard sells the shirts by mail-order.

Throughout this case Stanard has asserted that he intended only to poke fun at Nike's corporate identity. He intended to use his own name to play a witty prank upon the perception of the viewer. Whether a customer would also believe that MIKE was somehow affiliated with NIKE is a disputed issue of fact. On the record as it now stands we conclude that a jury could infer that Stanard intended to amuse, not confuse, and that MIKE was intended as a parody, not an imitation designed to be passed off to purchasers as a Nike product.

****

DISPARAGEMENT

The Lanham Act prohibits registration of trademarks that are disparaging, scandalous, or contemptuous. Most of the disparagement cases deal with language or symbols that are foul or sexually offensive. For example, in *Bromber v. Carmel Self Service* two women successfully opposed a chicken restaurant's attempt to register the slogan, "Only a breast in the mouth is better than a leg in the hand." A new line of challenges are emerging, however, which could dramatically impact all levels of sports.

For years various groups have complained that using words or symbols that pertain to native American Indians were demeaning. In 1992 several American Indians filed a petition, *Harjo v. Pro-Football*, claiming the trademark, "Redskins," used by the NFL's Washington Redskins, should be canceled. While the matter was pending the team did change the costumes of the cheerleaders and removed the lyrics, "scalp em" from the fight song. But, this was not enough to appease the petitioners. In April, 1999 the Trademark Trial and Appeal Board (TTAB) ruled the term was disparaging and canceled the trademark protection. The ruling did not stop the team from using the mark, but prevented the team from enforcing its exclusive rights. On appeal, the court reversed the decision and ruled that there was not sufficient evidence that the term "redskin" was derogatory.

Despite the loss, more attacks on similar mascots are anticipated. The Atlanta Braves and Chief Wahoo of the Cleveland Indians are obvious targets. A number of colleges began voluntarily changing from their Indian-like mascots. The NCAA followed up with a rule that required the change. The rule provoked an immediate reaction from the Seminole tribe in Florida that it supported Florida State's use of the Seminoles as its mascot. The Seminole's defense of the mascot was so powerful that the NCAA backed off and allowed an exception for Florida State. Many other schools, however, had to comply and adopt new mascots.

THE RIGHT OF PUBLICITY

Top athletes are extremely well known to the public. This identity provides the athlete with enormous marketing power. The association of athletes like Shaquille O'Neal and Tiger Woods with a product can bring instant recognition and, in many cases, a tremendous surge in sales. LeBron James reportedly signed a $90 million dollar endorsement agreement with Nike before he ever played his first professional basketball game. The player's identity is an extremely valuable right that belongs exclusively to the athlete. Like trademarks, however, the right of publicity must be protected from exploitation by others.

The unauthorized use of a person's name or likeness is often termed a "misappropriation" of property or an "appropriation" pursuant to an invasion of privacy action. In this material the legal action will be described as the right of publicity. That is, the right to control and profit from the use of one's name and likeness. A number of cases have recognized the right of an athlete to protect the rights associated with this type of action.

One of the earlier cases on an athlete's identity involved a famous football player, Elroy Hirsch, who had the nickname, "Crazy Legs." Hirsch objected to a company using the nickname on a moisturizing shaving gel for women. The court recognized Hirsch's property right in the nickname and the company discontinued the use of the term.

In a 1967 case, *Palmer v. Schonhorn,* Arnold Palmer and several other professional golfers filed suit to prevent the use of their name in a board game without their consent. The court ruled that the golfers themselves were the only ones who could make the decision as to the use of their name in the commercial field.

In a 1974 case, *Motschenbacher v. R.J. Reynolds Tobacco,* the court expanded the protection of a celebrity beyond his name or likeness. Motschenbacher was a professional race car driver. His personal trademark was his car which he individualized to set it apart from other drivers. Mostschenbacher sued the defendant for its television commercial which depicted a likeness of the plaintiff's car in the foreground and suggested the car was sponsored by Winston cigarettes. The court ruled that the plaintiff was identifiable in the commercial because of the use and identity of the similar car.

In 1978, in *Ali v. Playgirl,* Muhammad Ali sued Playgirl Magazine for its depiction of a nude black man seated in a corner of a boxing ring with a caption, "The Greatest." The court ruled that the magazine had infringed upon Ali's identity.

Dennis Rodman, the colorful ex-NBA basketball player, obtained an injunction against a New Jersey company, Fanatix Apparel. The court barred Fanatix from marketing a long-sleeve, cream-colored T-shirt that had images on the back, sleeves and front identical to Rodman's tattoos. Rodman stated he was "greatly offended and disturbed by having my tattoos, particularly my daughter's image, misappropriated and mass produced on a T-shirt and sold nationwide." The court found that the defendant was attempting to appropriate Rodman's likeness for its own benefit and granted the injunction.

Franklin Mint issued a "Tiger Woods Eyewitness Commemorative Medal" marking Woods' record breaking victory in the Masters (1997) without his permission. Woods filed suit to stop the sale of the medals. Franklin Mint argued it was a communications "medium" and that the medal is similar to a newspaper that is protected by the first amendment. The trial court disagreed and issued an injunction in favor of Woods.

Kareem Abdul-Jabbar is one of the greatest basketball players in college and NBA history. His name, however, was not always Kareem Abdul-Jabbar. The following case raised the novel issue as to rights in a previous name.

Abdul-Jabbar v. General Motors Corp.

Former basketball star Kareem Abdul-Jabbar appeals the district court's summary judgment in favor of General Motors Corporation ("GMC") and its advertising agency, Leo Burnett Co., in his action alleging violations of the Lanham Act, 15 U.S.C. § 1125(a), and California's statutory and common law right of publicity. Abdul-Jabbar argues that GMC violated his trademark and publicity rights by using his former name, Lew Alcindor, without his consent, in a television commercial aired during the 1993 NCAA men's basketball tournament. The district court based its judgment on all causes of action largely on its findings that Abdul-Jabbar had abandoned the name "Lew Alcindor," and that GMC's use of the name could not be construed as an endorsement of its product by Abdul-Jabbar.

Facts and Procedural History

This dispute concerns a GMC television commercial aired during the 1993 NCAA men's basketball tournament. The record includes a videotape of the spot, which plays as follows: A disembodied voice asks, "How 'bout some trivia?" This question is followed by the appearance of a screen bearing the printed words, "You're Talking to the Champ." The voice then asks, "Who holds the record for being voted the most outstanding player of this tournament?" In the screen appear the printed words, "Lew Alcindor, UCLA, '67, '68, '69." Next, the voice asks, "Has any car made the 'Consumer Digest's Best Buy' list more than once? [and responds:] The Oldsmobile Eighty-Eight has." A seven-second film clip of the automobile, with its price, follows. During the clip, the voice says, "In fact, it's made that list three years in a row. And now you can get this Eighty-Eight special edition for just $18,995." At the end of the clip, a message appears in print on the screen: "A Definite First Round Pick," accompanied by the voice saying, "it's your money." A final printed message appears: "Demand Better, 88 by Oldsmobile."

The following facts are undisputed. Kareem Abdul-Jabbar was named Ferdinand Lewis ("Lew") Alcindor at birth, and played basketball under that name throughout his college career and into his early years in the National Basketball Association ("NBA"). While in college, he converted to Islam and began to use the Muslim name "Kareem Abdul-Jabbar" among friends. Several years later, in 1971, he opted to record the name "Kareem Abdul-Jabbar" under an Illinois name recordation statute, and thereafter played basketball and endorsed products under that name. He has not used the name "Lew Alcindor" for commercial purposes in over ten years. GMC did not obtain Abdul-Jabbar's consent, nor did it pay him, to use his former name in the commercial described above. When Abdul-Jabbar complained to GMC about the commercial, the company promptly withdrew the ad. The ad aired about five or six times in March 1993 prior to its withdrawal. The parties dispute whether Abdul-Jabbar abandoned the name Lew Alcindor and whether the ad could be construed as an endorsement by Abdul-Jabbar of the 88 Oldsmobile.

Abdul-Jabbar brought suit in federal district court in May 1993, alleging claims under the Lanham Act and California's statutory and common law rights of publicity. The district court held a hearing on March 14, 1994. During the hearing, incorporated by reference into the order of summary judgment, the district court announced its "tentative finding that plaintiff has abandoned the name Lew Alcindor, and has abandoned the right to protect that name, and the right to assert any other rights that flow from his having had that name at one time in the past." This finding forms the basis for the district court's decision to grant summary judgment in favor of GMC on both the Lanham Act and the state law causes of action. Abdul-Jabbar timely appealed.

I. The Lanham Act

"An express purpose of the Lanham Act is to protect commercial parties against unfair competition." In *Waits*, we held as a matter of first impression that false endorsement claims are properly recognizable under section 43(a), 15 U.S.C. § 1125(a), of the Lanham Act. Id. at 1107. "Section 43(a). . . expressly prohibits, inter alias, the use of any symbol or device which is likely to deceive consumers as to the association, sponsorship, or approval of goods or services by another person." Accordingly, we held actionable:

> [a] false endorsement claim based on the unauthorized use of a celebrity's identity ... [which] alleges the misuse of a trademark, i.e., a symbol or device such as a visual likeness, vocal imitation, or other uniquely distinguishing characteristic, which is likely to confuse consumers as to the plaintiff's sponsorship or approval of the product.

Abdul-Jabbar contends that GMC's unauthorized use of his birth name, Lew Alcindor, was likely to confuse consumers as to his endorsement of the Olds 88, and thus violates the Lanham Act.

GMC offers two defenses in response to this claim: 1) Abdul-Jabbar lost his rights to the name Lew Alcindor when he "abandoned" it; and 2) GMC's use of the name Lew Alcindor was a nominative fair use which is not subject to the protection of the Lanham Act. The district court held both defenses applicable.

a) Abandonment under the Lanham Act

While the district court found that there was no dispute as to GMC's failure to seek or obtain Abdul-Jabbar's consent to use his former name in its commercial, and that "on its face, the Lanham Act applies," it held that GMC was entitled to summary judgment on the basis of its finding that Abdul-Jabbar had abandoned his former name through nonuse under the Lanham Act. Title 15 U.S.C. § 1127 (1992) provides in pertinent part:

A mark shall be deemed to be "abandoned" when either of the following occurs:

(1) When its use has been discontinued with intent not to resume such use. Intent not to resume may be inferred from circumstances. Nonuse for two consecutive years shall be prima facie evidence of abandonment. "Use" of a mark means the bona fide use of that mark made in the ordinary course of trade, and not merely to reserve a right in a mark.

(2) When any course of conduct of the owner, including acts of omission as well as commission, causes the mark to become ... generic. ...

Because Abdul-Jabbar acknowledged that he had not used the name Lew Alcindor in over ten years, and because the district court found that plaintiff's proffered religious reasons for nonuse were not applicable, the court held that Abdul-Jabbar had in effect abandoned the name.

Trademark law withdraws its protection from a mark that has become generic and deems it available for general use. Given that the primary cost of recognizing property rights in trademarks is the removal of words from (or perhaps non-entrance into) our language .... the holder of a trademark will be denied protection if it is (or becomes) generic, i.e., if it does not relate exclusively to the trademark owner's product. Similarly, the law ceases to protect the owner of an abandoned mark. Rather than countenancing the "removal" or retirement of the abandoned mark from commercial speech, trademark law allows it to be used by another. Accordingly, courts have held that an unused mark may not be held in abeyance by its original owner.

While the Lanham Act has been applied to cases alleging appropriation of a celebrity's identity, the abandonment defense has never to our knowledge been applied to a person's name or identity. We decline to stretch the federal law of trademark to encompass such a defense. One's birth name is an integral part of one's identity; it is not bestowed for commercial purposes, nor is it "kept alive" through commercial use. A proper name thus cannot be deemed "abandoned" throughout its possessor's life, despite his failure to use it, or continue to use it, commercially.

In other words, an individual's given name, unlike a trademark, has a life and a significance quite apart from the commercial realm. Use or nonuse of the name for commercial purposes does not dispel that significance. An individual's decision to use a name other than the birth name-whether the decision rests on religious, marital, or other personal considerations does not therefore imply intent to set aside the birth name, or the identity associated with that name.

While the issue of whether GMC's use of the name Lew Alcindor constituted an endorsement of its product is far from clear, we hold that GMC cannot rely on abandonment as a defense to Abdul-Jabbar's Lanham Act claim.

b) Lanham Act "fair use" doctrine

The district court cited the "fair use" defense, 15 U.S.C. § 1115(6)(4), as an alternative ground for dismissal of plaintiff's Lanham Act claim. We discussed this defense in *New Kids,* where we held that the use by two newspapers of the "New Kids" name to conduct phone-in polls measuring the group's popularity was a nominative or non-trademark "fair use" of the name not subject to protection under the Lanham Act.

Trademark law recognizes a defense where the mark is used only to describe the goods or services of [a] party, or their geographic origin. We cited the example of a Volkswagen repair shop which used the name "Volkswagen" in the sign advertising its business. There, we had recognized that it would be difficult, if not impossible ... to avoid altogether the use of the word "Volkswagen" or its abbreviation "VW" ... [to] signify appellant's cars. ... Therefore, his use of the Volkswagen trademark was not an infringing use.

We explained that "cases like these are best understood as involving a non-trademark use of a mark to which the infringement laws simply do not apply."

II. State Law Claims: Common Law and Statutory Rights of Privacy

"California has long recognized a common law right of privacy . . . [which includes protection against] appropriation, for the defendant's advantage, of the plaintiff's name or likeness. The right to be protected against such appropriations is also referred to as the "right of publicity."

The so-called right of publicity means in essence that the reaction of the public to name and likeness, which may be fortuitous or which may be managed and planned, endows the name and likeness of the person involved with commercially exploitable opportunities. The protection of name and likeness from unwarranted intrusion or exploitation is the heart of the law of privacy.

A common law cause of action for appropriation of name or likeness may be pleaded by alleging "(1) the defendant's use of plaintiff's identity; (2) the appropriation of plaintiff's name or likeness to defendant's advantage, commercially or otherwise; (3) lack of consent; and (4) resulting injury."

We hold that Abdul-Jabbar has alleged sufficient facts to state a claim under both California common law and section 3344. The statute's reference to "name or likeness" is not limited to present or current use. To the extent GMC's use of the plaintiff's birth name attracted television viewers' attention, GMC gained a commercial advantage. Whether or not Lew Alcindor "equals" Kareem Abdul-Jabbar in the sense that "'Here's Johnny' equaled Johnny Carson," or "'the greatest' equaled Muhammed Ali" or the glamorously dressed robot equaled Vanna White is a question for the jury.

While Lew Alcindor's basketball record may be said to be "newsworthy," its use is not automatically privileged. GMC used the information in the context of an automobile advertisement, not in a news or sports account. Hence GMC is not protected by section 3344(d).

For the reasons set out above, we reverse the judgment of the district court and remand for trial on the claims alleging violation of the California common law right of publicity and section 3344, as well as the claims alleging violation of the Lanham Act.

****

Several courts have ruled against athletes who have tried to stop the use of their likeness in a commercial product. The arguments in favor of allowing the use generally are based on free speech, public domain or that the use is transformative.

Tiger Woods tried to stop an artist who depicted Woods in an art work. Shortly after Tiger's historic victory at the Masters in 1997, won with a record score, sports artist, Rick Rush, created a new painting entitled "Masters of Augusta." In the art work Rush depicted Woods both swinging and crouching down behind a putt. Behind Woods is the famed club house at Augusta National Golf Club while six legendary golfers, including Jack Nicholas and Arnold Palmer, watch in the background. The prints were sold in a limited edition of lithographs through Jireh Publishing, a company that holds the exclusive rights to publish and distribute Rush's work. ETW Corporation, (Eldrick Tiger Woods) the exclusive licensing agent for the name, image and publicity rights of Tiger filed suit against Jireh. The suit alleged the art work was done without Tiger's consent and that the public was likely to mistakenly believe that Woods was affiliated with the product. The suit claimed the art work was a violation of Woods' trademark for his name. ETW holds a trademark for the term "Tiger Woods" for a variety of items including art prints. Even though Woods' name does not appear on the face of the painting it does appear in a narrative that accompanies the art work. The suit claimed unfair competition and false advertising in violation of state law. The trial court ruled that the defendant's art work was protected pursuant to the first amendment right to freedom of speech and the court of appeal affirmed the decision.

The news media can photograph players in a game and use the picture in the sports page without paying a fee. The media's conduct falls in what as known as the "news coverage exemption" and usually applies to contemporaneous events. *Sports Illustrated* featured a picture of Joe Namath, the once colorful quarterback for the New York Jets, after his 1969 Super Bowl upset victory—which he predicted. Several years later the magazine used the same picture to sell subscriptions to its magazine. Namath sued to stop the use of the photo for the sale of subscriptions, *Namath v. Sports Illustrated* (1976), but lost.

The following case involves a right of publicity dispute by Joe Montana, considered by many to be one of the best quarterbacks to ever play in the NFL.

Montana v. San Jose Mercury News, Inc.

On January 22, 1989, San Francisco 49'ers quarterback Joe Montana led his team to a 20-16 come-from-behind victory against the Cincinnati Bengals in Super Bowl XXIII. The following day, the San Jose Mercury News (SJMN) ran a front page story chronicling the 49'ers' feat and depicting four players, including Montana, celebrating on the field. The next year, the 49'ers were even more impressive in Super Bowl XXIV, sweeping past the Denver Broncos to a 55-10 win. Again, SJMN featured the 49'ers' accomplishment the next day in its front page story. The accompanying front page photograph showed Joe Montana "flying high in celebration with Guy McIntyre after a third-quarter touchdown pass to John Taylor."

The 1990 Super Bowl victory gave the 49'ers an unparalleled four championships in the 1980 to 1990 decade. To celebrate this accomplishment, SJMN issued a special "Souvenir Section" in its Sunday, February 4, 1990, edition, devoted exclusively to the 49'ers, a "team of destiny." The souvenir section, entitled "Trophy Hunters," carried an artist's rendition of Montana on the front page.

Each of these newspaper pages was reproduced in poster form within two weeks of its original printing in the newspaper and was made available for sale to the general public. Approximately 30 percent of the posters were sold for $5 each; SJMN gave away the remaining posters, mostly at charity events.

Almost two years after the last of these posters was produced, Montana brought an action against SJMN for common law and statutory commercial misappropriation of his name, photograph, and likeness. SJMN moved for summary judgment, arguing that Montana's action was barred by the First Amendment and by the applicable statute of limitations. The trial court granted SJMN's motion on First Amendment grounds. From the subsequent judgment, Montana appeals. We shall affirm the judgment.

For reasons we shall explain, we disagree. A cause of action for common law misappropriation of a plaintiff's name or likeness may be pled by alleging: "(I) the defendant's use of the plaintiff's identity; (2) the appropriation of plaintiff's name or likeness to defendant's advantage, commercially or otherwise; (3) lack of consent; and (4) resulting injury.

However, no cause of action will lie for the "[p]ublication of matters in the public interest, which rests on the right of the public to know and the freedom of the press to tell it ..." Furthermore, a matter in the public interest is not restricted to current events but may extend to the reproduction of past events.

In addition to the common law cause of action, California also has a statutory cause of a action for misappropriation. The statutory cause of action complements rather than codifies common law misappropriation and lies where the plaintiff can show that another "knowingly" used his or her "name, photograph, or likeness, in any manner, on or in products, merchandise, or goods, or for purposes of advertising or selling, or soliciting purchases of, products, merchandise, goods or services, without [the plaintiff's] prior consent . ..."

The Posters Reported on Newsworthy Events

In the instant case, there can be no question that the full page newspaper accounts of Super Bowls XXIII and XXIV and of the 49'ers' four championships in a single decade constituted publication of matters in the public interest entitled to First Amendment protection. Montana, indeed, concedes as much. The question he raises in this appeal is whether the relatively contemporaneous reproduction of these pages, in poster form, for resale, is similarly entitled to First Amendment protection. We conclude that it is. This is because Montana's name and likeness appeared in the posters for precisely the same reason they appeared on the original newspaper front pages: because Montana was a major player in contemporaneous news worthy sports events. Under these circumstances, Montana's claim that SJMN used his face and name solely to extract the commercial value from them fails.

When Joe Montana led his team to four Super Bowl championships in a single decade, it was clearly a newsworthy event. Posters portraying the 49'ers' victories are, like the poster in *Paulsen,* "form[s] of public interest presentation to which protection must be extended." A newspaper has a Constitutional right to promote itself by reproducing its news stories.

Additionally, SJMN had a right to republish its front page sports stories to show the quality of its work product. It is well established that "a person's photograph originally published in one issue of a periodical as a newsworthy subject (and therefore concededly exempt from the statutory prohibitions) may be republished subsequently in another medium as an advertisement for the periodical itself, illustrating the quality and content of the periodical, without the person's written consent." In the *Booth* case, the court held that actress Shirley Booth's right of publicity was not abridged by the publication of her photograph from an earlier edition of Holiday magazine in a later edition advertising the periodical.

At the hearing on the summary judgment motion in this case, SJMN submitted undisputed evidence that it sold the posters to advertise the quality and content of its newspaper. The posters were effective in this regard: they were exact reproductions of pages from the paper. They contained no additional information not included on the newspaper pages themselves, and they did not state or imply that Montana endorsed the newspaper. SJMN also submitted evidence showing it set the price of the posters with the intent simply to recover its costs. The fact that the posters were sold is without significance. "The First Amendment is not limited to those who publish without charge. Whether the activity involves newspaper publication or motion picture production, it does not lose its constitutional protection because it is undertaken for profit."

In summary, the First Amendment protects the posters complained about here for two distinct reasons: first, because the posters themselves report newsworthy items of public interest, and second, because a newspaper has a constitutional right to promote itself by reproducing its originally protected articles or photographs. Our conclusion on the First Amendment makes it unnecessary to discuss the alternative basis for upholding the judgment, the claim that the applicable statute of limitations bars recovery.

****

Gionfriddo v. Major League Baseball (2001)

The material facts underlying the summary judgment motion are not in dispute. Plaintiffs were four professional baseball players, who played in the major leagues for different periods between 1932 and 1948. Plaintiffs were paid for their performances during each of these seasons.

Defendant Major League Baseball is an unincorporated association whose members include the Major League Baseball Clubs (Clubs). The Clubs acted collectively to create the Office of the Commissioner which, in turn, produced and distributed media guides to the press at All-Star and World Series games.

Defendant Major League Baseball Properties, Inc. (MLBP), is a limited agent for each of the Clubs for certain purposes involving the use of the Clubs' trademarks. MLBP licenses the use of each Club's right to the game-related images of its current and former players. MLBP produces certain print and video publications including All-Star and World Series programs of its own. It also owns and controls the official Web site of Major League Baseball. Among other things, this site provides historical information about major league baseball including rosters, box scores, game summaries, lists of award winners, and video clips of historic moments from past games.

Defendant The PHoenix Communications Group, Inc. (PHoenix), was authorized by MLBP to produce and distribute audiovisual programs containing game performances and related activities. For 13 years between 1985 and 1998, PHoenix produced certain television shows including: *This Week in Baseball, Pennant Chase* and *Major League Baseball Magazine*, containing footage of earlier games. It also satisfied video footage requests made by third parties.

It is undisputed that plaintiffs brought great skill to the game of baseball and participated in memorable moments from baseball's past. Coscarart, Camilli and Crosetti appeared in All-Star games, and all four of them appeared in one or more World Series. Plaintiffs' games were played before thousands of spectators and plaintiffs knew their performances were being covered by the media. Their photographs and statistics and accounts of their play were widely disseminated to the public. Plaintiffs understood the important role this media publicity held in promoting interest in professional baseball.

By virtue of their accomplishments and team associations, Baseball has included plaintiffs' names and statistics with other former players in assorted All-Star game and World Series programs, or on its baseball Web sites. In some instances, plaintiffs' names have appeared within lists of team members or award winners such as the recipients of the "Most Valuable Player" award. In other instances, the references to plaintiffs have occurred in written accounts or video depictions of their play. Some plaintiffs have had still photographs from their playing days and footage of their performances included within video histories of major league baseball produced and/or distributed by defendants Phoenix and MLBP.

Plaintiffs filed this action, contending that these uses by Baseball were unauthorized and violated their rights of publicity. Plaintiffs pled the case originally as a putative class action on behalf of other retired players, alleging that Baseball had violated their statutory and common law right of publicity by using their "names, voices, signatures, photographs and/or likenesses" without their consent and without compensation. Their initial complaint was limited to persons who had played part of their major league careers prior to 1947, because that year the standard player contract was revised to add the following language:

> The Player agrees that his picture may be taken for still photographs,
> motion pictures or television at such times as the Club may designate and
> agrees that all rights in such pictures shall belong to the Club and may be
> used by the Club for publicity purposes in any manner it desires."

The complaint sought damages for the unauthorized uses, along with an injunction against such uses in the future, and a declaration that all members of the class were entitled to exploit commercially their own images in the uniforms in which they played.

In California the right of publicity is both a common law right and a statutory right. The common law right of publicity has been recognized in this state since 1931.

In 1971, the Legislature enacted section 3344, which authorized recovery of damages by any living person whose name, photograph, or likeness was used for commercial purposes without his or her consent. Eight years later, in *Lugosi v. Universal Pictures* (1979), our Supreme Court reaffirmed the common law right, which the statute was said to complement. However the Supreme Court held that, because the common law right of publicity derived from the right of privacy, it did not survive the death of the person whose identity was exploited and was not descendible to heirs or assignees. In 1984, the Legislature enacted a second statutory right of publicity that was "freely transferable" to the assignees or passed to the heirs of deceased persons.

The common law right of publicity derives from the fourth category of invasion of privacy identified by Dean Prosser, described as "appropriation" of a plaintiff's name or likeness for the defendant's advantage. Historically, courts were reluctant to permit celebrities to rely on this privacy right, since their fame seemed inconsistent with the injury to solitude or personal feelings implicitly required. In *Haelan Laboratories v. Topps Chewing Gum*, a court, for the first time, recognized a distinction between the personal right to be left alone and the economic right to exploit one's own fame. California recognizes the right to profit from the commercial value of one's identity as an aspect of the right of publicity.

Plaintiffs allege that Baseball appropriated their names and likenesses. The elements of this tort, at common law, are: "(1) the defendant's use of the plaintiff's identity; (2) the appropriation of plaintiff's name or likeness to defendant's advantage, commercially or otherwise; (3) lack of consent; and (4) resulting injury. Even if each of these elements is established, however, the common law right does not provide relief for every publication of a person's name or likeness. The First Amendment requires that the right to be protected from unauthorized publicity "be balanced against the public interest in the dissemination of news and information consistent with the democratic processes under the constitutional guaranties of freedom of speech and of the press.

In the uses challenged, Baseball is simply making historical facts available to the public through game programs, Web sites and video clips. The recitation and discussion of factual data concerning the athletic performance of these plaintiffs commands a substantial public interest, and, therefore, is a form of expression due substantial constitutional protection.

The uses challenged in this case are not "commercial speech." The term "commercial speech" has a special meaning in the context of the First Amendment. "[T]he 'core notion of commercial speech' is that it 'does no more than propose a commercial transaction.' " Here, the disputed uses were included as minor historical references to plaintiffs within game programs and Web sites and in videos documenting baseball's past, rather than in advertisements selling a product. As such, they are readily distinct from uses that *do no more than propose a commercial transaction*.

In addition, this is not a situation where Baseball affixed plaintiffs' names or images to merchandise such as T-shirts, lithographic prints, baseball souvenirs or other tangible products in order to market them to the public. Although plaintiffs alleged such activities in their pleadings, they were unable to present any evidence to the trial court of such uses by Baseball.

The uses at issue are entitled to receive the full constitutional protection accorded to noncommercial speech. Given the significant public interest in this sport, plaintiffs can only prevail if they demonstrate a substantial competing interest. They have not.

Here, the trial court found, among other grounds, that the complained of uses of plaintiffs' names, images and likenesses were all " 'in connection with [a] news, public affairs, or sports account' " within the meaning of section 3344, subdivision (d), and as such did not constitute uses for which consent is required under subdivision (a). We agree that these uses come within the "public affairs" exemption to consent provided in subdivision (d).

****

FANTASY SPORTS

In recent years a hobby known as "fantasy sports" has exploded in popularity and created a host of business opportunities. Fantasy sports allow the average consumer to become an "owner" or manager of a virtual team composed of real players that you and other owners select at the beginning of the season. How those players perform in real games over the course of the season determines your success in a fantasy league as you compete against your fellow owners. In 2006, about 16 million adults in American played in at least one fantasy sports league. Football, with over 12 million participants, led the way, with baseball's 5 million users holding second. NASCAR, golf, and basketball were also very popular, and fantasy leagues exist for many other sports, including curling, fishing, and waterskiing. Indeed, fantasy games have evolved beyond sports to encompass politics, celebrities' lives, and reality television shows such as American Idol.

With so many people playing, fantasy sports have created an entire industry. Some approximate the amount of business generated at a few billion dollars a year. A more conservative estimate is several hundred million dollars, but this does not include the advertising revenues that companies like ESPN, Yahoo, and CBS get from their fantasy sites or fantasy-related expenditures on mobile phones and wireless internet. Regardless, fantasy sports have become big enough to create conflicts over who owns the statistics used. Many fantasy services have historically paid licensing fees to avoid any potential trouble. However, Major League Baseball refused a license to CDM Fantasy Sports in 2005. CDM's subsidiary, C.B.C., filed suit. The question before the court was: "Who, if anyone, owns the combination of a player's name and their performance, as used in fantasy sports?" The case had enormous financial implications for anyone involved in the use of an athlete's identity.

C.B.C. Distrib. & Mktg. V. Major League Baseball Advanced Media

An action based on the right of publicity is a state-law claim. In Missouri, "the elements of a right of publicity action include: (1) That defendant used plaintiff's name as a symbol of his identity (2) without consent (3) and with the intent to obtain a commercial advantage." The parties all agree that CBC's continued use of the players' names and playing information after the expiration of the 2002 agreement was without consent. The district court concluded, however, that the evidence was insufficient to make out the other two elements of the claim, and we address each of these in turn.

With respect to the symbol-of-identity element, the Missouri Supreme Court has observed that " 'the name used by the defendant must be understood by the audience as referring to the plaintiff.'" The state court had further held that "[i]n resolving this issue, the fact-finder may consider evidence including 'the nature and extent of the identifying characteristics used by the defendant, the defendant's intent, the fame of the plaintiff, evidence of actual identification made by third persons, and surveys or other evidence Indicating the perceptions of the audience."

Here, we entertain no doubt that the players' names that CBC used are understood by it and its fantasy baseball subscribers as referring to actual major league baseball players. CBC itself admits that: In responding to the appellants' argument that "this element is met by the mere confirmation that the name used, in fact, refers to the famous person asserting the violation," CBC stated in its brief that "if this is all the element requires, CBC agrees that it is met." We think that by reasoning that "identity," rather than "mere use of a name," "is a critical element of the right of publicity," the district court did not understand that when a name alone is sufficient to establish identity, the defendant's use of that name satisfies the plaintiff's burden to show that a name was used as a symbol of identity.

It is true that with respect to the "commercial advantage" element of a cause of action for violating publicity rights, CBC's use does not fit neatly into the more traditional categories of commercial advantage, namely, using individuals' names for advertising and merchandising purposes in a way that states or intimates that the individuals are endorsing a product. But the Restatement, which the Missouri Supreme Court has recognized as authority in this kind of case, also says that a name is used for commercial advantage when it is used "in connection with services rendered by the user" and that the plaintiff need not show that "prospective purchasers are likely to believe" that he or she endorsed the product or service. We note, moreover, that in Missouri, "the commercial advantage element of the right of publicity focuses on the defendant's intent or purpose to obtain a commercial benefit from use of the plaintiff's identity." Because we think that it is clear that CBC uses baseball players' identities in its fantasy baseball products for purposes of profit, we believe that their identities are being used for commercial advantage and that the players therefore offered sufficient evidence to make out a cause of action for violation of their rights of publicity under Missouri law.

CBC argues that the first amendment nonetheless trumps the right-of-publicity action that Missouri law provides. Though this dispute is between private parties, the state action necessary for first amendment protections exists because the right-of-publicity claim exists only insofar as the courts enforce state-created obligations that were "never explicitly assumed" by CBC.

The Supreme Court has directed that state law rights of publicity must be balanced against first amendment considerations, and here we conclude that the former must give way to the latter. First, the information used in CBC's fantasy baseball games is all readily available in the public domain, and it would be strange law that a person would not have a first amendment right to use information that is available to everyone. It is true that CBC's use of the information is meant to provide entertainment, but "[s]peech that entertains, like speech that informs, is protected by the First Amendment because '[t]he line between the informing and the entertaining is too elusive for the protection of that basic right." We also find no merit in the argument that CBC's use of players' names and information in its fantasy baseball games is not speech at all. We have held that "the pictures, graphic design, concept art, sounds, music, stories, and narrative present in video games" is speech entitled to first amendment protection. Similarly, here CBC uses the "names, nicknames, likenesses, signatures, pictures, playing records, and/or biographical data of each player" in an interactive form in connection with its fantasy baseball products. This use is no less expressive than the use that was at issue in *Interactive Digital*.

Courts have also recognized the public value of information about the game of baseball and its players, referring to baseball as "the national pastime." A California court, in a case where Major League Baseball was itself defending its use of players' names, likenesses, and information against the players' asserted rights of publicity, observed, "Major league baseball is followed by millions of people across this country on a daily basis ... The public has an enduring fascination in the records set by former players and in memorable moments from previous games ... The records and statistics remain of interest to the public because they provide context that allows fans to better appreciate (or deprecate) today's performances." The Court in *Gionfriddo* concluded that the "recitation and discussion of factual data concerning the athletic performance of [players on Major League Baseball's website] command a substantial public interest, and, therefore, is a form of expression due substantial constitutional protection." We find these views persuasive.

In addition, the facts in this case barely, if at all, implicate the interests that states typically intend to vindicate by providing rights of publicity to individuals. Economic interests that states seek to promote include the right of an individual to reap the rewards of his or her endeavors and an individual's right to earn a living. Other motives for creating a publicity right are the desire to provide incentives to encourage a person's productive activities and to protect consumers from misleading advertising. But major league baseball players are rewarded, and handsomely, too, for their participation in games and can earn additional large sums from endorsements and sponsorship arrangements. Nor is there any danger here that consumers will be misled, because the fantasy baseball games depend on the inclusion of all players and thus cannot create a false impression that some particular player with "star power" is endorsing CBC's products. ...

Because we hold that CBC's first amendment rights in offering its fantasy baseball products supersede the players' rights of publicity, we need not reach CBC's alternative argument that federal copyright law preempts the players' state law rights of publicity.

****

The trial and court of appeal ruled in favor of C.B.C. Because of the high stakes MLB would not give up and asked the U.S. Supreme Court to hear the case. The NFL and NHL joined in MLB's request to the Supreme Court to overturn the decision. In June 2008 the Supreme Court denied the request. The decision will not only affect the parties in the C.B.C. case, but all other licensed fantasy leagues.

INTELLECTUAL PROPERTY
ON THE INTERNET

The Internet is having a profound impact on our culture. Every aspect of commerce has had to embrace this revolutionary medium. It took radio almost 40 years to reach 50 million people from its inception, television accomplished the same goal in 13 years and cable did it in 10 years. The Internet reached 50 million people in five years and is expected to have exponential growth in the foreseeable future.

The Internet is also a new frontier for legal issues. The courts are now facing a first wave of litigation involving the internet. There are few, if any, precedents to guide the courts in this uncharted area. The use of intellectual property on the Internet has raised a number of questions that are being addressed in court for the first time.

The Internet is an ideal setting for the exploitation of celebrities, especially star athletes. Anyone can register an unclaimed name with one of the clearinghouses. The cost is about nominal. At the present time domain names are registered on a first-come, first-served basis. A cottage industry has emerged of "cybersquatters" or "domain squatters," as they are affectionately called, who often obtain the domain name with the hope of selling it for a profit. Armed with little more than foresight the entrepreneurs register names of present or potential star athletes before it ever occurs to the individual. Venus Williams, Serena Williams, Sammy Sosa, Cal Ripkin, Warren Sapp and Stromile Swift are but a few of the athletes who learned their names had been registered by others without their permission. Typically the registrant sits back and waits for the athlete to discover that someone else has registered his or her name and attempts to negotiate a fee for the sale of the name. Some athletes refuse to pay any ransom and use other descriptions to register their identities, such as their jersey number. Some athletes have taken the matter to the courts.

In 1999 Congress passed an amendment to the Lanham Act referred to as the "Anticybersquatting Consumer Protection Act." The law prohibits an individual from registering or using a Web domain name that is identical to an existing trademark where the user has a bad faith intent to profit from that mark. The law authorizes the court to order the forfeiture or cancellation of the domain name or its transfer to the trademark owner. The law as written, however, does not protect the unregistered name of a celebrity.

In one of the first cases under the new law, *Quokka Sports v. Cup International*, a federal court in California ruled that the governing body of the America's Cup yacht races was entitled to an injunction preventing a Web site developer from using the address *www.americascup.com*. The American-registered trademark, "America's Cup" is held by America's Cup Properties. The shares in that company are transferred to the winners of the America's Cup after each race. The winner in 1966 was the Royal New Zealand Yacht Squadron and the rights were ultimately assigned by New Zealand to Quokka Sports. For some reason the name was just registered by New Zealand under the ".org" domain and not the ".com" domain. The defendant registered "americascup.com" and then offered to sell it to America's Cup Properties who refused and filed suit with Quokka. The court ruled that the site was likely to cause consumer confusion and ordered the defendant to shut down the site.

The NCAA and the Illinois High School Association won a court battle to stop SMI, the owners of the website, "marchmadness.com" from using the site. The NCAA's basketball tournament has been associated for a number of years with the brand "March Madness." In 1997 SMI began operating the site that included tournament brackets and the NCAA logo. The court found a strong likelihood of confusion and ordered SMI to cease and desist.

Another problem on the internet is that in addition to official sites there are numerous sites that are very similar to established domains, such as fan clubs, that attract and confuse the surfing public. Many of the sites are harmless, but some are designed for commercial purposes and can affect the revenue of the organization. Even more troubling is the fact that the authentic holder has no control over the contents of the counterfeiter. For example, someone visiting what they believe to be an official NFL site might encounter the pornography business.

COPYRIGHTS

Copyright law is designed to protect the original *expression* of ideas. A person who creates a work in *tangible* form obtains a copyright. The copyright entitles the owner to injunctive relief and actual damages for violation of the copyright. In order to obtain statutory damages and attorney fees, however, the copyright must be registered.

Books, music, movies and television programs are the most common types of works that are copyrighted. In an unusual case, *Production Contractor v. WGN Continental Broadcasting*, the court held that even a decorative parade float was subject to a copyright. In the sports context the most important copyrights pertain to the television broadcast of sporting events. In most cases the owner or organizer of the event, for example the professional leagues, the PGA or NASCAR control the rights to the contest. The owner contractually grants the right to a network to televise the event. The network creates and thereby obtains a copyright on the televised program of the event. Copying the program and using it in a commercial manner without authorization would violate the networks' copyright.

Hoopla Sports v. Nike illustrates what cannot be the subject of a copyright. Hoopla came up with the idea of an all-star high school basketball game. The game was called the "Father Liberty Game" and was described in an event profile which was sent to potential corporate sponsors. Nike accepted sponsorship and the game was held in June, 1994. In 1995 Hoopla learned that Nike was planning its own event, "Hoop Summit," which was described as an international all-star high school basketball game. CBS, who had agreed to broadcast the game, was announcing the event as the first of its kind. Hoopla sued Nike and CBS alleging trademark and copyright infringement. The court found an event could be considered a product under the Lanham Act, but the game belonged to Nike. The court stated that Nike took the idea of the game, not the labors involved in turning the game into an event. The court ruled that copyright law protects the expression of an idea, not the idea itself. The court further stated that copyright law does not extend to sports events.

Who owns the rights to view a sporting event? The answer is generally very easy. Teams can charge admissions to enter a stadium or arena. In addition, the owner can prevent spectators who do enter from filming the contest. But, what if someone can watch a game from another location, for example, a hill or rooftop overlooking the venue? What about a race route that travels along public streets? Can the event organizer prohibit someone from filming the race or the commercial use of the film? If the spectator films the race, but the organizer does not, is the spectator entitled to a copyright?

A six-year legal battle between the Chicago Bulls and the NBA was settled regarding the television rights to the Bulls' games. The Bulls and a Chicago television superstation, WGN, had a contract that allowed WGN to broadcast about 30 of Chicago's games outside the club's home market. The NBA contended that they had the exclusive control of the broadcast rights. The NBA argued that the broadcasts by WGN siphoned off viewers and ad dollars in other club's markets. Under the settlement, WGN reduced its broadcasts to 12 for the '96-'97 season and to 15 per season for the next four years. Chicago will pay the NBA an undisclosed amount for past broadcasts and will share future revenue with the league.

Another action in the NBA over rights to game information was *NBA v. Motorola*. The Sports Trax Pager created by Motorola provides real time in progress of NBA game information including the score, quarter, ball possession and time remaining. The device uses audible alerts to indicate the start of the game and the end of each period. The NBA filed suit claiming this was an appropriation of its property rights. The trial court ruled in favor of the NBA, but the appellate court reversed the decision.

PATENTS

A person who invents or discovers any new and useful process, or device or a new and useful improvement thereof, may obtain a patent. A patent is a grant from the federal government for the exclusive use of the invention. The inventor, however, has no rights until the patent is granted.

In sports, most patents pertain to the athletic equipment that is used. The Arena Indoor Football League, AFL, however, obtained a patent on some aspects of their game of indoor football. The issue of the AFL's patent on indoor football went to court in a dispute with a rival league, the Professional Indoor Football League, PIFL. The court denied part of the AFL's claims, but did recognize their exclusive right to the unique use of nets in the game.

The patent law includes protection for a process. Would that apply to an athlete's moves? Authors of books, composers of music and producers of movies are entitled to copyright protection for their creative works. Can an athlete who devises a new technique that revolutionizes a sport acquire a patent on the move? Consider how the "Fosbury Flop" revolutionized the sport of high jumping. Or, how soccer style kicking changed forever the way field goals and extra points are kicked in football.

CORPORATE SPONSORSHIP

The phenomenal growth and popularity of sports in the past 20 years has brought with it an unprecedented level of corporate involvement. The association of sports and business extends beyond licensing, endorsements and copyrights. A significant portion of corporate resources are now devoted to some form of sport sponsorship. There are critics of this commercial intrusion. But, it is undeniable that without the financial backing of the corporate community many leagues, sporting events and opportunities would not exist as we know them today.

Corporate sponsorship has a long, and well-accepted, relationship with professional golf and tennis. Corporate sponsorship of college bowl games, non-existent 20 years ago, is now well established. In 1998 only five of the 22 college bowl games did not have a corporate sponsor. Some of the larger bowls with corporate sponsors include the Tostitos Fiesta Bowl, the Allstate Sugar Bowl and the FedEx Orange Bowl. Even the Rose Bowl, one of the last holdouts, now has a corporate sponsor. Some companies are not just sponsors, but have their own bowls such as the Outback Bowl and the Champps Sports Bowl. Has the corporate involvement diminished the excitement and popularity of the games?

One of the most remarkable success stories in sports in the last several years has been the incredible growth of motorsports. Two hundred thousand fans regularly pack into the stadiums to watch races. The demand for new tracks and races has never been higher. No sport is more dependent on corporate sponsorship for its very existence and more demonstrative of that support. Numerous studies have shown that race fans are the most loyal and responsive with respect to race sponsors.

The form of corporate sponsorship is limited only by the imagination. Corporate signage in a stadium or arena or on the scoreboard has long been a standard practice. Using a corporate sponsors' name in connection with a half-time, a timeout, a score, a section of seats or a section of a parking lot are but a few examples of more recent forms of corporate sponsorship. Bank One was a major sponsor of the Arizona Diamondbacks, a Major League Baseball team. In addition to naming the stadium Bank One Ballpark, every home run hit in the team's park was announced as a "Bank One Boomer." The new Cleveland Browns NFL team has corporate names for each major gate entrance to their stadium. Major League Soccer features a team called the "New York Red Bulls" after the energy drink.

AMBUSH MARKETING

A common problem that arises in connection with corporate sponsorship of any event, and especially sports, is referred to as "ambush marketing." Usually one company pays a substantial fee to become a named sponsor of an event such as the Olympics, a marathon race or a college bowl game. The sponsorship is designed to brand the event and the sponsor together as much as possible with the spectators. However, a non-sponsoring competitor may try to circumvent or "ambush" the sponsorship by various means. For example, a non-sponsor may erect signs and displays in numerous places immediately adjacent to the sponsored supported Olympic village or marathon race route. The ambush actions will likely diminish or dilute the impact sought and paid for by the sponsor. The result will be an unhappy sponsor who may seek a refund or refuse to enter into future relations with the organizer of the event. Sponsors and event organizers must take every possible precaution to prevent ambush tactics and be prepared for a quick response at the first sign of such activity.

As Atlanta was getting ready for the 1996 Olympics, the city bustled with activity in preparation of the greatest sporting event in the world and its huge following. A number of companies made substantial investments with the USOC to use the Olympic name and symbols in their marketing. Companies who paid millions of dollars for the right to be designated as a "corporate sponsor" were not pleased with the fact that almost every business in Atlanta suddenly added a reference to the Olympics in their name. The USOC unleashed a trademark swat team and threatened every merchant using the Olympic name without authority. As a result, unauthorized references or use of the Olympic symbols were virtually eliminated.

Another form of ambush marketing arose between the NFL and Jerry Jones, owner of the Dallas Cowboys. According to the NFL, NFL Properties, the League's licensing division (not the individual teams) has the right to market merchandise pertaining to the teams through an agreement called the NFL Trust. Jones bitterly complained that Dallas generated approximately 25% of the revenue, but only received 1/30 of the money which was distributed evenly among the teams at the time. Jones broke ranks and cut his own deal by selling Pepsi, rather than Coke, the League's approved drink, at Dallas games. Jones also made his own deals with other companies including Nike, American Express and AT&T. The NFL had an agreement with Sprint making it the official telecommunications sponsor of the league and the then 30 teams. Jones' contract with AT&T diluted Sprint's contract with the NFL. Jones also signed a three-year contract with Nortel, a telecommunications company, to create a home page for the Cowboys on the Web. The League, however, had been working on a website arrangement with other companies for all 30 teams similar to the national television contracts.

The NFL filed suit against Jones and Jones filed a counter-claim against the League and all owners, except Al Davis of the Raiders. Jones' suit alleged that the agreement giving NFL Properties the right to control the licensing rights was an antitrust violation. Over $1 billion in damages were sought by the parties. A settlement was reached which allowed Jones to continue his individual marketing, but it required him to make some payments to the League from the money he generated.

A suit similar to the NFL-Dallas case involving Major League Baseball and the New York Yankees was also settled in 1998. George Steinbrenner, the owner of the Yankees, made a $95 million marketing agreement with *adidas*. The League claimed this was a violation of Major League licensing agreements and demanded the contract not be implemented. Steinbrenner filed an antitrust suit against the League's attempt to stop the *adidas's* deal. The case was also settled and the contract between New York and *adidas* was canceled.

NAMING RIGHTS OF SPORTS FACILITIES

One of the most striking trends in sports sponsorships is the naming rights of sports facilities. In 1973 a unique contract was reached between Rich Products Corporation and the County of Erie, New York. The agreement provided that the football stadium used by the NFL's Buffalo Bills would be called Rich Stadium. In return, Rich Corporation agreed to pay a total sum of $1.5 million over a 25 year period for the naming rights. The Rich Stadium deal attracted a lot of attention, but the concept was not copied--until the 1990s when naming rights became the rage on the national level. Currently there are over seventy (70) stadiums and arenas with corporate naming rights agreements—with more to come.

Naming rights on sports venues was originally confined to the largest companies on the facilities used by the four major professional team sports, the NFL, the NBA, the NHL and Major League Baseball. Smaller companies are, however, beginning to recognize that the benefits of a naming rights agreement are not limited to the Fortune 500 at facilities with national exposure. A second wave of deals is in progress with regional facilities such as minor league teams and colleges. The deals serve as a marketing platform for the companies and provide alternative sources to finance the construction or renovation of sports facilities.

Some of the benefits from a naming rights agreement include:

1. **EXPOSURE:** Naming rights can be an extremely cost-effective way for a company to advertise. The signage alone creates enormous exposure to everyone who enters or even sees the facility. In addition, television, radio and newspapers all refer to the company name when reporting on the events at the site. Depending on the agreement, tickets and team schedules may also include the company-facility name. With proper marketing, a multiple of "impressions" can be generated.

2. **EXCLUSIVITY:** The number of sports facilities, especially in a particular region, are limited. Branding with the facility is both unique and exclusive.

3. **GOODWILL:** The naming rights contract can and should be done in a way to demonstrate support of the teams who use the venue and the surrounding community. The relationship between the sponsor and facility can be a form of *cause* marketing.

4. **IDENTITY:** Naming rights are an ideal method to establish an immediate identity in a new area or when seeking to expand operations.

5. **CROSS PROMOTION:** The opportunities for cross promotion at the facility are unlimited.

6. **AMENITIES FOR CLIENTS OR EMPLOYEES:** Naming rights usually include tickets or other amenities at the facility. These benefits can be used to entertain clients, reward employees or serve as a prize to a sponsor-staged contest.

7. **TAX BENEFITS:** There may be tax advantages if the expenditures qualify for a business expense deduction as provided in Internal Revenue Code sec. 162(a).

The following list provides information on some naming rights agreements.

NAME	CITY	SOLD TO	PRICE	TERM
Adelphia Coliseum	Nashville, TN	Adelphia Telecommunications	$ 30,000,000	15
Air Canada Centre	Toronto, ON	Air Canada	$ 40,000,000	20
Allegheny Energy Dome	Pittsburgh, PA	Allegheny Energy Corp.	$ 5,000,000	
Alltel Arena	Little Rock, AR	Alltel Corp.	$ 7,000,000	
Alltel Stadium	Jacksonville, FL	Alltel Corp.	$ 6,200,000	10
America West Arena	Phoenix, AZ	America West Airlines	$ 26,000,000	30
American Airlines Arena	Miami, FL	American Airlines	$ 42,000,000	20
American Airlines Center	Dallas, TX	American Airlines	$195,000,000	30
Arco Arena	Sacramento, CA	Atlantic Richfield Co.	$ 7,000,000	10
Arrowhead Pond of Anaheim	Anaheim, CA	Arrowhead Mountain Spring Water	$ 19,500,000	13
Autozone Park	Memphis, TN	AutoZone	$ 4,300,000	25
Bank One Ballpark	Phoenix, AZ	Banc One Corp.	$ 33,100,000	30
Bi-Lo Center	Greensville, SC	Bi-Lo Corp.	$ 3,000,000	10
Blue Cross Arena at the War Memorial	Rochester, NY	Blue Cross	$ 3,975,000	15
Burns Stadium	Calgary, AB	Burns Meats Co.		
Canadian Airlines	Calgary, AB	Canadian Airlines	$ 20,000,000	20
Cinergy Field	Cincinnati, OH	Cinergy Corp.	$ 6,000,000	5
Coastal Federal Field	Myrtle Beach, SC	Coastal Federal Bank	$ 1,000,000	10
Comercia Park	Detroit, MI	Comercia Bank	$ 66,000,000	30
Compaq Center	Houston, TX	Compaq Computer Corp.	$ 5,400,000	6
Conseco Fieldhouse	Indianapolis, IN	Conseco, Inc.	$ 20,000,000	10
Continental Airlines Arena	East Rutherford, NJ	Continental Airlines	$ 29,000,000	12
Coors Field	Denver, CO	Coors Brewing Co.	$ 15,000,000	
Corel Centre	Ottawa, ON	Corel Corp.	$ 26,000,000	20
Edison International Field	Anaheim, CA	Edison International	$ 50,000,000	20
Enron Field	Houston, TX	Enron Corp.	$100,000,000	30
Ericcson Stadium	Charlotte, NC	Ericcson Electronics	$ 20,000,000	10
Ervin J. Nutter Center	Dayton, OH	Ervin J. Nutter	$ 2,800,000	
Fed Ex Stadium	Washington D.C.	Fed Ex	$205,000,000	27
Fieldcrest Cannon Stadium	Kannapolis, NC	Fieldcrest Cannon, Inc.		
First Union Center	Philadelphia, PA	First Union Corp.	$ 40,000,000	31
FleetCenter	Boston, MA	Fleet	$ 30,000,000	15
Florida Power Park	St. Petersburg, FL	Florida Power Co.	$ 3,000,000	10
Florida-Quest Field	Salt Lake City, UT	Franklin-Quest (recently changed to Franklin-Covey	$ 1,400,000	10
General Motors Place	Vancouver, BC	General Motors	$ 25,000,000	20
Great Western Forum	Los Angles, CA	Great Western Bank	$ 20,000,000	
Hawkinson Ford Field	Crestwood, IL	Hawkinson Ford	$ 3.5 million to the village and an undisclosed amount to the team	10

NAME	CITY	SOLD TO	PRICE	TERM
Houlihan's Stadium	Tampa, FL	Houlihan's	$ 10,000,000	10
JetForm park	Ottawa, ON	Jet Form Corporation	$ 1,700,000	15
John Thurman Field	Modesto, CA	Modesto Bee	$ 250,000	10
Key Arena	Seattle, WA	Key Corp	$ 15,000,000	15
Lowe's Motor Speedway	Charlotte, NC	Lowe's	$ 35,000,000	10
MCI	Washington, DC	MCI	$ 44,000,000	20
Marine Midland Arena	Buffalo, NY	Marine Midland Bank	$ 15,000,000	20
Miller Park	Milwaukee, WI	Miller Brewing Co.	$ 41,000,000	20
Mind Field	Winnipeg, MB	Mind Computer	$ 1,000,000	10
Minute Maid Park	Houston, TX	Minute Maid	$ 170,000,000	28
Monster Park	San Francisco, CA	Monster Cable	$ 6,000,000	4
National Car Rental Center	Sunrise, FL	National Car Rental	$ 25,000,000	10
Newman Outdoor Field	Fargo, ND	Newman Outdoor	$ 5,000,000	5
NorthAmeriCare Park	Buffalo, NY	NorthAmeriCare Products		
Old Kent Park	Comstock Park, MI	Old Kent Bank		
Oldsmobile Park	Lansing, MI	Oldsmobile		10
Pacific Bell park	San Francisco, CA	Pacific Bell	$ 50,000,000	24
Papa John's Cardinal Stadium	Louisville, KY	Papa John's Pizza	$ 5,000,000	
Pepsi Arena	Albany, NY	Pepsi	$ 3,000,000	10
Pepsi Center	Denver, CO	Pepsi	$ 68,000,000	20
Pepsi Coliseum	Indianapolis, IN	Pepsi	$ 650,000	5
Philips Arena	Atlanta, GA	Royal Philips Electronics	$168,000,000	20
PNC Park	Pittsburgh, PA	PNC Bank	$ 30,000,000	20
PSINet Stadium	Baltimore, MD	PSINet	$105,000,000	20
Pringles Park	Jackson, TN	Proctor & Gamble	$ 1,200,000	15
Pro Player Stadium	Miami, FL	Fruit of the Loom	$ 20,000,000	10
Qualcomm Stadium	San Diego, CA	Qualcomm	$ 18,000,000	20
RCA Dome	Indianapolis, IN	RCA	$ 10,000,000	10
Raymond James Stadium	Tampa, FL	Raymond James Financial	$ 32,000,000	13
Rich Stadium (NOTE: This deal has expired and is included for reference only)	Orchard Park, NY	Rich Products Corp.	$ 1,500,000	25
Safeco Field	Seattle, WA	Safeco	$ 40,000,000	20
Skyreach Center	Edmonton, AB	Skyreach Equip. Corp.	$ 3,306,500	5
ShopKo Hall	Green Bay, WI	ShopKo	$ 1,400,000	20
Southwestern Bell Bricktown Park	Oklahoma City, OK	Southwestern Bell		
Staples Center	Los Angles, CA	Staples, Inc.	$100,000,000	
TransWorld Dome	St. Louis, MO	TWA	$ 26,000,000	
Tucson Electric Park	Tucson, AZ	Tuscon Electric Co.		
United Center	Chicago, IL	United Airlines	$ 25,000,000	
University of Phoenix Stadium	Glendale, AZ	University of Phoenix	$ 154,000,000	20

Some of the naming rights agreements with colleges are listed below:

FACILITY	SCHOOL	TOTAL COST	ANNUAL VALUE	LENGTH	YEARS
Save Mart Center	Fresno State University	$40 million	$1.74 million	23 yrs.	2000-20022
Comcast Center	University of Maryland	$20 million	$800,000	25 yrs.	2001-2026
Jones Stadium	Texas Tech University	$20 million	$1 million	20 yrs.	2000-2019
Value City Arena	Ohio State University	$12.5 million	N/A	Indefinite	1998-Indefinite
Cox Arena	San Diego State University	$12 million	N/A	Indefinite	1998-Indefinite
United Spirit Center	Texas tech University	$10 million	$500,000	20 yrs.	1996-2015
Bank of America Arena	University of Washington	$5.1 million	$510,000	10 yrs.	1996-2009
Cox Pavilion	University of Nevada-Las Vegas	$5 million	$500,000	10 yrs.	2000-2009
Wells Fargo Arena	Arizona State University	$5 million	N/A	Indefinite	1998-Indefinite
Papa John's Cardinal Stadium	University of Louisville	$5 million	$333,333	15 yrs.	1998-2012
Coors Events Center	University of Colorado	$5 million	N/A	Indefinite	1991-Indefinite
Carrier Dome	Syracuse University	$2.75 million	N/A	Indefinite	1980-Indefinite
Alltel Arena	Virginia Commonwealth University	$2 million	$200,000	10 yrs.	1999-2008
Cesna Stadium	Wichita State University	$300,000	N/A	Indefinite	1969-Indefinite
Rawlings Stadium	Georgetown (Ky) College	$200,000	$50,000	Four years	1997-2003

The NFL's Houston Texans' has an agreement with Reliant Energy for the sum of $300 million for a thirty-year period; the NFL's St. Louis Rams' agreement with the Edward Jones Company provides for a twelve year naming-rights relationship with an average annual payment of $2.6 million; the NFL's Pittsburgh Steelers' agreement is with Heinz for twenty years with an average annual price of $2.85 million; the NFL's New England Patriots' fifteen year contract with CMGI was for an annual price of approximately $7 million; the NFL's Denver Broncos' twenty year agreement with Invesco Funds Group was for an average annual price of $6 million; MLB's Houston Astro's agreement is with Minute Maid for the sum of $100 million over a thirty year period.

Some naming-right companies have had problems with broadcasters. NBC refused to call the Charlotte Motor Speedway the "Lowes' Motor Speedway" unless Lowes bought advertising time during the race. The Fox Network refused to call Denver's hockey arena the Pepsi Center during the All-star Game due to the NHL's contract with Coke.

The naming-rights trend took some hits when some of the company sponsors went into bankruptcy. The rise and fall of Enron, who held the naming rights to the new baseball field for the Houston Astros, was probably the most dramatic. The Baltimore Ravens paid almost $6 million to reacquire the naming-rights held by PSINet after that company filed for Chapter 11 bankruptcy. The Tennessee Titans reached an agreement with Adelphia Business Solutions to pull that company's name off of its stadium in Nashville after Adelphia went into bankruptcy. Three Com Park and TWA Dome are two other naming-right deals that were lost due to the financial difficulties of the sponsoring company.

The revenue benefits of a naming rights deal has even reached the high school level. In 2002 Vernon Hills High School in Illinois got $100,000 for naming its stadium the Rust-Oleum Field. In 2004 the George Mason High School located in City of Falls, Virginia agreed to a 5-year, $50,000 naming rights deal for its stadium with a car dealership, Moore Cadillac.

Torts

A "tort" is a legal term generally defined as an unlawful, non-contractual injury to a person or his property. That is a very broad definition, but is necessary to describe the wide area of conduct encompassed by tort law. Almost any wrongful injury to a person or property, which is not of a contractual nature, may constitute a tort. Most torts involve "negligence," that is, unreasonable or careless conduct such as accidentally running a stop sign. Torts can also occur as a result of an intentional act, for example, deliberately striking someone.

Conduct which constitutes a tort, especially an intentional tort, can result in a criminal action. Tort law, however, refers to the civil (private) action that a victim has against the offender for damages.

In order to succeed in a tort action the following must be established:
1. A duty was owed by the defendant to the plaintiff.
2. The defendant breached the duty.
3. The plaintiff was injured.
4. The breach of the duty was a legal cause of the plaintiff's injury.

Torts often involve a physical injury to the plaintiff as a result of the defendant's conduct. The primary issue in most sports related tort actions is whether the defendant owed a duty to the plaintiff with respect to the particular conduct in question.

PARTICIPANT LIABILITY

In Ancient Greece, an athlete who killed another in competition was not punished. The offending athlete was required, however, to compensate the dead participant's family for the loss. The compensation was designed to reduce the harsh feelings and possibly avert a war between rival cities. Many sports involve contact among the participants. If a football player is severely injured as a result of a "bone-crushing" tackle, the injured player would not have a viable tort claim against the tackler. Two legal defenses, or legal justification for the conduct, may be asserted by the defendant to escape liability. The defenses are *consent* and *assumption of risk*. By participating in the contact sport, the plaintiff consented to being hit. The plaintiff also assumed the risk of injury from contact.

Dilger v. Moyles (1997)

Dorothy Dilger (appellant) was struck on the golf course by a ball hit by another golfer, David Moyles (respondent), whom she sued. She appeals the trial court's entry of summary judgment in his favor. We hold that the trial court was correct in finding that primary assumption of risk bars her lawsuit; accordingly, we affirm.

FACTS

On the morning of April 26, 1994, appellant and two companions were golfing at Sky West Golf Course in Hayward. After teeing off on the fifth tee, appellant, who was 78 years old at the time, drove her golf cart to where her ball had landed— approximately 95 yards down the fairway. She stopped her cart on the left side of the fairway, which borders the fairway of the sixth hole. After stopping her cart, appellant was struck in the mouth by a ball hit by respondent from the sixth fairway. At the time he hit the ball, respondent was standing behind a row of trees which separated the fifth and sixth Fairways. Respondent claimed trees blocked the line of sight to where appellant was located. Whether or not respondent yelled "fore" upon hitting his errant shot was disputed.

ANALYSIS

Appellant argues that the doctrine of assumption of risk is inappropriate as a defense for golfers. The California Supreme Court has found that participants generally do not have a duty to protect other participants against risks inherent in an active sport. *(Knight v. Jewett* (1992)) In Knight plaintiff's finger had to be amputated after defendant, a co-participant, accidentally stepped on it during a game of touch football. The court held that defendant's conduct did not breach any legal duty of care owed to plaintiff. The court found applicable the doctrine of assumption of risk to this sport because "vigorous participation in such sporting events likely would be chilled if legal liability were to be imposed on a participant on the basis of his or her ordinary careless conduct. ... [E]ven when a participant's conduct violates a rule of the game and may subject the violator to internal sanctions prescribed by the sport itself, imposition of legal liability far such conduct might well alter fundamentally the nature of the sport by deterring participants from vigorously engaging in activity that falls close to, but on the permissible side of, a prescribed rule." The court expressly declined to decide whether this rule should apply to less active sports such as golf: "Because the touch football game at issue in this case clearly falls within the rationale of this rule, we have no occasion to decide whether a comparable limited duty of care appropriately should be applied to other less active sports, such as archery or golf."

Nevertheless, the court's reasoning in limiting active sports participants' liability applies equally as well to the sport of golf.

While golf may not be as physically demanding as other more strenuous sports such as basketball or football, risk is nonetheless inherent in the sport. Hitting a golf ball at a high rate of speed involves the very real possibility that the ball will take flight in an unintended direction. If every ball behaved as the golfer wished, there would be little "sport" in the sport of golf. That shots go awry is a risk that all golfers; even the professionals, assume when they play.

Holding participants liable for missed hits would only encourage lawsuits and deter players from enjoying the sport. Golf offers many healthful advantages to both the golfer and the community. The physical exercise in the fresh air with the smell of the pines and eucalyptus renews the spirit and refreshes the body. The sport offers an opportunity for recreation with friends and the chance to meet other citizens with like interests. A foursome can be a very social event, relieving each golfer of the stresses of business and everyday urban life. Neighborhoods benefit by the scenic green belts golf brings to their communities, and wild life enjoy and flourish in a friendly habitat. Social policy dictates that the law should not discourage participation in such an activity whose benefits to the individual player and to the community at large are so great.

Golf etiquette requires that a player whose shot may endanger another warn the other by shouting "fore." But golf etiquette does not, necessarily rise to the level of a duty. If no duty was owed, the defense of primary assumption of risk completely bars recovery. Whether a duty exists depends on whether the activity in question was an "inherent risk" of the sport.

When the activity involved is an inherent risk of a sport, a participant owes no duty to coparticipants unless he "intentionally injures another player or engages in reckless conduct that is totally outside the range of the ordinary activity involved in the sport." We do not believe the failure to yell "fore" is that reckless or intentional conduct contemplated by the *Knight* court. Whether or not the golfer yells "fore" does not alter the inherent risk of the sport—being struck by a golf ball.

The grant of summary judgment is affirmed.

****

Athletes do not, however, consent or assume the risk of any and all contact by other players. There can be contact in competition that is so improper that an offending player may be found liable in a tort suit. Boxing is a violent sport, but certain punches are not allowed. Biting an opponent's ear is clearly against the rules of boxing. If Evander Holyfield had chosen to file a tort suit against Mike Tyson for the ear chomps, the case would have been an immediate knock-out in Holyfield's favor.

Tort law in sports, especially contact sports, is difficult to apply. The participants in sports know, or should know, that the event may involve hard physical contact with a player, equipment or playing surface. Injuries are an inherent risk in sports. The courts have had difficulty deciding what standard should apply to determine if the contact is so far outside of the game as to support a tort action.

The Supreme Court of New Jersey ruled in a case that involved informal men's softball, *Crawn v. Campo* (1996), that a plaintiff has a greater burden in a tort suit involving contact sports. The court held that in order for the defendant to be liable, the injury must have occurred as a result of "reckless disregard or intentional conduct." This approach seems to be an emerging view on the issue.

In *Nabozny v. Barnhill* (1975), an injured soccer goal keeper was awarded damages as a result of being kicked while he was in the penalty area. The fact that there was a specific rule which prohibited the conduct and that the rule was designed specifically for the safety of the keeper certainly influenced the decision. The court found that the actions of the defendant were deliberate, willful or with a reckless disregard for the safety of the player.

In *Bourque v. Duplechin* (1976), Bourque, the plaintiff, was playing softball for Boo Boo's Lounge. Bourque was well out of the baseline and had already thrown the ball toward first when the defendant ran into him at full speed near second base in an apparent attempt to break up a double play. The defendant did not slide, but brought his arm up under Bourque's chin breaking the plaintiff's jaw. The umpire evicted the defendant from the game. The trial court rendered a judgment in favor of the plaintiff. The Court of Appeal upheld the decision and ruled that the defendant breached his duty to play softball in an ordinary fashion. The court also held that the plaintiff did not assume the risk of the defendant going out of his way to collide with him at full speed when the plaintiff was at least five (5') feet away from the base.

Ginsberg v. Hontas (1989), is a case that arose out of a recreational softball game between faculty and staff at the Tulane Medical School. The plaintiff was playing shortstop and the defendant was batting. The defendant hit the ball in the field and slid into second base which the plaintiff was covering. As a result of the slide, there was a collision between the defendant-base runner and the plaintiff-shortstop. The plaintiff sustained a fracture of his right leg, which required two operations, hospitalization, a cast and physical therapy. The game was being umpired and played under major league rules which allowed sliding. The trial court dismissed the case. On appeal, the plaintiff contended that the defendant acted unreasonably by sliding, not head first into second base, but rather by throwing a roll block or cross body block while attempting to reach the base. Numerous expert witnesses testified with respect to the rules of the game and proper techniques for sliding into base. The umpire testified that sliding was permitted, but that players who threw roll or body blocks would have been expelled from the game. The umpire also testified that he did not expel the defendant and that he ruled the defendant was safe on base. The appellate court found no liability on the part of the base runner. The court would probably have found the runner liable if the evidence had shown that the collision was the result of a body-block rather than a slide.

A California appeals court addressed the issue of tort liability among ice skaters in *Staten v. Superior Court*, (1996). In *Staten*, the injury occurred when one skater collided with another during a practice session. California courts have ruled that, pursuant to the assumption of risk defense, a defendant owes no duty to protect a plaintiff against risks that are inherent in a contact sport. The plaintiff argued that ice skating was a solo sport, not a contact sport, and therefore the above doctrine should not apply. The court found that the doctrine had been applied in snow skiing, water skiing, sailing and even discuss throwing. The court reasoned that collisions with other skaters was an inherent risk in figure skating and dismissed the plaintiff's case.

In *Lestina v. West Bend Mutual Insurance*, a tennis instructor who was injured brought a negligence suit against the student who hit the ball and caused the injury. The court ruled that although a participant may consent to the inherent risk of being a participant in a sport, the consent did not encompass an injury that resulted from the negligence of another party. The student disregarded the instructions to hit the ball gently. The court said, under the circumstances, the hard swing was not an inherent risk of the sport.

Hackbart v. Cincinnati Bengals (1979), demonstrates that even in professional football some contact is outside the scope of the game and not an inherent risk. The suit was filed by Hackbart as a result of an incident which occurred in a 1973 exhibition game between the Denver Broncos and the Cincinnati Bengals. After a Denver interception, Cincinnati's Charles Clark, "acting out of anger and frustration, but without specific intent to injure," hit Hackbart on the back of his head with his forearm. No official saw the blow, but it was clear on the game film. Although he felt the impact, Hackbart continued to play for the remainder of the game. Hackbart was later diagnosed as having a neck injury and was eventually released by Denver. Hackbart filed suit against Cincinnati. The trial court said the emotional outburst by Clark was "part of the game" and dismissed the case. The appellate court ruled that the conduct was "reckless harm" and sent the matter back for trial. The appellate court's opinion included the following:

> The general customs of football do not approve the intentional punching or striking of others. That this is prohibited was supported by the testimony of all of the witnesses. They testified that the intentional striking of a player in the face or from the rear is prohibited by the playing rules as well as the general customs of the game. Punching or hitting with the arms is prohibited. Undoubtedly, these restraints are intended to establish reasonable boundaries so that one football player cannot intentionally inflict a serious injury on another. Therefore, the notion is not correct that all reason has been abandoned, whereby the only possible remedy for the person who has been the victim of an unlawful blow is retaliation.

In *McKichan v. St. Louis Hockey Club*, a Missouri appellate court decision illustrates how tolerant some courts are with respect to violent behavior in professional hockey. In *McKichan*, the plaintiff, a goalie, sustained serious injuries. A puck traveled over the goal and plexiglass and out of play. The linesman blew his whistle stopping play. As McKichan began to move away from the goal, Tony Twist, the defendant, smashed the plaintiff with his body and hockey stick rendering the plaintiff unconscious. It was well known in hockey circles that Twist's role on the ice was as an *enforcer*. Twist was suspended by the League for several games. McKichan filed suit against Twist and the St. Louis Hockey Club. Twist counterclaimed against McKichan. Both Twist and McKichan dismissed the claims against each other which left the St. Louis Hockey Club as the sole defender. The trial court found the hockey club culpable for the injury on the theory of vicarious liability. The court awarded a jury verdict of $175,000 compensation to McKichan. The Court of Appeal, however, reversed the decision. An extract from the Court of Appeal's decision is below:

> Reasonable men might argue that the physical punishment you incurred represents an inherent part and/or risk of the game. Whereas, others might claim that the pain and injury inflicted upon you surface outside the boundaries of an already violent game. However, your employers equipped you with the foremost quality of

protective equipment, designed to absorb a great amount of force. In addition, your coaches conditioned you so that your body was able to cushion additional energy. You, sir, a professional athlete, represent a highly compensated member of society. Your contract per year calls for more money than many people earn in a lifetime. Sir, here you appear before this court, seeking damages against another player for striking you. I am confident that you have probably struck someone before. After all, your game appears so violent. I must say that an athlete grossing $5 million a year does not need to seek damages for a smack in the face. The scar on your face will no doubt blend in with the scars you have already received playing the game. The teeth that you have lost will fit in with the three other teeth you have lost playing the game. Your salary compensates for the fear that you feel when taking the ice. You must have expected to be hit before you even took the ice. You assumed the risk of injury from an opponent who broke the safety rules. Verdict for the defendant. Good luck..

LIABILITY OF COACHES AND SCHOOLS

There are a number of theories which can be applied in a tort action against a coach, school or premise for an injured athlete, including failure to properly train, warn, or instruct. A coach or school may be liable if they knew or should have known that the equipment or facility was defective or insufficient. Two of the most notable cases against colleges arose out of the Hank Gathers and Marc Buoniconti incidents.

Gathers, a star basketball player for Loyola, had previously collapsed at a game due to an abnormal heart rhythm. The team acquired a defibrillator, a device to shock the heart back into normal rhythms, which was kept on the bench for an emergency. Gathers was also put on medication for the condition. The medication made Gathers sluggish. The team doctor, after discussions with Gathers and the coach, reduced the medications. Gathers' play improved and the team was successful--until Gathers dropped dead at a game. A settlement of approximately $2.6 million was reached with Loyola and the team doctor.

Buoniconti, a football player at Citadel, suffered multiple spinal abnormalities which increased the risk of a severe neck injury. He sustained persistent neck injuries throughout the 1985 season and was not able to practice for part of the week leading up to his permanent injury. The Citadel's trainer provided him with a special strap designed to prevent his neck from snapping back. At trial it was argued that the strap actually made the situation more dangerous. The school's insurer settled with Buoniconti for $800,000. The case against the doctor went to trial and the jury found the doctor not liable. At trial, the defense proved that Bouniconti had "speared" the ball carrier by leading the tackle with his head which is a violation of a NCAA rule that was passed specifically to minimize the risk of that sort of injury.

In *Besler v. West Windsor Plainsboro*, (2004) the plaintiff, a former high school player, filed suit for alleged abuse committed by her coach. A number of other players also testified that the coach screamed, swore and constantly berated them.

When the coach was not happy with the team's performance he became violent and would kick and bang on objects. That type of conduct may be viewed by many as common theatrics by a coach. The evidence showed that the coach singled out the plaintiff for much of his criticism and that he demanded that she loose 10 pounds in two weeks. The plaintiff alleged that the coach's abusive behavior and demands led to a long term eating disorder. The jury agreed and awarded the plaintiff almost $1.5 million. The court of appeal, however, reversed the decision and ruled in favor of the defendant.

In *Zalkin v. American Learning System*, (1994) a Florida appellate court ruled that a high school football player injured in a game may have "assumed the risk" inherent in the sport, but did not assume the risk of negligent supervision. The student had injured himself in the last regular season game. The coach advised the player to see a doctor and did not allow him to practice. Ten days later, the player advised the coach that he had not seen a doctor. He was, however, put into the game by the coach and suffered a severe aggravation to the injury. The appellate court held that it was improper to instruct the jury on "assumption of risks" because the student could not assume the risk of negligent supervision.

Woodson v. Irvington Board of Education, (1987) involved a track star who was recruited to play football for his speed. He was crippled when trying to make a tackle. The player had one practice session on tackling before the injury. There was considerable evidence at the trial that tackling is very dangerous and that one practice was grossly insufficient. One of the coaches admitted at trial that the only thing he knew about the player was his name. The evidence established the school and coaches were only concerned about "winning" and had little or no interest in safety for the players. A substantial award was made.

In *Mogabgab v. Orleans Parish School Board*, (1970) a high school football player began exhibiting signs of heat stroke, but the coach waited over two hours before seeking aid for the student. The student eventually collapsed and died. The coach's conduct was found to be negligent.

Understandably, a substantial duty is owed by the coaching staff with respect to the welfare of the players. The extent of the duty may vary based on the age of the athlete. The duty continues, however, even in the professional ranks. In *Krueger v. San Francisco Forty-Niners*, an appellate court held that a professional football team's conscious failure to inform a player that he risked a permanent knee injury by continuing to play was fraudulent concealment. The court found that the plaintiff was not informed by team physicians of the true nature and extent of his knee injuries. The court also found that the physician failed to warn the athlete about the consequences of steroid injection treatment, or the long-term dangers associated with playing professional football with this medical condition. It was clear to the court that the purpose of this nondisclosure was to induce the plaintiff to continue playing football despite his injuries, thereby constituting fraud. Krueger won a verdict of $2.36 million in damages in the trial court, but eventually settled his claim for a sum in excess of $1 million.

Dave Babych, who played for the NHL's Philadelphia Flyers, filed a medical malpractice suit against the Flyers' team doctor for the negligent treatment of his broken foot. Babych alleged that the doctor deviated from standard medical practice when he failed to inform Babych of the ramifications of playing with the injury. The jury awarded Babych $1.3 million dollars.

In 1996, a University of Miami football coach, Randy Shannon, was hit on the head with a trash can after a game against West Virginia University. The can, which was hurled from the upper deck at Mountaineer Field as the victorious Miami team left the field, caused severe injuries to Shannon. Shannon claimed the school failed to protect the visiting team from overzealous fans. The parties settled the case for the sum of $50,000.

Cheerleading has evolved over the years from yelling cheers and shaking pom-poms into a highly athletic and competitive sport. The entry of men into cheerleading allows routines which propel a cheerleader as high as three stories. The Consumer Product Safety Commission reported 15,600 visits by cheerleaders to hospital emergency rooms in 1993. In *Nova University v. Katz* (1993), a cheerleader fell while performing a cheer and severely injured her foot. She filed suit alleging negligence on the part of the school for failing to supply spotters and properly supervise. The jury returned a verdict in favor of the cheerleader, which was upheld by the appellate court.

In *Coyle v. Parish of Jefferson* (1997) the parents of a nine-year old baseball player was struck in the head when he misjudged a fly-ball hit to him. The parents filed suit alleging that the coaches were negligent. The trial and appellate court dismissed the case.

Harvey v. Ouachita Parish School Board (1994)

In this action against the head coach of the West Monroe High School football team and the Ouachita Parish School Board arising out of an injury sustained during a football game in 1986 by Michael Harvey, a WMHS player, the defendants, Coach Ross Davis and the School Board, appeal a judgment finding them 80 percent at fault for Harvey's injury, a ruptured cervical disc, and awarding Harvey about $215,000 in damages, subject to reduction by 20 percent for his share of fault.

While conceding they owed some vague legal duty to protect high school football players from the risk of injury, defendants primarily question the trial court's findings that Coach Davis had breached a duty to protect Harvey from the injury to his neck, which he sustained when tackled by players on the opposing team. Alternatively, defendants ask us to modify the trial court's allocation of fault and the assessment of Harvey's monetary damages.

Harvey argues in brief that he should not have been assessed with any fault, but he did not appeal or answer the appeal to preserve this issue for review.

Amending the judgment solely to correct what we believe is a mathematical error in the calculation of Harvey's damages, we reduce the total award to $180,866 and affirm the judgment as amended.

Harvey was injured on September 12, 1986, early in his senior year at WMHS, during a football game played in Shreveport against Booker T. Washington High School. A videotape of the game is in the record. By all accounts, the 17-year-old Harvey established himself as a gifted athlete and a "star player" for WMHS during his sophomore and junior years. Harvey played running back on offense and linebacker on defense.

In the third quarter of the game with BTWHS in Shreveport, Harvey, as a linebacker, intercepted a pass thrown by the BTW quarterback, successfully eluding BTW tacklers and returning the interception from the 10 to the 50 yard line. As Harvey approached mid-field, a BTW player grabbed Harvey's face mask, forcing his head downward and toward his left shoulder and placing Harvey on the ground in a seated position. A 15-yard penalty was assessed against BTW for this infraction.

As Harvey was forced to the ground by the face mask infraction and in the "seated" position, another BTW player, pursuing and seeking to ground Harvey, "piled on" the upper part of Harvey's body, slamming his body against Harvey, whose head and neck were being contorted downward and to the left by the face mask infraction. These combined forces caused a compression injury to Harvey's spine. This injury left Harvey lying on the field, fully conscious, but unable to feel or to move anything below his neck for about 15 minutes.

Fortunately, Harvey's paralysis was temporary. After he regained feeling and movement, Harvey was removed from the field and taken by ambulance to the emergency room at a Shreveport hospital. At the request of Harvey's parents, he was released from the ER on the night of the injury to return to West Monroe.

Harvey was then hospitalized at a West Monroe hospital for ten days, September 13-22, 1986. The initial diagnostic tests there being inconclusive, Harvey was returned to Shreveport for an MRI of the cervical spine, which was performed September 16, 1986.

The MRI showed that Harvey had a ruptured cervical disc at the C4-C5 interspace. Harvey's West Monroe neurosurgeon, Dr. Greer, referred Harvey to Dr. James Robertson, a Memphis neurosurgeon specializing in sports injuries. Dr. Robertson surgically removed the disc and fused the C4-C5 vertebrae with bone taken from Harvey's hip in November 1986.

After recuperating from the surgery, Harvey played baseball for WMHS during the spring of 1987, as he had done the year before. After graduating with his class, Harvey entered Louisiana Tech as a freshman on a football scholarship in the fall of 1987. His treating physicians cautiously or conditionally approved for Louisiana Tech Harvey's continuing his football career.

Notwithstanding his medical release to play football, Harvey was informed by his doctors that he faced a greater risk of reinjuring his neck, and of potentially permanent paralysis, than did players who had not undergone a cervical fusion. The doctors recommended that Harvey cease playing football if he experienced tingling or stinging in his arms or hands, leaving the final decision to Harvey.

Like other freshmen football players at Tech, Harvey was "red-shirted," being required to participate only in practices and scrimmages and not playing against opposing teams. In deference to his cervical fusion, Harvey wore a "neck roll" at all times in practice sessions and when scrimmaging. He sometimes experienced pain in his neck, and a stinging or burning sensation in his shoulders and thumbs, particularly after contact with another player. Fearing another neck injury, Harvey became less aggressive in his play, sometimes "holding back" and performing below his usual capabilities to avoid contact.

Harvey satisfactorily participated in the Tech football program in the fall of 1988, according to a Tech coach. He continued to experience pain and stinging, however, ceasing his college football career during the 1988 season because of his experience and his concern of more serious injury.

Before the 1986 high school injury, Harvey was being heavily recruited by several universities and colleges in Louisiana and other states to play college football.

Harvey brought his action for damages in Caddo Parish, joining as defendants the Caddo and Ouachita Parish School Boards, their respective high school football coaches, and the Louisiana High School Athletic Association. The LHSAA was dismissed on summary judgment. The Caddo School Board and coach were also dismissed before the trial.

The issues in this appeal hinge heavily on the factual circumstances leading up to Harvey's injury, as found by the trial court. Sometimes referring to appellants singularly as the Board, we summarize the trial court's findings, express and implied:

Trial Court Findings

-- Before his September 1986 injury, Harvey had suffered two prior, albeit minor, neck injuries as a football player for WMHS. His first minor injury occurred in a scrimmage in the spring of 1986, and his second in a pre-season jamboree game that August, preceding the regular season games. In each instance, Harvey told his father, a West Monroe doctor of chiropractic (D.C.), that he had "jammed" or strained his neck. Harvey's father observed and treated him for both injuries, noting that Harvey was free of symptoms within a week of each injury. Opinion evidence agreed that these injuries were minor, but had the effect of weakening to some degree Harvey's neck and increasing his susceptibility to more serious or severe neck injury.

-- The day after the August 1986 "jamboree" injury, Dr. Harvey telephoned Coach Davis, asking that Harvey be excused from football practice for a few days, during which time Dr. Harvey would treat the jamboree injury, and informing Coach Davis that Harvey had to wear a neck roll in all practices and games for an indefinite period of time to protect Harvey's neck from further injury.

-- Neck rolls were generally considered "optional" equipment for WMHS football players, unlike other protective equipment such as helmets, shoulder pads and knee pads, which each player was required to wear. The school furnished each player with the "standard" protective equipment, and carried spare items of such equipment when playing games away from West Monroe. The school generally did not furnish or carry replacements of "optional" protective equipment, but allowed players to use such equipment during games and practices if the players obtained the equipment for themselves.

-- Shortly after Harvey's August 1986 neck injury, Harvey's parents purchased for him from a local sporting goods store, a horseshoe-shaped neck roll. A neck roll is designed to be tied in several places to shoulder pads. The horseshoe neck roll limits movement of the head in all directions, especially to the back or to either side.

-- Harvey attached and wore the neck roll purchased by his parents in all practices, and in the first regular game of the season that was played the week before the BTW game.

-- Harvey wore the neck roll during the BTW game until it was forcibly torn from his shoulder pads by a BTW player in the second quarter of the game. A referee picked up the damaged neck roll, briefly waving it over his head before throwing it off the playing field. The neck roll was damaged to such an extent that it could not be reattached to the shoulder pads. Harvey played the rest of the second quarter without a neck roll. At half time, one of the WMHS student trainers, answering Harvey's inquiry about an extra neck roll, said he had none. Harvey did not ask any of his coaches for a neck roll. Harvey resumed play in the third quarter without a neck roll.

-- The coaching staff at the BTW game included Coach Davis and at least four assistant coaches: Aulds as offensive line coach, Smith and Moncrief as offensive backfield coaches, and Spears as defensive backfield coach. Aulds was also the team's equipment manager, but said he handled only "standard gear, not first aid supplies ... or injuries." Coach Davis relied on the assistant coaches, and on one or more uncompensated "student trainers" to assist him in fulfilling his duty as head coach, as he explained it, to monitor the players' medical needs and injuries.

-- Coach Davis knew, or should have been advised by his subordinate coaches and trainers, that Harvey's neck roll had been torn from him in the second quarter of the BTW game.

-- Coach Davis knew that Harvey's father did not want his son to play without a neck roll because of the prior neck injuries. Based on that knowledge, and by Coach Davis's own admission, a neck roll was not optional equipment for Harvey during the BTW game, but was "required equipment ... for his own benefit to prevent further possible injury to him and because of his parents' wishes."

More probably than not, the type of neck roll Harvey wore at the start of the BTW game would have protected him from the severe neck injury he suffered in that game.

In discussing Coach Davis's legal duty as head football coach, the trial court found that Davis and his assistant coaches had a duty to reasonably protect their players from injury during football games, which necessarily entail direct physical contact between players. This duty, in the trial court's view, included the duty of providing, or requiring players to wear, available protective equipment to minimize the risk of a player being injured when tackled, even by actions that violate game rules, such as the "face mask" and "late hit" infractions for which penalty flags are thrown.

The court found that Coach Davis and his staff breached their duty to Harvey in several respects: by generally having an attitude of indifference or ridicule toward players who expressed concerns for their own safety, by not having a clear designation of responsibility among the staff members for monitoring a particular player's susceptibility to injuries, and by their specific individual and collective conduct during the BTW game.

Harvey and two of his teammates testified that the coaching staff had sometimes ridiculed players who complained of injuries or requested additional protective equipment during games or practices, calling them "sissies" and telling them to "be tough." Coach Davis admitted that he sometimes "gigged" players who complained of minor injuries, such as bumps or bruises, but said he took all "legitimate" injuries seriously. The trial court described Davis's testimony on this issue as "troubling," and concluded that Davis and his staff "were not sufficiently concerned with their players' safety and complaints of problems."

According to Coach Davis, the entire coaching staff is responsible for monitoring students with injuries or with special equipment needs, yet no staff member noticed or inquired about the removal of Harvey's neck roll in the second quarter of the BTW game, even during half time when the coaches and the players convened in the visitors' locker room. In essence, the coaching staff's responsibility for monitoring the safety needs of the players in general, and of Harvey in particular, was assigned to everyone on the staff, but exercised by no one on the night in question.

From the totality of the evidence, the trial court concluded that Coach Davis was negligent in allowing Harvey, the team's "star" running back who also regularly played linebacker on defense, to continue playing in the BTW game without a neck roll. The court found that Harvey was also negligent because he knew his father did not want him to play without a neck roll.

The court's allocation of 80 percent fault to Coach Davis and 20 percent to Harvey obviously takes into account not only the conduct of the respective parties during the BTW game, but also the apparent lax attitude of Coach Davis and his staff toward the safety of the players, and the absence of any clear delineation of specific responsibility within the organizational structure of the coaching staff for monitoring and preventing player injuries.

In reasons for judgment, the court determined that Harvey was entitled to about $20,000 in special damages, $125,000 for the pain, suffering and disability associated with his ruptured disc and cervical fusion, and $35,000 for his "anguish and suffering due to the loss of ... opportunity" to play college football, subject to the 20 percent reduction. These awards total $180,866. The judgment, however, makes an in globo award of $215,866, without itemizing each element of damages. Appellants complain of a $35,000 "error" in the *in globo* award.

The Board's first two assignments of error, dealing with the existence and breach of a duty and with the trial court's allocation of fault, are premised on factual assertions which are in some respects contrary to and inconsistent with the factual findings made by the trial court. The Board has simply extracted those portions of the testimony which support its arguments, without attempting to demonstrate how and why the trial court was clearly wrong in accepting one of several permissible views of the evidence on the facts pertaining to duty, breach and fault allocation.

Our review of the record reveals ample support for the trial court's factual findings, which we have summarized. We particularly note that Coach Davis's credibility was significantly impeached by his having made inconsistent statements on several pertinent factual matters in his deposition, on the one hand, which was taken about two years after Harvey's injury, and at trial on the other, some seven years after the injury. Davis's attempt to "explain away" the inconsistencies, by saying his memory of the facts was refreshed when he heard other witnesses testify at the trial, apparently did little to help his cause.

The Board does not dispute that Coach Davis had a legal duty to reasonably supervise his players, nor does it dispute that the scope of such a broadly stated duty is necessarily fact-specific, to be determined on a case-by-case basis in light of the respective relationships and circumstances of the parties.

QUANTUM

In assessing Harvey's general damages, the trial court made separate awards for Harvey's initial and residual pain and suffering resulting from the cervical disc rupture and surgical repair ($125,000), and for his mental anguish over the loss of an "almost certain" opportunity to play college football ($35,000). The court rejected, as speculative, Harvey's additional claim for damages for the loss of earning capacity he might have enjoyed as a professional football player. (The appellate court upheld the award.)

HIGHTOWER, J., dissents with written reasons.

Under the circumstances presented in this case, the majority misconceives and overextends the duty of a coach. Will athletic mentors and boards of education, under today's ruling, be responsible to protect from injury any football player previously suffering from even a minor mishap?

Further, assuming arguendo a duty of care as expansive as that imposed here, Harvey himself stood in the best position to be directly aware of his situation and to avoid any risk of playing without a neck roll. Having failed to act accordingly, he should bear the majority of the fault for his injury.

****

Day v. Ouachita Parish School Board (2001)

The defendant, Ouachita Parish School Board and John Green, appeal a judgment in favor of the plaintiffs, Amy Day and her son, Morgan Day. The trial court found that defendants were liable for a back injury sustained by Morgan Day and awarded damages for his injuries. For the following reasons, we affirm and remand.

FACTS

In august 1997, Morgan Day ("Morgan") was a freshman at West Monroe High School ("WMHS). As a member of the freshman football team, Morgan was required to participate in a weight training class held during school hours. The weight lifting program was directed by the school's strength coach, John Sanders, who was assisted by coach John Green ("Green") and the two other coaches. The sixty student players were divided into four of five lifting groups, each of which was supervised by one of the coaches. Several senior students on the team assisted the coaches with supervising and instructing the class participants.

In October 1997, Morgan injured his back while lifting weights in class. The next day, Morgan played in a freshman football game even though his back was bothering him. On October 7, 1997, Morgan sought treatment from Dr. Douglas Brown, an orthopedic surgeon. After an examination, Dr. Brown diagnosed Morgan's injury as lumbar strain and a dehydrated L-5 disc. Dr. Brown provided Morgan with a written medical excuse, which state "(1) No football for 1 week (2) No weightlifting, squats or power cleans. Diagnosis-lumbar strain and injured L-5 disc."

Morgan presented the medical excuse to George Bell, the freshman coach, and the note was posted on a bulletin board in Coach Sanders' office. Coaches Bell, Green and Sanders testified that they interpreted the doctor's note to mean that Morgan could not participate in football or weightlifting for a period of one week. Morgan and his mother, Amy Day, testified that they interpreted the note to mean that he could not play football for one week and could not lift weight for an indefinite time period.According to Morgan, who did not recall the exact date, at some point after the medical excuse was posted he was observing in class but not lifting weights, when Green instructed him to perform a "dumbbell power clean push press." When

Morgan reminded Green that he was medically excused, the coach insisted that the lift was an upper body exercise and would not affect his lower back. After performing several repetitions of the lift, Morgan felt severe pain in his back and needed to lie down on a mat.

On October 21, 1997, Morgan again saw Dr. Brown with a complaint of back pain. Dr. Brown ordered an MRI of the lumber spine that indicated a disc protrusion between the fourth and fifth vertebrae. Dr. Brown diagnosed Morgan with a herniated disc at the L-4 level and issued another medical excuse that prohibited him from all weightlifting and football activities until further notice.

After the disc injury, Morgan was unable to play high school football or baseball. Morgan lost interest in school and failed his courses due to excessive absences. He withdrew from WMHS and enrolled in Richardson High School, an alternative school, where his grades improved.

Morgan's injury caused his mother to incur medical expenses of $7,485. Dr. Brown estimated that surgery to relieve the herniated disc would cost $16,000. As of the trial date, Morgan had not pursued the recommended series of epidural steroid injections or participated in physical therapy for his back.

The plaintiff, Amy Day, individually and as Tutrix of her minor son Morgan, filed a petition for damages against the defendants, Ouachita Parish School Board and John Green. Morgan was later added as a party plaintiff upon reaching the age of majority. After a trial, the court issued written reasons for judgment, finding that the defendants were liable for Morgan's back injury and awarding the plaintiffs damages of $7,485.45 for past medical expenses, $195,500 for pain and suffering, $30,000 for future medical expenses and $50,000 for loss of enjoyment of life. Judgment was rendered in favor of the plaintiffs. Defendant appeal the damage award.

In the present case, the testimony presented shows that as a result of his injury, Morgan lost a probably opportunity to participate in varsity football and baseball at WMHS, a goal for which he had trained and practiced since the sixth grade. The evidence also demonstrates that the loss of this opportunity caused Morgan emotional anguish. Dr. Ellis noted that the results of a psychological test indicated that Morgan was experiencing mild depression. Any Day testified that her son became "really depressed" after he was advised that he would be unable to play sports at the varsity level. Morgan stated that because his life was so centered on participating in school athletics, after learning that he could not participate in sports, he lost interest in his academic work, missed school and failed his classes. As the trial court noted, the opportunity to participate in high school athletics was a very significant part of Morgan's life and he cannot regain that lost opportunity.

The testimony also established that more probably than not, Morgan's injury will force him to give up the chance to participate in certain activities, including military service and any strenuous occupations. We note that Morgan has not sought psychological therapy or counseling and that despite his episodes of pain, Morgan has been able to play summer league baseball, serve as an umpire in youth games and work in a sporting goods store.

Based upon this record, we agree that loss of enjoyment of life is a compensable element of damages in this case. Further, we cannot say that the award of $50,000 for loss of enjoyment of life is excessive in light of the particular circumstances of this plaintiff's situation. Although the awards for pain and suffering and loss of enjoyment of life are on the high end of the spectrum, they do not exceed the highest amount reasonably within the trial court's broad discretion in assessing damages.

****

James v. Jackson and the Frederick Douglas Senior High School (2005)

At approximately 12:30 p.m. on September 21, 1998, Darrell James, a sixteen-year old student at Frederick Douglass Senior High School who weighed 327 pounds, collapsed during a physical education class. Darrell was then transported to St. Claude Medical Center where he was pronounced dead.

During the physical education class, which was conducted by substitute art teacher Donyea Allen, the students participated in a basketball game inside the Douglas gymnasium. The gymnasium was not air-conditioned and the temperature inside was at least ninety degrees during the class. After playing basketball for approximately twenty minutes, Darrell began complaining of a headache. After resting briefly, he collapsed and began having seizures.

In their third assignment of error the defendants contend that they did not breach any duty to Darrell James. Teachers have a duty to exercise reasonable care and supervision over students in their custody, and must therefore conduct their classes so as not to expose their students to an unreasonable risk of injury. Certain classes, such as physical education, involve dangerous activity, and due care must be exercised in instructing, preparing, and supervising students in these activities so as to minimize the risk of injury. Further, the law requires that supervision be reasonable and commensurate with the age of the student and the attendant circumstances. In the instant case, Darrell James, who weighed 327 pounds, was allowed to participate in a basketball game in a poorly ventilated gym where the temperature approached ninety degrees for approximately twenty minutes before any rest period was allowed. The substitute art teacher who was in charge of the class did not require that the students take any water breaks and participated in the game himself rather than observe and monitor the students as he should have under these conditions. Clearly, the defendants breached a duty to exercise reasonable care and supervision over Darrell James.

In the instant case, Dr. Douglas Singer, who is Board Certified in the areas of internal medicine and cardiology, opined that the specific heat related illness Darrell contracted was heat stroke and that Darrell suffered cardiac arrest due to a heat related illness. Signs of heat stroke which were exhibited by Darrell included headache and seizure. Both obesity and strenuous activity in the heat are predisposing factors to heat stroke. The defendants did not produce evidence that Darrell's death could not have been related to heat illness or heat stroke. Accordingly, we find that the trial court's finding on this factual finding was reasonable.

For the foregoing reasons, the judgment of the trial court (in favor or James' Mother) is affirmed.

****

Many states have laws which provide some liability protection for volunteer coaches. The Louisiana law is set forth below:

La. R.S. 9:2798:

A. Except as provided in Subsection B of this Section, no person shall have a cause of action against any volunteer athletic coach, manager, team physician, or sports team official for any loss or damage caused by any act or omission to act directly related to his responsibilities as a coach, manager, team physician, or official, while actively directing or participating in the sporting activities or in the practice thereof, unless the loss or damage was caused by the gross negligence of the coach, manager, team physician, or official.

B. Subsection A of this Section shall not be applicable unless the volunteer athletic coach, manager, team physician, or sports team official has participated in a safety orientation and training program established by the league or team with which he is affiliated. Participation in a safety orientation and training program by a coach, manager, team physician, or sports team official may be waived by the league prior to the individual's participation in the sporting activities or in the practice thereof upon submission of appropriate documented evidence as to that individual's proficiency in first aid and safety. A person who has been tested or trained, and sanctioned or admitted by a recognized league or association, shall be deemed to be in compliance with the Subsection. However, compliance with the requirements of this Subsection shall not be construed to create or impose on the volunteer any additional liability or higher standard of care based on participation in safety orientation and training or evidence of proficiency in first aid and safety.

C. The receipt of a small stipend or incidental compensation for volunteer services shall not exclude any person, who is otherwise covered, from the limitation of liability provided in Subsection A.

PRODUCT LIABILITY

In *Brett v. Hillerich & Bradsby d/b/a Louisville Slugger* the manufacturer of a high performance aluminum baseball bat agreed to pay a substantial settlement to a high school pitcher who was struck in the head by a ball that flew back at him so quickly that he didn't even have time to move. Evidence at the trial showed that consultants for Louisville Slugger had warned management that someone would get seriously hurt if the bat was not "detuned."

In *Sanchez v. Hillerich & Bradsby* (2002) a college baseball player was struck by a ball that was hit. The court held that assumption of risk did not bar a product liability suit against the bat manufacturer. The suit alleged that the "Air Attack" bat, a high tech aluminum bat designed to increase the speed at which the ball is hit, was unreasonably dangerous.

PREMISE LIABILITY AND SPECTATOR INJURY

Most of the cases dealing with spectator injuries arise from claims that relate to alleged defects or dangers with respect to the stadium or arena. A facility which is the host of an athletic contest, or any other event, assumes a degree of responsibility toward its patrons. The facility must not allow a condition to exist that would forseeably cause an injury. In addition, the facility should have adequate security and emergency medical services.

There are a number of cases holding that spectators who are injured as a result of foul balls hit into the stands during a baseball game cannot recover. The courts generally have found that the spectator *assumed-the-risk* of such an injury. Liability has been found on the part of teams or stadium owners if the screen behind home plate has holes that allows a ball to enter the spectator area. Years ago, when an extra point or field goal was kicked in the NFL the ball was allowed to go in the stands. Whoever caught the ball was permitted to keep it. Nets now prevent the ball from traveling in the stands. In all probability, the nets are not to save footballs for the NFL, but to prevent injuries and lawsuits that might result from a fight for the ball.

Does the risk of being hit in the stadium by a home run ball differ from the risk of being injured as a result of fans fighting for the ball? In an older case, *Lee v. National League Baseball* (1958), the court held that a baseball spectator who was injured as a result of being trampled on while fans pursued a foul ball was entitled to damages from the Milwaukee Braves club. The court made a distinction in assuming the risk for being struck by the ball, which is foreseeable, and being trampled by other spectators which, according to the court in this case, was not foreseeable.

Reider v. McNeese State University (2005)

On April 16, 1997, Heather Reider, desiring to attend a baseball game between McNeese State University and Rice University, approached the main entrance ticket booth along the third base line of McNeese's baseball field in Lake Charles, Calcasieu Parish, Louisiana. While Ms. Reider was approaching and near the ticket booth, she was struck in her right eye by an errant foul ball. The impact caused a complete fracture and implosion of the zygomatic structure of her right eye, laceration of the inner part of her right eyelid, and permanent macular blindness resulting in permanent 10/200 vision in her right eye. Ms. Reider sued McNeese for her personal injury and recovered damages.

The standard of care owed by McNeese to patrons of its baseball park is found in La.R.S. 9:2800. Under this statute, to carry her burden, Plaintiff must show: (1) the baseball field was in the care, custody and control of the Defendant; (2) the baseball park had a vice or defect which created an unreasonable risk of harm; (3) Plaintiff's injury was. caused by the, defect; and (4) the Defendant had actual or constructive knowledge of the dangerous condition.

There is no dispute that the baseball field was in the care, custody and control of the Defendant; however, Defendant argues that an unreasonable condition did not exist at the McNeese State University baseball park, and if one did, they had no prior knowledge of said unreasonably dangerous defect. McNeese argues that the Plaintiff was an experienced softball player herself and, therefore, was sufficiently aware of the dangers involved in attending such a sporting event. McNeese further argues that in twelve years since the construction of the baseball park, an accident of this nature has never occurred, thus, even if a dangerous condition existed, they had no prior knowledge of the defect.

Plaintiff contends that regardless of the dangers assumed by attending this sporting event, she had not yet entered the field and had not yet assumed any risk associated therein. Plaintiff further contends that in order to enter the baseball park she had to purchase the ticket by walking to the ticket booth through a dangerous area known by the Defendant to be susceptible to foul balls down the third base line.

Plaintiff testified she could not see the field of play. At the time she was struck, Plaintiff was not yet inside the baseball park, but was approaching the main entrance preparing to present her student identification card to the ticket booth operator.

The Director of Facilities and Planning Operations for McNeese State University, Mr. Richard Rhoden, testified that he was in charge of the design and construction of the McNeese baseball field during the relevant time period. Mr. Rhoden, a defense witness, admitted in his testimony on direct examination that he knew the entranceway to the baseball field was likely to, be struck by errant foul balls. Mr. Rhoden admitted that the ticket booth was purposely designed with extra wide eaves in order to protect its windows from being hit by foul balls. When Mr. Rhoden was asked by Plaintiff's counsel on cross examination if his design of the ticket booth with extra wide eaves meant he recognized the possibility that foul balls would be hit in the immediate area of the ticket booth, Mr. Rhoden stated, "[w]e ... knew that there's a possibility of foul balls, yes, sir." Thus, Defendant cannot successfully argue it did not have notice of the. defect when it specifically constructed extra wide eaves on the ticket booth to protect against errant foul balls. Defendant chose to protect the building but not the patrons.

Defendant's liability expert, Mr. Gene Moody, testified that a wooden, decorative fence constructed along the third base line in September of 1996, only seven months prior to this accident, completely obscured the view of the playing field from patron's entering at the main entrance. McNeese built the wooden decorative fence at a cost of $19,400.00. Plaintiff's liability expert, Dr. Leonard Lucienko, testified that a protective fence from ten feet to fifteen feet high along the entrance walkway would cost between $4,500.00 to $13,500.00. When asked by Plaintiff's counsel if he agreed that the construction of a protective fence as proposed by Dr. Lucienko would provide protection to patrons entering the park, Mr. Moody admitted, "[y]es . . . if they stayed under the overhang of the fence up close to it; then that would be a protection from fly balls-foul balls." The burden of prevention is slight and the gravity of the harm is great.

There will be foul balls as long as there are baseball games. Ball park owners cannot be held legally responsible for every foul ball in common areas of the ball park. But, there are certain areas of a ball park where protection is required. Obviously, the area behind home plate must be protected from anticipated foul balls. The area where people gather to purchase food and drink or go to the restroom should be protected. Another such area would be the main entrance ticket booth where people must go to purchase a ticket to enter the ball park to see the game. There is an unreasonable risk of harm, and an unreasonably dangerous condition, when patrons have to purchase their ticket at the main entrance ticket booth of the ball park along the third base line where one knows or, should know; and can reasonably anticipate, numerous and errant foul balls. This is an area, like the concession area, restroom area, and the area behind home plate, where there should be a reasonable expectation of protection. In the case at bar, Plaintiff, an innocent McNeese baseball fan outside the baseball park and in line to buy a ticket at the main entrance ticket booth, was unreasonably unprotected and struck by an errant foul ball down the third base line thereby sustaining a serious and permanent eye injury.

We are satisfied that the record contains a sufficient factual basis to support the jury's finding that the McNeese baseball park presented an unreasonably dangerous condition to patrons and that McNeese had notice of the existence of said defect. There was no manifest error and the jury was not clearly wrong.

****

In 1999, a Florida court ruled that Linda Postlethwaite should be compensated for injuries she suffered after being hit between the eyes by a ball thrown by a Philadelphia Phillies player in warmups. Testimony showed that a week before the incident, the net over the bullpen at Pro Player Stadium (then Joe Robbie Stadium) was lowered so it wouldn't block fans' views, and then ordered lowered a second time by Marlin's owner, H. Wayne Huizenga. The jury award was $2.7 million, although a number of defendants had already settled out of court. The fault of the parties was apportioned as follows: Huizenga--36.5%, Robbie Stadium--31.5%, the Marlins--27.5% and the Phillies--4.5%.

Gallagher v. Cleveland Browns (1989) involved an injury to a cameraman. Gallagher was a television station cameraman covering a Cleveland Browns' game in 1988. During the game players from the Browns and Oilers collided with Gallagher in the end zone. Gallagher sustained injuries and sued for negligence. The court held that because of his job he assumed the risk which caused the injury.

Selling drinks at a facility in a glass container would be an invitation for liability. The danger posed from broken glass or the use of the container as a missile would surely be found foreseeable by the courts if an injury occurred as a result of the object. A popular tradition which has been reduced, but not entirely eliminated from all colleges, is allowing fans to storm the field and tear down the goal post after a big victory. As unpopular as preventing this activity may be with the fans, such a chaotic demonstration by a large number of excited fans is fraught with danger. A school's tolerance of this type of conduct can result in serious injuries and lawsuits.

Conduct which might seem innocent enough may result in harm and liability. A jury awarded $25,000 to a woman who was five months pregnant when injured in a collision with the Philadelphia Phillies mascot, Philly Phanatic. In a similar case, the Miami Heat had to pay $10,000 in damages to a woman who was injured and humiliated by Burnie, the team's mascot when she was trying to watch a game.

In *Vann Dyke v. S.K.I. Limited*, 1998 a California appellate court held primary assumption of risk did not bar a skier's negligence claim where he skied into a warning sign posted by a ski resort that was not visible to him. The trial court granted the defendant's summary judgment, ruling the risk of hitting sign post is a primary assumption of risk of skiing. The appellate court rejected the ski resort's argument. The appellate court said that the typical case involved an injury caused by a natural feature of the terrain or a huge fabricated object plainly visible to skiers. The appellate court found that none of the cases cited by the defendant held that recovery for all skiing injuries was barred by assumption of risk. The appellate court also found that the defendants had a duty to use due care not to increase the risk to a participant over and above those inherent in the sport. The appellate court held that sufficient disputed facts existed and that the summary judgment was improper.

Bennett v. Hidden Valley Golf and Ski, Inc. (2003)

In the early morning of February 7, 1998, Bennett went with two older male friends to Hidden Valley for a midnight ski session. At the time Bennett was 16 years old and a high school student. She; had limited experience as a skier, all of which had been at Hidden Valley where she lead skied once before and had snowboarded twice.

While Bennett was skiing down a slope marked for intermediate difficulty, she fell at a spot which the parties have variously referred to as a bump, a ridge, a jump, a ramp, or a mogul. She was thrown about five feet forward and hit the ground limp. There was conflicting evidence as to whether she had hit a tree. Both sides agree that the bump on the slope had not been intentionally created by Hidden Valley, but had formed as skiers and snow boarders cut across the slope and moved the snow. Bennett claims injuries as a result of the accident, including brain damage and a diminished future earning capacity. Hidden Valley denied negligence and raised assumption of risk as a defense

Missouri recognizes three forms of assumption of risk: express, implied primary, and implied secondary. Only implied primary assumption of risk is at issue in this case. Express assumption of risk "occurs when the plaintiff expressly agrees in advance that the defendant owes him no duty" and both parties agree that Bennett made no such agreement. Implied secondary assumption of risk "occurs when the defendant owes a duty of care to the plaintiff but the plaintiff knowingly proceeds to encounter a known risk imposed by the defendant's breach of duty." Hidden Valley did not claim that Bennett knowingly proceeded to encounter the particular risks; it thus did not raise a defense of implied assumption of risk in the secondary sense.

Because the doctrine of implied primary assumption of risk focuses on whether the defendant owed a duty to the plaintiff with respect to the risk in question, it is not strictly an affirmative defense. ("Primary assumption of the risk is not really an affirmative defense; rather, it indicates that the defendant did not even owe the. plaintiff any duty of care."); ("Primary assumption of risk, express or implied, .relates to the initial issue of whether a defendant was negligent at all--that is, whether the defendant had any duty to protect the plaintiff from a risk of harm. It is not, therefore, an affirmative defense."); ("In its primary sense the plaintiffs assumption of a risk is only the counterpoint of the defendant's lack of duty to protect the plaintiff from that risk.").

We conclude that under Missouri law, a voluntary skier assumes the risks inherent in or incidental to skiing, regardless of her subjective knowledge of those risks. This principle can also be put in terms of duty: the proprietor of a ski area has no duty to protect a skier from those risks inherent in or incidental to skiing. Implied primary assumption of risk does not of course relieve a defendant of liability for negligence, because inherent risks "are not those created by a defendant's negligence but rather by the nature of the activity itself." ("[R]isk ... posed by a ski resort's negligence[] clearly is not a risk []inherent in the sport . ... "). By directing the jury to find for Hidden Valley if it determined that the conditions on the ski slope at the time Bennett was injured were inherent risks of skiing, Instruction 7 fairly and adequately submitted the issue to the jury. The district court therefore did not abuse its discretion by giving this charge.

****

EXCULPATORY PROVISIONS

A discussion of tort law would not be complete without some explanation of exculpatory clauses. An exculpatory agreement is language which purports to excuse one party, the provider, from legal liability for an injury to another party, the participant. An exculpatory provision is often referred to as a "waiver of liability" agreement. With an exculpatory clause, the participant agrees in advance that, if he is injured in the activity, he will not pursue a legal claim against the provider. The exculpatory language may be a part of a larger contract or it may be the sole contents of a document.

Exculpatory clauses are often used with connection with school athletics. In order to participate in sports, schools often require parents to sign a form which provides that the parents will not pursue legal action against the school in the event the child is injured.

Are exculpatory clauses valid? The answer is not simple or absolute. Exculpatory clauses should always be used, but the provider should realize that in many cases the agreements will not be enforced by the court. The law varies among the states. A number of courts have upheld the validity of exculpatory clauses when written properly. Three states, Louisiana, Montana and Virginia, generally deem exculpatory clauses unenforceable.

Courts are especially reluctant to enforce an exculpatory clause against a minor, even if signed by the child's parents. Some courts have found the language in exculpatory agreements unclear or that the provision failed to address the particular harm which occurred.

In *Shaner v. State Systems of Higher Education*, 1998, a Pennsylvania trial court held a waiver of liability form signed by a minor and her father did not prevent the minor from recovering damages for injuries sustained during a university softball camp. The fourteen (14) year old girl broke her leg while participating in camp run by the university softball coach and staffed by university employees. The trial court granted a directed verdict in favor of the defendants holding that the release and waiver prevented or barred the plaintiff's claim. The trial court later vacated its order and found that the release could not be enforced against the girl's claim for damages because she was a minor when she signed the release and thus incompetent and her father did not have the authority, simply by virtue of being a parent, to release the girl's claim against the defendant. Treating the release of liability as a type of contract, the court cited the general rule that a minor is not competent to enter into a valid contract and noted that contracts with minors are voidable upon the minor's disaffirmance.

In *Cooper v. Aspen Skiing*, 2002, the Colorado Supreme Court refused to uphold waiver signed by the minor's mother. David Cooper was a 17-year-old involved in competitive skiing. While training for a high-speed alpine race he ran into a tree and was severely injured. The coach, allegedly, had moved the run to an unfamiliar course and failed to install safety netting. The Court found that a minor should be protected not only from his own release, but also from unwise decisions of his parents.

In *Sharon v. City of Newton*, 2002, however, a Massachusetts court upheld a student's waiver that was executed by her father to participate as a cheerleader. The court found that to declare such "permission" slips invalid would "eventually force schools to abandon activities in which students might be injured."

Another approach other than a waiver to minimize, if not negate, liability is to have participants execute an Agreement to Participate. The Agreement to Participate should fully describe the various risks and dangers of the event. An Agreement to Participate, unlike a waiver, does not seek to have the participant release rights or excuse the negligence of the provider. It does, however, prevent the participant from claiming later that he was not aware of the hazards.

EDUCATIONAL MALPRACTICE

The chapter on contracts discussed the lawsuit Kevin Ross filed against Creighton University, the school he attended on an athletic scholarship. Ross was an excellent basketball player, but woefully unprepared for college courses. School officials, however, managed to keep him enrolled and on the team for a period of time. Efforts to keep Ross eligible included offering courses on ceramics and enrollment for remedial courses at an elementary school. Ross' suit alleged a number of theories against the university, including tort, or what the court characterized as an educational malpractice action.

Ross v. Creighton University (1990)

. . . Ross says his tort claim is a hybrid of "negligent infliction of emotional distress" and "educational malpractice." These strands of tort law "intertwine" to form the novel tort of "negligence in recruiting and repeatedly re-enrolling an athlete utterly incapable—without substantial tutoring and other support—of performing the academic work required to make educational progress," exacerbated by the enrollment of plaintiff in a school with children half his age and size. Before considering the merits of this tort, the Court must unravel its separate threads.

Educational malpractice is a tort theory beloved of commentators, but not of courts. While often proposed as a remedy for those who think themselves wronged by educators, educational malpractice has been repeatedly rejected by the American courts.

Whether to create a cause of action for educational malpractice is, of course, a question for the Court, which determines as a matter of law whether a duty runs from defendant to plaintiff. It is a matter of considering sound social policy, guided by looking to " '[t]he likelihood of injury, the magnitude of the burden of guarding against it and the consequences of placing that burden upon defendant.' "

This Court believes the same general concerns would lead the Illinois courts to reject the tort of educational malpractice. Admittedly, the term "educational malpractice" has a seductive ring to it; after all, if doctors, lawyers, accountants and other professionals can be held liable for failing to exercise due care, why can't teachers? The answer is that the nature of education radically differs from other professions. Education is an intensely collaborative process, requiring the interaction of student with teacher. A good student can learn from a poor teacher; a poor student can close his mind to a good teacher. Without effort by a student, he cannot be educated. Good teaching methods may vary with the needs of the individual student. In other professions, by contrast, client cooperation is far less important; given a modicum of cooperation, a competent professional in other fields can control the results obtained. But, in education, the ultimate responsibility for success remains always with the student. Both the process and the result are subjective, and proof or disproof extremely difficult.

It also must be remembered that education is a service rendered on an immensely greater scale than other professional services. If every failed student could seek tort damages against any teacher, administrator and school he feels may have shortchanged him at some point in his education, the courts could be deluged and schools shut down. The Court believes that Illinois courts would avert the flood and the educational loss. This is not to say that the mere worry that litigation will increase justifies a court's refusal to remedy a wrong; it is to say that the real danger of an unrestrained multiplication of lawsuits shows the disutility of the proposed remedy. If poor education (or student laziness) is to be corrected, a common law action for negligence is not a practical means of going about it.

Ross's inability to plead a cause of action under existing law strongly counsels against creating a new cause of action in his favor. Rules serve little purpose if they are not reasonably predictable and if they do not apply across the board, for one cannot conform behavior to the unknowable. Even a new rule declared through the evolutionary process of the common law ought fairly be deduced from existing doctrine-something that cannot be said for ROSS'S claim. The policy reasons considered by the Illinois courts further counsel against recognition of this new duty. Schools would be forced to undertake the delphic science of diagnosing the mental condition of potential recruits. And why should the cause of action be limited to student-athletes? Shouldn't all students who actually pay tuition also have an equal right to recover if they are negligently admitted, and once negligently admitted, have a right to recover if the school negligently counsels and educates them? To allow Ross to recover might redress a wrong (assuming, for sake of argument, that he was in fact exploited), but it would also endanger the admissions prospects of thousands of marginal students, as schools scrambled to factor into their admissions calculations whether a potentially "negligent admission" now could cost unforeseeable tort damages later. The Court should not and will not craft a new tort for Ross.

****

The Right to Play

Colleges, secondary schools and recreational organizations are put in a difficult position when a student with a physical impairment wants to compete in athletics. If the student is allowed to play, the sponsor may be viewed as morally and legally responsible for a related injury. If the school denies the student the right-to-play the school may be accused of morally and legally discriminating against the impaired student.

There have been a number of court battles over a student's right to participate in sports. Some of the factors considered by the courts on the issue are the age of the athlete, the nature of the sport, the medical risk and the position or role of the parents. In *Pendergast v. Sewanhaka Central High School* (1975), the school ruled a student could not play because he had only one testicle. The court reversed the school because 1) the organ could be protected, 2) participation did not increase the risk of other parts of his body or other players and 3) the missing organ was not functionally necessary for sport participation. In *Colombo v. Sewanhaka Central High School* (1976), a school refused to let a deaf student play, and in *Spitaleri v. Nyquist* (1973) a student with only one eye was prohibited from participating. The sport in each case was football. The students challenged the refusal, but the schools' decisions were upheld. In *Kampmeier v. Harris* (1978) a female high school student with vision in one eye successfully challenged the school's denial of her right to participate in a non-contact sport. In *Southeastern Community College v. Davis* (1979), the court ruled that the mere possession of a "handicap" was not sufficient grounds for the denial of a right-to-play sports. In *Poole v. South Plainfield Board of Education* (1980), the court held that a student with one kidney should be permitted to participate in wrestling. The court held that the school's duty was to properly advise the student and his family of the danger, not to impose its view of the proper course of conduct. In its opinion, the court noted that "life has risks." The court stressed that both the student and his parents were well informed of the risk and were willing to sign a waiver (exculpatory agreement) releasing the school from legal liability. In *Grube v. Bethlehem Area School* (1982), which involved a high school football player with one kidney, and in *Wright v. Columbia University* (1981), which concerned a football player with vision in one eye, the courts ruled that the students could not be denied the right to participate because of their impairments.

In *Neeld v. American Hockey League* a hockey player challenged the league's policy banning one-eyed players as a violation of the U.S. Constitution's Equal

Protection Clause. The court found that the action was private and therefore not subject to constitutional scrutiny. The court indicated that a student player in college would have a claim because of the state action. In addition to Equal Protection arguments, several actions have been brought pursuant to the Due Process Clause of the Constitution. Most courts have held, however, that there is no Constitutional liberty or property interest in playing interscholastic or intercollegiate sports.

FEDERAL LEGISLATION

Most of the court challenges taken by athletes who have been denied the right to participate in sports because of a physical condition have focused on federal legislation designed to prohibit discrimination against persons with physical, and to some extent, mental, impairments. Three laws pertaining to this issue are:

1. **The Individuals with Disabilities Education Act (IDEA), 20 U.S.C. sec. 1400 et. seq.** The IDEA requires support services and accommodations for impaired students with special needs.
2. **The Rehabilitation Act of 1973, (RA) 29 U.S.C. sec. 701 et. seq.** The RA prohibits programs which receive federal funds from discriminating against a person with an impairment who is "otherwise qualified." The RA applies to persons who 1) have a physical or mental impairment which substantially limits one or more "major life activities," or 2) have a record of such impairment, or 3) are perceived as having such an impairment.
3. **The American With Disabilities Act (ADA) 42 U.S.C. sec. 1201 et. seq.** The ADA expanded the provisions of the Rehabilitation Act to private employers and "public facilities."

The Rehabilitation Act and the ADA are designed to prohibit discrimination against individuals on the basis of a handicap. A major term in both laws is "major life activities" which is defined as basic functions of life such as caring for one's self, performing manual tasks, walking, seeing, hearing, speaking, breathing, learning and working. The ADA was passed in 1990 in part to expand the coverage of Section 504 of the RA to the private sector, including public entities and places of public accommodation. As a result private schools, universities and professional facilities for professional sporting events are covered even though they may not receive federal funds.

The ADA is very broad and is divided into three major titles. Title I applies to private employment situations. Title II applies to state and local governments and Title III applies to privately operated places of public accommodation.

The Code of Federal Regulations (CFR) includes participation in athletics as activities covered by the ADA. The ADA's public accommodations and public services provisions require all secular public schools, private schools and secular colleges to comply with its mandates. Public schools and state universities fall under the public service provisions and are considered public entities. Private schools and organizations fall under the public accommodations mandates.

The definition of "disability" is the same under the ADA and the RA, and prohibits using criteria to screen out individuals with disabilities "unless it can be shown to be necessary for the provisions of the goods, services, facilities, privileges, advantages, practices and procedures." The law requires reasonable accommodation unless the accommodation would result in a "fundamental modification" of the services or program or cause an "undue burden" on the public entity. The ADA requires individual evaluation to determine if the person is qualified in spite of their disability. The RA law states that a person is not entitled to the accommodation required by the law if it would endanger the health and safety of the individual or others. The ADA law does not contain this specific provision, but the courts would probably apply it if faced with the issue.

PHYSICAL IMPAIRMENTS

Nicholas Knapp signed an athletic scholarship with Northwestern University to play basketball. A few months later Knapp collapsed during a pick-up basketball game as a result of heart failure. Knapp's incident is referred to as "sudden death" by cardiologists. Knapp was revived and had a defibrillator implanted in his abdomen. A defibrillator is designed to shock the heart back into normal rhythm if necessary. Knapp attended Northwestern on the scholarship, but was ruled ineligible to play by a team doctor. In his second year Knapp was again ruled ineligible. Knapp went to court asserting the ineligibility ruling was a violation of the federal Rehabilitation Act. Two doctors testified in favor of Knapp and two in favor of the school. The latter's position was that although they recommend exercise to their patients with Knapp's condition, they would never condone the high intensity exercise Knapp would experience in collegiate basketball. In a preliminary ruling, the trial court ruled in favor of Knapp and ordered that he be allowed to play. The court of appeal reversed and ruled the school did not have to let him play on the school's team.

State ex. rel. Lambert v. West Virginia State Board of Education was a suit filed by a deaf high school student who was on the basketball team. Lambert claimed she was entitled to a sign language interpreter to assist her ability in playing. The school had provided her with an interpreter for her academic courses, but would not do so for vocational classes or extracurricular activities. She had played on the school's team for the previous two years without an interpreter. In ruling in favor of Lambert, the court relied on federal regulations of the IDEA which provide that "each public agency shall take steps to provide nonacademic and extracurricular services to afford children with disabilities an equal opportunity for participation in those services and activities," 34 C.F.R. sec. 300.306(a). The court also cited regulations on the RA which provides that a school "that operates or sponsors interscholastic, club, or intramural athletics shall provide to qualified handicapped students and equal opportunity for participation in these activities," 34 C.F.R. sec. 104.37(C)(1).

There are a number of deaf athletes in many sports who require little or no accommodation. Quite often the opposing players are not even aware of their condition. The athlete's coaches and teammates use visual signals to let the hearing impaired players know when to discontinue play. At Gallaudet University, a school for students with impaired hearing, players compete against hearing athletes regularly in many sports. Some historians credit Gallaudet with the start of the football "huddle" which was apparently necessary to conceal their sign-language play calling.

What about a deaf swimmer who can't hear the starter's gun? Swimmers at indoor meets watch the pool surface to see the reflection of the starter's gun going off. At outdoor meets, allowing hearing impaired swimmers to turn their head to see smoke from the gun is a slight, but sufficient accommodation. NCAA rules prohibits swimmers from grabbing lane lines to pull themselves forward, but allows blind swimmers to graze against the lines with their hands to judge their place in the lane. The blind swimmers can also have a tapper at the end of the pool. The tapper has a cane with a tennis ball on the end of it and taps the athlete on the head or shoulder to tell them when to start their turn. Sight impaired athletes are accommodated in both wrestling and judo by a rule that requires the sighted athletes to maintain body contact with the blind athletes. What about a blind runner? Would it be permissible to allow the runner to run along side or immediately behind an assistant who guides the runner with a cane?

MENTAL IMPAIRMENTS AND AGE LIMITS

The challenges on eligibility are not limited to physical impairments. A major issue at the high school and collegiate level is the possible conflict between the application of federal laws and academic requirements imposed by schools or organizations such as the NCAA.

Chad Ganden was a state champion high school swimmer. Ganden had a learning disability and took special classes for learning-disabled students. Ganden and his parents engaged in a long battle with the NCAA regarding his eligibility for collegiate sports. The NCAA initially ruled that Ganden's failure to have taken the necessary core courses precluded him from accepting school paid recruiting trips to Arizona St. and Michigan St. The U.S. Justice Department began an investigation after being contacted by the Gandens to determine if the NCAA rules violate the RA or the ADA law. As a result of pressure from the Justice Department, the NCAA agreed to propose a modification of its rules for students who have learning disabilities. Ganden was given a scholarship by Michigan State. The NCAA initially ruled that Ganden was not eligible because he lacked the NCAA 13-core course requirement. An appeal with the NCAA was taken and Ganden was granted a partial waiver and classified as a "partial qualifier" due to his grades and ACT score. That is, Ganden could practice, but not compete with the team during his first year. Ganden filed suit, but the trial court upheld the NCAA's decision.

Two high school students who ran track for three years were denied the right to compete in their senior year because they did not meet the age requirements set forth by the state athletic high school association. The students were diagnosed with learning disabilities at an early age and entered school two grades behind their age group. The students filed suit, *Sandison v. Michigan High School Athletic Association* (1995), asserting the denial was a violation of the RA and ADA laws. The trial court ruled in favor of the students. On appeal, however, the appellate court reversed and upheld the denial. The appellate court found that, to be successful under the Rehabilitation law, a plaintiff must prove:

1. The plaintiff is "handicapped" under the law.
2. The plaintiff is "otherwise qualified."
3. The plaintiff is being excluded solely due to the handicap.
4. The program receives federal funds.

The appellate court found the plaintiffs proved the requirements noted in 1 and 4, but failed in proving elements 2 and 3. The court found that the students were permitted to participate for 3 years in the program despite their disability. The court ruled it was not their disability that rendered them ineligible, but the passage of time. In its analysis the court reasoned that the students, absent the disability, would still be ineligible.

The following two cases present similar issues with different results from the courts in Michigan and Indiana.

McPherson v. Michigan High School Athletic Association, Inc., (1997)

The Michigan High School Athletic Association appeals the district court's entry of a preliminary injunction forbidding the MHSAA from enforcing its eight-semester eligibility rule against the plaintiff, Dion R. McPherson, and further forbidding the MHSAA from invoking any penalty against the school district for which McPherson played basketball. The district court entered the injunction after concluding that enforcement of the rule in this case violated the Americans with Disabilities Act, 42 U.S.C. §§ 12101-12213, and Section 504 of the Rehabilitation Act of 1973, 29 U.S.C. § 794. We conclude that, although McPherson has now graduated from high school, the case is not moot. We also conclude that the district court abused its discretion in entering the preliminary injunction, and therefore reverse.

I.

Dion McPherson attended Huron High School in the Ann Arbor Public School District. Huron, like virtually all private and public secondary schools in Michigan, is a member of the Michigan High School Athletic Association. The principal function of the MHSAA is to promulgate regulations for its member schools that will promote fair athletic competition; the regulations are formulated by consensus of the member schools. As a member of the MHSAA, the Ann Arbor school district has adopted the regulations and has agreed to abide by them.

The MHSAA Handbook makes any student who has completed eight semesters of high school ineligible for interscholastic sports competition:

A student shall not compete in any branch of athletics who has been enrolled in grades nine to twelve, inclusive, for more than eight semesters.

Regulation I, § 4. The Constitution of the MHSAA provides, however, that the so-called eight-semester rule may be waived:

Except for the eligibility rule in regard to age, the Executive Committee shall have the authority to set aside the effect of any regulation governing eligibility of students or the competition between schools *when in its opinion the rule fails to accomplish the purpose for which it is intended, or when the rule works an undue hardship upon the student or school.*

There are a number of purposes for the eight-semester rule. As a member of the MHSAA's Executive Committee testified below, "[t]he eight-semester rule creates a fair sense of competition" by limiting the level of athletic experience and skill of the players in order to create a more even playing field for the competitors. The member further testified that the absence of such a rule would lead, as it has in other states, to red-shirting of players, in which a player is deliberately held back for a year in order to allow the student to gain greater physical and athletic maturity, leading in turn, presumably, to greater athletic ability. The assistant director of the MHSAA testified that the rule was "essential to preserving the philosophy that students attend school primarily for the classroom education and only secondarily to participate in interscholastic athletics," thus encouraging student-athletes to graduate in four years. He, too, opined that red-shirting abuses would become common in the absence of the eight-semester rule. The Executive Committee member testified that the rule was "essential" to the functioning of the MHSAA, and that it was "basic . . . to the administration of the athletics in keeping the playing field level." Acknowledging, however, that waivers had been granted in the past, the member testified that the circumstances were narrow; they had been limited to cases in which the waiver was applied for, *prior* to the expiration of the eight semesters, and to cases in which students had been physically unable to attend school for a medical reason, or had been limited to taking a small number of courses, which limitations would result in attending high school more than eight semesters.

McPherson was not a high academic achiever during high school. He originally entered the eleventh grade in 1992, but had to repeat that grade during the 1993-94 school year. Thus, the 1993-94 school year represented McPherson's seventh and eighth semesters in high school. It was while repeating the eleventh grade that McPherson participated in varsity basketball for the first time. Before that time, he was ineligible to participate in sports because he failed to meet a grade point average requirement of the Ann Arbor school district—a requirement separate and apart from requirements of the MHSAA. His grades improved, however, while repeating the eleventh grade, making him eligible to play under Ann Arbor standards.

In September 1994, McPherson was diagnosed as having Attention Deficit Hyperactivity Disorder, and later was diagnosed as also having a seizure disorder. Both diagnoses were made at the beginning of his ninth semester in high school and after he had exhausted his athletic eligibility under the eight-semester rule. As a result, McPherson was classified under state law as having a "specific learning disability." McPherson had never been referred for special education testing prior to the 1994-95 school year.

McPherson wanted to participate in basketball during the 1994-95 school year, but the eight-semester rule barred his participation. He filed a request with the MHSAA for a waiver. The MHSAA initially considered the waiver request in November 1994. The Executive Committee noted that it "was provided no information regarding this student's physical stature or his athletic experience or ability in comparison to teammates or opponents." It further noted additional reasons for its reluctance to grant the waiver:

It is plain that the controversy addressed by the part of the preliminary injunction ordering that McPherson be allowed to compete during the 1995 basketball season is moot. As we observed in an earlier case presenting strikingly similar issues, the season is over, and there are no more games to be played.

We nonetheless conclude that the case as a whole is not moot. McPherson's complaint specifically requested that the district court "restrain[] the MHSAA from taking any action which would cause the Defendant school district to be penalized for Plaintiff's participation in interscholastic athletic competition, including . . . requiring that any games in which Plaintiff competes be forfeited." Moreover, the district court's injunction provided that the MHSAA was prohibited from taking "any action which would cause the school district to be penalized for Plaintiff's participation in interscholastic athletic competition." As discussed above, if a student is ineligible under MHSAA rules but is nonetheless allowed to play because of a court-ordered injunction, the MHSAA shall "require that team victories [be] forfeited to opponents," and may vacate or strike "that individual or team records and performances achieved during participation by such ineligibles," if the "injunction is subsequently . . . reversed or finally determined by the courts that injunctive relief is not or was not justified."

Requiring a waiver of the eight-semester rule, under the circumstances present here, would work a fundamental alteration in Michigan high school sports programs. Moreover, requiring a waiver under these circumstances would impose an immense financial and administrative burden on the MHSAA, by forcing it to make "near-impossible determinations" about a particular student's physical and athletic maturity. One could argue, of course, that the fact that the MHSAA allows for waivers under some circumstances demonstrates its judgment that these determinations are not unduly burdensome. While that point has a superficial appeal, we find an important distinction between the class of waiver cases contemplated by the MHSAA and the type of relief the plaintiff asks us to impose. The plaintiff would have us require waivers for all learning-disabled students who remain in school more than eight semesters. That, of course, would have the potential of opening floodgates for waivers, while until now, there have been only a handful of cases deemed appropriate for waivers. Assessing one or two students pales in comparison to the task of assessing a large number of students; an increase in number will both increase the cost of making the assessments, as well as increase the importance of doing so correctly. Having one student who is unfairly advantaged may be problematic, but having increasing numbers of such students obviously runs the risk of irrevocably altering the nature of high-school sports.

In sum, we conclude that the plaintiff has not made out a successful claim under the ADA. As already discussed, the elements of a Rehabilitation Act claim are largely similar to those of an ADA claim, with the additional requirement that the defendant be shown to receive federal financial assistance.

****

Washington, et al. v Indiana HS Athletic Assoc., Inc. (1999)

Mr. Washington is a learning disabled student at Central Catholic High School ("Central Catholic") in Lafayette, Indiana. Throughout elementary school, he had been allowed to advance to the next grade despite academic insufficiency. He was held back, however, in the eighth grade. During the first semester of the 1994-95 academic year, while he was repeating the eighth grade, he continued to receive failing grades. School officials then decided that he might do better if he stayed with his class, and they therefore advanced him to the ninth grade at Lafayette Jefferson High School at the beginning of the second semester during the 1994-95 academic year. In this new environment, Mr. Washington continued to fail during that semester and throughout the following academic year. Early in the 1996-97 academic year, a school counselor suggested that Mr. Washington drop out of high school. Mr. Washington took that advice.

In the summer of 1997, Mr. Washington participated in a three-on-three basketball tournament sponsored by Central Catholic. At the tournament, Mr. Washington met the coach of the Central Catholic basketball team, Chad Dunwoody. Mr. Dunwoody was also a teacher at the school. After conversations with Dunwoody, Mr. Washington decided to attend Central Catholic. Mr. Washington entered school and began playing basketball. Mr. Dunwoody, who also became Mr. Washington's academic mentor at Central Catholic, suggested that Mr. Washington be tested for learning disabilities. Although Mr. Washington had previously been tested and found not to be learning disabled, a January 1998 test indicated that he was in fact learning disabled.

The IHSAA has a rule that limits a student's athletic eligibility to the first eight semesters following the student's commencement of the ninth grade ("the eight semester rule"). The purposes of that rule, according to the IHSAA, include discouraging redshirting, promoting competitive equality, protecting students' safety, creating opportunities for younger students and promoting the idea that academics are more important than athletics. Under the rule in question, because Mr. Washington entered the ninth grade during the second semester of the 1994-95 academic year, he would no longer be eligible to play basketball in the second semester of the 1998-99 year (nine semesters after he began the ninth grade).

Central Catholic applied for a waiver of the eight semester rule for Mr. Washington. It requested that the IHSAA not count the semesters that he was not enrolled in any high school for purposes of eligibility under the eight semester rule. It requested a waiver under IHSAA Rule C- 12-3, which allows an exemption "if a student is injured which necessitates the student's complete withdrawal from the school or prohibits enrollment in the school for that semester, and the student does not receive any academic credit for that semester." Central Catholic also requested a waiver under IHSAA Rule 17-8, referred to by the parties as "the hardship rule." That rule allows the IHSAA not to enforce a rule if strict enforcement in the particular case would not serve to accomplish the purpose of the rule, the spirit of the rule would not be violated, and there is a showing of undue hardship in the particular case. Even though it had granted waivers for physical injuries in the past, the IHSAA denied Mr. Washington's application. Mr. Washington appealed the denial to the IHSAA Executive Committee, which denied the appeal.

Mr. Washington will be ineligible to play high school basketball during the 1999-2000 school year because his participation will violate another eligibility rule that limits the maximum age at which a student-athlete may compete ("the age limit rule"). No challenge is made to that rule in this lawsuit. Rather, the focus is exclusively on the eight semester rule; it is challenged on the ground that failure to grant a waiver of the eight semester rule in this case violates Title II of the Americans with Disabilities Act, 42 U.S.C. sec. 12132.

The district court granted a preliminary injunction against the enforcement of the Rule against Mr. Washington.

This court has no difficulty determining that this plaintiff will suffer irreparable harm for which he has no adequate remedy at law if this injunction is denied. The loss of the remainder of the basketball season, and with that, most likely the loss of any future playing opportunities and the loss of the desire to continue academically, are harms which cannot be repaired, for which Eric cannot be adequately compensated.

There must be a causal connection between the disability and Mr. Washington's ineligibility. The IHSAA submits that no such causality exists and that it is the mere passage of time, and not the disability, that caused Mr. Washington's ineligibility in this case. The IHSAA relies upon McPherson and Sandison v. Michigan High School Athletic Ass'n, 64 F.3d 1026, 1029 (6th Cir. 1995), to support its argument.

At the outset, it must be noted that the eight semester rule that the Sixth Circuit refused to waive in McPherson and the eight semester rule in this case are distinct in a very material respect. The Michigan rule restricts eligibility to eight semesters of enrollment, while the Indiana rule creates ineligibility automatically eight semesters from the first day of enrollment, even if the student was not enrolled for the full eight semesters. Under the Indiana rule, the eligibility "clock" therefore continues to "tick" when a student drops out of school; the clock does not tick for the Michigan student who drops out of school. Notably, Mr. Washington requested only that the semesters that he was absent from school because of his disability not count toward his eight semesters of eligibility; he did not ask that the IHSAA be prohibited from allowing the eligibility clock to run while he was enrolled. Indeed, he is merely asking that the IHSAA apply a rule identical to the rule the MHSAA applies to its students.

We believe that the district court was on solid ground in determining that waiver of the eight semester rule in Mr. Washington's case would not create a fundamental alteration of the eight semester rule. Such a minimal request for a rule modification is much more reasonable and less fundamental than the waiver requested in McPherson. The IHSAA's argument to the contrary is particularly unpersuasive because it has granted waivers of the eight semester rule in the past, thereby establishing that waivers do not always work fundamental alterations of the rule. Moreover, none of the dangers that motivated adoption of the rule is present in this case. The primary goals of the rule are to control redshirting, to prevent the preeminence of athletics over academics, and to keep larger, more advanced players from dominating competition. Mr. Washington was clearly not redshirted--nobody was interested in his basketball abilities until he had already left school. Moreover, waiver of the rule in Mr. Washington's case does not indicate that athletics is valued over education. Indeed, waiver of the rule in Mr. Washington's case has promoted his education. Mr. Washington has re- entered school because of basketball, has improved his grades in part due to the influence of basketball and his coach, and is even considering going to college. Application of the eight semester rule to Mr. Washington does not appear to add anything to the protections provided by the IHSAA's age limit rule, which generally limits the size, strength and athletic maturity of student-athletes.

The district court found that Mr. Washington would be irreparably harmed if he did not obtain an injunction, because if he were not allowed to play, he would lose out on the chance to obtain a college scholarship and he would have a diminished academic motivation. The IHSAA's first argument is that the loss of a potential college scholarship is too speculative to constitute irreparable harm. However, Purdue University basketball coach Gene Keady testified at the preliminary injunction hearing that Mr. Washington would be harmed by an inability to play basketball in his high school games because basketball scouts would not have an opportunity to view him playing. Dunwoody, Mr. Washington's coach and academic mentor, testified to the same effect. The district court's finding is therefore not clear error.

The IHSAA also argues that the district court erred in determining that irreparable harm would stem from Mr. Washington's loss of academic motivation if he were declared ineligible. The IHSAA notes that Mr. Washington would not be prohibited from continuing to attend Central Catholic, or any other school, if he had been ineligible to play basketball. The district court did not commit clear error in finding that Mr. Washington would suffer irreparable harm from a lost academic desire. Zello, the school psychologist, testified that basketball is an important part of Mr. Washington's academic success at Central Catholic. Before he started at Central Catholic, Mr. Washington had experienced a career of academic failure due to his learning disability. His lack of self confidence prevented him from performing well academically. By giving him something at which he could excel, basketball improved his confidence in other areas of life, including education. When asked what the consequence would be if Mr. Washington were not allowed to play basketball, Zello stated:

> "I think it would be difficult. This is a child who has been thoroughly frustrated academically, socially, family problem from that, who now gets a taste of success, and then we're going to pull that away from him? ... I think it would be devastating."

For the foregoing reasons, we affirm the judgment of the district court.

****

Like most state high school athletic associations, the Louisiana High School Athletic Association (LHSAA) permits students to participate in sports for eight (8) consecutive semesters while in high school. Students in Louisiana become ineligible if they reach their nineteenth birthday before September 1, of that school year. In 1997 the LHSAA adopted a controversial ban on "hold backs" in junior high school. The rule was prompted by complaints that some junior high schools were holding back students, not for academic reasons, but solely to enhance the students' athletic career. One school had reportedly "red shirted" nineteen (19) junior high school students in one year. The rule also provides for sanctions against coaches and principals who violate the ban.

Bingham v. Oregon School Activities Association was a successful challenge to Oregon's eight-semester rule. Bingham met the age requirements for athletic competition in his senior year, but had repeated the tenth grade and was therefore ineligible pursuant to the eight-semester rule. Bingham claimed he had to repeat the tenth grade because he suffered from an attention deficit disorder. The Association denied Bingham's request for an accommodation in the form of a waiver of the eight-semester rule. The court ruled in favor of Bingham. It was probably significant that the court found that Bingham was not a highly skilled player that would give his team a competitive advantage.

Home-schooling appears to be gaining favor among parents and their children. The home-schooled student does not have the athletic opportunities available at traditional schools. In *Jones v. West Virginia* (2005) the parents chose to home-school their children, but wanted their children to participate in the public school's athletic activities. The school district had a rule that limited participation in interscholastic athletic programs in the public school to students enrolled full-time, and thereby excluded home-schooled children from participation in interscholastic athletics. The parents challenged the rule in court.

The court found that the rule did not violate equal protection under the state constitution. The court concluded that the parents made a voluntary choice not to have their children participate in the public school system, and therefore, to forego the benefits incidental to a public education. Furthermore, the court found that the rule was rationally related to the state's interest in promoting academics over athletics, in that enrolled students were required to maintain a minimum grade point average in order to participate in school athletic programs, while home-schooled children might have been taught a completely different curriculum and been graded differently. The rule was also rationally related to the state's concern that public schools would suffer financially from participation of home-schooled children in interscholastic *sports,* because the school board received funding for athletic programs based in part on the average daily attendance and enrollment numbers.

The following case is a United States Supreme Court decision that could have a significant impact on high school athletic associations.

Brentwood Academy v. Tennessee Secondary School Athletic Association
Supreme Court of the United States, 2001

The issue is whether a statewide association incorporated to regulate interscholastic athletic competition among public and private secondary schools may be regarded as engaging in state action when it enforces a rule against a member school. The association in question here includes most public schools located within the State, acts through their representatives, draws its officers from them, is largely funded by their dues and income received in their stead, and has historically been seen to regulate in lieu of the State Board of Education's exercise of its own authority. We hold that the association's regulatory activity may and should be treated as state action owing to the pervasive entwinement of state school officials in the structure of the association, there being no offsetting reason to see the association's acts in any other way.

Respondent Tennessee Secondary School Athletic Association (Association) is a not-for-profit membership corporation organized to regulate interscholastic sport among the public and private high schools in Tennessee that belong to it. No school is forced to join, but without any other authority actually regulating interscholastic athletics, it enjoys the memberships of almost all the State's public high schools (some 290 of them or 84% of the Association's voting membership), far outnumbering the 55 private schools that belong. A member school's team may play or scrimmage only against the team of another member, absent a dispensation.

The Association's rulemaking arm is its legislative council, while its board of control tends to administration. The voting membership of each of these nine-person committees is limited under the Association's bylaws to high school principals, assistant principals, and superintendents elected by the member schools, and the public school administrators who so serve typically attend meetings during regular school hours. Although the Association's staff members are not paid by the State, they are eligible to join the State's public retirement system for its employees. Member schools pay dues to the Association, though the bulk of its revenue is gate receipts at member teams' football and basketball tournaments, many of them held in public arenas rented by the Association.

The constitution, bylaws, and rules of the Association set standards of school membership and the eligibility of students to play in interscholastic games. Each school, for example, is regulated in awarding financial aid, most coaches must have a Tennessee state teaching license, and players must meet minimum academic standards and hew to limits on student employment. Under the bylaws, "in all matters pertaining to the athletic relations of his school," the principal is responsible to the Association, which has the power "to suspend, to fine, or otherwise penalize any member school for the violation of any of the rules of the Association or for other just cause."

The action before us responds to a 1997 regulatory enforcement proceeding brought against petitioner, Brentwood Academy, a private parochial high school member of the Association. The Association's board of control found that Brentwood violated a rule prohibiting "undue influence" in recruiting athletes, when it wrote to incoming students and their parents about spring football practice. The Association accordingly placed Brentwood's athletic program on probation for four years, declared its football and boys' basketball teams ineligible to compete in playoffs for two years, and imposed a $3,000 fine. When these penalties were imposed, all the voting members of the board of control and legislative council were public school administrators.

Brentwood sued the Association and its executive director in federal court . . . claiming that enforcement of the Rule was state action and a violation of the First and Fourteenth Amendments. The District Court entered summary judgment for Brentwood and enjoined the Association from enforcing the Rule.

The United States Court of Appeals for the Sixth Circuit reversed. It recognized that there is no single test to identify state actions and state actors but applied three criteria . . . and found no state action under any of them. It said the District Court was mistaken in seeing a symbiotic relationship between the State and the Association, it emphasized that the Association was neither engaging in a traditional and exclusive public function nor responding to state compulsion

We granted certiorari, to resolve the conflict and now reverse.

Thus, we say that state action may be found if, though only if, there is such a "close nexus between the State and the challenged action" that seemingly private behavior "may be fairly treated as that of the State itself."

We have, for example, held that a challenged activity may be state action when it results from the State's exercise of "coercive power," when the State provides "significant encouragement, either overt or covert," or when a private actor operates as a "willful participant in joint activity with the State or its agents." We have treated a nominally private entity as a state actor when it is controlled by an "agency of the State," when it has been delegated a public function by the State, when it is "entwined with governmental policies" or when government is "entwined in its management or control."

The "necessarily fact-bound inquiry," leads to the conclusion of state action here. The nominally private character of the Association is overborne by the pervasive entwinement of public institutions and public officials in its composition and workings, and there is no substantial reason to claim unfairness in applying constitutional standards to it.

The Association is not an organization of natural persons acting on their own, but of schools, and of public schools to the extent of 84% of the total. Under the Association's bylaws, each member school is represented by its principal or a faculty member, who has a vote in selecting members of the governing legislative council and board of control from eligible principals, assistant principals and superintendents.

Although the findings and prior opinions in this case include no express conclusion of law that public school officials act within the scope of their duties when they represent their institutions, no other view would be rational, the official nature of their involvement being shown in any number of ways. Interscholastic athletics obviously play an integral part in the public education of Tennessee, where nearly every public high school spends money on competitions among schools. Since a pickup system of interscholastic games would not do, these public teams need some mechanism to produce rules and regulate competition. The mechanism is an organization overwhelmingly composed of public school officials who select representatives (all of them public officials at the time in question here), who in turn adopt and enforce the rules that make the system work. Thus, by giving these jobs to the Association, the 290 public schools of Tennessee belonging to it can sensibly be seen as exercising their own authority to meet their own responsibilities. Unsurprisingly, then, the record indicates that half the council or board meetings documented here were held during official school hours, and that public schools have largely provided for the Association's financial support. A small portion of the Association's revenue comes from membership dues paid by the schools, and the principal part from gate receipts at tournaments among the member schools. Unlike mere public buyers of contract services, whose payments for services rendered do not convert the service providers into public actors, the schools here obtain membership in the service organization and give up sources of their own income to their collective association. The Association thus exercises the authority of the predominantly public schools to charge for admission to their games; the Association does not receive this money from the schools, but enjoys the schools' moneymaking capacity as its own.

In sum, to the extent of 84% of its membership, the Association is an organization of public schools represented by their officials acting in their official capacity to provide an integral element of secondary public schooling. There would be no recognizable Association, legal or tangible, without the public school officials, who do not merely control but overwhelmingly perform all but the purely ministerial acts by which the Association exists and functions in practical terms. Only the 16% minority of private school memberships prevents this entwinement of the Association and the public school system from being total and their identities totally indistinguishable.

To complement the entwinement of public school officials with the Association from the bottom up, the State of Tennessee has provided for entwinement from top down. State Board members are assigned ex officio to serve as members of the board of control and legislative council, and the Association's ministerial employees are treated as state employees to the extent of being eligible for membership in the state retirement system.

The entwinement down from the State Board is therefore unmistakable, just as the entwinement up from the member public schools is overwhelming. Entwinement will support a conclusion that an ostensibly private organization ought to be charged with a public character and judged by constitutional standards; entwinement to the degree shown here requires it.

The judgment of the Court of Appeals for the Sixth Circuit is reversed, and the case is remanded for further proceedings consistent with this opinion.

It is so ordered.

****

The issues in *Brentwood* are similar to those which were raised in the *Tarkanian* decision involving the NCAA. In *Tarkanian* the Supreme Court found that the NCAA was not a state actor. In *Brentwood* the court noted that the TSSAA was confined to one state and that its relationship with Tennessee was more direct than the NCAA's involvement with colleges. The *Brentwood* decision will require many state athletic associations to reconsider their organization and procedures. In the *Brentwood* case, the anti-recruiting rule was vague and the punishment quite harsh under the due process standard. The *Brentwood* decision will require state athletic high school associations to provide due process rights when seeking to punish its members.

In *Indiana High school Athletic Association v. Durham* the plaintiff was a high school student-athlete participating in track and cross-country who transferred from a private school to a public school in his district because of his parents' divorce. After the divorce his mother could no longer afford to send him to a private school. Plaintiff submitted an IHSAA Transfer Form so he could continue participating in sports at the new school. IHSAA granted only limited eligibility which prevented the student from competing at the varsity level and denied him a hardship exception. The plaintiff filed suit asking that the IHSAA's decision be overturned and a permanent injunction be issued. The trial court granted the injunction and the IHSAA appealed. The appellate court found the decision of the lower court was correct and found that the IHSAA's decision was arbitrary and capricious. The appellate court found that the IHSAA ignored its own rules and injected a condition of undue hardship not found in the rules. The appellate court said the IHSAA should not be in the business of second guessing personal financial decisions by a family.

Johansen v. Louisiana High School
Athletic Association (2005)

The plaintiffs, Neal Johansen and Linda Johansen, appeal the judgment of the 19th Judicial District Court dismissing their petition for injunctive relief and damages on the peremptory exception of no cause of action of the defendants, the Louisiana High School Athletic Association, Inc. Tommy Henry, Mac Chauvin, and B.J. Guzzardo. We dismiss the appeal in part as moot, and otherwise affirm in part, reverse in part, and remand the case to the trial court, for the reasons stated below.

Plaintiffs are the parents, of Krystin Johansen, a minor enrolled as a student in Maurepas High School in Livingston Parish during the 2001-2002 school year. Krystin participated in interscholastic basketball at that school. Plaintiffs then resided in the community of Maurepas on a 10½ acre tract on which their residence, a barn, and dog kennels were situated. In June 2002, plaintiffs purportedly decided to change their residence to St. John the Baptist Parish in order to serve special educational needs of their minor son. They rented an apartment in LaPlace that month, but did not establish it as their residence until September 2002. Plaintiffs then placed a sign on their Maurepas property, advertising it for sale, and also placed a newspaper advertisement. They left some personal items which could not be moved to their LaPlace apartment due to their condition or size. They also changed their mailing address and discontinued their telephone service in Maurepas, although Mrs. Johansen continued to use the property in operating a dog breeding kennel. Krystin and her brother were enrolled as students at Reserve Christian School, a private school.

Reserve Christian School is a member of the Louisiana High School Athletic Association, Inc. (the LHSAA). The LHSAA is a nonprofit corporation first organized as an association in 1920. There are presently over member schools, and the LHSAA certifies the eligibility of approximately 70,000 student athletes annually. Although not a state agency the state of Louisiana has left to the LHSAA the enforcement of the administration of interscholastic athletic competition between its member schools.

Upon enrolling their children at Reserve Christian School, plaintiffs met with the principal to specifically discuss the issue of Krystin's eligibility to play girls' varsity basketball under the LHSAA's transfer rule and its related rule on bona fide changes of residence. Upon reviewing the facts provided by plaintiffs relating to their purported change of residence, the principal advised plaintiffs that he felt plaintiffs were in compliance with those rules.

Thereafter, the LHSAA received a complaint charging Reserve Christian School, as an LHSAA member, with violation of the transfer and bona fide change of residence rules regarding Krystin's eligibility. The LHSAA retained a private investigator to investigate plaintiffs' residence status and to conduct surveillance of the Maurepas property. LHSAA assistant commissioners Mac Chauvin and B.J. Guzzardo undertook further investigation, interviewing the principal and requesting that plaintiffs meet them at the Maurepas property. According to plaintiffs' petition, the assistant commissioners demanded access to the house in order to search it, with the threat to immediately declare Krystin ineligible to participate in interscholastic athletics if permission was denied. Plaintiffs then consented to their entry into the house, and the assistant commissioners conducted an inspection of the premises.

On January 22, 2003, the LHSAA issued an LHSAA Rule Infraction Notification and the ruling of its commissioner, Tommy Henry, that Reserve Christian School violated the LHSAA transfer and bona fide change of residence rules by permitting Krystin to play girls' varsity basketball. In addition to being placed on administrative probation, the school was fined and assessed the cost of the private investigator, and forfeited the fifteen games in which Krystin played between October 25, 2002, and December 28, 2002, to the opposing schools.

Reserve Christian School appealed Commissioner Henry's ruling to the LHSAA executive committee, which conducted a hearing on January 29, 2003. The school and plaintiffs were permitted to present evidence in support of their contention that there was a bona fide change of residence and that the LHSAA's rules were not violated. The executive committee ultimately upheld Commissioner Henry's ruling.

On February 5, 2003, plaintiffs instituted the present civil action by filing a petition seeking injunctive relief and damages based upon the LHSAA's action.

The transfer rule provides that a student athlete must be enrolled in a school in the LHSAA zone where her parents reside in order to be eligible to play during the first year of that student's attendance at that school. If the student transfers to a school outside the zone of parents' residence, then the student is ineligible to play during the first year of attendance at that school. The bona fide change of residence rule, Rule 1.11.11, requires that any change of residence from one zone to another by parents be an actual, bona fide change of permanent residence, in order to avoid the evils of recruiting by schools to obtain unfair advantage over competing schools. Rule 1.11.11. 1.1 provides that two legal residences are not permitted under the rule. Rule 1.11.11.8 also provides that a change of residence made for the purpose of creating eligibility to play is not considered a bona fide change of residence, and the student athlete shall be ineligible to compete at all LHSAA schools for a year. Rule 1.11.11.5 sets out the nonexclusive criteria governing the determination of a bona . fide change of permanent residence, including, among other circumstances, (1) the abandonment as a residence and sale or other disposal of the original residence; (2) the removal of all personal belongings and furniture appropriate to the circumstances; and (3) change of mailing address and telephone service.

Plaintiffs contend that their petition adequately sets forth a cause of action for defendants' violation of the rights of procedural and substantive due process under the Fourteenth Amendment of the United States Constitution and La. Const. art. I, § 2. To prevail on their due process claim, plaintiffs must show the existence of some property or liberty interest which has been adversely affected by state action.

To have a property interest protected by due process, a person must have more than an abstract need or desire for it. He must have a legitimate claim of entitlement to it rather than a unilateral expectation of it. Id. The due process clause of the Fourteenth Amendment does not insulate a citizen from every injury at the hands of the state. Id. In *Walsh* v. *Louisiana High School Athletic Association*, the plaintiff parents challenged the LHSAA's transfer rule. In rejecting the challenge as "outside the protection of due process," the court squarely held that "[a] student's interest in participating in a single year of interscholastic athletics amounts to a mere expectation rather than a constitutionally protected claim of entitlement." Id. at 159.

Plaintiffs alleged in their petition that Krystin "had an *opportunity* for an athletic scholarship to college," and that defendants' actions, if upheld, would "preclude her *ability to be considered* for such scholarship because she will not be playing the sport," being then a junior. (Emphasis supplied.) The possibility of obtaining a college athletic scholarship based upon participation in high school athletics simply does not constitute such a property interest or right, but rather a "speculative and uncertain" expectation or opportunity.

****

PROFESSIONAL SPORTS

Interestingly, there are age restraint issues which have arisen in professional sports. In 1999 the parents of 14-year-old tennis star, Monique Viele, threatened to sue the Women's Tennis Association (WTA). The issue was the WTA's restricting tournament entries of young players. The rules allow 14 year olds to play in only four events sanctioned by the International Tennis Federation and barred the youngsters from playing in any of the Grand Slam tournaments and regular stops. The WTA's position was that it needed to protect the younger players from emotional problems that were detrimental to some young players before the restrictions were in place. The parents claimed that the rules were an unlawful restraint of trade.

The RA and IDEA address the right to participate in programs that receive federal funds and applies to almost all schools. Professional sports do not receive federal funds and are, therefore, exempt from these statutes. The ADA, however, is broader and prohibits employment discrimination in the private sector by employers with 15 or more employees. The law also prohibits discrimination in places of public accommodation which includes stadiums and arenas used for professional sporting events. Before 1997 there were no reported ADA claims by professional athletes. This was the first ADA action filed by a professional athlete and it generated enormous media attention and sparked a national debate. It was reported that an out-of-court compromise was reached in the matter.

THE CASEY MARTIN SAGA

The Casey Martin case is discussed in another chapter. Martin, who played collegiate golf at Stanford with Tiger Woods, has a rare circulatory disorder called Klippel-Trenaunay-Weber Syndrome. He is missing an important vein that runs along the bone of the lower leg reducing the blood flow to his leg. As a result, blood is forced to travel to his heart by way of a series of smaller veins near the surface of the leg. Under stress, such as walking for extended periods of time, the overworked veins bleed into Martin's knee and cause his shrunken leg to swell. He is in constant risk of fracturing his weakened leg which could result in amputation. Carts are not allowed in collegiate golf, but Martin was allowed to use a cart while at Stanford pursuant to accommodation rules by the NCAA and the PAC-10 conference.

The PGA Tour, Inc., is a non-profit organization that consists of professional golfers. It serves as the sponsor of golf events in the PGA tour, the Seniors PGA and what was for many years the Nike Tour. There are a number of ways to qualify in each tour, but the most common is to compete in the PGA three-stage qualifying school (Q school) tournament. The first two stages of Q school and the PGA Senior Tour allow the use of carts. The third stage of Q school and the PGA Tour prohibit the use of carts.

In 1997 Martin entered Q school and filed a petition seeking a court order to allow him the use of a cart for the remainder of the tournament. His suit alleged that the PGA's refusal to let him use a cart would be a violation of the ADA because: a) the PGA Tour was a public accommodation, b) the PGA Tour offered, "examinations of courses related to applications, licensing certificates or credentials for professional or trade purposes" as provided in the law and, c) the PGA Tour was his employer.

The court held that the PGA Tour was a commercial enterprise, not a private club, and that the Tour was a place of public accommodation and subject to the ADA. The ADA does not require accommodation if the result would fundamentally alter the program. The court essentially found that nothing in the rules of golf require or define walking as part of the game and ruled in favor of Martin.

The PGA lost the case and suffered a public relations nightmare. Public support was overwhelming in favor of Martin. Ironically, the PGA's slogan for the Tour before Martin filed his claim was "anything's possible." The Tour dropped the slogan after Martin's suit. Even the PGA conceded Martin's impairment was serious and his determination was admirable.

Not everyone agreed with the court's decision in the Martin case. The ruling prompted immediate and unequivocal criticism from widely respected people in golf and other sports. Central to the complaints was the concern that the law and the courts should not be telling sports organizations how to conduct their games. Many felt that the ADA was unconstitutional if it allowed the courts to determine how sports are played. Martin's victory was upheld on appeal.

At the same time that Martin's case was making national headlines an almost identical suit, *Olinger v. United States Golf Association,* was going through the courts unnoticed. Fred Olinger, like Martin, was an accomplished golfer who suffered from a disability that impaired his ability to walk. Olinger filed suit to obtain an exemption from the USGA's walking-only rule in the Open qualifying round. The court found that the ADA did apply to the USGA and that Olinger's request for a cart was reasonable. The court recognized that even with a cart Olinger would likely be more fatigued than other healthy golfers who walked the court. The court, however, found that the use of a cart would fundamentally alter the nature of the U.S. Open competition and could be withheld without violating the ADA. The U.S. Supreme Court reversed the lower courts, however, and ruled in Olinger's favor.

Martin and Olinger were not the first athletes with impairments to compete in professional or highly competitive sports. Jim Abbot was a University of Michigan baseball player who was born without a right hand. Abbot became a major league pitcher with the New York Yankees. Tom Dolan, a collegiate swimmer, won a gold medal in the 400 meter individual medley at the 1996 Olympic Games in Atlantic despite having asthma and a windpipe half the size of most adults. Ronda Miller, a deaf athlete from Gallaudet University, a school for deaf students, was named honorable mention All American in basketball and who holds the NCAA Division III women's volleyball record for most kills in a season. Marla Runyon, one of the top ten U.S. women in the Pentathlon at 1996 U.S. Olympic trials, is legally blind. She did not make the '96 Olympics, but set a record in the Women's 800 Meter Run portion of the Pentathlon.

The chapter on Individual Sports discusses the Oscar Pistorius and LZR Race swimsuit controversies. That is, whether the use of certain technology provides an unfair advantage to an athlete. It is likely that the sports world will face many more such challenges in the future.

SPECTATOR RIGHTS

The impact of the ADA on sports is not limited to participants, but includes spectators. Public facilities are regulated by the ADA. Title III of the ADA prohibits discrimination against an individual on the basis of a disability with respect to the "full enjoyment of the goods, services, facilities, privileges, advantages, or accommodations by any person who owns, leases, or operates a place of public accommodation." The law encompasses theaters, arenas, golf courses, ski resorts, arenas and stadiums, including those used by professional teams.

Generally, the law requires the removal of barriers that obstruct impaired persons from all aspects of the facility. Facilities built or renovated prior to January 1992 are required to comply to the extent it is "readily achievable." Construction or alterations after that date must be in strict compliance with the Americans With Disabilities Act Accessibility Guidelines" (ADAAG). The ADA does not require a facility to be brought into total compliance if any renovations are made. If something is replaced, however, such as a toilet, it should be done in compliance with the Act. The guidelines require that if the "primary function area" is altered, 20 percent of the total cost spent on the alteration must be spent to improve access.

The ADAAG requires that wheelchair locations shall be equal to one percent (1%) of total seating capacity plus one additional space for each location. Accessible seats for the impaired must be located throughout the facility and be dispersed if fixed seating exceeds 300 people.

One problem area is the "line of sight" issue. During excited moments of play fans often stand and, consequently, block the view of wheelchair spectators. The Justice Department has indicated that it believes that wheelchair observers should be situated so that they can continue to watch the event when others are standing. A suit was filed against the managers of the Oakland Coliseum and the professional football and baseball teams that play there by a group of disabled persons. The suit alleged that the disabled fans were unable to see the playing field when fans in front stand up. The outcome of the suit is unknown.

Seating for wheelchair bound persons should be available throughout the facility. Michigan State was alleged to have violated the ADA when renovations were made to its stadium in 1994. An elite section, known as the Stadium Club, did not provide seating for persons with mobility impairments. Several suits have been filed regarding the one extra seat limitation. Some wheelchair confined persons are alleging that they are prevented from sitting with their families under the current guidelines.

The NFL's television blackout rule survived a court challenge that the rule was a violation of the ADA. In *Stoutenborough v. NFL*(1996), a suit was filed on behalf of a group of hearing impaired individuals. The plaintiffs contended the rule prevented hearing impaired individuals from being granted substantially equal access to NFL games since they could not listen to the game on the radio like an unimpaired person. The court ruled that the blackout rule had nothing to do with radio broadcast and did not discriminate since the blackout applied to all persons. The court also questioned if the ADA applied because the NFL and the television stations which cover games are not places of "public accommodation."

DRUG TESTING

Drug testing of athletes is a largely accepted, yet controversial, practice that raises state and federal constitutional issues. Cases involving NCAA regulations on drug testing were presented in an earlier chapter. Drug testing disputes are not, however, limited to collegiate athletes.

A major decision with respect to drug testing high school athletes was rendered in 1995 by the U.S. Supreme Court in *Vernonia School District v. Acton*. In *Acton* the school enacted a drug testing policy due to disciplinary and drug use problems in the school. The policy, applicable only to athletes, required athletes and parents to sign a form authorizing a drug test before the season and to consent to random weekly testing during the school year. If the test revealed drug use, a second test would be administered. If the second test was positive, the player had the option to either undergo a 6-week drug counseling program or be suspended for the current and next season. If the student failed a subsequent test the student would not have an option, but would be suspended for two seasons. Refusal to sign the form would preclude the athlete from participating in athletics.

Acton, a seventh-grader, was not suspected of drug use or disruptive behavior. He and his parents refused to sign the form and took the suspension to court asserting it was a violation of their federal and state constitutional rights pertaining to search and seizure and his right to privacy. The trial court ruled in favor of the school. The appellate court reversed and ruled in favor of Acton. In its opinion, the appellate court stated:

> Children, students, do not surrender their rights to privacy in order to secure their right to participate in athletics.

The U.S. Supreme Court reversed the appellate court and upheld the drug testing policy stating:

> Legitimate privacy expectations are even less with regard to student-athletes. School sports are not for the bashful. They require "suiting up" before each practice or event, and showering and changing afterwards. Public school locker rooms, the usual sites for these activities, are not notable for the privacy they afford. The locker rooms in Vernonia are typical: No individual dressing rooms are provided; shower heads are lined up along a wall, unseparated by any sort of partition or curtain; not even all the toilet stalls have doors. As the United States Court of Appeals for the Seventh Circuit has noted, there is "an element of 'communal undress' inherent in athletic participation."

The Supreme Court cited 4 factors to consider on the issue:
1. The importance of the governmental interest.
2. The degree of physical and psychological intrusion.
3. The degree of discretion vested in the governmental officials.
4. How well the procedure contributes to reaching the goal.

The Supreme Court found that the public policy against drug use outweighed the rights of the student-athletes. The Supreme Court held that athletes could be held to a heightened disciplinary system and that they had less of an expectation of privacy than the general student population. Would the *Acton* reasoning support random drug testing of cheerleaders, members of the band or teachers?

In *Earls by Earls v. Board of Education*, a case decided after *Acton*, the trial court upheld a school's drug testing policy that applied to all students who participated in extra-curricular activities, including the choir, Future Farmers of America and athletics. The Court of Appeal reversed and held that the policy violated the Fourth Amendment's protection from unreasonable search and seizures. The Court of Appeals in the *Earls'* decision distinguished *Vernonia* on the basis that the Vernonia school district established a compelling need to address the drug problem that was not shown in the *Earls'* case. In 2002 the U. S. Supreme Court reversed the Court of Appeal and found that the drug testing policy was constitutional. The U.S. Supreme Court stated that the reasonableness of a search must be determined by balancing the nature of the intrusion on the individual's privacy against the promotion of the government's interest. The Court emphasized the custodial responsibility schools maintain over students. The Court also stressed that the intrusion was minimal and that the test results were not turned over to law enforcement or used to discipline the student.

In *University of Colorado v. Derdeyn* (1993), a case decided before the *Acton* and *Earls'* decisions were rendered, the Colorado Supreme Court struck down a random drug testing policy of college athletes. In *Acton* and *Earls* the Supreme Court was dealing with minors. Would the age difference dictate a different result at the college level?

The "Quality Assurance in Drug Testing Act" is a bill that has been introduced in Congress to amend the Public Health Service Act, 42 U.S.C. 201 by adding Title XXVII. The bill is designed to ensure the security and quality of drug testing programs for private employers. Section 2714 of the law would, however, specifically exempt professional sports leagues.

RELIGIOUS FREEDOM

NCAA rule 92(a)(1)(d) was designed to stop players from showing off, taunting other players or engaging in other unsportsmanlike conduct. The rule stated that no player, "shall use ... language or gestures or engage in acts that provoke ill will or is demeaning to an opponent ... any delayed, excessive or attention to himself." The NCAA made it clear that game officials would strictly enforce the rules and give penalties for violations. The NCAA distributed literature and a film demonstrating various conduct that would be unacceptable. The rule was interpreted by some that a player who kneeled in the end zone for a prayer after a touchdown could be penalized because this was a form of posing and could focus attention on one person. Before the 1995 season began, players from Jerry Falwell's Liberty University filed suit against the NCAA asserting that enforcement of the rule was be a violation of their first amendment right to freedom of religion. Immediately after the suit was filed, the NCAA issued a memo that the rule was not intended to stop prayer.

Can the NBA require a player to stand during the playing of this country's National Anthem before a game if the player asserts it is against his religion? Should the issue be based on what the player believes his religion stands for or should opinions of experts on the particular religion be considered? The Sikh religion requires members to cover their head while in public. Could an official disqualify a Sikh soccer player because he wore a bandanna on his head?

In *Hadley v. Rush Henrietta Cental School District* the school attempted to prevent the Hadley's child from participating on the lacrosse team because he had failed, or religious grounds, to obtain the required tetanus vaccination. The Hadley's had obtained a waiver with respect to attendance at school. The school maintained that the waiver did not apply to extra curricular activities. The court found that extra-curricular sport activities are a fundamental part of the education process and was therefore included in the waiver granted by the school. A preliminary injunction in favor of Hadley was granted.

Most high school athletic associations have transfer rules designed to prevent recruiting of athletes. In *Walsh v. Louisiana High School Athletic Assoc.* (1977), several students wanted to transfer to a Lutheran school outside of their district. The rule applicable at the time stated that if a student attended school outside of his residential district he was ineligible to play sports. The students argued that the rule violated their first amendment right to religion. The court found that the rule did not prevent students from attending the religious school, but only prevented participation in athletics and upheld the rule.

ACADEMIC RULES

NCAA academic rules were addressed in a previous chapter. Similar issues exist at the secondary school level regarding academic requirements for student-athletes. There have been a number of challenges to the regulations, but the courts have generally upheld the school's rules. The courts have found that the academic standards have a rational government purpose to withstand constitutional challenges. In *Biley v. Truly* (1984), a rule was challenged that required a secondary student to have at least a "C" average to play sports. The court upheld the rule. The dissenting judge argued that the rule was a violation of equal protection because students who wanted to join 4-H, the debate team, the school newspaper and many other organizations did not have to meet the same standard. More court challenges may be filed on the issue of whether a school can require athletes to maintain higher grades to play than is required of students who participate in other school activities or the remaining general student population.

CHAPTER 17

Workers' Compensation

Workers' compensation laws pertain to the obligation an employer owes to an employee for an injury the employee sustained "within the course and scope" of employment. Compensation laws vary in each state, but basically require the employer to pay compensation benefits, which are usually a percentage of the injured employee's wages, during the disability period. In addition, the compensation laws require an employer to pay for necessary medical treatment. Generally an employer who is obligated to pay an injured employee workers' compensation benefits is immune from a tort suit by the employee.

PROFESSIONAL ATHLETES

The concept of paying workers' compensation benefits to professional athletes has caused considerable debate. Injuries are regarded as unavoidable consequences of professional sports. In addition, the huge salaries many athletes earn makes it difficult to sympathize with the injured player. Some states, including Florida, Massachusetts, Missouri, Pennsylvania, Texas, and Washington, have laws which exclude or limit the right of professional athletes to workers' compensation. For various reasons, compensation actions by professional athletes injured in the course of their employment have been rare. Some players are, however, beginning to seek relief under workers compensation laws.

In April 1998, the Illinois Industrial Commission ruled that a professional football career is not a temporary job. The ruling came in a compensation claim filed by Cap Boso, who played tight end for the Chicago Bears until a knee injury forced him to retire. Under Illinois compensation law, the ruling, if upheld, would mean the Bears would have to pay Boso an $18,000 a year lifetime annuity. The Bears argued that, because the career of a professional football player is limited to several years, disability payments should be limited to the remaining duration of a player's career. The Commission rejected the argument.

Doug Williams was a quarterback for the Washington Redskins and won an MVP award in the Super Bowl several years ago. Williams also won a compensation award that could, over a 25-year period, be worth almost a million dollars.

Williams hurt his back while working out on a treadmill during the off-season. The injury was such that it prevented him from continuing his career in football. His employer, the Redskins, claimed the injury was not within the course of his employment. Williams proved, however, that the team had asked him to get the treadmill and do the workouts. Williams will receive $513 per week as long as the injury prevents him from earning what he previously made with the Redskins, which was in excess of $1 million per year.

Palmer v. Kansas City Chiefs (1981) was a workers' compensation filed by Palmer, an offensive lineman for the Chiefs, for a game injury. The administrative law judge denied Palmer's claim. The Industrial Commission reversed and ruled in favor of Palmer finding that the injury was due to an abnormal back strain in the course of employment. On appeal to the courts, however, Palmer's claim was denied. The court found that under the applicable state law compensation was due for injuries that arose from an unforeseen event. The court held that the deliberate collision that was part of the game was not an unexpected event.

Most worker compensation laws provide for a credit or offset of compensation benefits if the injured employee is receiving payments from other sources such as social security or disability benefits. The offset may be based on the time of the payments or a dollar-for-dollar credit. Contracts between the parties can influence the method of the offset and the consequences can be substantial.

Green v. the New Orleans Saints (2000)

We granted a writ in this workers' compensation case to determine whether the lower courts correctly determined that the employer, the New Orleans Saints football team (the "Saints"), is entitled to an offset for a payment made to the plaintiff, Paul E. Green ("Green"), pursuant to an August 19, 1997 "Agreement and Release," against workers' compensation benefits based upon a time period rather than a dollar-for-dollar basis as provided for in La. R.S. 23:1225(D). After reviewing the record and the applicable law, we reverse the lower courts and find that the Saints are entitled to an offset for the full amount of the "Agreement and Release" payment on a dollar-for-dollar basis under La. R.S. 23:1225(D).

Facts and Procedural History

Green entered into a contract to play professional football with the Saints for the 1997 football season (the "Contract"). The Contract went into effect on April 7, 1997 and was to end on February 29, 1998, unless extended, terminated, or renewed. Green's base salary was $105,000.00. Green sustained a right knee injury on July 14, 1997, and shortly thereafter, although the exact date is unclear, suffered a hernia injury, both prior to the start of the 1997 season. He underwent a hernia repair and an arthroscopy on his right knee on August 20, 1997. On August 19, 1997, the Saints and Green entered into a "Agreement and Release," acknowledging that Green had an inguinal hernia, that his convalescence period would be 4-6 weeks, and that in exchange for a payment of $38,210.88, plus reasonable and customary medical and rehabilitation expenses for his hernia injury, Green released the Saints "from any and all claims arising from or related to [his] employment" and "any medical care incident to such employment." In addition, Green released the Saints from their obligation to pay his salary and medical expenses under Paragraphs 5 and 9 of the Contract, effectively terminating Green's contract with the Saints. On July 8, 1998, Green filed a LDOL-WC 1008 alleging entitlement to workers' compensation benefits for knee and hernia injuries. He has not returned to playing professional football.

In his workers' compensation suit, Green alleged that he was entitled to the a maximum workers' compensation benefits of $341.002 per week from August 19, 1997 minus a four to six weeks offset, representing the period of time for which he was paid the $38,210.88 settlement. He contends that the Saints can utilize their dollar-for-dollar offset only against the amount due under workers' compensation for the 4-6 week recuperative period of time as set forth in the Agreement and Release and Contract, and not against a future workers' compensation benefit. The Saints contend that they are entitled to a dollar-for-dollar credit for the $38,210.88 paid to the claimant and that they are not obligated to pay weekly indemnity benefits until the $38,210.88 is exhausted If Green is awarded $341.00 per week as he has requested, he would receive approximately $17,732.00 per year, meaning that under the Saint's theory, Green would not begin to receive workers' compensation benefits for over two years from August 19, 1997, while under Green's theory, he would begin to receive these benefits six weeks after August 19, 1997.

The case was submitted on briefs, with the parties stipulating that the only triable issue was whether the Saints were entitled to an offset, and if so, for how much. The workers' compensation judge agreed with Green on the offset issue and found that the Saints were entitled to a dollar-for-dollar credit for workers' compensation benefits due during the six weeks time period which was paid pursuant to the Agreement and Release. The workers' compensation judge also found that Green was "entitled to weekly workers' compensation benefits in the amount of Three Hundred Forty One Dollars ($341.00) per week after the expiration of the six week period, for his knee injury and related medical expenses." The court of appeal affirmed the workers' compensation judge's ruling on the offset issue, but appears to have remanded all other issues, including Green's entitlement to SEB's, back to the workers' compensation judge for further proceedings.' *Green v New Orleans Saints,* *99* 1057 (La. App. 5 Cir. 2/16/2000), 757 So. 2d 36. We granted the Saints' writ to decide the offset issue. *Green v New Orleans* Saints, 00-0795 (La. 5/5/2000), 760 So. 2d 1185.

La. R.S. 23:1225(I5) provides:

The compensation benefits payable to a professional athlete under any provision of this Chapter shall be reduced or offset by an amount equal to the total amount of benefits, wages, or other type of payment mentioned in any part of this provision on a dollar-for-dollar basis and not just on a week-to-week basis, if a professional athlete receives payment or remuneration from any of the following or payment of any type from any of the following:

(1) Any wages or benefits payable or paid to the athlete.
(2) A collective bargaining agreement.
(3) A contract of hire of any type.
(4) Any type of severance pay.
(5) Any type of injured reserve pay.
(6) Any type of termination pay.
(7) Any grievance or settlement pay.
(8) Any worker's compensation benefit of any type.
(9) Any other payment made to the professional athlete by the employer pursuant
     to any contract or agreement whatsoever.

This is a workers' compensation statute that applies only to "professional athletes." It allows an offset against workers' compensation benefits of a broad range of payments made to the player, including any wages, any grievance or settlement payments, or "any other payment . . pursuant to any contract or agreement whatsoever." As both lower courts recognized, under La. R.S. 23:1225(D), the Saints would clearly be entitled to an offset for the total amount of the $38,210.88 payment, as the statute provides for an offset by an amount equal to the total amount of the payment paid on a dollar-for-dollar basis.

However, the workers' compensation judge found that the Contract between Green and the Saints provided Green with rights in excess of La. RS. 23:1225(D).

The Contract was prepared by the National Football League and the NFL Players' Association and is the standard contract used by all teams in the NFL. Paragraph 10 of the Contract provides:

> WORKERS' COMPENSATION. *Any compensation paid to Player under this contract* or under any collective bargaining agreement in existence during the term of this contract *for a period during which he is entitled to workers' cm-Mnsation benefits* by reason of temporary total, permanent total, temporary partial, or permanent partial disability will be *deemed an advance payment of* workers' compensation benefits due Player, *and Club will be entitled to be reimbursed the amount of such payment out of any award of workers' compensation.* (Emphasis added.)

Recently, the First Circuit was presented with the same issue in *Dombrowski v. New Orleans Saints.* In that case, Jim Dombrowski was injured during a football game on November 17, 1996 and did not play during the 1997 season. In lieu of his regular salary for the 1997 season, he received $200,000 pursuant to an injury protection provision contained in a Collective Bargaining Agreement. He began receiving weekly compensation benefits of $341.00 at the conclusion of the 1997 season and the Saints sought a credit for the $200,000 on a dollar-for-dollar basis, rather that a week to week basis. The First Circuit, expressly disagreeing with the Fourth Circuit's opinion in Rickets, held that paragraph 10 of the Contract was clear and explicit and did not amount to a waiver of the statutory dollar-for-dollar offset set forth in La. R.S. 23:1225(D). We agree.

While the parties may disagree as to the interpretation of paragraph 10 of the Contract and there are sound arguments for interpreting the provision to provide the player with greater rights than those afforded by La. RS. 23:1225(D), we find that the language of paragraph 10 of the Contract is in fact consistent with the language of La. R.S. 23:1225(D). Under paragraph 10, "[a]ny compensation paid to [Green] under this contract … for a period during which he is entitled to workers' compensation benefits … will be deemed an advance payment of workers' compensation benefits due [Green], and [the Saints] will be entitled to be reimbursed the amount of such payment out of any award of workers' compensation." The $38,210.88 represents "compensation paid to [Green] under this contract … for a period during which he is entitled to workers' compensation benefits." Under paragraph 10, the Saints are entitled to be reimbursed the amount of such payment $38,210.88. The time period reflected in paragraph 10 merely categorizes payments made during that time period as an advance of workers' compensation benefits; it does not limit the employer to an offset against workers' compensation awards for the specified period of time during which the player was still under contract. If this provision was intended to limit the offset for a period of time, the last line of the provision would not have so clearly said otherwise.

The Louisiana Legislature created a dollar-for-dollar credit for payments made to a professional athlete as specified under La. R.S. 23:1225(D). Paragraph 10 of the Contract does not provide a contractual right greater than this statutory dollar-for-dollar offset. Accordingly, the Saints are entitled to a dollar-for-dollar credit for the $38,210.88 paid to Green pursuant to the "Agreement and Release" and they are not obligated to pay weekly indemnity benefits until the $38,210.88 is exhausted. To the extent that Ricketts holds otherwise, it is overruled. Finally, if not already accomplished by the court of appeal's somewhat inconsistent judgment, we remand the case to the workers' compensation judge to determine Green's entitlement to workers' compensation benefits.

For the foregoing reasons, the judgment of the court of appeal is reversed and the case is remanded to the workers' compensation judge for further proceedings. REVERSED AND REMANDED.

****

Wade R. Gibson v. Lake Charles Ice Pirates (2001)

Wade Gibson, a professional hockey player, was involved in an accident in the course and scope of his employment with the Lake Charles Ice Pirates (Ice Pirates) on January 20, 1998, when he attempted to block a shot in an ice hockey game and was struck with a hockey puck in the area of his left eye. He sustained orbital fractures, facial fractures, cuts, scarring, loss of central vision, and a significant reduction in depth perception. Gibson underwent two surgical procedures in connection with his injuries, one of which involved the installation of titanium plates and screws. The Ice Pirates continued paying Gibson's wages until the end of the hockey season, and thereafter, the Ice Pirates' compensation carrier, Virginia Surety Company, paid temporary total disability benefits of $333.35 from April 19, 1998, through October 17, 1998.

Gibson filed a claim for compensation, and the matter went to trial on various issues, including Gibson's entitlement to additional indemnity benefits and the defendants' entitlement to a credit/refund. The workers' compensation judge awarded Gibson 100 weeks of permanent partial disability benefits for scarring and disfigurement, 100 weeks of permanent partial disability benefits for loss of vision in his left eye, and temporary total disability benefits at the maximum rate of $350.00 per week "from the date of injury until released to return to work." The workers' compensation judge also awarded the defendants a credit in the amount of $1,000.00, representing the amount of profits Gibson's lawn care business netted. The defendants have appealed, contending that the workers' compensation judge erred in (1) failing to find that, pursuant to La.R.S. 23:1081(1)(c), no compensation was due because Gibson failed to use a face shield; (2) failing to find that, pursuant to La.R.S. 23:1208, Gibson forfeited his benefits for giving false statements or representations for the purpose of obtaining workers' compensation benefits; (3) failing to require that, pursuant to La.R.S. 23:1208(D), Gibson make restitution for violating La.R.S. 23:1208 and pay civil penalties; (4) failing to grant them a credit/refund for overpayment of benefits; (5) awarding permanent partial disability benefits under both La.R.S. 23:1221(4)(I) for loss of vision in the left eye and La.R.S. 23:1221(4)(p) for scarring and disfigurement; (6) awarding maximum permanent partial disability benefits under La.R.S. 23:1221(4) without deducting the number of weeks of compensation previously paid under La.R.S. 23:1221(1) as temporary total disability benefits; (7) awarding maximum permanent partial disability benefits for a minor scar; (8) awarding permanent partial disability benefits for loss of use of the left eye where appropriate evidence was not submitted to support the award; (9) awarding temporary total disability benefits when Gibson returned to work as a professional hockey player immediately after benefits were terminated; and (10) holding that the maximum compensation rate is applicable in this case.

La.R.S. 23:1081(1)(c) provides that compensation shall not be allowed for an injury caused "by the injured employee's deliberate failure to use an adequate guard or protection against accident provided for him." The defendants contend that the workers' compensation judge was clearly wrong in failing to find that the La.R.S. 23:1081(1)(c) defense applied in this case where Gibson made a deliberate decision not to use a face shield while playing hockey.

A face shield covers the area from the bridge of the nose to the top of the forehead. The parties stipulated that a face shield was made available to Gibson prior to and at the time of his injury and that he did not use the face shield. However, it appears that the parties used the phrase "was made available" to mean "could be obtained" rather than to mean "was on hand." Gibson testified that he was never offered a face shield and that if a player asked for a shield it would have to be ordered. He stated: "When you walk in the dressing room you have your equipment provided. There is a helmet and there is no face shield under it unless you ask for it." Even Robert Loucks, the coach of the Ice Pirates at the time of Gibson's injury, testified that "[o]nce you become a professional, it's optional. It's your choice, and very few players wear them because they tend to fog up and impair vision." Gibson testified that the face shield is an impediment to his play and that he does not have clear vision through the face shield: "During play it will fog up. If you get chunked in the boards, perspiration or snow or water will splash on the visor, and you know, then you're trying to wipe it off while you are playing. So, it does get in the way. It's bothersome."

The employer has the burden of proving the defense. La.R.S. 23:1081(2). Initially, in light of the liberal construction afforded the employee in workers' compensation law, we do not find that the Ice Pirates proved that the face shield was actually "provided" to Gibson and as required by the statute. While the face shield was obtainable through the Ice Pirates by an employee, it was not on hand for immediate use.

Moreover, we find no merit to the defendants' contention that the defense is applicable, because the injury would not have occurred if Gibson had been wearing the face shield, which he currently wears while playing. We have declined to hold that a claimant's recovery is barred by his mere failure to use an adequate guard against injury, since such a holding would abrogate the rule that ordinary or contributory negligence constitutes no bar to recovery in workers' compensation. Rather, "[t]he defenses of LSA-R.S. 23:1081, strictly construed, relieve employers of liability only for injuries that are intended by individuals or that result from an individual's intoxication, as the latter constitutes no less than a voluntary self-removal from the world of reason." In fact, "[t]he employer must prove that the employee had a willful and wanton intention to injure himself." The defenses simply do not prohibit an employee's recovery on grounds of contributory negligence, and, in fact, the defenses do not even defeat a claim for injuries resulting from stupidity or foolishness or even recklessness. In the instant case, the Ice Pirates did not require the use of the face shield, and the evidence does not support that Gibson's failure to use the face shield was due to a willful and wanton intention to injure himself. Rather, the evidence shows that Gibson's failure to use the face shield was due to the fact that it was an impediment to his job performance. Thus, we find no error in the workers' compensation judge's rejection of the La.R.S. 23:1081(1)(c) defense.

****

COLLEGE ATHLETES

In one old case, *Van Horn v. Industrial Accident Commission*, 1963, the court held that the student-athlete was an employee and, therefore, entitled to workers compensation coverage for a sports related injury. Other courts have, however, ruled student-athletes are not employees and therefore not entitled to workers compensation protection unless additional employment duties beyond athletic participation are involved.

Fred Rensing was a student-athlete on football scholarship with Indiana State. Rensing was permanently paralyzed as a result of an injury during spring practice. Rensing brought a compensation action against the school. *Rensing v. Indiana State University* (1982). The critical issue was whether Rensing, by virtue of his scholarship, was an employee of Indiana State. The appellate court ruled in favor of Rensing.

Additionally, the Trustees also retained their right to terminate their agreement for Rensing's services under certain prescribed conditions, a factor tending to distinguish his grant from an outright gift and which has previously been noted by this Court as a significant indicia of an employer-employee or master-servant relationship. … From these facts, the conclusion is compelling that Rensing and the Trustees bargained for an exchange in the manner of employer and employee of Rensing's football talents for certain scholarship benefits.

The Indiana Supreme Court, however, found that a student-athlete is not an employee and reversed the decision.

All of the above facts show that, in this case, Rensing did not receive "pay" for playing football at the University within the meaning of the Workmens' Compensation Act; therefore, an essential element of the employer-employee relationship was missing in addition to the lack of intent. Furthermore, under the applicable rules of the NCAA, Rensing's benefits could not be reduced or withdrawn because of his athletic ability or his contribution to the team's success. Thus, the ordinary employer's right to discharge on the basis of performance was also missing. While there was an agreement between Rensing and the Trustees which established certain obligations for both parties, the agreement was not a contract of employment.

California has enacted a law which provides that student-athletes are not employees and are not covered by workers' compensation insurance.

NFLPA Standard
Representation Agreement

This AGREEMENT made this ___ day of _____, _____, by and between _____ (hereinafter "Player") and _____ (hereinafter "Contract Advisor")

WITNESSETH:

In consideration of the mutual promises hereinafter made by each to the other, Player and Contract advisor agree as follows:

1. General Principles

This Agreement is entered into pursuant to and in accordance with the National Football League Players Association (hereinafter "NFLPA") Regulations Governing contract advisors (hereinafter "the Regulations") effective December 1, 1994, and as amended thereafter from time to time.

2. Representations

Contract Advisor represents that in advance of executing this Agreement, he/she has been duly certified as a Contract Advisor by the NFLPA. Player acknowledges that the NFLPA certification of the contract Advisor is neither a recommendation of the Contract Advisor, nor a warranty by NFLPA of the Contract Advisor's competence, honesty, skills, or qualifications.

Contract Advisor hereby discloses that he/she (check one): [ ] represents or has represented; [ ] does not represent and has not represented NFL management personnel in matters pertaining to their employment by or association with any NFL club. (If Contract Advisor responds in the affirmative, Contract Advisor must attach a written addendum to this Agreement listing names and position of those NFL Personnel represented).

3. Contract Services

Player hereby retains Contract Advisor to represent, advise, counsel, and assist Player in the negotiation, execution, and enforcement of his playing contract(s) in the National Football League.

In performing these services, Contract Advisor acknowledges that he/she is acting in a fiduciary capacity on behalf of Player and agrees to act in such manner as to protect the best interests of Player and assure effective representation of Player in individual contract negotiations with NFL Clubs. Contract Advisor shall be the exclusive representative for the purpose of negotiating player contracts for Player. However, Contract Advisor shall not have the authority to bind or commit Player to enter into any contract without actual execution thereof by Player. Once Player agrees to and executes his player contract, Contract Advisor agrees to also sign the player contract and send a copy (by facsimile or overnight mail) to the NFLPA and the NFL Club within 48 hours of execution by Player.

If Player and Contract Advisor have entered into any other agreements or contracts relating to services other than the individual negotiating services described in this Section, describe the nature of the other services covered by the separate agreements:

_____

_____

4. Compensation for Services

If Contract Advisor succeeds in negotiating a NFL Player contract acceptable to Player and signed by Player during the term hereof, contract Advisor shall receive a fee of three percent (3%) of the compensation received by Player for each such playing season, unless a lesser percent (%) or amount has been agreed to by the parties and is noted in the space below.

The parties hereto have agreed to the following lesser fee:

_____

_____

_____

In computing the allowable fee pursuant to this Section 4 the term "compensation" shall include only base salaries, signing bonuses, reporting bonuses, roster bonuses and any performance incentives actually received by Player. The term "compensation" shall not include any "honor" incentive bonuses (i.e., ALL PRO, PRO BOWL, Rookie of the Year), or any collectively bargained benefits.

5. Payment of Contract Advisor's Fee

Contract Advisor shall not be entitled to receive any fee for the performance of his/her services pursuant to this Agreement until Player receives the compensation upon which the fee is based.

However, Player may enter into an agreement with Contract Advisor to pay any fee attributable to deferred compensation due and payable to Player in advance of when the deferred compensation is paid to Player, provided that Player has performed the services necessary under his contract to entitle him to the deferred compensation. Such fee shall be reduced to its present value as specified in the NFLPA Regulations (see Section 4(b)). Such an agreement must also be in writing, with a copy sent to the NFLPA.

In no case shall Contract Advisor accept, directly or indirectly, payment of any fees hereunder from Player's club. Further, Contract Advisor is prohibited from discussing any aspect of his/her fee arrangement hereunder with any club.

6. Expenses

Player shall reimburse Contract Advisor for all reasonable and necessary communication expenses (i.e., telephone and postage) actually incurred by Contract Advisor in connection with the negotiation of Player's NFL contract. Player also shall reimburse Contract Advisor for all reasonable and necessary travel expenses actually incurred by contract Advisor during the term hereof in the negotiation of Player's NFL contract, but only if such expenses and approximate amounts thereof are approved in advance by Player. Player shall promptly pay all such expenses upon receipt of an itemized, written statement from Contract Advisor.

After each NFL season and prior to the first day of May following each season for which Contract Advisor has received fees and expenses, Contract Advisor must send to Player (with a copy to the NFLPA) an itemized statement covering the period March 1 through February 28th or 29th of that year. Such statement shall set forth both the fees charged to Player for, and any expenses incurred in connection with, the performance of the following services: (a) individual player salary negotiation, (b) management of the player's assets, (c) financial, investment, legal, tax and/or other advice, and (d) any other miscellaneous services.

7. Disclaimer of Liability

Player and Contract Advisor agree that they are not subject to the control or direction of any other person with respect to the timing, place, manner or fashion in which individual negotiations are to be conducted pursuant to this Agreement (except to the extent that Contract Advisor shall comply with NFLPA Regulations) and that they will save and hold harmless the NFLPA, its officers, employees and representatives from any liability whatsoever with respect to their conduct or activities relating to or in connection with this Agreement or such individual negotiations.

8. Disputes

Any and all disputes between Player and Contract Advisor involving the meaning, interpretation, application, or enforcement of this Agreement or the obligations of the parties under this Agreement shall be resolved exclusively through the arbitration procedures set forth in Section 5 of the NFLPA Regulations Governing Contract Advisors.

9. **Notices**

All notices hereunder shall be effective if sent by certified mail, postage prepaid to the following addresses. If to the Contract Advisor:_____

_____

If to the Player:_____

_____

110. **Entire Agreement**

This Agreement, along with the NFLPA Regulations, sets forth the entire agreement between the parties hereto and cannot be amended, modified or changed orally, Any written amendments or changes shall be effective only to the extent that they are consistent with the Standard Representation Agreement as approved by the NFLPA.

11. **Filing**

This contract is signed in triplicate. Contract Advisor agrees to deliver one (1) copy to the NFLPA within five (5) days of its execution; one (1) copy to the Player; and retain one (1) copy for his/her files. Contract advisor further agrees to submit any other executed agreements between Player and Contract Advisor to NFLPA.

12. **Term**

The term of this Agreement shall begin on the date hereof and shall continue for the term of any player contract executed pursuant to this Agreement; provided, however, that either party may terminate this Agreement effective five (5) days after written notice of termination is given to the other party. Notice shall be effective for purposes of this paragraph if sent by certified mail, postage prepaid, return receipt requested to the appropriate address contained in this Agreement.

If termination pursuant to the above provision occurs prior to the completion of negotiations for an NFL player contract(s) acceptable to Player and signed by Player, Contract Advisor shall be entitled to compensation for the reasonable value of the services performed in the attempted negotiation of such contract (s) provided such services and time spent thereon are adequately documented by Contract Advisor. If termination pursuant to the above provision occurs after Player has signed an NFL player contract negotiated by Contract Advisor, Contract Advisor shall be entitled to the fee prescribed in Section 4 above for negotiation of such contract(s).

In the event that Player is able to renegotiate any contract(s) previously negotiated by contract Advisor prior to expiration thereof, Contract Advisor shall still be entitled to the fee he/she would have been paid pursuant to Section 4 above as if such original contract(s) had not been renegotiated. If contract Advisor represents Player in renegotiation of the original contract(s), the fee for such renegotiation shall be based solely upon the amount by which the compensation in the renegotiated contract(s) exceeds the compensation in the original contract(s), whether or not contract Advisor negotiated the original contract(s).

If the Contract Advisor's certification is suspended or revoked by the NFLPA or the Contract Advisor is otherwise prohibited by the NFLPA from performing the services he/she has agreed to perform herein, this Agreement shall automatically terminate, effective as of the date of such suspension or termination.

13. **Governing Law**

This Agreement shall be construed, interpreted and enforced according to the laws of the State of Louisiana.

Contract Advisor and Player recognize that certain state statutes regulating sports agents require specified language in the player/agent contract. The parties therefore agree to the following additional language as required by state statute:

"NOTICE TO CLIENTS"

(1) THIS ATHLETE AGENT IS REGISTERED WITH THE SECRETARY OF STATE OF LOUISIANA. REGISTRATION DOES NOT IMPLY APPROVAL OR ENDORSEMENT BY THE SECRETARY OF STATE OF THE SPECIFIC TERMS AND CONDITIONS OF THIS CONTRACT OR THE COMPETENCE OF THE ATHLETE AGENT.

(2) DO NOT SIGN THIS CONTRACT UNTIL YOU HAVE READ IT OR IF IT CONTAINS BLANK SPACES.

(3) IF YOU DECIDE THAT YOU DO NOT WISH TO PURCHASE THE SERVICES OF THE ATHLETE AGENT, YOU MAY CANCEL THIS CONTRACT BY NOTIFYING THE ATHLETE AGENT IN WRITING OF YOUR DESIRE TO CANCEL THE CONTRACT NOT LATER THAN THE SIXTEENTH DAY AFTER THE DATE ON WHICH THIS CONTRACT IS FILED WITH THE SECRETARY OF STATE.

EXAMINE THIS CONTRACT CAREFULLY BEFORE SIGNING IT

IN WITNESS WHEREOF, the parties hereto have hereunder signed their names as hereinafter set forth.

_____
(CONTRACT ADVISOR)

_____
(Street Address)   (City, State, Zip Code)

_____
(Telephone)   (Fax Number)

_____
(PLAYER)

_____
(Street or P.O. Box)   (City, State, Zip Code)

_____
(In-Season Telephone)   (Off-Season Telephone)

Player's Date of Birth: _____
                              (Month/Day/Year)

_____
Print Name and Signature of PARENT or GUARDIAN (if Player is under 21 Years of Age)
_____
(Address and Telephone)

NFL Player Contract

THIS CONTRACT is between _____, hereinafter "Player," and _____,
a _____ corporation
(limited partnership) (partnership), hereinafter "Club," operating under the name
of the_____ as a member of the National Football
League, hereinafter "League." In consideration of the promises made by each to the
other, Player and Club agree as follows:

1. TERM. This contract covers football season(s), and will begin on the date of
execution or March 1, _____, whichever is later, and end on February 28 or
29, _____,
unless extended, terminated, or renewed as specified elsewhere in this contract.

2. EMPLOYMENT AND SERVICES. Club employs Player as a skilled football
player. Player accepts such employment. He agrees to give his best efforts and loyalty to the Club, agrees to conduct himself on and off the held with appropriate
recognition of the fact that the success of professional football depends largely on
public respect for and approval of those associated with the game. Player will report promptly for and participate fully in Club's official mandatory mini-camp(s),
official pre-season training camp, all club meetings and practice sessions, and all
pre-season, regular season and post-season football games scheduled for or by Club.
If invited, Player will practice for and play in any all-star football game sponsored
by the League. Player will not participate in any football game not sponsored by the
League unless the game is first approved by the League.

3. OTHER ACTIVITIES. Without prior written consent of the Club Player will
not play football or engage in activities related to football otherwise than for Club
or engage in any activity other than football which may involve a significant risk of
personal injury. Player represents that he has special exceptional and unique knowledge, skill, ability, and experience as a football player, the loss of which cannot be
estimated with any certainty and cannot be fairly or adequately compensated by
damages. Player therefore agrees that Club will have the right, in addition to any
other right which Club may possess, to enjoin Player by appropriate proceedings
from playing football or engaging in football-related activities other than for Club

or from engaging in any activity other than football which may involve a significant-risk of personal injury.

4. PUBLICITY AND NFLPA GROUP LICENSING PROGRAM. (a) Player grants to Club and the League, separately and together, the authority to use his name and picture for publicity and the promotion of NFL Football, the League or any of its member clubs in newspapers, magazines, motion pictures, game programs and roster manuals, broadcasts and telecasts, and all other publicity, and advertising media, provided such publicity and promotion does not constitute an endorsement by, Player of a commercial product. Player will cooperate with the news media, and will participate upon request in reasonable activities to promote the Club and the League. Player and National Football League Players Association, hereinafter "NFLPA," will not contest the rights of the League and its member clubs to telecast, broadcast, or otherwise transmit NFL Football or the right of NFL Films to produce, sell, market, or distribute football game film footage, except insofar as such broadcast, telecast, or transmission of footage is used in any commercially marketable game or interactive use. The League and its member clubs, and Player and the NFLPA, reserve their respective rights as to the use of such broadcasts, telecasts or transmissions of footage in such games or interactive uses, which shall be unaffected by this subparagraph.

(b) Player hereby assigns to the NFLPA and its licensing affiliates, if any, the exclusive right to use and to grant to persons, firms, or corporations (collectively "licensees") the right to use his name, signature, facsimile, voice, picture, photograph, likeness, and/or biographical information (collectively "image") in group licensing programs. Group licensing programs are defined as those licensing programs in which a licensee utilizes a total of six (6) or more NFL player images on products that are sold at retail or used as promotional or premium items. Player retains the right to grant permission to a licensee to utilize his image if that licensee is not concurrently utilizing the images of five (5) or more other NFL players on products that are sold at retail or are used as promotional or premium items. If Player's inclusion in a particular NFLPA program is precluded by an individual exclusive endorsement agreement, and Player provides the NFLPA with timely written notice of that preclusion, the NFLPA will exclude Player from that particular program. In consideration for this assignment of rights, the NFLPA will use the revenues it receives from group licensing programs to support the objectives as set forth in the By-laws of the NFLPA. The NFLPA will use its best efforts to promote the use of NFL player images in group licensing programs, to provide group licensing opportunities to all NFL players, and to ensure that no entity utilizes the group licensing rights granted to the NFLPA without first obtaining a license from the NFLPA. This paragraph shall be construed under New York law without reference to conflicts of law principles. The assignment in this paragraph shall expire on December 31 of the later of (a) the third year following the execution of this contract, or (b) the year in which this contract expires. Neither Club nor the League is a party to the terms of this paragraph, which is included herein solely for the administrative convenience and benefit of Player and the NFLPA. The terms of this subparagraph apply unless, at the time of execution of this contract, Player indicates by staking out this sub-paragraph (b) and marking his initials adjacent to the stricken language his intention to not participate in the NFLPA Group Licensing Program. Nothing in this subparagraph shall be construed to supersede or any way broaden, expand, detract from, or otherwise alter in any way whatsoever, the rights of NFL Properties, Inc. as permitted under Article V (Union Security), Section 4 of the 1993 Collective Bargaining Agreement ("CBA").

5. COMPENSATION. For performance of Player's services and all other promises of Player, Club will pay Player a yearly salary as follows:

$ _____ for the 200_____ season;

$ _____ for the 200_____ season;

$ _____ for the 200_____ season;

$ _____ for the 200_____ season;

$ _____ for the 200_____ season;

In addition, Club will pay Player such earned performance bonuses may be called for in this contract; Player's necessary traveling expenses from his residence to training camp; Player's reasonable board and lodging expenses during pre-season training and in connection with playing pre-season, regular season, and post-season football games outside Club's home city; Player's necessary traveling expenses to and from pre-season, regular season, and post-season football games outside Club's home city; Player's necessary traveling expenses to his residence if this contract is terminated by Club; and such additional compensation, benefits and reimbursement of expenses as may be called for in any collective bargaining agreement in existence during; the term of this contract. (For purposes of this contract, a collective bargaining agreement will be deemed to be "in existence" during its stated term or during any period for which the parties to that agreement agree to extend it.)

6. PAYMENT. Unless this contract or any collective bargaining agreement in existence during the term of this contract specifically provides otherwise, Player will be paid 100% of his yearly salary under this contract in equal weekly or bi-weekly installments over the course of the applicable regular season period, commencing with the first regular season game played by Club in each season. Unless this contract specifically provides otherwise, if this contract is executed or Player is activated after the beginning of the regular season, the yearly salary payable to Player will be reduced proportionately and Player will be paid the weekly or bi-weekly portions of his yearly salary becoming due and payable after he is activated. Unless this contract specifically provides otherwise, if this contract is terminated after the beginning of the regular season, the yearly salary payable to Player will be reduced proportionately and Player will be paid the weekly or bi-weekly portions of his yearly salary having become due and payable up to the time of termination.

7. DEDUCTIONS. Any advance made to Player will be repaid to Club, and any properly levied Club fine or commissioner fine against Player will be paid, its cash, can demand or by means of deductions from payments conning due to the Player under this contract, the amount of such deductions to be determined by Club unless this contract or any collective bargaining agreement in existence during the term of this contract specifically provides otherwise.

8. PHYSICAL CONDITION. Player represents to Club that he is and will maintain himself in excellent physical condition. Player will undergo a complete physical examination by the Club physician upon Club request, during which physical examination Player agrees to make full and complete disclosure of any physical or mental condition known to him which might impair his performance under this contract and to respond fully and in good faith when questioned by the Club physician about such condition. If Player fails to establish or maintain his excellent physical condition to the satisfaction of the Club physician, or make the required full and complete disclosure and good faith responses to the Club physician, then Club may terminate this contract.

9. INJURY. Unless this contract specifically provides otherwise, if Player is injured in the performance of his services under this contract and promptly reports such injury to the Club physician or trainer, then Player will receive such medical and hospital care during the term of this contract as the Club physician may deem necessary, and will continue to receive his yearly salary for so long, during the season of injury only and for no subsequent period covered by this contract, as Player is physically unable to perform the services required of him by this contract because of such injury. If Player's injury in the performance of his services under this contract results in his death, the unpaid balance of his yearly salary for the season of injury will be paid to his stated beneficiary, or in the absence of a stated beneficiary, to his estate.

10. WORKERS' COMPENSATION. Any compensation paid to Player under this contract or under any collective bargaining agreement in existence during the term of this contract [or a period during which he is entitled to workers' compensation benefits by reason of temporary total, permanent total, temporary partial, or permanent partial disability] will be deemed an advance payment of workers' compensation benefits due Player and club will be entitled to be reimbursed the amount of such payment out of any award of workers' compensation.

11. SKILL, PERFORMANCE AND CONDUCT. Player understands that he is competing with other players for a position on Club's roster with-in the applicable player limits. If at any time, in the sole judgment of Club, Player's skill or performance has been unsatisfactory as compared with that of other players competing for positions on Club's roster, or if Player has engaged in personal conduct reasonably judged by Club to adversely affect or reflect on Club, then Club may terminate this contract. In addition, during the period any salary cap is legally in effect, this contract may be terminated if, in Club's opinion, Player is anticipated to make less of a contribution to Club's ability to compete on the playing field than another

player or players whom Club intends to sign or attempts to sign, or another player or players who is or are already on Club's roster, and for whom Club needs room.

12. TERMINATION. The rights of termination set forth in this contract will be in addition to any other rights of termination allowed either party by law. Termination will be effective upon the giving of written notice, except that Player's death, other than as a result of injury incurred in the performance of his services under this contract, will automatically terminate this contract. If this contract is terminated by Club and either Player or Club so requests, Player will promptly undergo a complete physical examination by the Club physician.

13. INJURY GRIEVANCE. Unless a collective bargaining-agreement in existence at the time of termination of this contract by Club provides otherwise, the following injury grievance procedure will apply: If Player believes that at the time of termination of this contract by Club he was physically unable to perform the services required of him by this contract because of an injury incurred in the performance of his services under this contract, Player may, within 60 days after examination by the Club physician, submit at his own expense to examination by a physician of his choice. If the opinion of Player's physician with respect to his physical ability to perform the services required of him by this contract is contrary to that of the Club's physician, the dispute will be submitted within a reasonable time to final and binding arbitration by an arbitrator selected by Club and Player or, if they are unable to agree, one selected in accordance with the procedures of the American Arbitration Association on application by either party.

14. RULES. Player will comply with and be bound by all reasonable Club rules and regulations in effect during the term of this contract which are not inconsistent with the provisions of this contract or of any collective bargaining agreement in existence during the term of this contract. Player's attention is also called to the fact that the League functions with certain rules and procedures expressive of its operation as a joint venture among its member clubs and that these rules and practices may affect Player's relationship to the League and its member clubs independently of the provisions of this contract.

15. INTEGRITY OF GAME. Player recognizes the detriment to the League and professional football that would result from impairment of public confidence in the honest and orderly conduct of NFL games or to integrity and good character of NFL players. Player therefore acknowledges his awareness that if he accepts a bribe or agrees to throw or fix an NFL game; fails to promptly report a bribe offer or an attempt to throw or fix an NFL game; bets on an NFL game; knowingly associates with gamblers or gambling activity; uses or provides other players with stimulants or other drugs for the purpose of attempting to enhance on-field performance; or is guilty of any other form of conduct reasonably judged by the League Commissioner to be detrimental to the League or professional football, the Commissioner will have the right, but only after giving Player the opportunity for a hearing at which he may be represented by counsel of his choice, to fine Player in a reasonable amount; to suspend Player for a period certain or indefinitely; and/or to terminate this contract.

16. EXTENSION. Unless this contract specifically provides otherwise, if Player becomes a member of the Armed Forces of the United States or any other country, or retires from professional football as an active player; or otherwise fails or refuses to perform his services under this contract, then this contract will be tolled between the date of Player's induction into the Armed Forces, or his retirement, or his failure or refusal to perform, and the later date of his return to professional football. During the period of this contract is tolled, Player will not be entitled to any compensation or benefits. On Player's return to professional football, the term of his contract will be extended for a period of time equal to the number of seasons (to the nearest multiple of one) remaining at the time the contract was tolled. The right of renewal, if any, contained in this contract will remain in effect until the end of any such extended term.

17. ASSIGNMENT. Unless this contract specifically provides otherwise, Club may assign this contract and Player's services under this contract to any successor to Club's franchise or to any other Club in the League. Player will report to the assignee Club promptly upon being informed of the assignment of his contract and will faithfully perform his services under this contract. The assignee club will pay Player's necessary traveling expenses in reporting to it and will faithfully perform this contract with Players

18. FILING. This contract will be valid and binding upon Player and Club immediately upon execution. A copy of this contract, including any attachment to it, will be filed by Club with the League Commissioner within 10 days after execution. The Commissioner will have the right to disapprove this contract on reasonable grounds, including but not limited to an attempt by the parties to abridge or impair the rights of any other club, uncertainty or incompleteness in expression of the parties' respective rights and obligations, or conflict between the terms of this contract and any collective bargaining agreement then in existence. Approval will be automatic unless, within 10 days after receipt of this contract in his office, the Commissioner notifies the parties either of disapproval or of extension of this 10-day period for purposes of investigation or clarification pending his decision. On the receipt of notice of disapproval and termination, both parties will be relieved of their respective rights and obligations under this contract.

19. DISPUTES. During the term of any collective bargaining agreement, any dispute between Player and Club involving the interpretation or application of any provision of this contract will be submitted to final and binding arbitration in accordance with the procedure called for in any collective-bargaining agreement in existence at the time the event giving rise to any such dispute, occurs.

20. NOTICE. Any notice; request, approval or consent under this contract will be sufficiently given if in writing and delivered in person or mailed (certified or first class) by one party to the other at the address set forth in this contract or to such other address as the recipient may subsequently have furnished in writing to the sender.

21. OTHER AGREEMENTS. This contract, including any attachment to it, sets forth the entire agreement between Player and Cub and cannot be modified or supplemented orally. Player and Club represent that no other agreement, oral or written, except as attached to or specifically incorporated in this contract, exists between them. The provisions' of this contract will govern the relationship between Player' and Club unless there are conflicting provisions in any collective bargaining Agreement in existence during the term of this contract, in which case the provisions of the collective bargaining agreement will take precedence over convicting provisions of this contract relating to the rights or obligations of either party.

22. LAW. This contract is made under and shall be governed by the laws of the State of

23. WAIVER AND RELEASE. Player waives and releases any claims that he may have arising out of, related to, or asserted in the lawsuit entitled White v. National Football League, including, but not limited to, any such claim regarding least NFL Rules, the College Draft, Plan B, the first refusal/compensation system, the NFL Player Contract, pre-season compensation, or any other term or conditions of employment, except any claims asserted in Brown v. Pro Football. Inc. This waiver and release also extends to any conduct engaged in pursuant to the Stipulation and Settlement Agreement in White ("Settlement Agreement") during tile express term of that Settlement Agreement or any portion thereof. This waiver and release shall not limit any rights Player may have to performance by the Club under this Contract or Player's rights as a member of the White class to object to the Settlement Agreement during its review by the court in Minnesota. This waiver and release is subject to Article XIV (NFL Player Contract), Section 3(c) of the CBA.

24. OTHER PROVISIONS. (a) Each of the undersigned hereby confirms that (i) this contract, renegotiation, extension or amendment sets forth all components of the player's remuneration for playing professional football (whether such compensation is being furnished directly by the Club or by a-related or affiliated entity); and (ii) there are not undisclosed agreements of any kind, whether express or implied, oral or written, and there are no promises, undertakings, representations, commitments, inducements, assurances of intent, or understandings of any kind that have not been disclosed to the NFL involving consideration of any kind to be paid, furnished or made available to Player or any entity or person owned or controlled by, affiliated with, or related to Player, either during the term of this contract or thereafter.

(b) Each of the undersigned further confirms that, except insofar as any of the undersigned may describe in an addendum to this contract, to the best of their, knowledge, no conduct in violation of the Anti-Collusion rules of the Settlement Agreement took place with respect to this contract. Each of the undersigned further confirms that nothing in this contract is designed or intended to defeat or circumvent any provisions of the Settlement Agreement, including but not limited to the Rookie Pool and Salary Cap provisions; however, any conduct permitted by the CBA and/or the Settlement Agreement shall not be considered a violation of this confirmation.

(c) The Club further confirms that any information regarding the negotiation of this contract that it provided to the Neutral Verifier was, at the time the information was provided, true and correct in all material respects.

25. SPECIAL PROVISIONS.

THIS CONTRACT is executed in six (6) copies. Player acknowledges that before signing this contract he was given the opportunity to seek advice from or be represented by persons of his own selection.

PLAYER   CLUB

_____   _____
Home Address   By
                                       _____
_____   Club Address
Telephone Number   _____

_____   _____
Date   Date

_____
PLAYER'S CERTIFIED AGENT

_____
Address

_____

_____
Telephone number

_____
Date